The Unknown Life of the Shah

The Unknown Life of the Shah

Amir Taheri

HUTCHINSON
London Sydney Auckland Johannesburg

© Amir Taheri 1991

The right of Amir Taheri to be identified as Author
of this work has been asserted by Amir Taheri in
accordance with the Copyright, Designs and Patents Act, 1988

This edition first published in 1991 by
Hutchinson

Random Century Group Ltd
20 Vauxhall Bridge Road, London SW1V 2SA

Random Century Australia (Pty) Ltd
20 Alfred Street, Milsons Point, Sydney, NSW 2061, Australia

Random Century New Zealand Ltd
PO Box 40–086, Glenfield, Auckland 10, New Zealand

Random Century South Africa (Pty) Ltd
 PO Box 337, Bergvlei, 2012, South Africa

British Library Cataloguing in Publication Data
Taheri, Amir
  The unknown life of the Shah.
  I. Title
  955.05092

  ISBN 0–09–174860–7

Photoset in Sabon by Speedset Ltd, Ellesmere Port
Printed and bound in Great Britain by
Mackays of Chatham PLC, Chatham, Kent

In this world you are a slave –
not a king.
In name only are you a king.
Kingship, power, government, authority
are just other names for pain and death.
You are not king to your own beard – which
grows white regardless of your wishes.
Do not, do not call yourself king.
How can man reign over Good and Evil?

Rumi

Contents

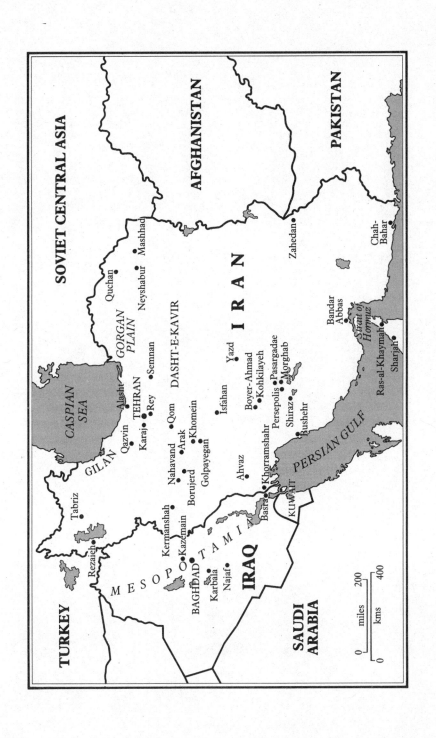

Illustrations

Ayatollah Ruhollah Khomeini
The Shah and Empress Farah with President and Mrs Carter in Washington, 1977
Revolutionary crowds march in the streets of Tehran
Amir Abbas Hoveyda
The Shah with his eldest son Reza in Panama in 1980
The Shah in exile on the island of Contadora in 1980
The exiled Shah with Princess Leila Pahlavi
President Nixon escorts Empress Farah during the Shah's funeral, Cairo 1980

Introduction

At a mosque in the heart of Cairo's bustling bazaar part of the prayer hall is cordoned off with sheets of plywood beyond which visitors are not admitted without special permission. At the centre of the secluded area is a low tomb covered with a dusty Persian carpet on which stand a number of nondescript vases of long-withered flowers. A sleepy guardian – who allows a visitor to enter without special permission in exchange for a handful of Egyptian banknotes – describes the place as 'the house of the end'.

It is dark but further generosity from the visitor persuades the guardian to light a few candles, revealing an ivory inlay frame, the work, no doubt, of an Isfahani master craftsman. The frame contains the portrait of a middle-aged man with thick, salt and pepper hair. The man is smiling an almost boyish smile, obliterated by the aggressive sadness of the eyes.

A notice scribbled in a hurried hand and containing a number of spelling errors, tells the visitor that this is 'the temporary abode of the mortal remains of The Holiest Essence, The Superior Presence His Imperial Majesty Mohammad-Reza Shah, Aryan Sun, King of Kings of Iran'. The Shah's last wish was that his remains be buried in Iranian soil. More than a decade after his death, however, that last wish remained unfulfilled. In the 1940s The Rifa'i Mosque, where the Shah's temporary tomb is located, had also housed the mortal remains of his father Reza Shah. He too died in exile and wished to be buried in Iran. His wish had eventually come true.

The contrast between the dismal aspect of the makeshift mausoleum in downtown Cairo and the lofty titles that precede his name illustrates the principal feature of Mohammad-Reza Shah Pahlavi's eventful reign: a reign of sharp contrasts in which high drama and boulevard farce often represented the two faces of the same coin. His was a truly dramatic life, marked by violent convulsions punctuated with almost Ubuesque contretemps.

Mohammad-Reza Shah sat on the Peacock Throne of Persia for more than thirty-seven years. He died in 1980 a hunted exile. He reached the end of his road in Cairo after eighteen months of wandering in which he was chased from one country after another. Even his closest friends described him as 'the Flying Dutchman' of modern times.[1] His death in exile marked the end of a whole era in Iran's turbulent history, an era of high hopes and bitter disillusionments, and the start of a new age of revolution and war that brought the entire region to the brink of disaster.

The Shah was plunged into the turmoil of Iranian politics in 1941 when he was barely 22 years old. The country was under foreign military occupation – the British in the south, the Russians in the north – with the army and the administration created by his father in disarray. Iran's independence was no more than a cypher and, until the mid-1940s, the nation experienced periodic famines of the kind usually associated with the poorest regions of Africa. 'What is the good of being king in so miserable a land?' he once asked.

Foreign occupation humiliated the nation and encouraged secessionist movements inspired and financed by rival foreign powers. The young Shah was a plaything of ambitious, older politicians who wished to turn him into a powerless prisoner. Whenever he tried to seek a decision-making role the Shah was told that since under the Constitution of 1906 he had no responsibility he could have no power either. His struggle to gain real political power without scrapping the Constitution was to become one of the central themes of Iranian politics until the late 1970s.

At the start of the 1950s Iran nationalised its principal natural resource, oil, and began to reassert her independence. This provoked a period of confrontation with Britain that led to almost a decade of conflict during which the Shah nearly lost his throne. In the 1960s the Shah launched his White Revolution – a programme of limited but, under the circumstances, audacious reforms that gave some land to the peasants and tried to enhance the status of women. In the 1970s, acting through OPEC, the Shah promoted a campaign aimed at raising oil prices. Iran's income from oil more than quadrupled and gave the Shah the financial means necessary for an ambitious industrialisation programme combined with an unprecedented military build-up. Iran, the 'sick man of the Middle East' in the 1940s and 1950s, was established as a regional superpower. Following British military withdrawal from East of Suez, Iran assumed the role of 'policeman of the Persian Gulf'. Using his rising military might, economic power and international prestige, the Shah challenged Soviet expansionism in Afghanistan, the Indian subcontinent, the Arabian Peninsula and the Horn of Africa. In 1973 he used military threat to persuade the Iraqis, led by Saddam Hussein, to abandon their dream of annexing Kuwait. He asserted his role as guarantor of stability in a region that contained two-thirds of the world's oil reserves.

The man buried in the solitary tomb at Rifa'i became one of the contemporary world's most experienced and powerful rulers. He conducted business with virtually every leading personality in international politics after 1941. As a young monarch he played host to Churchill and Roosevelt. Stalin himself called at the royal palace to pay his respects. In later years a steady stream of distinguished visitors gave Tehran the status of an important centre of international politics, attracting presidents Eisenhower, Johnson,[2] Nixon and Carter, as well as British visitors including the Queen, Edward Heath, James Callaghan and Margaret Thatcher. Among visitors from France were General de Gaulle, Georges Pompidou, and Valéry Giscard d'Estaing. Statesmen from both left and right, from both East and West as well as from the non-aligned movement, called on the Shah and praised his 'wisdom and leadership'. Leonid Brezhnev, Deng Xiao-Ping, Marshal Tito, Indira Gandhi, Willy Brandt, Emperor Haile Selassie, King Faisal of Saudia Arabia and Helmut Schmidt were among visitors to Tehran, as were Henry Kissinger and Ronald Reagan. Virtually every crowned head in the world included him among their personal friends as the Pahlavis, despite the fact of being a new dynasty, were eventually recognised by other royal families as legitimate members of their restricted club. And yet as he desperately searched for a safe haven in exile, few people were prepared to come to his aid.

The Shah regarded politics as the province of demagoguery, an art in which only charlatans could excel. He had no time for what he saw as the tedious process of achieving consensus through debate and discussion and tried to justify his solitary exercise of power by insisting it was what Iran needed to catch up with lost time. He believed that he was more patriotic than anyone else and needed no advice on how best to promote and protect the highest interests of the nation. He suffered during much of the 1940s and a good part of the 1950s, as he was denied a share in running the country. He was bored in his cold, uncomfortable palaces where frequent dalliance with the fairer sex provided only partial solace.

The Shah evoked and provoked intense emotions. There were those who loved him passionately: the Azeri peasants who wanted to sacrifice their children on his path in the 1960s; the young officers who were ready to kill and to die in his name until the very end; the many thousands of ordinary folk who wrote to him from all over the world to offer him love and affection when he was being refused a visa by his former friends and partners. But there were also those who hated him: Ayatollah Khomeini, who claimed that Muslim prayers would not be complete without the slogan 'Death to the Shah', the keynote of his Islamic Revolution; Saddam Hussein, who described the day the Shah left Iran as 'the happiest day in my life'; tens of thousands of Marxist-Leninist militants who regarded the Shah as the main obstacle to proletarian revolution in the Middle East. There were also the many ordinary Iranian folk who, in the end, could not understand why their Shah decided to abandon the country and fly his entire family to safety while many of his most faithful associates were left behind to face Khomeini's death squads. At least some of the hundreds of thousands of Iranians who marched against his regime for nearly a year must have hated him passionately. To those who idolised him he could do no wrong: the mere fact that he was heir to the throne of Cyrus the Great put him beyond judgment, but to those who hated him he was the incarnation of evil. One thing was certain: one had to be for him or against him; no one was allowed to remain indifferent or to try to assess his record as a leader objectively.

In 1961 at a Paris restaurant a friend and I overheard a conversation between two elderly French gentlemen at the next table. They were talking about Iran and the Shah. Within minutes the tone of the conversation changed and the two respectable-looking gentlemen began to shout abuse at each other. When calm was restored I told my friend how amazed I was to see that conflicting views about the Shah, the leader of a remote and backward land with virtually no role in world politics and certainly no important relations with France, could provoke such passions thousands of miles from Tehran. Within minutes it was the turn of my friend and me to quarrel about the Shah. 'Are you for him or against him?' my friend asked in a rising tone of anger. When I refused to give a yes or no answer he began to sulk and was soon too angry to wait for coffee. I was left with the bill and knew that I had lost a friend. Later he turned his hatred of the Shah into a religion and refused to go back to Iran until the monarchy had been overthrown. He returned to Tehran just days after Khomeini had seized power and a few months later was executed on orders from the ayatollah after being accused of 'warring against Allah.'

The Shah described the modernisation of Iran as the principal goal of his life, and yet he adamantly refused to see that there could be no veritable modernisation without democracy. He often referred to his Swiss education as part of his credentials as a profoundly committed democrat, but was, at the same time, convinced that Iran was not yet ripe for democracy, and that it was his duty as 'the father of the nation' to save the Iranians from a slothful life of prayer, pilgrimage, small commerce, backward farming and cottage industry. He wanted to turn Iran into a second Japan, make her one of the five or six major world powers by the end of the century. He regarded himself as the custodian of Iran's grandeur and freedom and in later years he extended his self-proclaimed mission of saving Iran to include the entire world. He ordered the creation of a Universal Welfare Legion whose task was to combat and, in time, eliminate poverty, hunger, disease and ignorance from the entire globe.

The Shah also created an advisory committee whose task was to prevent the world from being conquered by Communism.[3] The committee held its first full meeting at a Caspian Sea resort in the summer of 1978 when Iran herself was passing through a revolutionary crisis. Had the participants at the meeting opened their windows they could have heard the crowds shouting 'Death to the Shah' outside.

There were other occasions when the Shah's many enterprises offered both high drama and pure farce. In the mid-1960s the Shah dispatched his newly-created navy to show the flag round the Arabian Peninsula and down to the Horn of Africa, but the first flotilla that set out amid massive propaganda ran out of petrol in the middle of the Arabian Sea and had to be rescued with help from passing British merchant vessels.

In 1971 the Shah organised the Persepolis ceremonies to mark the twenty-fifth centenary of the Persian Empire and the return of Iran to the international scene as a regional military power. But before the ceremonies could begin the Imperial Guard, the flower of the Shah's new army, had to launch a campaign against the millions of poisonous snakes that populated the desert and whose sting could have killed the distinguished guests. The guards suffered more casualties in that campaign than ever before in battle. During the ceremony itself the guests admired the beauty of finely choreographed parades, but at one point the camels, frightened by accompanying fireworks, bolted and sent a wave of panic through the world leaders present.

More than a decade after the Shah's death it is no longer necessary to be for or against him on all matters. How could one be for or against everything that happened during a reign of nearly thirty-eight years? How could Iranians not be for him when he fought over Azerbaijan or when he gave the royal assent to the bill that nationalised Iran's oil? How could one be against the principle of land reform or the enhancement of women's status? And did he not deserve support when he fought for a more just system of production and pricing for oil, which he called 'a noble substance'? But how could anyone be for him when he closed all doors on discussion and debate and effectively drove many intelligent and patriotic Iranians into the arms of reactionary mullahs? And how could one approve of the unchecked intervention of the SAVAK secret police in virtually all aspects of life, especially in the 1970s? Last but not least, it would be difficult to understand, much less to justify, his almost pathological belief that only the major powers were capable of either protecting or destablising his regime. In the mid-1950s he had obtained a written guarantee from Britain and the United States not to recognise any new Iranian regime that might come to power as a result of a *coup d'état* that overthrew the Shah. In 1979 he counted on that dated – and by then worthless – piece of paper to calm down the situation in Iran. For a while after he had gone into exile he continued to entertain illusions about an early return with help of foreign friends. And right to the end he remained convinced, or pretended to be, that he had been brought down as a result of foreign conspiracy.

I first thought of writing a biography of the Shah in 1971 as a means of coming to grips with the many political questions that plagued my life and

the life of at least two Iranian generations. I wanted to know who the
Shah really was, what made him tick so to speak. I abandoned the idea
when I realised that I would not be able to offer an objective account
without running the risk of being forced into exile. In 1979, when the
Shah himself was in exile, I thought of the project once again. By then,
however, an objective biography would have provoked the wrath of
Iran's new ruler, Ayatollah Khomeini. By 1988 both the Shah and
Khomeini were gone, but the drama in which they had been the principal
protagonists continued to dominate Iran's life as a nation in search of its
own way into the modern world. Both men are still eminently relevant to
the course of political development not only in Iran but throughout the
Middle East and beyond. The two offer mutually exclusive models that
have supporters and opponents in most Muslim countries. Having told
the story of Khomeini's life,* I tried to discover the unknown Shah.

Since the Persian monarchy began some 2550 years ago, Iran has had
more than 350 kings. No fewer than half of them were either assassinated
or killed in battle. Many went into exile to escape death. Iran's long
history is full of fallen crowns and shattered imperial dreams. Of
Mohammad-Reza Shah's five immediate predecessors, one was assassinated and three were forced into exile. What makes Mohammad-Reza
Shah's tragedy special is that he was, perhaps, the first Iranian king in
more than a century to have a real possibility of ending his reign
peacefully and dying in his own country. That this was not the case was,
to a large extent, the result of Iran's chronic political underdevelopment.
But the Shah's own failure to operate within the realities of Iranian society
– unpleasant as they undoubtedly were – contributed to his downfall and
its dramatic consequences for the nation as a whole. The fall of the Shah
was, in a sense, the prelude to more than a decade of instability in the
region, culminating in the Iraqi invasion of Kuwait and the subsequent
massacre of Kurds and shi'ites in Mesopotamia. It may take Iran and her
region many more years before the shockwaves unleased by the fall of the
Shah are fully absorbed.

The day the Shah flew out of Tehran, never to return, his opponents
gathered in the streets of the capital to burn his portrait. The fires thus
raised reminded me of the ordeal of Siavash, Iran's mythological hero,
who also had to pass through fire in order to receive the judgment of
Ahura Mazda, the God of the ancient Persians. Mohammad-Reza Shah
suffered a far more painful ordeal as a result of the physical pain and
moral humiliation of exile. He is beyond the judgment of mortals and
here I have simply tried to tell his unknown story.

*The Spirit of Allah – Khomeini and the Islamic Revolution, published by Hutchinson,
1985.

I

The Giant

Reza Khan had just put on his uniform and was waiting for his breakfast of dry bread and tea when his orderly, the excitable Abbas Beyg, swept in in a gyrating mass of enthusiastic gestures and incoherent words. 'Good news! Good news!' the orderly shouted as his master, half amused and half annoyed, tried to restrain him.

The scene was Reza Khan's tent deep in the dense subtropical Caspian forest. It was the end of October 1919. For more than a year the forest had been the scene of bloody battles between an expeditionary force of just over 1000 soldiers from Tehran and the elusive guerrillas of the so-called Movement of the Jungle. The movement was led by Mirza Kuchak Khan, an ex-mullah turned rebel general, who had concluded an alliance with Lenin, the new master of Russia, and declared the creation of a Soviet republic in parts of the Iranian coast on the Caspian.

Reza Khan, a professional soldier, commanded the expeditionary force. His mission was to kill or capture the charismatic Mirza whose passionate message of freedom and equality was spreading like wildfire. Thus the best news Reza Khan could receive would be the capture or death of the ever-elusive Mirza. But Abbas Beyg's good news had nothing to do with the war. A messenger had just arrived from Tehran to inform Reza Khan that his wife had given birth to twins – a boy and a girl – three days earlier on 26 October in the capital. Reza Khan was on horseback a few hours later on his way to Tehran. In his absence one of his loyal lieutenants, Fazlallah Khan, took command.[1]

Reza Khan must have been exceptionally happy that day. His first son had been born and, according to Persian tradition, he was now a 'full father'. He had already fathered two daughters, one from each of his two wives, and loved them both,[2] but only the birth of a son could fully establish a man's status as a father.

Because there were no roads between Tehran and the Caspian forest belt at the time, the journey, through the Alborz mountain gorges, lasted three days for a distance of less than 200 miles. On arrival in Tehran, Reza

Khan first went to a public bath to wash away the dirt and fatigue of a rough journey. He was returning home to his young wife after an absence of more than six months.

Home was a mudbrick one-storey edifice at the end of a narrow cobblestone alley known as Kucheh Roghani or Greasy Lane. It intersected with the wider Khalabad (Tattooville) Street where no sane person would venture after dark. Down the middle of Greasy Lane ran an open gutter which, once every other week, was filled with a brownish liquid that was often the cause of violent disputes in the neighbourhood. People killed and died over how to share the gift of the gutter, the much-coveted liquid that came from the melting snows of the Towchal mountains some 15 miles away. On its way through many villages and the best part of a chaotic city it collected an assortment of debris. By the time it reached Greasy Lane this unique body of water was almost too thick to flow further. On warmer days the gutter spread an aggressive odour of decay throughout the neighbourhood. The water from the gutter was stored in reservoirs built in the basement of every house.

This part of the city was known as Darvazeh Qazvin (Qazvin Gate) and consisted of a jigsaw puzzle of crooked alleys just inside the ruins of what had once been the city wall. From the rooftops one could still see the moat just beyond the wall. Now dry, the moat served as a rubbish dump where stray cats and dogs fought noisy nocturnal battles. Beyond the moat was the desert, the universe of highwaymen, adventurers and wandering dervishes, where caravans of camels were often attacked and robbed, travellers' throats were slit and fortunes were made and lost. The only law in force beyond the Tehran walls was not that of the King of Kings; it was the law of violence. The only order that reigned throughout the country was that of anarchy. Every now and then the desert bandits would attack parts of the capital itself, stealing, killing, and kidnapping. Some of the kidnapped children – usually girls – were then dispatched to Khivah, in Central Asia, where they were sold as slaves.[3]

Reza Khan's house, although one of the better-built in that forlorn part of Tehran, was still too modest for a man who had just been promoted one of the most senior officers in the only organised military force that the Persian King of Kings had at his disposal at that time.[4] Surrounded by a ten-foot mud wall, the house belonged to a bazaar merchant who let it for the equivalent of £10 a year. It consisted of four rooms of which only one had windows. The building opened on a desolate courtyard where a lone persimmon tree leaned over an empty pond like a witch staring into a desecrated tomb. It was in the windowed room that the twins had been born with the help of a group of weeping, shrieking and ululating women. Outside the house had gathered a crowd of beggars, witchdoctors, ventriloquists, bear-dancers, fire-eaters, fortune-tellers and exorcists to mark the happy occasion in exchange for a bowl of broth or a few coins. The birth of a boy often attracted such crowds in Tehran at the time.

A birth is always something of an adventure, even under the most propitious of circumstances. For the newly-born twins that freezing autumn it was more than an adventure: it was a life and death gamble. In the Iran of 1919 the odds favoured death over life. One in four babies was stillborn and of those who were born alive only one in three lived beyond a second birthday. Of the babies who survived the first two years of existence only one in two had a chance of reaching the age of 21. Average life expectancy was just under 30. Smallpox, malaria, whooping cough, diphtheria, mumps, measles, typhoid and meningitis reaped a rich harvest each year. There was only one hospital in the whole of the country, with no more than three or four trained doctors.

Survival in itself did not guarantee a rewarding life even for the children of wealthy aristocratic families. In a country with 99 per cent illiteracy, very few children received any form of schooling. Virtually no girls were allowed to learn to read and write and boys attended Qur'anic schools where a rudimentary and dogmatic education was offered. Iran had just one secondary school and no universities.[5]

In 1919 the romantic Persia of Western travellers existed only in the imagination. The country was passing through what many historians saw as one of the darkest phases in its thrice-millennial history. The period, named by later Iranian scholars as the Age of Decline,[6] had begun nearly a century earlier with a series of military defeats suffered by the reigning Qajar monarchs at the hands of Tsarist armies. In 1808 Persia lost to Russia as the Tsars pushed their southern borders down to the River Aras. From 1850 onwards Russia speeded up its territorial expansion in Central Asia and captured the last of the small semi-autonomous khanates and fiefdoms that had paid nominal allegiance to the Persian monarch in Tehran.

During the same period Iran also lost territory in the east. Parts of Iranian Baluchistan were detached by Great Britain and incorporated into the British Raj. Britain also used a combination of trade pressures and military threats to force the Shah to accept the loss of Herat to Pushtun warlords who had created the Afghan kingdom in the eighteenth century.

Between 1840 and 1870 Iran suffered a series of unprecedented famines. These were only partly due to adverse climatic conditions in a land where a single season of insufficient rain spelled disaster. Recent research has established that the worst of these famines were man made. The major landowners – always supported by the mullahs –artificially reduced supply in order to push up prices. At the same time the various tribal chiefs who controlled the country's few roads attacked and looted caravans carrying grain to cities. Harvested wheat and rice were deliberately burned to prevent prices from falling. According to conservative estimates, these famines reduced the population of the country by nearly a third as hundreds of thousands of people perished from hunger. In some parts of the country cannibalism was recorded on an alarmingly large scale. Tens of thousands of families just walked across the border into territories held by the Tsar or the Ottoman sultan in a reversal of the previous trends.*

A week after their birth, the twins were formally named at a ceremony that cost Reza Khan almost all of his meagre savings. Food was served to a large gathering of relatives and friends, as well as to the beggars of Tattooville who had besieged the house. A blind sithar player provided entertainment and Abbas Beyg was persuaded to offer his own version of Caucasian dances. A mullah murmured a few verses of the Qur'an into the ears of the new-born and the boy – it went without saying – had to be named Mohammad after the Prophet of Islam. (In those days, Mohammad was the most popular name for first-born sons of Persian families regardless of social background and economic station.[7]) Reza Khan, however, insisted that his own name be added to that of the Prophet to give the new-born boy the unusual name of Mohammad-Reza.[8] His twin sister, born only half an hour after him, was named Ashraf, an aristocratic name which means 'the noblest'. The girl's presence, however, was totally eclipsed by that of her twin brother who, in a male-dominated society, enjoyed countless privileges as the future head of the family.

Like other Persian fathers, Reza Khan must have had big dreams for his first-born son. He was a taciturn, even secretive, man, with virtually no close friends in whom he would confide, but it is safe to speculate that he dreamed of a military career for Mohammad-Reza. Reza Khan was himself a professional soldier and the son of a professional soldier. What is certain, though is that Reza Khan could not have dreamed of his son as a future King of Kings, a successor to the 2500-year-old throne of Cyrus the Great. There was nothing in the rough forests of the Caspian or the desolate landscape of Tattooville to inspire those kind of dreams.

Reza Khan might have even had doubts about his ability to pay for Mohammad-Reza's education. People often wondered why Reza Khan, a senior officer, lived in a rented house on Greasy Lane. Some accused him of demagoguery, saying he wanted to build up an image as a man of the people. The real reason was that Reza Khan could hardly make ends meet. Most of his officers corps peers were from aristocratic backgrounds and independently wealthy. The salary the King of Kings paid to his officers allowed them no surpluses for venturing beyond the bare minimum. The most senior officers, including Reza Khan, received the equivalent of £10 in monthly salary. NCOs were paid the equivalent of £3

*Previously ethnic Iranians had fled Tsarist rule while some shi'ite subjects of the Ottoman sultan, the Caliph of the sunni Muslims, also emigrated to Iran to live under the shi'ite monarch. The nineteenth-century famines were so severe as to make people disregard their ethnic loyalties and religious beliefs.

a month. Ordinary soldiers, although theoretically employed by the Crown for life, received no salary at all. They had to be content with food and shelter plus the occasional gift of a uniform. Some soldiers received pocket money from wealthier relatives, but the vast majority had to spend their weekly day-off as well as all their leave doing odd jobs to earn cash. They worked as stone-masons or barbers, sold watermelons, chopped wood, built furniture and slit the throat of sacrificial sheep or camel at religious festivals. Every now and then the King of Kings would present his soldiers with gifts in kind: chickens or eggs or even mudbricks that could be sold in the bazaar. Many returned to their villages at harvest time.

That Reza Khan managed to maintain a certain standard of living, meaning that his family did not starve, was in part due to a small fortune inherited by his second wife, Taj al-Moluk, Mohammad-Reza's mother. Taj al-Moluk's family belonged to a branch of the Ayramlu clan from Nakhichevan. With the fall of Nakhichevan to the Tsar in 1826, a number of Ayramlu families – all Turkic speaking and fanatical shi'ites – crossed the River Aras into Iran and eventually settled in Tehran. Thus Taj al-Moluk, whose name means the Crown of the Kings but who was usually called Taji, the Coronet, was born in Tehran. Two of her brothers were officers in the same force as Reza Khan and it was through them that the marriage was eventually arranged.

Taji's beauty had become proverbial in family circles. Her long, curly tresses and her deep black eyes made her a typical Persian beauty of the kind one sees in Qajar period paintings. She was probably 20 when she married Reza Khan, an unusually late age at the time. Many girls were married off at the age of nine and most had already become mothers in their teens. In their occasional quarrels, Reza Khan and his wife did not agree on Taj al-Moluk's age at the time of her marriage. 'I was only sixteen when I married you and didn't know better!' Taj al-Moluk would shout at her husband. 'Sixteen? Come on, come on! You were at least twenty-six!' Reza Khan would shout back, half in jest. The exchange would end with Taj al-Moluk bursting into tears and withdrawing to her room.[9]

Taji had one decisive advantage over her husband: she was fully literate, having learned to read and write at an early age, later applying herself to a study of the Qur'an. Delicate, well-mannered and respectful of the intricate formalities that pervade every aspect of Persian life, Taji was the opposite of her husband in virtually every domain. Reza Khan had remained illiterate until the age of thirty and had received virtually no education in either classical learning or social manners. Ignorant of the flowery style of Persian discourse, Reza Khan had no time for the verbal gymnastics that gave the ancient language much of its charm. His limited vocabulary of, perhaps, a couple of thousand words would not allow him to venture beyond the beaten track of stark expression.

The husband and wife were also poles apart on the crucial subject of religion. Taji was a devout shi'ite Muslim who spent much of her time reading the Qur'an and the standard duodecimal textbooks.[10] She had also performed the important pilgrimages of Mashhad and Qom in the company of her parents. At least once a year she also went to Shah Abdul-Azim's shrine in Rey, south of Tehran, for a day of prayer and pilgrimage. Reza Khan on the other hand, was never known for his firm Islamic convictions. Taji made fun of her husband because he could not even remember the names of all the twelve Imams of Iranian shi'ism. In those early years Reza Khan did not advertise his irreverence and at times even participated in some of the religious ceremonies organised by Taj al-Moluk. But he never performed the five daily prayers of Islam; nor did he observe the fasting rites of Ramadan. As for pilgrimages to shi'ite shrines, it was not until much later that Reza Khan visited Mashhad and Qom.

Reza Khan and his wife differed in still other fields. While Taj al-Moluk was sociable, her husband was a loner. Taj al-Moluk enjoyed elaborate Persian cooking and always wanted to organise dinner parties. Reza Khan preferred simple food and was often content with a meal of bread, goat's cheese and grapes. In later years, when he had more money, he had two meals of rice and chicken every day, at noon and shortly after sunset, remaining faithful to this rather limited diet for the best part of twenty years. For Reza Khan, eating was a physical need that had to be satisfied in a few minutes. For Taj al-Moluk, a meal provided an occasion for conviviality.

Reza Khan believed that listening to music was either a waste of time or even potentially dangerous because it dampened the fighting ardour of young men. Taj al-Moluk was something of an expert in the complex styles of classical Persian music and had even learned to play the sithar. Taj al-Moluk shared only one of her husband's passions: his love of Persian cats. Their house was often full of cats that came and went as they pleased.

People who saw the couple on the rare occasions that they appeared together in public – in practice this meant at gatherings of the Ayramlu clan – often commented on the contrast in their physical appearances. Taj al-Moluk, short and petite, appeared almost fragile, but behind this deceptive appearance lay a strong personality; by all accounts she was the only person capable of standing up to Reza Khan and forcing him to retreat in an argument. Reza Khan stood 6 feet tall with broad shoulders and an unusually large head. At a time when most Iranians were either short or of medium height, he appeared a veritable giant. In contemporary photographs, the first of which dates back to 1911, he stands head and shoulder above everyone else.

Taj al-Moluk boasted about her family tree and claimed a number of minor military and civilian leaders of the Caucasus among her ancestors. Reza Khan's origins were more obscure. In later years much effort was spent on manufacturing a pedigree for Reza Khan. His son Mohammad-Reza tried to trace his ancestry to 'the earliest Aryan tribes' who settled the Iranian Plateau. This was how Mohammad-Reza described his father's background:

> My family comes from the ancient and famous Caspian province of Mazandaran, one of the original homelands of the Aryan tribes . . . About 1500 BC the hardy Aryan races moved from the steppes of Central Asia and settled down in my country. It is they who gave my country its name – Iran, the land of the Aryans. . . They were highly civilised, possessed horses, wheeled wagons and military chariots. They knew how to write and how to rule, and they put up a state which lasted nearly 2500 years. These Aryans gave Iran some of the finest and most famous kings and warriors know to history, from Jamsheed to Faridoon, Gustasp to Kavus, Rustom to Sohrab [sic] of whose glories Firdousi [sic] sings in his Shahnamah [sic].[11]

Later the enemies of Reza Khan and Mohammad-Reza were to conjure fanciful stories of their own in order to demolish 'the father and the son'.[12] Much of the independent research carried out into Reza Khan's background could not be published before the 1979 revolution.

Reza Khan was born in the village of Alasht in the Savadkuh (Black Mountain) district of the province of Mazandaran on the Caspian in or around 1878. In 1925 an official date for his birth was established: 16 March 1878. But it was not until 1972 that the house in which he was supposed to have been born was identified, renovated and turned into a museum. Journalists invited to visit the village for the occasion found almost no one who could claim to have even the remotest memory of Reza Khan's family. In a society of extended families and close clan relations this could mean only one thing: Reza Khan's family had no roots in Alasht and must have briefly settled there for some obscure reason. Had Reza Khan's parents come to Alasht from somewhere else? If so, where? Reza Khan himself almost never spoke of his ancestors. Did he bear them a grudge for having left him destitute and at the mercy of fate?

Mohammad-Reza had no doubt that his family was connected to the Bavand clan of Savadkuh, known for its martial traditions. He wrote: 'My great-grandfather, Major Murad-Ali Khan, took part in the siege of Herat against the Afghans and was killed in 1856. . . .My grandfather, Abbas-Ali Khan [sic], was a colonel in the Iranian regiment who distinguished himself by his gallantry.'[13] These vague assertions are based on accounts put in circulation in the 1920s after Reza Khan had already attained power. They raise more questions than they pretend to answer. Mohammad-Reza gives his grandfather's name incorrectly and omits the latter's title of Dadash-Beyg. The grandfather's real name was Abbas-Qoli, suggesting a Turkic background. The title Dadash-Beyg is also Turkic; meaning Chief Elder Brother. It was often given to men of a certain age who took charge of raising orphan children.[14] The ranks of colonel and major that Mohammad-Reza mentions did not exist at the time as Iran had no regular army.

The principal objective of the stories concocted by court historians was to sustain the claim that Reza Khan was the first 'true Iranian' to lead the nation after several centuries of 'alien rule' by dynasties of Turkic extraction. Reza Khan had to be portrayed as the quintessential 'Aryan' saviour, in contrast to the Turcoman Qajar rulers who had led Iran into decline and humiliation. Reza Khan also had to be portrayed as the true heir of a long-established martial tradition, again in contrast with the Qajar rulers who spend much of their time in European brothels or at hashish and opium parties in Tehran.

The 'Aryan' claim is so gross that one need not dwell long on the task of refuting it. The Iranian nation today is a curious mixture of more than 3000 years of constant metissage. Even if the notion of race had any concrete meaning it would be virtually impossible for most Iranians to trace their 'Aryan' roots accurately.

As for the martial background of the family, one should not make a great deal of the claims made. During the nineteenth century Iran was almost constantly at war against the Russians, the Afghans, the British and the Ottomans, and when there were no foreign enemies available, the Iranians engaged in one of their seemingly endless civil wars. Tribal feuds and armed rebellions by provincial chieftains against the Crown were permanent features of Iranian life. While there were countless private armies throughout the country, the King of Kings lacked an army of his own. When a foreign war threatened he just appealed to the chiefs of the private, largely tribal, armies to join forces under the command of one of the princes, usually the Crown Prince, and fight in the name of Islam. At the end of each war the Iranian army disbanded and the warriors and their chiefs returned to the provinces. The village of Alasht where Reza Khan was born is too small to have housed an army garrison of any size. Alasht, with a population of around 1000 in 1978, could not have been much larger a century earlier. Because of its strategic location the village might have had a gendarmerie post and Reza Khan's father could have been a gendarme serving in Alasht when his son was born. Alternatively, Abbas-Qoli might have been a soldier of fortune who fought on the side of the highest bidder. He would not have been alone. Thousands of men with a taste for fighting made a career of serving in the private armies maintained by provincial warlords.

At any rate Reza Khan was only forty days old when his father died of unspecified causes. Until 1973 official accounts spoke only of 'a sudden death' and gave no details, Later some court historians began to suggest that Abbas-Qoli Khan was killed in combat. But what combat? Mystery again. Alasht and the entire Savadkuh region were quite peaceful at the time and there was no major conflict anywhere else in the country. At the time of Abbas-Qoli's death, the Qajar monarch, Nassereddin Shah, was on one of his European tours and the whole Iranian nation was preparing for the new year celebrations.[15]

There is at least one other mystery regarding those murky days of Reza Khan's early existence: his mother suddenly decided to take her new-born baby and leave Alasht. Together with her brother, she joined a small caravan that left Savadkuh for Tehran sometime in April 1878. Why the haste? And why did the widow choose to go to Tehran where we know she had no relatives or friends? Did she feel that she and her son might be in danger in Alasht? The journey from the forests of Mazandaran to Tehran was one of the most arduous – and often dangerous – for the caravans of the time, having to pass through steep mountain paths in order to cross the permanently snow-capped Alborz mountains. The better-off travellers made the journey on the backs of mules or donkeys. Others, the vast majority, simply followed on foot, covering their feet with rolled felt to escape frostbite. Some perished before reaching their destination. The risk of death was so strongly present in any caravan journey that safar-kardan – meaning to travel – also meant to die. Travellers paid a small fee in exchange for the guidance and protection the caravan offered and the better-organised caravans were accompanied by armed escorts to protect travellers and merchandise from attacks by wild animals or the bandits who were present on every route. The caravan also included a mullah whose task was to avert all danger thanks to his special contacts with the Hidden Imam.[16] In practice many caravans were attacked and robbed and travellers left destitute on arrival at destinations.

The Savadkuh caravan was not attacked that April, but Reza Khan, less than two months old at the time, nearly froze to death in one of the mountain passes near Tehran where temperatures remain well below zero until June. Reza Khan's uncle was convinced that the baby had already died and wanted to bury him on the spot, but Reza's mother refused and continued to warm him up as best she could until they arrived at an inn where he 'returned to life as if in a miracle'.[17]

Reza Khan's early years in Tehran remain undocumented. What is certain is that he and his mother survived largely thanks to his uncle. The family was not wealthy enough to pay for Reza's schooling even at a local maktab, the school run by a mullah. Reza's uncle taught him the rudiments of arithmetic but he did not learn to read and write until he was in his twenties. Some accounts have even suggested that he was over thirty when he became literate thanks to the ministrations of a private tutor. How did he spend his childhood? One can only speculate. At that time childhood and adolescence were not recognised distinct phases of life that, in any case, was not that long. Girls were put to work, for example, weaving carpets at the age of four or five and were married off by the time they had turned nine or ten. Boys began to work on the farm or in shops from the age of five or six and married at sixteen. Like other boys of his age, Reza must have helped win the family bread by doing a variety of odd jobs. His enemies have suggested that he spent his childhood driving donkeys.[18] This is unlikely because the donkey drivers of those days were the equivalent of today's truck drivers, ensuring the distribution of an incredible variety of commodities, including drinking water, throughout Tehran and other major cities. A donkey driver's position was too elevated for a poor village boy.

The first we hear again of Reza is when, aged 14, he begins his military career. Here again official accounts differ from unofficial – and more plausible – ones. Mohammad-Reza writes that his father joined the Cossack Brigade at the age of 14.[19] The Cossack Brigade had been created by the Qajar Shah in the 1880s as the first step towards the creation of a national army capable of controlling the country on behalf of the central government. The new force was patterned on Tsarist army units and commanded by Russian, Ukrainian and Polish officers seconded by Saint Petersburg. A highly-disciplined force by the then existing Persian standards, the Cossack Brigade, which quickly created garrisons in a number of other cities as well, kept excellent records at its Tehran headquarters. These records first mention Reza Khan in November 1900 when he was at least 22. Thus Reza's military career did not begin with the Cossacks. Recent research shows that Reza joined the Savadkuh fowj in 1892. His uncle must have been able to secure him a place there thanks to contacts he still had in the region. The unit was commanded by Ali-Asghar Khan Amin-Sultan, a Qajar prince, and was stationed at Savadkuh with the task of keeping an eye on the perpetually rebellious Turcomans to the northeast.

In 1895, aged 17, Reza was financially independent enough to take a bride, Maryam Khanom, Reza's 15-year-old cousin. She gave Reza a daughter in 1904 and died a few days later.[20] When by 1900 Reza had gained enough military experience to think of joining the larger and more prestigious Cossack Brigade, he was instantly accepted. His impressive physique, his natural talent for command and his boundless energy soon set him in a class apart. The brigade had no Iranian officers as yet, and the young natives who joined the force were invariably assigned routine tasks. During his first year with the Cossacks, therefore, Reza went through a number of frustrating assignments including two long spells as police guard for the German and Belgian embassies in Tehran. In 1903 Reza was promoted lieutenant and was among the few Iranians who were trained in the use of the new Maxim machineguns that the brigade had just purchased. A year or so later he had occasion to use one of the two Maxims in battle against Kurdish tribal rebels in the Kermanshah region. The Cossacks won a dramatic victory in that battle and Reza the nickname of Maxim.

Over the following five years Reza spent his time fighting various tribal rebels in the four corners of Persia. This gave him a direct understanding of the way things worked in a country that had teetered on the brink of anarchy for several decades. Reza's bravery, his exemplary discipline and unusual abhorrence of luxury made him something of a hero with the men who served under him. The Russian Revolution of 1905 and the Iranian Constitutional Revolution of 1906 injected an unprecedented dose of politics into the previously anodyne conversations of the Cossacks. In 1908 Mohammad-Ali Shah, the new Qajar King, tried to cancel the Constitution granted by his father, Mozaffareddin Shah two years earlier. Mohammad-Ali, supported by the Tsar, ordered the Cossacks to bombard the newly-created parliament and restore traditional despotism. The Russian commander of the Brigade, Vselevod Liyakhov, performed with such zeal that he and his force were quickly established as symbols of Iran's humiliation by foreign powers. The Constitutionalists, who raised partisan armies and fought the Shah's Cossacks in the three-year-long civil war that followed, did all they could to win the Persian officers and NCOs of the Brigade over to their cause. Mohammad-Ali Shah's subsequent defeat and exile to Russia confirmed the triumph of the Constitutionalists and, at the same time, led to a major purge of the Cossacks Brigade high command. The brigade was no longer the Shah's private force but a branch of the constitutional government and responsible to the Majlis.

The purge of the Russian officers meant rapid promotion for Iranians serving in the force. Reza was promoted captain. For the first time it was possible for Iranians to dream of one day expelling all the Russians and assuming full command themselves.

The upheavals of 1908–11 that had kept Reza busy in various parts of the country also helped awaken his taste for politics. It was after 1908 when he was already over 30, that he began to educate himself in earnest. He took lessons in calligraphy, literature and history, also spending some time studying mathematics and geography. Between 1908 and 1911 he enjoyed the services of more then 20 private tutors. By 1911 he had no difficulty reading even very long and complex texts. He devoured history books and read as many newspapers as he could find in the remote provinces where he was often stationed. During the leave that he spent in Tehran he observed the capital's political scene and tried to understand how the machinery of government worked.

Left a widower by the death of Maryam Khanom in 1904, Reza Khan did not think of a second marriage until 1915. By that time Iran had been sucked into the First World War. Within a few weeks the whole country was aflame. German agents in the south succeeded in inciting local tribes to revolt. The British landed troops at Bushehr and, through their tribal allies among the Bakhtiars, cut off the province of Khuzestan, where oil had been discovered in 1908, from the rest of the country. The Ottomans invaded Iran from the west, using Mesopotamia, then part of the empire of the Sublime Porte, as a base for their aggression. The Russians marched into Khorassan and Gorgan and landed an expeditionary force on the

Iranian coast of the Caspian Sea. Between 1915 and 1918 the Cossack Brigade was largely confined to its barracks as foreign armies fought one another on Iranian soil.

The collapse of the Tsarist empire in 1917 knocked Russia out of Iranian politics for the first time in more than a century. The new Bolshevik regime later renounced all the imperial advantages the Tsars had acquired in Iran by force, bribery and intrigue. The Bolshevik Revolution and the civil war it provoked in Russia also divided the Russian, Ukranian and Polish officers of the Cossack Brigade. Some officers sided with the Bolsheviks while the vast majority left Iran and joined the White forces in the Russian civil war. The departure of these officers paved the way for speedier promotion of the Persian officers and by the end of 1918 Reza Khan had been made a colonel and put in command of a unit at Kermanshah.[21] In the meantime he had a second daughter, Shams, by his second wife.

In 1919 Britain seized the opportunity offered by Russia's withdrawal and dictated a treaty to the Qajar monarch that made Iran a virtual protectorate. The ruling classes, concerned about the possibility of Bolshevism spreading to Iran, believed that only Britain could save the country from annexation by revolutionary Russia. However, the Persian intelligentsia and the middle classes deeply resented the 1919 treaty and openly called for its cancellation and Reza Khan could not have been unsympathetic to the country's growing mood of nationalism. Some nationalists felt so outraged that they committed suicide.[22]

From 1918 onwards Reza had his own circle of confidants and admirers. These were mostly recruited among recently promoted army officers, but also included a number of young politicians and bazaar merchants. By 1920, when Reza Khan was put in command of the Qazvin garrison, his reputation as a potential national leader had already been established in the capital's political circles. The Qazvin assignment was of crucial importance. That strategic city, situated only 60 miles west of the capital, also controlled the network of roads leading west, northwest and to the Caspian coast. Proximity to Tehran enabled Reza Khan to visit the capital almost every week and to entertain potential friends and supporters who travelled to his Qazvin base. Simultaneously Reza Khan put increasing pressure on Tehran to sack the remaining Russian officers and replace them with Iranians.

In November 1920, apparently without the prior accord of either the Shah or his Grand Vizir (Sadr 'Azam), Reza Khan took it upon himself to sack General Clerge, the Russian commander of the Cossack Brigade. The operation was a simple one. Reza Khan, accompanied by half a dozen heavily armed Cossacks, arrived at General Clerge's sumptuous residence in Tehran one evening while the Russian general was having tea. He was manifestly surprised to see one of his subordinates suddenly appear in front of him. Politely but firmly, Reza informed General Clerge that a coach was waiting outside to take him to the port of Enzeli: 'There, General, you shall board a ship and return home to Russia.' The Russian officer knew that the game was up and did as he was told. Within twenty-four hours there were almost no foreigners within the Cossack Brigade. Reza Khan declared himself Commander of the force, a *fait accompli* which was instantly approved by the Qajar king who promoted the audacious officer to the rank of brigadier-general (Mir-Panj).

Reza Khan now installed himself at his newly-acquired home on Amirieh Street, not far from the royal palaces. He now had a monthly income of over £30 and a far higher standard of living. His house became something of a political club where nationalist officers and reformist politicians gathered to discuss the nation's seemingly endless problems. This was a typical Iranian dowreh or salon, informal associations that assumed some of the functions of the political parties which did not exist.[23] Taj al-Moluk was, of course, not allowed to attend any of the sessions: politics were not for women. Nevertheless, she had the task of running a household that was rapidly being established as a veritable centre of power in the capital.

The bright star among Reza Khan's political associates was a 35-year-old journalist named Sayyed Zia-eddin Tabataba'i. Born to a traditional religious family, the Sayyed, as he was generally called, had trained to become a mullah,[24] but before attaining the title of Hojat al-Islam (Vicar of Islam), he had exchanged his mullah's garb for a European-style suit. A fiery speaker and a writer with a vitriolic pen, the Sayyed had created an influential circle of young politicians around his newspaper *R'ad* (The Thunder). The mullahs hated him as a renegade and resented his emphasis on nationalism rather than Islam as a means of mobilising the energies of the Iranian people at a crucial moment in the history of the country. The Sayyed, after a brief flirtation with socialism, had concluded that only a firm alliance with Britain could keep the Bolsheviks out of Iran. In his contacts with the British he argued that Iran needed strong, nationalistic leadership capable of standing up to the threat of Communist subversion.

The 1919 treaty saw an increase in the British military presence in Iran. Britain also tried to fill in the gap left by the expulsion of the Russian officers from the Cossack Brigade. General Ironside, the commander of the British military mission in Iran, soon realised that Britain alone would be unable to prevent the spread of Bolshevism to Iran by the force of arms. Iran had been the first country in the world to recognise the new Bolshevik regime in 1918 and an Iranian delegation had been dispatched to Moscow to talk to the new masters of Russia in 1919. The Russians, however, seemed reluctant to enter into formal agreements with a regime they must have regarded as a fading force. In his frequent contacts with Sayyed Zia-eddin Tabataba'i, Ironside must have learned about Reza Khan's personality and ambitions. Reza Khan and Ironside had also met during a courtesy visit paid by the British general to the Cossack Brigade headquarters at the end of 1920.

Did Ironside encourage a military move on the part of the Cossacks? There is no evidence to support such a contention although later critics of Reza Khan tried to portray him as a tool of the British. What is certain is that when the move was eventually made, Ironside was no longer in Tehran; he had left for Cairo and the aircraft that carried him had crashed half way.

Reza Khan made his move on 20 February 1921, marching to Tehran from Qazvin at the head of a force of 1500 Cossacks. The force reached the capital shortly before midnight and entered it through the Gomrok (Customs) Gate without meeting any resistance. The Cossacks who had been assigned to defend the capital would not fire at their own commander-in-chief. When a snowbound Tehran woke up the following day the putsch had succeeded in seizing control of all government buildings as well as the many royal palaces. A half-hearted attempt at resistance had been made by Crown Prince Mohammad-Hassan Mirza who had ended up abandoned even by his trusted bodyguards and fled into hiding. The central gendarmerie station at Tupkhaneh (Cannon House) Square had also tried to resist but had capitulated after barely an hour. Three gendarmes were killed in the engagement; they were the only casualties of an otherwise bloodless *coup d'état*.

On the morning of 21 February the Qajar King was told that he could keep his throne provided he did what he was told. Ahmad Shah, a weak man interested mostly in building up his personal fortune, had no intentions of resisting. He consulted the British Embassy and was told that this was an internal Iranian problem and that he should handle it himself. Forty-eight hours later he signed two decrees: one appointing Sayyed Zia-eddin as Grand Vizir and the other named Reza Khan Commander-in-Chief (Sardar Sepah). This was the first time in more than half a century that an Iranian had commanded the Iranian armed forces.

Reza Khan was too busy to go home and visit his family. He had to supervise the rounding up of potential opponents – more than 80 were arrested – and help the Sayyed choose his ministers. At noon on 21 February a communiqué signed by Reza Khan was read at street intersections by public criers and pasted onto walls. It was written in a terse, direct language in sharp contrast with the pseudo-scholarly and flowery jargon of the Persian bureaucracy during the Qajar era. The communiqué said: 'I command that all be obedient and keep quiet. Those who refuse to obey will be punished.' It was clear that despite the presence of Sayyed Zia-eddin and more than a dozen other civilians in the new Cabinet, real power rested with the military.

The new Cabinet moved quickly to handle some of the nation's most pressing problems. Six days after it took over a treaty was signed with the Bolshevik government in Moscow under which Russia renounced all colonial claims against Iran and cancelled Iranian debts to the Tsarist state. In exchange Iran undertook never to allow its territory to be used as a base for aggression against the new Soviet power. At the same time steps were taken to improve the living standards of the poor and to curb bureaucratic and royal corruption. The security situation in the capital and other major cities improved beyond recognition.

The new Cabinet was formally presented to Ahmad Shah on 24 April 1921, two months after seizing power. Reza Khan held the post of War Minister in the new Cabinet and was immediately identified as the new regime's strongman.

As prime minister, Sayyed Zia-eddin soon proved far less effective than he had been as a propagandist and conspirator. His Achilles heel, in the context of the nationalistic atmosphere he himself had helped create, remained his close contacts with the British. Within the Cabinet Reza Khan had emerged as leader of a faction that wanted the 1919 treaty with Britain scrapped. The group argued that because Soviet Russia no longer posed a military threat against Iran, there was no point in turning the country into a virtual protectorate of Great Britain. Indeed, the presence of British troops in southeast Iran and almost open British intervention in Iranian politics constituted provocation against Soviet Russia. The Sayyed, however, was opposed to an early cancellation of the 1919 treaty, arguing that the new regime needed support from a major power in order to establish itself and test Russian intentions in practice. By May 1921 the clash between the Anglophile Sayyed and the faction led by Reza Khan had come to a head and Ahmad Shah had to choose between them.

He had no real choice. His palace was surrounded by Reza Khan's heavily armed Cossacks. The Sayyed resigned and immediately fled to Baghdad which was then under British control. Had he stayed on he would, almost certainly, have been arrested. On 23 June 1921 Ahmad Shah formally repudiated the 1919 treaty and Britain was asked to withdraw its troops from Iranian territory, providing an occasion for nationwide jubilation.

One might have expected Reza Khan to take over as prime minister immediately, but he had not yet fully established a nationwide power base for himself. As prime minister he would have been obliged to spend most of his time in Tehran, preventing him from personally surpervising the many campaigns launched by his Cossacks against various rebel leaders in the four corners of the country. In the 30 months that followed the Sayyed's eviction Reza Khan served as War Minister and Commander-in-Chief in eight different Cabinets under three different prime ministers. During that period he succeeded in crushing major rebellions in Gilan, the Gorgan Plain, Baluchistan, Bakhtiari, Luristan and Khuzestan, using a mixture of cunning and brutality to achieve his objectives. In the Gorgan Plain he had more than 100 Turcoman chiefs hanged in public and ordered the destruction of villages that had served as bases for the rebels.

The highway to Mashhad, Iran's principal holy city, was thus reopened after some 30 years of control by Turcoman marauders. In Baluchistan he divided the warring tribes against one another, thus achieving a number of easy victories. In Khuzestan he lured Shaikh Khaz'al, the Arab chieftain who had set up an almost autonomous shaikhdom in Muhammarah (Khorramshahr) into a trap. The shaikh was invited to a ship anchored at Khor Mussa bay for negotiations. Once he was safely aboard the ship lifted anchor and made for the Persian Gulf. The shaikh ended up a prisoner. The toughest rebels were the Lur and Boyer-Ahmad tribes. They continued to fight for the best part of a decade and were eventually crushed when Reza Khan managed to bring in a number of aircraft – the very first in Iran's history – to bombard rebel positions.*

The campaign of pacification helped the Cossack Brigade to become a veritable army. Its officers gained experience in combat, and the force acquired new weapons by absorbing more than a dozen semi-official armies into its ranks. Before the end of 1923 Cossack garrisons were present in virtually all provincial centres. A new central command (Arkan Harb) had been created and two new divisions raised. As War Minister Reza Khan levied special taxes whose proceeds were used to strengthen the armed forces. Most of these taxes were, strictly speaking, illegal but no one dared say so and almost everyone agreed that the country needed a credible army.

In his frequent visits to the provinces Reza Khan extended his network of friends and supporters. He was especially popular among the merchant classes and the small but influential intellectual elite. Qajar society was blocked by its own inner contradictions that none of the factions that together formed the ruling elite could fully comprehend. What was needed was an outsider capable of standing above antagonistic vested interests and feuding factions. Reza Khan was that quintessential outsider. Power was shared among the princes, the mullahs, the great compradores (who were often citizens of foreign powers), the landlords who owned more than 80 per cent of all farms, the top bureaucrats who were often linked with this or that foreign embassy and, last but not least, the tribal chiefs. Reza Khan did not belong to any of these groups. He was a new man, untainted by decaying traditions and unencumbered by ideology. His power base – the army – was also a new force in Iranian politics. The military had never played an independent political role in Iran and, until at least 1923, few people expected Reza Khan to use the army for the purpose of winning exclusive political power.

Reza Khan's busy public life did not prevent him from an active pursuit of his own private affairs. In 1922 he built himself a new house and it was there that Taj al-Moluk gave birth to her second son, Ali-Reza, on 4 April 1922.[25]

*A French mercenary, Charles Banel, helped organise the rudimentary Air Force and flew some of the first sorties against rebel positions. He settled in Iran and lived in Isfahan until the Islamic Revolution of 1979.

The birth of his new son did not discourage Reza Khan from extra-marital affairs. For a while his name was linked with Aziz Khanom, the darling of wealthy Tehranis in the 1920s, but he soon realised that such an illicit liaison could damage his reputation and thus his long-term political plans. He therefore decided to take advantage of the Islamic law under which men are allowed up to four wives (and as many concubines as they can afford)[26] and in 1922 he took a third wife: Turan Khanom, a daughter of the Qajar prince Majd ad-Dowleh. In 1923 Turan Khanom bore Reza Khan a son who was named Gholam-Reza. A few months later Reza Khan married another Qajar princess, Esmat Khanom, who bore him four sons and one daughter.

Reza Khan's three wives could not, largely because of Taj al-Moluk's bitter opposition, live under the same roof. She would not accept the traditional harem system even though she was recognised by everyone as the senior wife and thus deserving of special respect. The problem was partly solved when Reza Khan divorced Turan Khanom barely a year after their marriage, but Esmat Khanom, who was, by all accounts, his favourite, still had to be housed and it was with a loan from his in-laws that Reza Khan purchased a new house. Reza Khan stopped sharing a home with Taj al-Moluk towards the end of 1923 and from then on visited her only twice a week when he spent the nights with her. The rest of the time he lived in Esmat Khanom's house.

Esmat was only sixteen when Reza Khan married her and she became his true love. Every visit to Taj al-Moluk's house by Reza Khan was an occasion for scenes of conjugal discord. Taj al-Moluk never fully reconciled herself to the idea of sharing her husband with another woman. In these scenes the attack invariably came from Taj al-Moluk while Reza Khan often tried to laugh the whole thing off. 'What a pity that I wasted my youth and beauty on you!' was the sentence Taj al-Moluk most often threw at her husband during these disputes.[28]

The presence of Mohammad-Reza, the first-born son, was something of an insurance policy for Taj al-Moluk: it was unthinkable for a Persian father to divorce the wife that had born him a first son, who was automatically entitled to the title of 'dadash' (elder brother) and enjoyed vast prestige and a high degree of deference within the family. Every Persian husband considered his first son as his own 'crown prince'.

By October 1923 it was clear that political power had become concentrated in Reza Khan's hand. Ahmad Shah had no choice but to formally acknowledge this fact by appointing Reza Khan to the post of 'Sadr 'Azam (Grand Vizir). They met on 20 October ostensibly for Reza Khan to bid farewell to Ahmad Shah who was about to leave on his third and last trip to Europe. When the Shah offered Reza Khan the premiership the latter accepted with one condition: the Shah should not return to Iran without the prior approval of the Cabinet. That sounded like exile to the Shah but the Qajar monarch had virtually no choice.

Theoretically he could have dismissed Reza Khan and even crushed him with the help of the vast network of Qajar connections and their hangers-on. But Ahmad Shah had no stomach for a fight and could not wait to get away from a country that had already sent his father into exile. As the meeting ended Reza Khan made another request: that he begin his premiership on 26 October. This was a special date for Reza Khan, coinciding with the fourth anniversary of Mohammad-Reza's birth. The Shah agreed and left the country a week later. Reza Khan had removed his principal obstacle to absolute power.[29]

But what exactly did he want? 'I don't ask to be loved,' he used to say. 'But I insist on being obeyed.'[30] In 1923 he was thinking of turning Iran into a republic along the lines proposed by Mustafa Kemal (Atatürk) who had abolished the Caliphate and declared himself president in neighbouring Turkey. The vested interests, however, were still strong enough to fight Reza Khan every step of the way to the top. In April 1924 Reza Khan decided to provoke confrontation with the remnants of the Qajar establishment. He announced his resignation suddenly, citing 'constant intrigue by agents of foreign powers' as the cause but in fact the whole thing had been carefully stage-managed.

On the announcement of his resignation the whole country was plunged into confusion and protest. Many bazaars closed as the mullahs called from the pulpits for Reza Khan's return. Reza Khan had withdrawn to a summer residence he had acquired near Tehran. It was there that he received a parliamentary delegation who had come to beg him to return. The delegation spokesman was one Dr Mohammad Mossadeq who in later years became a fierce opponent of Reza Khan and his son.

Reza Khan's week-long retreat, principally caused by the rejection of his republican plans by the Majlis (parliament) and the bureaucracy as well as the mullahs, ended in his triumph. At the same time, however, he understood that Iran was not ready for republican government. Apparently, regardless of their social background and political beliefs, the Iranians could not do without a Shah, so Reza Khan decided to give them one: himself. On 31 October 1925 the Majlis approved a bill removing the Qajars and appointing Reza Khan as monarch on a provisional basis.[31] Only five of the Majlis' 96 members spoke and voted against the bill.[32]

The Constituent Assembly that was subsequently elected to choose a new reigning family was, naturally, filled with Reza Khan's supporters. On 12 December 1925 the assembly unanimously named Reza Khan the new Shahanshah (King of Kings). For the occasion, Reza Khan gave himself a family name, Pahlavi, and it was to the new Pahlavi Dynasty that the Constituent Assembly transferred the 'divine gift' of reigning over the kingdom. Pahlavi, meaning 'heroic' in middle-Persian languages, also denoted the literary language in which some of the most ancient

Iranian texts had been written before the Arab invasion in the seventh century.

The choice of Pahlavi as the name of the new dynasty was not fortuitous. Reza Khan, who became Reza Shah Pahlavi on 15 December 1925 after taking the oath of office at a session of the Majlis, had already decided to present himself as the true heir of Iran's pre-Islamic monarchs.

The Constituent Assembly and the Majlis had taken two other important decisions. The first was to bar anyone with blood relationship with the deposed Qajars from sitting on the throne of Persia. This meant that Reza Shah's sons from his third and fourth wives were automatically barred from succession, which was to have a dramatic effect on the life of his first son, Mohammad-Reza, many years later. The second decision taken by the parliamentary organs was to officially designate Mohammad-Reza as Crown Prince and thus as heir to the throne. The first practical consequence of this decision was that Mohammad-Reza, age six, was separated from his mother and his two sisters and younger brother and housed in a palace within the compound of palaces known as Golestan (Rose Garden).

On 25 April 1926 Reza Shah Pahlavi formally crowned himself at a state ceremony in the Museum Hall of Golestan Palace. He sat on the Peacock Throne and wore a crown that included the darya-ye-nur (Sea of Light), the sister diamond of kuh-i-nur which is part of the British Crown jewels.[33] Crown Prince Mohammad-Reza, named a colonel of the Cossacks and fully dressed in a uniform fitting with his new military rank, took the salute and played his role during more than three hours of elaborate ceremonies. The coronation must have been a physical ordeal for the child-prince who had never been in robust health and had barely recovered from a strong cold complicated by fever. He had not been born a prince but had quickly learned to act as one.

2

Child Exile

Reza Khan's transformation into Reza Shah at first introduced few major changes in the daily life of the members of the new royal family. They moved into Golestan in the centre of Tehran and as the Pahlavis had very few possessions the move took only a day or two: the bulk of the cheap furniture that the family had used in its non-royal days was thrown away.

For Reza Shah life continued as before. Politically, he had become the nation's effective ruler at least two years before being named King of Kings. He continued to wear his military uniform, made of a rough, home-woven cloth, and spent most of his time in the company of soldiers. He slept on a mattress on the floor in a bare room and continued to rise at dawn as he had always done. There were no state banquets and the new King of Kings continued to take most of his meals, boiled chicken and rice twice a day, alone in his office. He smoked his ill-smelling Persian cigarettes and foul-mouthed all who dared displease him as he had done in his Cossack days. It was not until years later that Reza Shah gradually agreed to have a court, complete with officials and courtiers.

The family routine also continued unchanged. Taj al-Moluk, who now had the title of Malakeh Pahlavi (The Pahlavi Queen), was addressed as Her Majesty by relatives and servants. But she still lived in a separate house where she and her children received Reza Shah twice a week. Esmat Khanom, Reza Shah's fourth wife and favourite also had her own house where she lived with her children. She was not Queen and was simply addressed as Vala-Hazrat (Your Highness), but she had an advantage over Taj al-Moluk: Reza Shah visited his fourth wife five times a week. The various princes and princesses who lived with their respective mothers were too young to feel that by becoming royal their lives had been altered beyond recognition.

Only one life was dramatically, one might almost say brutally, changed as a result of Reza Khan's ascending the Peacock Throne. That life belonged to Mohammad-Reza, the new Crown Prince. Immediately after the coronation he was separated from his mother and his sisters and brothers and housed in one of the palaces within the compound. A butler, Hashem Agha, was assigned to his service, and a French-born governess, Madame Arfa, was charged with the task of supervising his social and cultural education. The trouble was that Agha was a Turkic speaker while Madame Arfa, a stern lady, insisted that the Crown Prince speak only French.

At the same time Reza Shah wanted his designated heir to have a 'manly education' and this, for him, meant a military upbringing. It was for this purpose that the Shah created a special military school within the compound of Golestan palaces. There were only two classes. The Crown Prince was enrolled in the senior class of 23 pupils. His full-brother Ali-Reza and half-brothers Gholam-Reza and Abdul-Reza attended the junior class together with some 20 other children.

Reza Shah had picked all the pupils and teachers of what he intended to be a model school for his successor. All instruction at the model military school was in the army's version of the Persian language. Determined to revive Iran's 'Aryan' past, the army created by Reza Khan in 1921[1] considered it a duty to purge the Persian language of as many borrowed Arabic words as possible. The result was a 'pure' vocabulary that was, at times, totally incomprehensible to most average Iranians. Faced with a French governess, a Turkic butler and a dozen 'purist' military teachers, the Crown Prince had little opportunity to hear the language of the real people.

Even Mohammad-Reza's parents no longer talked to him in what could be considered a normal way. His father addressed him as 'Sir' and used the plural form 'shoma' (you) instead of the singular 'taw' (thou), which made their conversations unnecessarily formal. His mother addressed him as Vala-Hazrat ('Your Highness') and rose as soon as he entered the room. The family's other children were also acutely aware of Mohammad-Reza's special position and knew that they had to pay special deference to him.

As Crown Prince, Mohammad-Reza had a strict weekly schedule. He visited his mother for an hour every day, reserving another hour for his father. Six hours were spent at the military school each day except Fridays. Madame Arfa occupied a further two daily hours of the Crown Prince's time. These she spent on teaching him not only the French language and manners, but also French history and literature. Years later, Mohammad-Reza wrote: 'To her I owe the advantage of being able to speak and read French as if it were my own language; and beyond this, she opened my mind to the spirit of Western culture. She also introduced me to French food. I shall always remain indebted to Madame Arfa.'[2]

Thursday afternoons and sometimes the whole of Fridays were reserved for horseback riding. Mohammad-Reza's instructor was Abol-Fatah Atabay who had served as the riding instructor to the Qajar Crown Prince until 1921. The stablemaster had strict instructions from Reza

Shah not to let Mohammad-Reza jump hurdles on his horse, but the young prince quickly persuaded Atabay to ignore the royal command and the two had 'great fun' doing 'all sorts of dangerous gymnastics with horses, especially the coltish ones.'[3] It was on horseback that Mohammad-Reza felt he could get away from it all and enjoy some of the freedom that fate and his father had denied him.

The children took their meals, lunch at noon and dinner at six, in the presence of their father. The Shah's two wives stayed in their respective palaces and dined alone or with lady friends. Reza Shah's conversation at table was limited to a few constantly repeated injunctions: do your homework and maintain discipline! He would never embrace any of the children nor address them in the exaggeratedly sentimental terms used by most Persian fathers. The most he could manage was to put his heavy hand on a child's head and say 'You are a naughty one, aren't you?'[4] He treated Mohammad-Reza as a grown up and had him served before anyone else. Besides the Crown Prince it was only Princess Shams who enjoyed special attentions from Reza Shah. A shy, sweet and extremely kind girl, Shams was Reza Shah's undisputed favourite among his four daughters.

At the military school Mohammad-Reza picked as his special friend one Hossein Fardust, the son of an army lieutenant. Though this was to become a life-long friendship, it is difficult to see what attracted Mohammad-Reza to Fardust who was shy, withdrawn and extremely secretive. As a rule, however, Mohammad-Reza did not like expansive boys who were often bullies and mischief-makers. This was the type that his brother Ali-Reza liked to hang around with. While Mohammad-Reza stayed aloof and played his royal role, Ali-Reza had the time of his life with fist fights and practical jokes.

A few weeks after the coronation Mohammad-Reza fell ill with typhoid fever, a disease that killed a good percentage of Iranian children until the 1960s. For weeks he hovered between life and death. Reza Shah spent much of his time at Mohammad-Reza's bedside while Taj al-Moluk organised a series of prayer sessions, pilgrimages to the local holy shrines and the distribution of alms among the poor. She even enlisted the help of charm-breakers because of a belief that Mohammad-Reza, having so distinguished himself during the coronation, had attracted the attention of someone with an evil eye. On at least one occasion the child was so delirious that the court physician, Dr Amir Alam, believed that all was lost. Reza Shah was present when Dr Alam presented his gloomy report. The King of Kings listened to the report with 'the face of a poker-player'. After the physician had taken his leave, however, Reza Shah burst into tears; the first time anyone had seen him in such a state.[5]

The crisis was over within forty days and Dr Alam claimed credit for the Western-made medicine he had managed to bring from Paris. Taj al-Moluk was sure that her efforts to frustrate the designs of the Evil Eye had borne fruit. Reza Shah convinced himself that it had been Mohammad-Reza's inner strength and will to live that had seen him through the ordeal. The Crown Prince, however, attributed his recovery to another, totally different, cause. He had no doubt that he had been saved by Imam Ali Ibn Abi-Talib, the first of the twelve Imams of shi'ite Islam.

One night when he was running a high temperature Mohammad-Reza saw the Imam in a dream holding his famous two-pronged sword (Zulfiqar) in one hand. In another hand he held a bowl containing a liquid. The Imam 'told me to drink, which I did. The next day, the crisis of my fever was over, and I was on the road to rapid recovery.'[6]

Mohammad-Reza did not dare relate the story to his father. Reza Shah considered much of religion as little more than superstition and had endeavoured to give his son a secular education. Taj al-Moluk, however, fully believed her son and sent a special donation to Ali's shrine in Mesopotamia.

The dream was the first of a series of 'visions' that persuaded Mohammad-Reza of his 'mystic connections'. This is how he relates his second vision:

Almost every summer my family and I made an excursion to Emam-Zadeh Dawood, a lovely spot in the mountains above Tehran. To reach it one had to follow a steep trail on foot or on horseback; and since I was so young, a relative who was an army officer placed me in front of him on the saddle of his horse. Some way up the trail the horse slipped and I was plunged head first on to a jagged rock. I fainted. When I regained consciousness, the members of the party were expressing astonishment that I had not even a scratch. I told them that as I fell I had clearly seen one of our saints, named Abbas,* and that I had felt him holding me and preventing me from crashing my head against the rock.[7]

This was not the kind of story one could tell Reza Shah. Nevertheless, since the prince had related his experience in front of so many people, Reza Shah ended up hearing about it. For the first time he was in a rage against his favourite son and heir. Mohammad-Reza made matters worse by also relating his earlier vision of Ali. 'Rubbish, sir,' the angry Shah commented. 'If those saints could make miracles they would have saved themselves from being killed like chickens.'[8] Mohammad-Reza had to accept his father's verdict. Years later, he wrote: 'Knowing my father to be a very strong-willed man, I did not argue with him, but I never doubted that I had seen Saint Abbas.'[9]

Mohammad-Reza's third vision came a few weeks later when he was walking near the royal summer palace in Shemiran, north of Tehran, with the butler, Hashem Agha. This is how Mohammad-Reza told the story some fifty years later:

*Abbas, a half-brother of Hossein, the third Imam, is always portrayed in Persian naive paintings as a man without hands because both his arms were cut off by the Umayyid soldiers who captured him during the battle of Karbala.

Our path lay along a picturesque cobbled street. Suddenly I clearly saw before me a man with a halo around his head – much as in some of the great paintings, by Western masters, of Jesus. As we passed one another, I knew him at once. He was the Imam or the descendent of Mohammad who, according to our faith, disappeared but is expected to come again to save the world. I asked my guardian: 'Did you see him?' 'Who?' he enquired. 'No one was here?' How could I see someone who was not there?' I felt so certain of what I had seen that his reply did not bother me in the least.[10]

It is interesting that Mohammad-Reza saw the shi'ite saint in an almost-Western, Christian setting, complete with a halo which does not exist in Islamic imagery. The vision was so outlandish that Mohammad-Reza did not dare tell his father about it and after that he never had another but he was already convinced that he had acquired a special relationship with God:

From the time I was six or seven, I have felt that there is a Supreme Being who is guiding me. . . Sometimes the thought disturbs me because then, I ask myself, "what is my own personality?" and "am I possessed of free will?" Still, I often reflect, if I am driven – or perhaps I should say supported – by another force, there must be a reason.[11]

In later years Mohammad-Reza interpreted a series of other incidents as so many manifestations of his special ties with the Almighty. He wrote: 'In whatever I have done, and whatever I do in the future, I consider myself merely as an agent of the Will of God, and I pray that He may guide me in the fulfilment of His Will, and keep me from error.'[12]

Reza Shah, awe-inspiring as he was, had clearly failed to inculcate his own irreverence, not to say positive aversion for religion into the mind of his son and heir. Mohammad-Reza had been more impressed by Taj al-Moluk's traditional religiosity. Madame Arfa, a devout Catholic, had also played her part, albeit indirectly and with great tact, to give the child prince a religious bent. This was at a time when Reza Shah was stepping up his campaign against the mullahs and encouraging the development of a new image of Iran as an ancient Aryan nation in whose long history Islam represented no more than an unfortunate accident.

Reza Shah's deep dislike of the mullahs was a sentiment shared by many army officers and a good number of intellectuals. The mullahs were held responsible for Iran's disastrous wars against Tsarist Russia. Many people remembered the role played by one Ayatollah Mohammad Mujahed, a shady mullah who had come to Tehran from Mesopotamia, in provoking the second Russo-Iranian war by declaring jihad (Holy War) on the Tsar. The declaration of jihad had come at the worst possible time for Iran and in 1824 the Tsarist forces inflicted a crushing defeat on the ill-prepared forces of the Qajar monarch. Once the war was over and Russia had gobbled up large chunks of Persian territory, the ayatollah simply vanished like the Hidden Imam. It was not until years later that he reappeared, this time in Saint Petersburg and wearing European clothes. It turned out that he had declared the jihad in exchange for a substantial bribe from the Russians who had also promised him safety in Saint Petersburg.

During the Constitutional Revolution of 1906–11, many mullahs sided with supporters of despotism with Russia's encouragement. Britain, however, had its own clients among the mullahs and, through them, gave her support to the constitutionalists. In this environment many people saw the mullahs as agents of foreign powers and objective opponents of Iranian modernisation. Atatürk's abolition of the Turkish Caliphate and the secularisation movement that he started on becoming president in 1922 found sympathetic echoes among Iran's small modernising elite. The version of Islam represented by the mullahs was seen as decadent and degrading. Direct or indirect attacks on mullahs provided a major theme of Persian literature – both poetry and prose – from 1911 onwards.[13] Ahmad Shah, although not a religious man himself, had retained an ambiguous attitude towards the mullahs. Many turbaned heads continued to frequent his court where they wielded considerable influence. Reza Shah ended all that and openly committed the court and the machinery of the state to a relentless war against what he described as the 'shameful superstitions upon which mullahs feed like flies on a dung heap'.[14] Reza Shah was not an atheist and could best be described as an agnostic. He was, for a while, fascinated by the teachings of Zoroaster, Iran's pre-Islamic prophet, but this fascination should be understood in the context of his old soldier's dream of restoring Iran to its ancient grandeur.

Mohammad-Reza, on the other hand, was deeply religious, even to the point of rejecting all free will. 'I have always had the sentiment that only what is written will come to pass,' he noted, towards the end of his life.[15] And his fatalistic view of the universe was shaped by his religious beliefs. 'My faith has always dictated my conduct – both as man and statesman. And I have always believed that one of my principal duties was to give to our religion the place it merited. . . . Religion is the cement that permits the social edifice to stand.'[16]

In June 1931 Reza Shah announced that he intended to send the Crown Prince to Europe for further studies. Mohammad-Reza had just completed the six-year course offered at the military primary school and in October he would celebrate his twelfth birthday. Reza Shah consulted a number of people about the choice of European country. Some theoreticians of Aryanism suggested Germany (Nazi ideas had not yet taken their disastrous final shape) and many of Iran's Aryanists had been Germanophile long before Nazism appeared on the international scene. Mohammad-Reza, however, shuddered at the thought. His French governess Madam Arfa, who manifested 'a visceral hatred of Germans' had already told him about the barbarous life-style of those 'savages' from across the Rhine.[17]

Quite naturally, Madame Arfa's choice was France. She had done a good job of turning the Crown Prince into an ardent francophile. He later commented:

> I must say that I was always enthusiastic about French history. I admired Saint Louis who administered justice under an oak tree in the Vincennes wood . . . Henry IV, the Sun King, Napoleon – a truly extraordinary personality in my opinion – fascinated me. With keen interest I (also) studied the role of the cardinals – Richelieu, Mazarin and even Dubois – who, despite their defects (of character?) had served France. Among the great men I admired Charles Quint, magnificent warrior and political sage, Peter the Great, Catherine the Great, Elizabeth of England, Frederick the Great . . .[18]

It is worth remarking that the 12-year old prince did not include a single Iranian in his list of admired historical figures.

Reza Shah rejected both Germany and France as countries where his son might be educated for practical political reasons. The choice of either country would have appeared a deliberate provocation of Great Britain which was still considered as the dominant foreign power in Iran. A few of the Shah's advisers suggested the United States but that country appeared simply too far away. Switzerland appeared the ideal choice. It was both an advanced country and a neutral power. It had no political ambitions in Iran and was not involved in the international power struggle. Moreover, the Crown Prince could continue his studies in French, a language he spoke effortlessly thanks to Madame Arfa's patience and persistence.

The decision to send Mohammad-Reza abroad was crucial, both for him and for the country he would later rule. He was the very first Shahanshah to be educated outside Iran. The Qajars had established a clever tradition of dispatching the Crown Prince to Tabriz, capital of Azerbaijan, after the age of twelve. In Tabriz, the Crown Prince would learn to speak Turkic, a language used by nearly a quarter of all Iranians. he would also be close to the Russian border from whence the greatest threats to Iran had come since the end of the eighteenth century. The presence of the Crown Prince would, at the same time, honour the country's second most-populous city.[19] In Azerbaijan the Crown Prince would also come into direct contact with peasant life. Reza Shah himself had never lived in Azerbaijan before he became king but he spoke Turkic fluently and had a direct understanding of the life of the Iranian peasantry. Mohammad-Reza was to be the first Shah of Iran in probably a thousand years not to know Turkic. He was also the first to be fluent in a Western language.

The Swiss school chosen for Mohammad-Reza's education was Le Rosey, near Rolle, between Lucerne and Geneva. In those days Le Rosey's reputation attracted the children of the rich from more than 20 countries, including a large contingent from the United States.

Before leaving Mohammad-Reza spent the whole summer with his mother, sisters and brothers in Mazandaran on the Caspian. Reza Shah came to stay with them as often as he could. In September 1931 the whole family, with Reza Shah himself in the lead, joined in the official send-off at Enzeli, a Caspian fishing port. Mohammad-Reza's younger full-brother, Ali-Reza, was also sent to Switzerland together with Mehrpur Teymurtash, the son of one of Reza Shah's ministers and confidants at that time. Hossein Fardust, Mohammad-Reza's closest school-friend, joined the party, which also numbered a teacher of Persian calligraphy and a supervisor, Dr Moaddeb Nafisi, whose responsibilities included looking after the physical and moral welfare of the Crown Prince and his companions. By the end of the ceremony, with Taj al-Moluk and Princess Ashraf in tears, the Crown Prince and his party boarded a fishing boat that took them to a Soviet steamer anchored some distance off shore. The steamer took the party to Baku, the capital of Soviet Azerbaijan, where the Soviet authorities gave the Crown Prince and his entourage an official reception. The Persian party travelled from Baku to Warsaw on a Soviet train, then on to Berlin. Three weeks after leaving Enzeli, the Crown Prince and his party arrived in Lucerne. At every stop on the way Mohammad-Reza and Ali-Reza sent postcards, written in French, to their father in Tehran. Shams and Ashraf translated the cards into Persian for Reza Shah and Taj al-Moluk. It took Ashraf weeks to cope with separation from her twin brother and for three months she cried every night and wrote her brother a letter every day.

On arrival in Switzerland Mohammad-Reza and his younger brother were housed in a private *pension* run by a Mr and Mrs Mercier who had three sons and two daughters. The Persian boys quickly made friends with the Mercier children and this helped attenuate their feeling of homesickness. Fardust and Teymurtash were accommodated at the boarding house run by the local school. All the boys had to prepare for a school entrance examination before being enrolled at Le Rosey. The nine months of hard work was made more difficult for the Iranians by the fact that, in addition to the courses required under the Swiss curriculum, they had to study Persian and practice calligraphy every day.

Dr Nafisi was a stern supervisor. Before leaving Enzeli Reza Shah had told him: 'Take these boys and bring them back as men!' And Nafisi was convinced that a good handwriting was essential to being a man. The Persian teacher, Mr Mostashar, offered a general course for all the boys and a special one designed for Mohammad-Reza. This meant that the Crown Prince had to do more homework in Persian than his companions. He and Fardust were also the only ones in the party to pray every day.

The preparatory course took nine months at the end of which Mohammad-Reza and the other boys sat Le Rosey's entrance examination, all passing, none with special distinction. In September 1932, nearly a year after their arrival in Switzerland, the Persian boys were admitted to Le Rosey as boarders and Dr Nafisi and Mr Mostashar took up residence in two apartments near the school.

Le Rosey's headmaster was Henri Carnac, the son of the school's founder, but the real power in the school was Carnac's American-born wife. Because it charged exorbitant fees – around £1000 per pupil per annum – the school was able to employ outstanding teachers of many nationalities. During the winter it also offered its pupils special skiing courses in the Alps or the Jura. Although all teaching was in French, the pupils had also to learn English as a mandatory second language. Alongside the large contingent of pupils from the United States, there were also many children of reigning or deposed royal families from India, Egypt, Austro-Hungary and Poland.

Mr and Mrs Carnac had received a letter from Reza Shah asking them not to give the Crown Prince any special treatment. 'I want him to grow up like other boys and to learn to stand on his own two feet.' The Carnacs had, in any case, no intention of offering Mohammad-Reza any special favours. But neither did they envisage the possibility of the Persian Crown Prince being beaten up on his first day, but this is exactly what happened.

Mohammad-Reza, flanked by the ever-present Dr Nafisi as well as the Iranian Ambassador to Switzerland arrived at the school in a Hispano-Suiza, one of the flashiest cars of the time, and was given an official reception by the Carnacs. The other boys watched the Persian prince personally supervise the transfer of half a dozen suitcases from the car to his room. Every now and then he cast half a glance at his future classmates. Having inspected the school, Mohammad-Reza said goodbye to Dr Nafisi and the ambassador while the Carnacs also returned to their offices. Ali-Reza, Fardust and the Teymurtash boys also went to their rooms leaving Mohammad-Reza alone.

The Crown Prince apparently wanted to walk around the school when he ran into a group of American boys in the garden. He wanted to sit on a bench and the Americans would not let him. A fight ensued between him and one of the American boys and he was thrown to the ground and roundly beaten. Some 20 other American boys watched as the Crown Prince, his nose bleeding and his shirt torn, begged to be pardoned. The strange scene was over within less than a minute and Mohammad-Reza was on his feet, smiling. He then stretched his hand towards his adversary. 'Let's shake hands and be friends,' he suggested. The American agreed with a smile.[20] Mohammad-Reza had fought and lost his first fight. Later when Ali-Reza and the other Persian boys learned of the incident they suggested revenge. Mohammad-Reza refused.

One fact that shocked Mohammad-Reza during his first year in Switzerland was the general ignorance about Iran. Almost no one with whom Mohammad-Reza came into contact had heard about Iran and many thought it was somewhere in the Americas. He very quickly learned that despite the fact that he had been given the largest and best-furnished room in the boarding school, his position as Crown Prince of an almost unknown country guaranteed him no special status at Le Rosey. In Tehran he had always received the highest marks in all subjects at school. At Le Rosey he had to be content with pass marks in most subjects and quickly realised that, contrary to what he had been told by sycophantic teachers at home, he did not have a scholarly mind. Within weeks he discovered his taste and talent for sport and began to build up his physical strength.

Like all Iranian children of his generation, at home he had suffered from a variety of illnesses, including diphtheria, typhoid, whooping cough and an acute attack of malaria from which he never fully recovered. In Switzerland, however, he became all health and energy. He participated in virtually all sports activities offered at Le Rosey and was particularly good at the discus, the javelin, the shot, the high jump, the long jump and the 100 metres. He also played tennis and hockey but his real passion was football which he enjoyed practically every day. He became captain of Le Rosey's football team and helped the school win the Swiss Schools' Football Association Cup for two consecutive years. This did not make him a bully, though. His contemporaries remember him as a gentle and likeable boy who never initiated a fight and almost always entered one in defence of a weaker schoolmate. The real bully was Ali-Reza who never missed an opportunity for punching someone's nose. The two brothers, together with the other Persian boys, received special training in boxing and soon became a formidable force at the school.

Pictures of Mohammad-Reza during his time at Le Rosey show him as a healthy and athletic adolescent with his father's Roman nose and his mother's deep, sad eyes. Was he happy at Le Rosey? Probably not. In later years he tried to remember his Swiss school days with a mixture of realism and nostalgia, but he bitterly complained about the strict discipline imposed on him by Dr Nafisi, presumably on Reza Shah's orders. Mohammad-Reza was never allowed to leave the school unless accompanied by Dr Nafisi or other escorts and officials. Of all the boys at Le Rosey he was the only one not allowed to ski; Reza Shah had apparently concluded that his son might be hurt in a skiing accident and it was, perhaps, to make up for those years of frustration that Mohammad-Reza became a keen skier in later years.[21] Nearly 30 years later Mohammad-Reza recalled:

> I was like a prisoner. When my comrades had free time they would go merrily into town, but I was not allowed to accompany them. During the Christmas and New Year holidays they went to parties and balls in some of the hotels, but I could not go. My friends were having fun, laughing and dancing while I was sitting alone in my room. I had a radio and gramophone to keep me company,

but what fun were they compared with the festivities my friends enjoyed? I think it was quite wrong . . .[22]

Mohammad-Reza tried to alleviate his solitude by giving parties in his room, the largest in the residential hall. Boys would gather there for an hour or two to drink fruit juice and listen to the latest French records. And yet, Mohammad-Reza had few real friends. Hossein Fardust was still close to him but could not behave towards him as if he were an equal. He loved his younger brother Ali-Reza but could never feel close to him. The two were poles apart in character, Mohammad-Reza shy, taciturn and always anxious not to offend, Ali-Reza a practical joker and a rebel. Gholam-Reza and Abdul-Reza, two half-brothers who joined him at Le Rosey a year later, never grew close to him. Gholam-Reza was simply too dull and showed little interest in sports. Abdul-Reza, a hardworking pupil, preferred his own, younger circle. Mohammad-Reza's closest schoolfriend was probably the Swiss Hubert Piquete, the future journalist and banker. Two American boys were also close: Henry Pearson, who became a successful businessman, and Richard Helms, the future head of the American Central Intelligence Agency or CIA.

Once a week Mohammad-Reza spent a couple of hours writing to his father. These long letters, written in beautifully calligraphed Persian, contained full reports of his activities which Mr Mostashar must have helped the young prince draft. He also wrote to his mother and sisters whenever he felt in the mood. All these letters reflect his feelings of solitude and unhappiness which grew still more intense during holidays when almost all the boys at Le Rosey either returned home or travelled to other parts of Switzerland. Mohammad-Resa had to stay behind in the company of Dr Nafisi and Mr Mostashar to catch up with his Persian studies. On one occasion he indirectly suggested that he might spend part of a summer holiday in Tehran so that he could be with his family. Reza Shah instantly rejected the idea and instead dispatched Taj al-Moluk, Shams and Ashraf to Switzerland. The Queen and the two princesses spent six weeks getting to Switzerland via Baku, Moscow, Warsaw and Berlin and in the German capital they were surprised by the warm reception they received from the new Nazi regime. It was 1934 and the royal ladies spent three months in Switzerland.

During that time Reza Shah went on a state visit to Turkey, his first and last trip outside Iran. From Istanbul the Shah was able to put in a telephone call to Mohammad-Reza, the first time in almost two years that father and son had heard each other's voices. In those days Iran did not have a telephone system outside the capital and people who wished to make international calls had to go either to Baku or to Istanbul.

As summer ended Ashraf tried to stay in Switzerland and cabled her father for permission to enrol at a girls' school not far from her twin's establishment. Reza Shah's reply arrived within 48 hours: permission refused, return home immediately. Clearly, the King of Kings was not convinced that girls should enjoy the same educational opportunities as boys. The Pahlavi contingent at Le Rosey continued to grow, however. Prince Ahmad-Reza and Hamid-Reza also entering the Swiss school.

Mohammad-Reza took advantage of his mother's visit to air some complaints, but his mother and sisters could do no more than express their understanding. No one dared raise the subject with Reza Shah. Mohammad-Reza ended his litany of complaints with a philosophical observation: 'I suppose this is my fate and no one can escape what is written!'[23] He also said: 'They want me to grow like a yogi; I feel I am serving a prison term.'[24] He sought comfort in prayers and meditation with 'real fervour and conviction'.[25] Religion must have given him some solace for he resolved that 'when later I come to the throne, my conduct would always be guided by a true religious sense'.[26]

During his lonely hours Mohammad-Reza tried to pass the time by dreaming about his own future as king. One thing he decided he would do was to 'let each peasant family amass a little fortune'. He also resolved to install a public complaints box in which people could drop their anonymous letters without fear of punishment. Only the King of Kings himself would have direct access to the box.[27]

Once a month Mohammad-Reza went on a shopping spree, always flanked by the inevitable Dr Nafisi. Although there were few occasions for dressing up, the Crown Prince liked to buy as many expensive clothes as Dr Nafisi would allow. He also collected neckties, mostly of provocative colour and design. On his sixteenth birthday he bought himself a large American sedan, a Lincoln, on his father's behalf, marking the start of Mohammad-Reza's passion for luxury cars. This passion remained with him well into the 1960s, despite the fact that the Lincoln remained virtually unused in the Le Rosey courtyard. Its owner had very few occasions to leave his 'prison'.

In the meantime, Mohammad-Reza had lost one friend and gained another. The friend he lost was Mehrpur Teymurtash who had been with him since the time of the military primary school in Tehran. Mehrpur's father, who had served as Reza Shah's Royal Court Minister, had suddenly fallen from grace and was even accused of plotting against the state. Disgrace was followed by prison and a social boycott of anyone connected with the former minister. Unaware of his father's fate, Mehrpur was in tears when he came to say goodbye to Mohammad-Reza before leaving for the long journey back to Iran. The parting was charged with emotion as the two boys had been close for nearly six years. Mohammad-Reza made a few attempts at finding out what had happened in his father's mysterious capital many thousand miles away but quickly realised that he should not pursue the matter any further: Mehrpur and his family had suddenly ceased to exist and that was that. Once again,

Mohammad-Reza's belief that all is written must have helped him to absorb the shock of his friend's sudden disappearance.[28]

Mehrpur's loss was quickly compensated by Ernest Perron. At first glance Perron had little to recommend him as a friend and confidant for a prince. He was the son of one of the Le Rosey janitors and lived in the servants' quarter of the compound. His task was to help his father in the garden and he hardly came into contact with the boys.

A childhood accident resulting in a permanent limp made Perron an easy victim for bored bullies. Although he was 24 years old when he met Mohammad-Reza, Perron looked like an undernourished teenager, short and thin, almost a midget, with frightened eyes. One day as Mohammad-Reza was passing through the school garden he saw Perron surrounded by a number of boys who had overturned his trolley of rubbish and were dancing and shrieking around him. The frightened Perron was desperately trying to break out of the threatening circle around him. Mohammad-Reza told the bullies that they had had enough fun, then helped Perron put his trolley upright and apologised on behalf of the other boys.[29] The following day Perron arrived at the door of Mohammad-Reza's room with a bouquet of flowers. This was the start of a friendship that was to last until 1961 when Perron died of cancer.

Perron turned out to be a pleasant and profitable companion for the Crown Prince. The janitor's son had not gone beyond primary school but had continued to educate himself with the help of the books he bought with his meagre allowance. Over the years he had become fairly well read in French literature so he was able to help Mohammad-Reza improve his marks in French. His two favourite writers were Rabelais and Chateaubriand, as different one from the other as any two writers could be, and they soon became Mohammad-Reza's bedside companions too. Within a week or so of Perron's encounter with the Crown Prince the two had become intimate friends. Perron would go to Mohammad-Reza's room every evening after dinner and would stay until lights-out. He would help Mohammad-Reza with his French homework but they would also discuss the political events of the day throughout the world. Every now and then, Perron would read his latest poetic compositions to his royal friend.

In May 1936, shortly before he was due to take his leaving examinations, Mohammad-Reza received a cable from his father summoning him to Tehran. He did not even think of asking why he should return with so much haste. Nor did he dare suggest that he postpone his return until after the examinations for which he had worked so hard. Reza Shah had to be obeyed without question. One favour Mohammad-Reza did dare ask his father was for permission to bring Ernest Perron with him. Reza Shah, generally suspicious of foreigners to the point of xenophobia, instantly agreed. Mohammad-Reza did not know it at the time but his father loved him above all else and would have granted him virtually anything he might have cared to ask for.

The presence of Ernest Perron in the Crown Prince's entourage led, as might have been expected, to an orgy of rumours in Tehran's political circles. The favourite was variously described as a British agent secretly planted next to Iran's future king and as a vulgar go-between whose task was to ensure the redamselling of Mohammad-Reza's voracious bed. It is possible that Britain – or other powers – tried to recruit Perron in later years as it was almost standard practice for foreign intelligence services to seek well-placed informers inside royal palaces. Perron, the only person with access to the Crown Prince at virtually all times of day and night, would have been an ideal spy,[30] but it is almost certain that the initial encounter and the friendship that ensued were the results not of a Machiavellian British *mise-en-scène*, but of pure chance. The pimp-for-the-prince theory is equally unsustainable. Mohammad-Reza was in his teens and under constant watch by guardians, butlers and security agents appointed by his father. He hardly ever left the school grounds, except for sports matches or special outings in the company of Dr Nafisi.

A third, much more shortlived, rumour that the Crown Prince and Perron had been homosexual lovers evaporated as soon as people saw Perron in person. Moreover, Mohammad-Reza lost no time in manifesting his passion for female company shortly after his return to Tehran.

The friendship between the two men might never be fully explained, but it is possible to suggest that Perron offered Mohammad-Reza genuine and boundless gratitude and admiration, sentiments that the future king ardently sought throughout his life. With most other people Mohammad-Reza could never be quite sure whether he was loved and admired for his own person or as a means of reaping the favours that his position offered. Mohammad-Reza always questioned the sincerity of those with whom he came into contact. He would, for example, ask his wife whether or not this or that politician or intellectual was 'genuinely loyal to us or just pretending?'[31] Perron, however, did not need to pretend as it was Mohammad-Reza who first chose him as a friend. And the son of the Swiss janitor knew well that he could never become a high official of the Iranian state even if Mohammad-Reza wished to make him one. Perron retained his Swiss nationality and received no official appointment in Iran where he spent the last 25 years of his life. In the 1950s he played a number of supporting, though by no means insignificant, roles in Mohammad-Reza's private and public lives, but it was always clear that he would do nothing without the express orders of his friend. At one point, Perron was attacked by Tehran's pro-Soviet press as 'the new Rasputin' while many years later his expulsion became a major demand for opposition circles in the mosques and the bazaars.

During his six years' absence Mohammad-Reza had missed some of the most dramatic events in the saga of change that Reza Shah had imposed on a deeply conservative country. The Crown Prince witnessed some of the results of the change in Iran's international standing during his journey back home. At every stop – from Berlin to Baku via Warsaw and Moscow – he and his party received full official honours from the local authorities. The train from Berlin was full of German businessmen, technicians and, almost certainly, secret agents, on their way to Tehran. The Soviet Caspian steamship that carried the Crown Prince and his party to the Iranian coast was escorted by a Soviet patrol boat to Iranian territorial waters.

The Iranian port of Enzeil where they docked had, in the meantime, been renamed Bandar Pahlavi (Port Pahlavi), but it was not only the name of the place that had changed. The port city now had a modern dock capable of receiving large boats, and scores of official buildings copied from edifices erected by Communists in Baku gave the previously humble fishing port a new skyline fit for Iran's most important northern port. Wide, tree-lined, asphalted boulevards had replaced the narrow, crooked alleys that turned into gutters of mud and sleet every time it rained. More important still the city now enjoyed electrical power. The Crown Prince could not believe his eyes. 'It's like Europe,' he commented, with some excitement.[32]

Reza Shah was present at the head of a large welcoming party that included all members of the family plus high civilian and military officials. There was even a brass band – something that had not existed before Mohammad-Reza's departure for Switzerland – and it played the nation's new anthem, a hymn to the glory of the Pahlavis who had made Iran 'a hundred times better than in ancient times'.[33] Reza Shah barely managed to control his tears and Taj al-Moluk cried profusely as she embraced her son, but there was no lessening of the strict protocol enforced during the ceremony. Reza Shah was no longer the simple soldier playing the role of the king. He was treated as the Shahanshah, the King of Kings, by officials dressed in tailcoats and wearing top hats. Half a dozen generals, their chests covered with medals, stood to attention, resembling toy soldiers in their bright new uniforms.

After a day's rest at a brand new luxury hotel at a resort called Ramsar, the royal party travelled on to Tehran on a new road that cut through the rugged Alborz mountains and, at some points, reached a height of more than 2000 metres. That road was in itself a sign that Iran had changed. Mohammad-Reza learned that two other roads between the Caspian and Tehran were also under construction and that work on Iran's first railway, designed to link the Caspian to the Persian Gulf, was already well advanced. At both Bandar Pahlavi and Ramsar, as well as the many villages through which the royal party passed, Mohammad-Reza was surprised to see that traditional dress had all but disappeared. Men now wore Western-style suits complete with European hats which they called shapoo from the French *chapeau*. In 1935 a law had been passed to make the wearing of traditional local and tribal clothes an offence punishable by a prison term. The army and the gendarmerie had then roamed the country to enforce the law and, as part of the Shah's campaign, to distribute tens of thousands of European-style suits in towns and villages.

Reza Shah had also banned turbans which he regarded as symbols of the degeneration that Islam had imposed on the country.[33] Turban-burning ceremonies had been organised in many parts of the country in 1936 and early 1937. The veil had also been abolished after a dramatic scene at a ceremony in Tehran in December 1935. Reza Shah had appeared at a graduation ceremony at the teachers' training college in Tehran in the company of Taj al-Moluk and princesses Shams and Ashraf. This was the first time the royal ladies had been seen at a state ceremony and they were unveiled. In a brief speech Reza Shah said that all Iranian women should follow the example set by their Queen and her daughters and 'cast their veils, this symbol of injustice and shame, to the fires of oblivion'.[34] Pictures of the unveiled royal ladies were published in all the newspapers and shown at cinemas as part of a newsreel. Many women, mostly from urban upper- and middle-class families followed the royal example with great enthusiasm. Peasant women did not feel concerned since they had never been veiled nor had ever saved enough money to buy a chador. Trouble came with the womenfolk of the bazaaris and the mullahs whose veils and chadors were removed by soldiers and gendarmes by force and burned in public. Tens of thousands of families decided to keep their womenfolk locked up at home rather than risk having them dishonoured by the loss of the veil and the chador. Upper- and middle-class ladies formed a nationwide association to persuade the 'hiding women' to appear in public without the veil.[35]

The anti-veil campaign provoked bitter confrontation with the mullahs. Most grand ayatollahs, the high-ranking ecclesiastics who controlled the spiritual life of the shi'ites, chose to go into exile rather than risk going to prison. Many of the mullahs who decided to stay in Iran practised the tactic of 'inner exile': they were physically in the country but tried to reduce their contact with society to a bare minimum. The mullahs were also outraged by Reza Shah's decision to ban beards. Units of the armed forces poured into cities and villages and shaved millions of men. In most cases the owners of the beards agreed to be shaved, after finding out that the alternative could be prison. In some cases, however, men had to be handcuffed and chained first. Reza Shah allowed, and even encouraged, the sporting of moustaches as a sign of manliness. But beards he considered symptomatic of decadence and 'Arab degeneration'.[36]

Reza Shah's war against the mullahs was not limited to outward appearances. He had abolished the Qur'anic schools run by the shi'ite clergy and, instead, created a network of compulsory secular education offering an entirely different ideology. They portrayed Iran as a great Aryan nation that had, as a result of internecine feuds and mismanagement by the last Sassanid monarchs, fallen 'victim' to a seventh century

Islamic invasion. It was now time for Iran to regain its 'true personality', rebuild its past glory and claim its rightful place among the leaders of the civilised world. It was a pity that 'alien races' such as Turks and Arabs had separated Iran from its European racial kith and kin. Happiness could be achieved only through education, hard work, discipline and patriotism. The new ideology also preached a cult of the fatherland in direct opposition to Islam's historic internationalism. Reza Shah invited Iranians to deify their mountains, their rivers and their deserts, saying that true Iranians should be prepared to give their lives for Iran's frontiers.[37] Much to the mullahs's chagrin, there was no mention of dying for the Islamic faith.

Reza Shah also banned public religious ceremonies. For the first time in centuries Iranians were prevented from performing ta'azieh ceremonies to mark the martyrdom of Hussein, the grandson of the Prophet. These ceremonies had always been accompanied with scenes of collective delirium in which women beat their chests to the point of bleeding while men opened their own heads with tiny knives or chains, a masochistic exercise which often ended in the death of some participants.

The King of Kings also opposed what he believed was a squandering of scarce financial resources on the building of mosques. When he became king in 1926 there were more than 400 mosques in Tehran: at the end of his reign in 1941 there were only 24 mosques. The rest had disappeared after falling into ruin as a result of a ban on repair work. The sites of most mosques were used for building new primary and secondary schools and on the site of one large mosque Reza Shah built Iran's very first opera house.[38] Control of holy shrines considered part of the national heritage was wrested away from the mullahs and entrusted to a new government department called the Endowments Office or Awqaf, thus depriving the mullahs of a major source of income.

To counterbalance his campaign against the mullahs, Reza Shah ordered a major programme of conservation and renovation that saved hundreds of shrines – some of them among the finest examples of Persian architecture – from destruction. The holy city of Mashhad was especially favoured and soon emerged as a rival for the shi'ite pilgrimage centres of Mesopotamia. Reza Shah also tried to control the training of shi'ite clerics by creating a special faculty of divinity at Tehran University, the country's first centre of higher education, inaugurated on 4 February 1935.

Reza Shah's campaign against the mullahs was part of a broader attack against virtually all sections of traditional Iranian society. Convinced that only a strong central government under his own command could save Iran from decline and possible disintegration, he set out to eliminate all potential sources of challenge to state authority. The mullahs had to be crushed because on countless occasions they had shown their ability to dictate to the Qajar monarchs and alter basic policies. Indeed, the mullahs could paralyse the economies of Tehran and other major cities whenever they wished. Worse still, they claimed to represent the sole legitimate authority in the country on behalf of the Hidden Imam.

The mullahs were not the only powerful group that Reza Shah wanted to destroy. He also set out to break up the power base of the tribal chiefs. Some of these chiefs commanded fairly large private armies that, at times of crisis, were instantly armed by foreign powers as a means of exerting pressure on Tehran. By 1937 the tribal structure had all but been broken and the private armies disarmed. More than 100,000 guns of all descriptions were seized from more than 800 tribal forces. No fewer than 6000 tribal chiefs and other leaders were rounded up and brought to Tehran where they lived under close surveillance. Hundreds of chiefs were executed to set an example and discourage thoughts of revolt against the central government. From 1926 onwards the central government also pursued a policy of enforced settlement of the tribes who represented nearly a third of the country's total population. Here, however, only limited success was achieved. The Pahlavi state was not yet rich enough and organised enough to change the life styles of more than five million people at that time.

The third power group that Reza Shah set out to crush consisted of large landowners. A few dozen families, all related to one another and connected with the Qajars by blood or marriage, owned almost all rural Iran. This gave them enough money and local political power to ignore or get around central government policies whenever they wished. They also used their position during general elections for the purpose of securing seats in the Majlis for themselves or their agents. Some families had even put themselves under foreign protection as a further sign of their disdain for the government. Officials sent from Tehran to the 'feudal' fiefs were either bribed into working for the landlords or were driven off or murdered.

By the time Mohammad-Reza returned home his father had created a Bonapartist state capable of standing above – even outside – traditional social and economic classes of Iranian society. The new regime was strongly backed by a good portion of the merchant classes who appreciated the creation of a national market and the secure roads that resulted from efficient policing. The backbone of support for the Pahlavi state, however, was provided by the new and expanding bureaucracy and its powerful and especially privileged military arm. The new regime had established a number of industrial concerns and opened up numerous development projects, all under direct state control. This, added to the fact that the central government received virtually all of Iran's oil income, made the Pahlavi state the dominant economic force in the country. By 1936 more than half a million people were directly or indirectly in government employ. With their families they represented a force of some three million people, almost one fifth of the total population. A good part of the new bureaucracy consisted of old Qajar elites, but the new schools, supported by schemes started in 1926 for training Iranian experts in Europe, also produced new crops of administrators and managers from a variety of social backgrounds. Around them a new middle class came into being which, as soon as it developed a minimum of selfconsciousness, began to oppose Reza Shah's authoritarian and paternalistic style of rule.

Mohammad-Reza found it hard to recognise Tehran. The city now had a number of broad, and well-lit, tree-lined avenues and boulevards. Half a dozen cinemas offered a variety of foreign feature films to growing audiences. The first Iranian feature films had already been made and shown to enthusiastic fans who often came up from the provinces specifically to go to the cinema. An embittered mullah commented: 'Pahlavi closes our shrines and opens cinemas which are the places of perdition and sin.'[39] The capital now had a number of modern hotels where none had existed before. The Darband Hotel, in the foothills of Tehran, included a dance-floor and a casino, two symbols of 'satanism' in the eyes of the mullahs. Mohammad-Reza, however, would not complain. He was determined to make up for his years of solitude in Switzerland by going out as much as he dared.

A list of the changes implemented in Iran's national life under Reza Shah would cover virtually every aspect of the country's economy and social organisation. A new system of justice was created, replacing the courts run by the mullahs. Capitulation that granted various foreign powers extraterritorial judicial privileges in Iran were cancelled and the right of issuing banknotes, hitherto the monopoly of a British bank, was handed over to the newly-created National Bank of Iran.[40] For the first time in its history Iran was given a system of compulsory national service. Also for the first time in more than two centuries, Iran built itself a Navy in the Persian Gulf.[41]

The finance for some of these ventures was obtained when, during Mohammad-Reza's absence, his father cancelled the oil agreement signed by the Qajars with a British businessman and adventurer. A new contract was negotiated and approved in November 1933, giving Iran a larger share of the income of her oil industry. Reza Shah also imposed a policy of 'Iranisation' which led to the entry of Iranian managers and technicians at the lower and middle levels of the oil industry. Almost all the foreign experts who had helped manage several government departments – including finance, customs, the gendarmerie, police and post and telegraph – were dismissed and replaced by nationals.

Nevertheless, the number of foreigners working in Iran also grew sharply between 1930 and 1940. Thousands of engineers, foremen and other skilled workers were recruited in Europe – mostly Germans and Danes – to help build the Trans-Iranian Railway and operate the new factories that signalled Iran's modest entry into the industrial age. The presence of these expatriate workers and their families gave Tehran and a number of other major cities an international flavour they did not previously have. Partly because of their patronage and partly as a result of the earlier influx of thousands of White Russians fleeing the Bolshevik Revolution, certain parts of Tehran developed a European air. The city now had a number of good cafés and restaurants where none had existed before, and European-style shops appeared side by side with traditional Persian bazaars. Young Mohammad-Reza could, for example, go to Café Naderi, owned and managed by White Russians, and feel that he was in a Europe that, as the years passed, he began to remember almost with nostalgia.

Yes, Iran had changed – in some areas beyond recognition. A people that had lived in accordance with the natural rhythm of the seasons and the various stations of the sun and the moon had now learned to organise its life on the basis of an official calendar and with an eye on the clock. The vast majority of Iranians had never seen a clock and had great difficulty mastering the concept of time with its arbitrary division into seconds, minutes and hours. People were bitterly hurt when they missed coaches that had left dead on time: in the old days the driver and his passengers would have waited for the last straggler to show up. Government offices that had worked according to the mood of those who managed them were also obliged to respect the clock. On a number of occasions ministers who came late to work were simply locked out of their offices and told to report to Reza Shah. The King of Kings hated disorder and indiscipline.

The Tehran of the Qajar era had been a shapeless city with a few cobbled streets where camels, donkeys, horse-drawn coaches and a few motorcars tried to negotiate their paths through a mass of jaywalkers. Under Reza Shah the streets were widened and provided with sidewalks for pedestrians. But it took some years for most people to accept the new rule under which the middle of a street was reserved for motor vehicles and the sidewalks for pedestrians. Soldiers, whip in hand, had to be stationed in every street to help people understand. In 1932 special pedestrian crossings were also introduced in major streets and jaywalking was declared a crime punishable by imprisonment. As for the beasts of burden that had played a key role in the distribution of goods for centuries, the Shah wanted none of them. He ordained that the camel, which he regarded as a symbol of Arabism and thus unacceptable in an Aryan nation, should simply disappear from the face of Iran and in the initial phases of the campaign hundreds of camels were slaughtered. Most owners managed to hide their beasts in safety, however, until the storm had passed. The entry of donkeys and other beasts of burden into Tehran was subject to strict regulation and the issuance of special permits by the gendarmerie.

Reza Shah scrapped the lunar calendar and adopted a solar one, thus upsetting many religious and traditional habits. This was a further move designed to distance Iran from the Arabs. The programme of 're-Aryanising' Iran went even further. People were encouraged to give old

Persian, non-Islamic, names to their children. And now that it had become obligatory for everyone to have a surname, many people, especially within the armed forces and the bureaucracy, imitated Reza Shah himself and chose 'Aryan' appellations. Teams of 'glory hunters', often helped by European archaeologists, were dispatched throughout Iran to identify ancient ruins and tombs of great Iranians. It was thus that Persepolis, the tomb of Cyrus the Great at Pasargad, the ruins of the temple of Anahita in Hamaden, the Sassanid palaces of Kermanshah and numerous other symbols of Iran's pre-Islamic history were officially recognised and registered as part of the national heritage. The Shah also wanted to do something for Ferdowsi, Iran's national poet and the author of Shahnameh (the Book of Kings). A team of scholars dutifully identified a spot in the village of Tus as Ferdowsi's burial place. A magnificent mausoleum was duly constructed and an international conference was convened in Tehran to mark the millennium of the poet's birth.

The Farhangestan (Iranian Academy) created in 1935 was charged with the task of de-Arabising the Persian language and rewriting the nations's history to magnify the Aryan past at the expense of the Islamic present. Many towns and villages regained their pre-Islamic names and numerous streets and other public places were named after Achaemenian or Sassanid emperors of ancient Persia. In contrast, nothing was named after the Prophet of Islam or the 12 Imams of shi'ism, even in the holy cities of Mashhad and Qom.

The reform programme upset the people's traditional patterns of life in many other ways. Ramadan was no longer a month of holidays: government offices, schools and universities, public enterprises and courts of law continued to function normally. Even the bazaars and other private enterprises were not allowed to close for the whole of Ramadan.[42] Traditionally, most Iranians had spent the lunar months of Moharram and Safar mourning the martyrs of shi'ism and accomplishing pilgrimages to one or more of the many thousands of holy shrines that dotted the country. As a result, the nation's economy, such as it was, came to a virtual halt. The Royal Court and the government also observed the period of mourning and the Shah of the day spent much of his time appearing at services organised by the mullahs. Under Reza Shah the period of mourning was reduced to only three days. Many devout shi'ites felt that the Shah had thus deprived them of the chance of securing a place in paradise by mourning the Imams for sixty days each year. The new, time-regulated style of life also prevented many Iranians, especially in the urban areas, from observing the five daily prayers of Islam. Most had to be content with just two prayers, at dawn and after sunset.

Another pleasant tradition that had to be scrapped was the afternoon siesta. For centuries, most Iranians had taken their main daily meal shortly before noon and had then enjoyed one or two hours rest before returning to work. It was considered more than bad manners to disturb a man's siesta. Reza Shah, however, did precisely that. He was especially hard on the army officers, making a point of suddenly appearing at a barracks or an officers' club shortly after lunch to make sure that no one was taking an illicit nap. Those caught napping faced public humiliation, demotion and virtual exile to remote military garrisons.

Many of Reza Shah's changes were achieved in the interest of the nation as a whole, but against the wishes of the wide majority who had simply lost the will to change. They felt threatened by the Shah's reforms although in reality they benefited from them. Thus the very success of the Shah's programme made him increasingly unpopular. Reza Shah had changed Iran but had also been changed by it. In 1936 he was no longer the man Mohammad-Reza had embraced on a Caspian jetty before leaving for Europe five years earlier.

Reza Shah, man of the people and simple soldier who had wanted to turn Iran into a republic, had become the object of an unprecedented personality cult. His portraits, busts and statues were everywhere and everything was done in his name. In every city the widest streets and the central square were named after him. Even the new national anthem was a hymn to his glory, making virtually no mention of the supposed historical grandeur of the Persian peoples. He had dispatched his heir to Europe to learn about Western democratic traditions, but he himself had gradually become an almost classical Oriental autocrat. He now had a secret police that informed on everyone, including high officials of the state, and by 1936 there were two dozen or so political prisoners in Iran, the first since the overthrow of the Qajars eleven years earlier. A number of other opponents of the regime were banished to remote regions of the country or forced to go into exile in Europe.

The Shah had also developed a taste for acquiring wealth, becoming one of Iran's largest landlords. He owned no fewer than 3480 villages, mostly in the Caspian region. The Shah had also become the country's main hotel proprietor and an important restaurateur. Not finding the decadent atmosphere of Qajar palaces to his liking, Reza Shah built himself more than 30 palaces in Tehran and a number of other cities. some of the land he appropriated belonged to major landowners or tribal chiefs who had defied the authority of the state and been punished through arbitrary expropriation. The Shah also came to own much land by reclaiming the so-called mawat (uncultivated) areas that belonged to the government: the law at that time allowed anyone who brought a hitherto uncultivated piece of land under cultivation to claim ownership. Much of the land reclaimed on behalf of Reza Shah thus represented genuine investment. But here, too, it was difficult to know what part of the capital used came from the national treasury and what part from the Shah's own pocket. Reza Shah justified the extension of his private estate by arguing that his presence as landlord in an area gave it a better chance of being developed. This was partly true: the various government agencies were more likely to allocate resources to regions where the Shah had a direct stake. As a result the twin provinces of Gilan and Mazandaran experienced faster economic growth than the remoter Sistan and Baluchistan where the Pahlavis had no property. Many government projects were designed or altered to offer direct services to regions where the Shah's estates were situated.

The simple life-style of the family was gradually abandoned after 1931. The princesses had their clothes imported from Paris where Chanel was a favourite. Each prince and each princess received a Model T Ford as birthday presents between 1931 and 1939 – the Crown Prince himself had a flashy yellow one – and the vehicles were used for joyrides in Tehran at a time when there were no more than 100 or so private motorcars in the whole capital. At home the royal children spoke mostly French.

Reza Shah himself continued to shun luxury and maintained his soldierly austerity; the only compromise he made with the corrupt Qajar traditions was the occasional poker game. Otherwise he continued to don his uniform of rough cloth and worked fourteen hours a day. It was when it came to his family that Reza Shah was uncharacteristically over-generous. A tight-fisted man if there ever was one, Reza Shah was quite prepared to finance the acquisition of superficial luxuries for his eleven sons and daughters. Furthermore, the decision to send all his sons to study abroad was not received as quite the vote of confidence he wanted others to cast for his new system of Iranian education.

The growing presence of the military, at first universally welcomed as an antidote to anarchy and insecurity, in time became a source of resentment, especially in rural areas. Peasants needed their sons to help them till the land, but the Shah wanted rural boys to increase the size of his army from a mere 12,000 to nearly 200,000 in a decade and a half. In some provinces, especially those near the Persian Gulf, many families chose wholesale emigration, mostly to the Arab side of the water, to avoid having their sons taken away by the army.

The father who had welcomed the son at Bandar Pahlavi had appeared perfectly healthy and in robust mood. Reza Shah still stood head and shoulders above the Crown Prince. At the first grand family reunion at the palace in Tehran he had, in fact, showed his physical strength by inviting both Mohammad-Reza and Ali-Reza to fight him as Taj al-Moluk and the royal children watched with a mixture of concern and expectation. 'Well boys!' the Shah had loudly announced, 'I'm told you were sports champions in Europe. Come and see if you can beat an old man. Come, both of you!'[43] Before the boys knew what attitude to adopt the Shah had picked them both up and was spinning them round his head and roaring with laughter. Nevertheless, all was not well with the Shah. Although only in his late fifties, Reza Shah had lived 'more than a hundred years of intense life.'[44] His long military career that included personal partici-pation in scores of battles over a period of 40 years had left many physical and spiritual scars. Mohammad-Reza could not have known it at the time but his father was tired and unwell. The Shah suffered from an extended ulcer which he would not allow his doctors to treat properly and at times of exceptionally intense pain he simply smoked opium to alleviate his suffering. He thought that a Shah who is known to be unwell would not be properly obeyed by his people and refused to go to hospital or even take a few days of rest at the palace. Such moves, he thought, would be signs of weakness and Iran could not afford another weak Shah.

He spent many long hours talking to a son he had not seen for years. How did he judge the results of Mohammad-Reza's European education? He would, of course, never discuss the subject, even with his closest advisers. From the moves he made after Mohammad-Reza's return, however, it is possible to speculate that the old Shah was not quite satisfied with what Europe had done to the Crown Prince. Shortly after the family reunion in Tehran, Reza Shah announced that Mohammad-Reza and Ali-Reza should enrol at the newly-created Military Academy. 'The good life is over my friends,' he told the two princes. 'From now on you are soldiers!' One day, soon after his return from Switzerland, Mohammad-Reza asked the Shah what he would single out as his main objective. Reza Shah's reply was simple but highly significant: to leave behind a state machinery strong and well-organised enough to carry on the business of government without him. 'What does he mean?' Mohammad-Reza asked himself. 'Does he think that if he were gone I couldn't take over and continue his work?' The most important lesson Reza Shah had learned from his own reading of Iranian history was a simple – and simplistic – one: with a strong Shah Iran might regain its place as a world leader, but with a weak ruler it risked disintegration.

The question uppermost in Reza Shah's mind was: would Mohammad-Reza be a strong or a weak Shah?

3

Playing King

During his stay in Switzerland Crown Prince Mohammad-Reza had acquired a fairly large collection of expensive clothes. Back in Tehran he soon found that he would have virtually no opportunity to dress up. On his father's order he was quickly enrolled at the newly-created Officers' Faculty, a military institution modelled on France's famous Saint-Cyr school near Paris. Like other cadets the Crown Prince had Thursday afternoon and Friday off, but even this truncated Persian weekend had to be largely spent on official duties. Thursday afternoon was spent on a special course of Persian grammar under the ever-vigilant Abdol-Azim Qarib. Friday lunch was taken with his sisters and brothers in the presence of Reza Shah, leaving only the afternoon and evening of Friday free. Mohammad-Reza spent this free time driving one of the several fast cars he had acquired since his return. Among his favourite cars was a Mercedes sent to him as a birthday present by Adolf Hitler, the German Chancellor. On Friday evenings the Crown Prince made his weekly round of Tehran's few nightclubs: the Kolbeh at Darband, which belonged to Reza Shah himself, the Tehran Palace on Istanbul Avenue, the Park Hotel and the Café Naderi run by White Russians.

Mohammad-Reza's Swiss friend Ernest Perron had been quietly exiled by Reza Shah – who never quite accepted his presence – to Ramsar on the Caspian Sea where he worked as General Manager of a luxury resort that belonged to His Majesty. Hossein Fardust had followed the Crown Prince to the Officers' Faculty and was, therefore, constantly in his company. Mohammad-Reza also made friends with two other cadets: Abdul-Karim Ayadi, who later became his personal physician and confidant, and Assadallah Sani'i, his future War Minister.

In the spring of 1938 Mohammad-Reza graduated from the Officers' Faculty as a second lieutenant. During his two years at the school he had not only learned the rudiments of command but had fallen in love with the very idea of the army. As a child he had often played with lead soldiers. In Switzerland he had discovered electric trains for which he developed a lifelong passion. As a teenage officer – he was just under nineteen when he graduated – he brought his lead soldiers and electrical trains together and, whenever he had the time, played one of the many variations of the Blitzkrieg that he himself invented.

War, however, was not the only game the Crown Prince liked to play in his spare time and in his large but rather sad palace he was introduced to a never-ending stream of society debutantes who aspired after a match that would one day make them the Empress of Persia. These encounters took place at semi-official tea parties often organised with Taj al-Moluk's consent. There was no question of leaving the prince alone with any of the debutantes; that would have immediately led to scandal at a time when a mere kiss exchanged outside marriage could be seen as a prelude to perdition. An army of stately matrons was, somehow, always present whenever the Crown Prince appeared with a girlfriend at a nightclub. For more intimate relationships Mohammad-Reza had to address himself to professionals. Reza Shah must have heard about these activities but showed no reaction. Instead he set to work quietly looking for a bride for his son.

Mohammad-Reza has often been described as an almost insatiable skirt-chaser in those days. But, leaving aside the three or four professional ladies, it is virtually certain that he had only one intimate relationship, with a Tehran debutante early in 1939. She was one Miss 'Azam Divshalli who, for obscure reasons, believed that Mohammad-Reza would marry her.

Tehran high society in 1938 and 1939 was convinced that the Crown Prince preferred blondes with short hair, in sharp contrast with the traditional Iranian admiration for very long, jet black hair. Accordingly hairdressers' scissors were set to work and a large number of debutantes wearing short, bleached hair appeared on the scene. A Greek barber and tooth-extractor in south Tehran made a fortune by moving uptown and setting up shop as a 'European hairdresser'.

Debutantes who were courted by Mohammad-Reza in those days describe him as shy, sweet and extremely polite. 'What came as an immediate surprise was the fact that he treated girls as equals,' relates a woman who was Mohammad-Reza's frequent escort in 1938 and early 1939. 'Most other Iranian men at the time – and even much later – did not know how to behave in the company of women; they either became aggressive or were frightened. Mohammad-Reza was a perfect companion. He put you at ease immediately. And then he always had something interesting to talk about.'[1] His position, his wealth, his good looks and his athletic physique would have been sufficient to make Mohammad-Reza attractive to most girls. That he was an entertaining companion made him almost irresistible.

He thirsted for sympathy and badly wanted to be loved for himself. He tried to impress his companions with his Western education and his knowledge of European music and literature.[2] He had never truly experienced love and affection. He had been removed from his mother's care at the age of seven and his father hardly ever demonstrated his emotions.

The Crown Prince had hoped to marry for love, but for Reza Shah love was an invention of sentimentalists who wished to soften and corrupt society. The Shah regarded his son's marriage as a military campaign that had to be carefully planned with precise objectives. Like a battle plan, everything about it had to remain secret until the very last moment. Reza Shah was not looking for a sweet little blonde girl who could win Mohammad-Reza's heart. He had begun thinking about his son's marriage from the middle of 1935, long before Mohammad-Reza's return from Switzerland.

Reza Shah had discussed the matter with only two or three close confidants. The would-be bride had to help the King of Kings achieve two objectives. First she should link the Pahlavi family, which had no historical roots, with older and more-established royal dynasties. The Western royal families had to be excluded right from the start. None of them would allow any of their members to convert to Islam in order to become Empress of Persia. And Iran's Constitution explicitly forbade the marriage of the heir to the throne to a non-Muslim.* For a brief moment Reza Shah toyed with the idea of seeking the hand of one of the daughters of Ahmad Shah, the Qajar monarch he himself had overthrown. That would have merged the new dynasty with the older one and strengthened links with the Qajar elite, which continued to play the dominant political role in the country, with the Pahlavis. This option, Reza Shah rejected for two reasons: he was genuinely convinced that the 132-year Qajar rule had been one of the darkest periods in Iran's long history and was best forgotten; furthermore, the Qajars traced their origins to Chengiz Khan, the hated Mongol conqueror, and could have no place within the new Aryan nationalism that Reza Shah promoted. Thus the would-be bride had to be found within the royal families of the Muslim countries, but here too there were several difficulties. Reza Shah had made it his mission to de-Arabise Iran. Thus, an Arab princess could not be a suitable choice as the future Empress of Persia, the birthplace of the Aryans. An Afghan princess would have been the ideal choice; both Aryan and Muslim, she would have fulfilled the conditions set by Reza Shah and the Iranian Constitution. This choice, however, was quickly ruled out. Most Afghan princesses were either too young or simply illiterate.

Reza Shah's second objective in deciding the choice of a wife for his son was to ensure succession with the birth of a new prince. From 1938 onwards Reza Shah had begun thinking about abdicating in favour of

* In fact the Iranian Constitution explicitly stated that the consort of a ruling monarch of Persia must be of Persian origin. For this reason, Mohammad-Reza's eventual Egyptian bride, Princess Fawziah, had 'the quality of Persianness' bestowed upon her by a special session of the parliament in Tehran.

Mohammad-Reza. His plan, never clearly formulated, envisaged his retirement in 1940. Mohammad-Reza would become king and his father would stay in the background as an elder statesman, offering advice and guidance. The success of such an enterprise partly depended on Mohammad-Reza being settled and already assured of an heir.

The idea of consulting Mohammad-Reza himself about the project never crossed Reza Shah's mind and by the end of 1938 he had made up his mind: an Egyptian princess was to become Mohammad-Reza's wife. The princess was chosen on the basis of a single photograph and two brief reports prepared by the Turkish Ambassador to Cairo, Rushdi Eres. The choice of a Turkish diplomat for such a delicate mission reflected Reza Shah's close personal friendship with Atatürk, which had been further strengthened by his state visit to Ankara in 1934. The formal demand for marriage, however, was put to Farouk by Iran's own ambassador to Egypt, Ahmad Rad.

The Egyptian princess was Fawziah, the 17-year-old sister of King Farouk. Reza Shah, however, had to convince himself that Fawziah was, somehow, of Aryan origin. Court experts studied the matter and quickly came up with the kind of report the Shah wanted. They showed that the Egyptian royal family founded by Mohammad-Ali Pasha, had arrived in the Nile valley from Daghestan via Albania. Since Daghestan was – and still is – populated by people of Iranic origin, Princess Fawziah was, therefore, not an Arab but an Aryan!

Mohammad-Reza was shown the photo of his bride-to-be and asked to prepare for the trip to Cairo during which the Muslim rites of marriage would be performed in the presence of Farouk. Even the amateur photo sent from Cairo showed Fawziah to be a great beauty. She was a brunette with deep blue eyes which the black-and-white photo could not fully represent. At least one admirer saw her as a new version of the Botticelli Venus.[3] Like Mohammad-Reza himself, Fawziah had been educated in Switzerland and had never worn the veil; she was a thoroughly modern girl who had been a guest at many European courts including that of Saint James. The idea of going to Tehran must have come as a shock to her: Iran was still considered to be one of the most backward countries in the world and the Pahlavis were sneered at as upstarts. The Egyptian Queen Mother, Nazli, was especially opposed to her daughter's marriage, believing that such a link might hurt the prestige of the Egyptian Royal Family. Her husband, however, was a strong supporter of the marriage. Farouk had developed the dream of reviving the Caliphate that had been abolished by Atatürk fourteen years earlier. The revival of the Caliphate would, Farouk hoped, give him the position of the Caliph. The Egyptian ruler was also involved in negotiations aimed at marrying his two other sisters, Fa'ezeh, to Crown Prince Talal of Jordan and King Faisal of Iraq respectively.

The final problem to be overcome was religious: Iran was a shi'ite country while Egypt, thanks to the presence of the al-Azhar theological school in Cairo, was the centre of sunni Islam. In the lengthy negotiations that preceded the marriage accord, the two sides agreed to work for a 'convergence' of the different versions of Islam. The first step to that end, it was agreed, should be the recognition by the sunnis of Shi'ism as a legitimate 'way' of Islam.[4]

Early in March 1939 Mohammad-Reza, accompanied by a large delegation of dignitaries and courtiers (including Dr Nafisi who had been his guardian in Switzerland and now served as his *chef de cabinet*) travelled to Cairo. The Islamic marriage ceremony took place at the Abdin Palace in Cairo and was conducted by Shaikh al-Maghrabi, the Rector of al-Azhar, in Farouk's presence. The Crown Prince and his future bride had met only once, in the presence of the official delegations of both countries, before the marriage ceremony took place. After the ceremony the marriage could not be consummated and the couple had to wait until a second marriage ceremony had been performed in Tehran according to shi'ite rites.

The couple flew to Tehran on 16 March, where a jubilant Reza Shah and a curious Taj al-Moluk awaited them at the airport at the head of a huge gathering of family members and officials. Reza Shah kissed Fawziah on the forehead and presented her to those present. 'Here is your future queen,' he said. Then turning to Fawziah he added: 'Well, my daughter, this is your country and here is your people.'

The aircraft that brought the royal couple from Cairo also carried Fawziah's personal effects which were packed in no fewer than 200 trunks and suitcases. The arrival of Fawziah's belongings at the Marble Palace where the couple were to be housed after their marriage ceremony caused a sensation. The suitcases contained over 200 dresses, 160 pairs of shoes, 7 fur coats, a large variety of jewellery and scores of baubles that the princess needed for decorating her new palace. A few days later the bridal dress ordered from Paris also arrived. It had cost Reza Shah over £10,000, the single biggest item of personal expenditure the stringent Shah – who had a habit of turning off lights in the palace – had ever consented to.

The shi'ite ceremony took place at the Shah Mosque in the centre of Tehran and was followed by the traditional Persian wedding ceremonies lasting seven days and seven nights. Hundreds of prisoners were released for the occasion and food and money was distributed among the poor in Tehran and several other cities. Mohammad-Reza and his bride then left for their honeymoon on the Caspian where Fawziah contracted malaria.

By the end of the summer when Mohammad-Reza and Fawziah settled in their special palace in the centre of Tehran the atmosphere in the capital had changed. The war that had broken out in Europe had created a sense of unease among Iranian leaders. Reza Shah and his aides had not forgotten that the previous European war had led to an invasion of Iran in

1915. The new war opposed Great Britain, which controlled the Khuzestan oil, Iran's single largest source of income, and Germany, which had emerged as the nation's main trading partner since 1936. Between 2000 and 3000 Germans lived and worked in Iran as technicians, merchants, teachers, military instructors and researchers. It is almost certain that quite a few of them were Nazi secret agents. The moment Britain declared war on Germany the expulsion of all German nationals from Iran became a major British demand.

The Shah, of course, refused to comply. For one thing the expulsion demand was never put to him formally until much later. Also, the departure of the Germans, without having them replaced by an equal number of technicians and instructors, would have paralysed parts of the economy and the army's logistics. At no point did Britain suggest filling such a gap with its own subjects. In any case such a move would have provoked a strong backlash in Iran where Britain remained extremely unpopular as an imperialist power that had constantly tried to destroy Iran's independence.

The first year of war in Europe had little direct effect on Iran except for a series of price increases followed by shortages of imported goods. There were sporadic demonstrations of pro-Nazi sentiment, especially among the military. All accounts concur that during the period 1939–40, the majority of Iranian army officers, including some senior commanders, were sympathetic to the German cause. Crown Prince Mohammad-Reza, whose official title now was that of Army Inspector, could not have ignored the presence of a pro-Nazi undercurrent in the officer corps. There was, however, no pro-Nazi organisation on any serious level: Reza Shah would not have tolerated that.

As Army Inspector Mohammad-Reza travelled to many parts of the country, at times in his father's company. But his official duties did not prevent him from pursuing a marital life that he clearly enjoyed at the time. Princess Fawziah was both beautiful and entertaining when she wanted to be. The couple were never really in love but were, almost certainly, quite fond of each other. Fawziah spent most of her time lazing in bed or playing cards with court ladies. She kept her relations with her in-laws to a minimum. Only Princess Shams managed to develop something approaching a friendly relationship with the 'Egyptian bride', as Fawziah was, no doubt disparagingly, referred to by the Pahlavi womenfolk.

In September 1940 Reza Shah was given the good news that Fawziah was expecting a child. Everyone, including the Shah himself, hoped that the coming child would be a boy. Reza Shah had even intimated his intention to name his would-be grandson Massud-Reza, meaning Reza's happiness. In the event Fawziah gave birth to a daughter on 10 October 1940. She was named Shahnaz (The Grace of the Shah).

Some reports have claimed that Reza Shah was deeply unhappy at the birth of a girl. This might initially have been true, but later Reza Shah grew extremely fond of his granddaughter and missed no opportunity of visiting her. As for Mohammad-Reza himself, the birth of Shahnaz was to become 'the happiest moment' of his life with Fawziah.

In March 1941 the newly-born Princess Shahnaz was the star of the family reunion organised to celebrate the Iranian New Year (Now-Ruz). This was to be the very last time that all the Pahlavis came together under one roof. It was also on this occasion that the Crown Prince first met a man who was to become a friend and close associate until the very end: Amir-Assadallah Alam, the son of a landowner and chieftain from the remote region of Birjand on the Afghan frontier. Young Alam, who had roamed around the court for several months in search of a precise post, was brought in to photograph Princess Shahnaz. He stayed on to have tea with the Crown Prince and was 'fully noticed'.

As the war raged in Europe Iran took virtually no steps to prepare herself for coping with the possibility of being sucked into the conflict. The military budget increased sharply and some frontier posts were fortified, but there was no overall strategic planning as the Shah and his senior officers hoped for the best, hiding behind the solemn pledge of neutrality Iran had declared as the war began. Iran was a member of the Saadabad Pact which also included Turkey and Afghanistan, but it was clear that neither Turkey nor Afghanistan would be in a position to help Iran repulse an attack by a major European power. The conclusion of the Russo–German alliance added a new dimension to Iran's problems. Would the Russians move into northern Iran while Britain, which had oil interests in the south of the country, was fighting Hitler in Europe?

The Soviet Union, acting through the Comintern, had created an ideological base for itself in Iran from 1931 onwards. A law passed by the parliament in that year, however, made all Communist activity illegal. As a result a number of secret cells, all indirectly controlled by agents of the Comintern, were created in the capital.[5] While pro-Soviet political activity was severely checked by the police and led to the arrest of many intellectuals, pro-German propaganda was discreetly encouraged by the authorities. General Ayrom, the chief of police and a brother of Taj al-Moluk, made no secret of his admiration for Hitler and deemed it his mission to protect Iran against the disease of Communism.

Probably a majority of Iran's intellectual elite and military leadership of the time could be described as pro-German. A large number of Iranians had studied in Germany since 1931 and Britain and the USSR were disliked and distrusted because of their past record of colonial bullying of Iran. Hitler's 'Aryanism' was seen as an endorsement of Iran's own nationalism promoted by Reza Shah. At the same time German business interests in Iran had established extensive and profitable links with many leading families. The Persian-language programmes of Berlin Radio, supervised by an 'Aryanist' Iranian known as Bahram Shahrokh, also played a role in whipping up anti-British and pro-Hitler sentiments.

Relations between Reza Shah and the British had never been smooth and after 1939 London increasingly regarded the Iranian king as a potential enemy rather than a future ally. The British envoy in Tehran, Sir Reader Bullard, who hated virtually everything Persian, had a role in portraying Reza Shah as a secret admirer of Hitler and an objective ally of the Nazis. Such allegations, however, are difficult to prove. Indeed we now know that Reza Shah, although he admired Germany's industrial might and national discipline, had no warm feelings for Hitler. He never took up an invitation by Hitler to visit Germany and refused to reorganise the Iranian armed forces on the German model. He found Hitler's anti-Semitism especially odious and in 1938 he instructed the Iranian Ambassador to Berlin, Mohsen Ra'is, to invite the German Jewish professors who had lost their positions to come and work in Iran.[6] During his visit to Turkey Reza Shah had heard a great deal about the 'arrogant behaviour' of Germans who had been allies of the Ottoman Empire during the First World War, and in 1939, a few days after war had broken out in Europe, he told his children that Germany wanted to 'set the whole world on fire'.[7]

Numerous German attempts at establishing a close personal relationship with the Shah had produced no positive results and by the summer of 1941, after Germany's invasion of the USSR, Berlin was thinking of staging a *coup d'état* against Reza Shah. They were especially angry with the Shah's renewed declaration of neutrality. The German candidate for Reza Shah's succession as strongman in Tehran was none other than General Ayrom, the Shah's brother-in-law.[8] The so-called Rosenberg Plan prepared by the German high command envisaged the invasion and occupation of Iran. Germany wanted to capture the oilfields of the entire Persian Gulf region and, at a later stage, invade British India.

From the end of June 1941 onwards, Russia and Britain sent a stream of 'friendly warnings' and protest notes to Reza Shah on the subject of the German presence in Iran. They claimed that German agents were preparing tribal revolts in the south with the aim of stopping the flow of oil to Britain. They warned the Shah that Nazi agitators and saboteurs could blow up the newly-completed Trans-Iranian Railway, an easy target with its numerous bridges and tunnels over a distance of some 1200 kilometres. It is almost certain that Reza Shah was unable to correctly interpret the real motive behind what was an orchestrated diplomatic campaign as his ministers and advisers couched the Anglo-Russian threats in terms that would not displease him. They dared not tell the stern autocrat that his very throne was now in danger and as a result Reza Shah did not see the bite that was hidden behind the bark. He replied to Allied notes by saying that he was fully able to prevent the Germans from misbehaving and that there were, in any case, at least as many citizens of the Allied nations as there were Germans in Iran.

The fact that not a single act of sabotage was carried out anywhere in Iran showed that Allied fears were groundless. Under the Rosenberg Plan, Germany was determined to use Iran's oil resources and transport facilities for its own ends; there was, thus, no point in destroying either. The German calculation was that Nazi forces would capture the whole of the Caucasus by the spring of 1942 and then enter Iran and use it as a base for the invasion of the Middle East and India.

The Allies must have known all that, yet they needed a pretext for their own invasion of Iran. A cursory glance at the world map would show that Iran was the most logical way of supplying Russia with the arms and foodstuffs she required to continue her war against Germany. This is how Winston Churchill, the British prime minister at the time, spelled out the Allied position:

> The need to pass munitions and supplies of all kinds to the Soviet Government, and the extreme difficulties of the Arctic route, together with future strategic possibilities, made it eminently desirable to open the fullest communication with Russia through Persia . . . The Persian oilfields were a prime war factor, and if Russia were defeated we would have to be ready to occupy them ourselves. And then there was the threat to India.[9]

Accordingly, early in August 1941, Churchill appointed a special committee to plan the invasion of Iran. A final protest note, dated 17 August, was sent to Reza Shah, but the invasion date had already been fixed for 25 August. The note was not different in content from several others that had preceded it over a period of 10 months, but it was more menacing in tone. On the day it was presented to the Shah, the British Broadcasting Corporation's newly-created Persian service, broadcast from Cyprus, launched a major campaign against Reza Shah. The founder of the Pahlavi dynasty was presented as a former donkey-driver turned dictator and the Iranian people were invited to overthrow him.

Reza Shah now understood that the Allies meant to get rid of him but did not know how they would proceed to achieve that end. He began to seek ways of soothing the Allies. He instructed his minister in London to formally ask the British Government for a full explanation of their precise demands. There was no answer. It was too late. The invasion machine had been put in motion. Nothing could stop it.

Many years later, Mohammad-Reza argued that his father would have given the Allies what they wanted had he been asked in the proper manner:

> My father was a reasonable man. If the Allies had abandoned their circumlocution and had given Reza Shah an honest picture of their strategic predicament in its relation to Iran's interests, I think he would have seen the point . . . My father would have either accepted the Allied proposal or stepped aside so that I could do so.[10]

History can always be rewritten with 'ifs' and 'buts'. Reza Shah had, as we have already noted, thought of abdicating in favour of his son long before the Allied invasion, but it is difficult to imagine Reza Shah either in the role of collaborator with foreigners occupying Iran or as an *éminence grise* in his son's court while the Allies effectively controlled the country. The Allies were correct in their view that their invasion and occupation of Iran had to be accompanied by Reza Shah's dethronement and exile.

Reza Shah appointed the Anglophile Ali Mansur as prime minister, partly in the hope of allaying British suspicions, but Mansur quickly told his British friends that the Shah would never accept becoming a British stooge. Mansur did not inform Reza Shah of a formal note sent by the Allies informing the Iranian Government that Iran had been invaded. By the time the Shah learned the truth virtually all effective resistance had ceased on the Iranian side and Soviet forces were speeding towards Tehran. Through Mansur, Reza Shah informed the British envoy Bullard and his Russian counterpart Smirnov that Iran would expel all remaining German citizens and would also let the Allies use the Trans-Iranian Railway for the shipment of supplies to the USSR. His offer, however, provoked nothing but laughter and derision. Mansur was told that the Allies would first conquer Tehran and only then decide whom they would deal with as representing authority in Iran.

The BBC meanwhile continued to call for Reza Shah's 'expulsion'. The dictator who had plundered the nation's wealth had to go, the radio told its growing audience. 'And before he leaves, search his luggage to make sure he does not take what does not belong to him,' the propaganda programme insisted.[11]

Reza Shah's last desperate bid to stop the Allies from entering Tehran came in the form of a cable he sent to President Franklin D. Roosevelt of the United States on 25 August. The move was almost certainly made with encouragement from the Crown Prince. In it Reza Shah wrote:

> I consider it my duty, on the basis of declarations which Your Excellency has made several times regarding the necessity of defending principles of international justice and the rights of people to liberty, to request Your Excellency to be good enough to interest yourself in this incident which brings into war a neutral and pacific country which has had no other care than the safeguarding of tranquillity and the reform of society. I beg Your Excellency to take efficacious and urgent humanitarian steps to put an end to these acts of aggression.

Roosevelt's reply came 10 days later and told the sinking Shah not to expect anything from Washington.[12]

Meanwhile on 27 August Mansur suddenly resigned after signing the last expulsion order against the remaining German citizens in Iran. Mohammad-Reza, who had not left his father's side since the Allied invasion had begun, continued to press Reza Shah to join the camp of the

Allies and to consult them about the choice of a new prime minister.[13] Reza Shah would have none of this and during one discussion took his son by the shoulders and shouted: 'How do you see me, a reigning monarch, taking orders from a little Russian or British captain?'[14] He continued to refuse a ceasefire and would not cancel his order to the armed forces to resist the invasion despite the fact that all real fighting had come to an end within the first 48 hours. 'I know that our forces cannot offer serious resistance,' he told Mohammad-Reza, 'but my orders to them to fight on will ensure our good name in the future. It will be remembered as a positive and brave act.'[15]

In the evening of 27 August Reza Shah entered his car and ordered the driver Sadeq Agha to take him to an address in central Tehran. This was an unusual step. The Shah had no escort and was not accompanied even by a secretary. He was going to find himself a prime minister. The royal car stopped at the door of a modest house. The Shah got out of the car and rang the bell. The door was opened by a young boy who immediately recognised the monarch. The boy led the Shah upstairs to where an astonished old man received the unexpected guest. The old man was Mohammad-Ali Foroughi, a scholar and statesman. He had been one of Reza Shah's closest aides and had even served as prime minister in the late 1920s. He had suffered royal disgrace because of his opposition to what he had seen as Reza Shah's increasingly authoritarian style of rule. The Shah had thrown him out of the palace after a heated argument in which Foroughi, who always sported a goatee, had been described as 'a bearded woman' by the angry monarch.

'Please help me!' Reza Shah asked Foroughi before the latter could recover from his shock.

The two men spent nearly two hours together at the end of which Reza Shah had agreed to a ceasefire and Foroughi had accepted the post of prime minister. The Shah had also said he was ready to abdicate provided he could be assured of his son's succession. Foroughi promised to try his best to put Mohammad-Reza on the throne[16] and within hours he had announced a ceasefire and the imposition of martial law in Tehran.

Three days later the Allies announced that they had divided Iran into three zones: the northern part would be under Russian control while the British occupied the south. The third zone would consist of a narrow band in which Tehran was situated.

Foroughi's appointment and his acceptance of a ceasefire had not pacified the invaders. They wanted Reza Shah to go and this message was now hammered out not only by the BBC but also by a British-controlled Persian language radio in Baghdad as well as Soviet radios in Baku and Moscow. The Allies, especially the British, adopted a hostile attitude even towards the Crown Prince. For a brief moment they tried to persuade Foroughi himself to become interim head of state after sending Reza Shah and his entire family into exile. Foroughi, of course, dismissed the idea out of hand. The Russians tried to promote Mohammad Sa'ed, Iran's Ambassador to Moscow, as head of a provisional government in Tehran, but Sa'ed also refused to back any scheme that would involve a betrayal of his oath of loyalty to the Pahlavis. After lengthy negotiations with the British and Russian ambassadors, Forughi succeeded in shaping a compromise: Reza Shah would abdicate and leave the country and the Crown Prince would be sworn in as the new monarch. Iran would then formally join the Allied camp.

Unknown to Forughi, who was thinking in terms of several weeks preparation before Reza Shah's abdication was announced, the monarch himself had decided to speed up the process. On 14 September the Shah spent several hours with his son to brief the future king about major issues. At the end of the session he asked the court photographer to take a series of pictures of him and the Crown Prince at the Saadabad Palace. According to at least one account the Allies, acting through Bullard and Smirnov, had given Reza Shah until 17 August to abdicate or face 'the use of force'.[17]

On 15 September Forughi was summoned to the Royal Palace at 7am. The Shah received his prime minister in the special imperial cabinet room. Reza Shah, his tired eyes indicating his lack of sleep, leaning against his desk, presented the prime minister with a rather untidy bundle of papers before inviting him to sit in an armchair. 'Here is my letter of abdication,' the Shah said. 'See what you think of it.'

The letter of abdication began with a line of poetry to the effect that future generations would be the best judges of His Majesty's actions. It then went into several pages of bitter invective against Britain and Russia, Iran's traditional enemies. Finally, the Shah recalled his many services to the country and invited all patriots to support his son as the new Shahanshah.

Forughi found the text too long and too abrasive regarding the Allies. He argued that one could not insult the Allies and at the same time expect them to accept the Crown Prince's accession to the throne.[18] After a brief discussion Reza Shah asked Forughi to sit behind the imperial desk and prepare a new and more acceptable text. The exercise lasted more than an hour and Forughi had to rewrite it twice before the Shah would accept it. It was brief, dramatic and moving. Forughi wrote the final version on paper bearing the royal letterhead in his own hand. The Shah signed and sealed it. The next move was clear: the prime minister had to rush to the Majlis (Parliament) where one of three ordinary sessions held each week would begin at around 9am.

A few minutes after the start of the session, in the presence of British and Russian ambassadors as well as the rest of the corps diplomatique, Forughi was invited by the speaker, Mohatasham Saltaneh Esfandiari to take the floor. The prime minister, with the briefest of preliminaries, read the Shah's letter of abdication and asked for a vote. It took a stunned house more than half an hour before a vote could be conducted. Many deputies were crying, a few had even fainted. Most were glued to their seats in a state of shock. When the vote came it was unanimous. Reza Shah's abdication was approved and Mohammad-Reza's succession duly recognised. The Allied diplomats watched the whole procedure with impassive, expressionless faces.[19]

The Majlis session had guaranteed the success of only half of the plan for Mohammad-Reza's accession. He now had to appear in front of the parliament and take the oath of office before he could begin to exercise his new function. Reza Shah and Foroughi knew that they could not delay until the regular session of the Majlis the following week. That was too long to wait in the context of Iran's explosive politics at a time when Allied armies continued to move towards the capital. An extraordinary session was, therefore, arranged for the following day. It was clear that Reza Shah and Foroughi wished to speed things up so as not to leave the Allies enough time to work out a response which might have come in the form of advising the parliamentarians not to convene or simply to reject Mohammad-Reza as the new Shah.

Reza Shah and Foroughi had also been informed by Iran's Ambassador to London, Hassan Taqizadeh, that the British had for some time been looking at the possibility of putting one of the Qajars back on the throne. The scheme had not made much progress because it was found out that the potential Qajar pretender, a son of Mohammed-Hassan Mirza who had been Crown Prince during Ahmad Shah's reign, had converted to Christianity and acquired British citizenship, even changing his name and joining the Royal Navy as a petty officer. Taqizadeh, however, was convinced that British hatred for the Pahlavis was such that London would continue to seek ways of bringing the new dynasty to an end.

On 17 September the Majlis met in an atmosphere of dramatic suspense. The urgency of the situation was understood by all as Foroughi had been informed by the Allies that their troops would enter Tehran the same day. Rumours were rife about the possibility of the Crown Prince being assassinated or prevented from attending the ceremony by the Allies. Some members of the parliament had already packed their suitcases to return to the relative safety of their provinces and there was a possibility that a quorum would not be obtained, making the swearing-in ceremony impossible. Foroughi, however, used a mixture of threat and cajolement to make sure that most deputies showed up.

From the earliest hours of the morning a large crowd had gathered at Baharestan Square where the parliament building was situated. The city had been thrown in disarray by the announcement of Reza Shah's abdication. The fact that all members of the royal family with the exception of Reza Shah, the Crown Prince and Princess Fawziah had been sent to Isfahan several days earlier was seen by many people in Tehran as a sure sign that the capital was no longer safe.

The task of getting the Crown Prince to the Majlis was entrusted to Major Ali Nejati who had served as Reza Shah's personal bodyguard for some time. And it was in a white rented Chrysler that Nejati arrived at the White Palace (Kakh Abyaz) early that morning, ostensibly to deliver a package. When the car left the Crown Prince was in it hidden under a blanket on the back seat. Although no one followed the car Nejati took the precaution of taking a roundabout route to the Golestan Palace where the Crown Prince, emerging from under the blanket, freshened up and donned his uniform of commander-in-chief. He also rehearsed the text of his speech, written by Forughi, until he knew it by heart. It was around 3 pm that Mohammad-Reza, in full state regalia, boarded the official royal limousine, a Pierce Arrow, and drove to the Majlis where impatient deputies were threatening to leave the building.

In later years Mohammad-Reza recalled that his state limousine had been carried shoulder high by a crowd of supporters at Baharestan Square. There is little independent evidence to support this but most accounts agree that the Crown Prince received an enthusiastic reception from the crowd and was, indeed, carried shoulder high – though not in his limousine – to the entrance of the parliament building. There he was greeted by Forughi and Speaker Esfandiari. The Allied diplomats had boycotted the session, but this did not affect Mohammad-Reza's composure. In a calm, firm and reassuring voice he read the text of his speech and offered the promise that Iran's miseries would soon be over. He was given a standing ovation by the 193 deputies present. Nejati then telephoned the palace to inform Reza Shah that all was over. The old king had already packed his suitcases and was waiting for the signal to leave for Isfahan to join his two wives and ten of his children. He would leave Mohammad-Reza in charge alone. Reza Shah was never to see his son again.

From the Majlis Mohammad-Reza Shah drove to Saadabad Palace where he was told that his father had left less than an hour earlier. Mohammad-Reza entered his father's office where every piece of furniture evoked memories of the old man. The new Shah could not bring himself to sit in his father's chair for several days. Although he had long been prepared for the job, he quickly found that the actual exercise of political power was quite different from theoretical preparation for it. Reza Shah had been a powerful leader only partly because of his position, and Mohammad-Reza was fully conscious of the fact that he had few of his father's natural assets. The new Shah had received a democratic training which meant that he knew that there were different views on every issue and that reality could be contemplated from many different angles: this made him hesitant and indecisive where his father had been determined and resolute. Mohammad-Reza wanted to be loved for his person: Reza Shah never knew what love was, asking only to be obeyed. The new Shah was polite and shy and anxious not to offend: the old Shah deliberately terrorised members of his entourage in order to keep them constantly on their guard. Reza Shah had been a born leader; the new Shah had to learn to become one. Reza Shah always seemed to know exactly what he wanted: his son began his kingship by asking Forughi and other ministers what was to be done.

Forughi regarded two issues as urgent. The first was to find some legal basis for the presence of the Allies in Iran in exchange for an Allied recognition of Iranian independence and sovereignty. The second was to work out a treaty under which the Allies would agree to withdraw from Iran at the end of the war. The new Shah, now that he was Commander-in-Chief at the age of 22, added a third issue of importance to the agenda set by the prime minister: saving what was left of the armed forces.

The military machine created by Reza Shah with great patience and at enormous expense had been all but broken as a result of the Allied invasion. The entire Iranian war fleet had been sunk by the Royal Navy in the Persian Gulf on the first day of hostilities. The embryonic Air Force had disintegrated after some aircraft were destroyed on the ground and others rendered inoperative for lack of spare parts: the departure of German technicians and a number of foreign pilots completed the destruction. All the army's conscripts had simply returned home and hundreds of officers and NCOs had resigned in disgust. The young Shah was Commander-in-Chief of a largely fictitious army.

Meanwhile Reza Shah had arrived in Isfahan after a long and arduous journey from the capital. On the way his Rolls-Royce had broken down and he had been obliged to complete his journey in a taxi. He was alone and broken with stooping shoulders and a shrivelled face covered with white stubble. The taxi driver had not recognised him. When he arrived at the Governor's Residence where the royal family was now housed he had to introduce himself to the guards before he was admitted. 'We had left him in Tehran a towering figure,' one of his daughters later recalled. 'In Isfahan he came to us as an old and sick man.'[20]

One of Reza Shah's first acts on arrival in Isfahan was to send his son a cable. It was a simple message: 'Your Majesty! Never fear anything!' This done, the old Shah began to prepare for exile as the Allies continued to press for his departure. Did they fear that he might be used as a focal point for a resistance movement? Or were they merely being vengeful against a man who had defied them for so long?

The list of those accompanying Reza Shah into exile was handed over to the Allies two days later. It included his favourite wife, Esmat, together with Princesses Shams and Fatemeh. Princes Ali-Reza, Gholam-Reza, Abdul-Reza, Mahmud-Reza, Ahmad-Reza and Hamid-Reza would also be of the party. Taj al-Moluk would be left behind, ostensibly to help Mohammad-Reza Shah in his early days as king. More significantly, Reza Shah also ordered Princess Ashraf, Mohammad-Reza's twin sister, to return to Tehran and stay at her brother's side. Reza Shah's third wife,

Turan, was not included in the exile party because she had been repudiated by the king several years ago and was no longer a member of the Pahlavi family.[21]

The former Shah and his party then travelled to Kerman where they stayed for more than a week pending the arrival of a British ship at Bandar Abbas on the Persian Gulf. The ship was to take the exiles to Canada. In Kerman, Reza Shah spent much of his time transferring the deeds of his many lands, villages and properties in urban areas to Mohammad-Reza. This was a gigantic task and involved several days of hard work by a team of lawyers and notaries headed by one Mohammad-Kazem Dast-Ghayb. The estate transferred to the new Shah included more than 3000 villages with a registered book value of more than £60 million.[22]

Very little has leaked from the long private sessions that Forughi and Mohammad-Reza Shah had together in those early days, but from sporadic accounts given by both men, as well as their confidants, it is possible to see that a relationship of teacher and pupil emerged between the old prime minister and the young monarch. Forughi, a past master of Iranian techniques of cool patience at times of adversity, must have restrained some of the more dangerous ambitions of the second Pahlavi. Mohammad-Reza had briefly flirted with the idea of ordering some dramatic action as a means of forestalling any charge of Pahlavi collaboration with the invading armies. Years later he spelled out his sentiments succinctly: 'We could have mined all the bridges, railroads and major highways so that Iran could not be considered a communications link for the invading armies. We should have taken measures aimed at denying our vital oil resources to the invader.'[23]

Finally, however, Mohammad-Reza Shah was never a man to take risks unless he was sure of having at least an even chance of winning. Even in poker, a game he enjoyed playing until the 1970s, he would not allow the stakes to rise above nominal sums. In those humiliating days of occupation, no doubt encouraged by Forughi, he swallowed his pride and wore the smile of 'kitman' (dissimulation) in his dealings with the invaders. He went out of his way to appear an enthusiastic supporter of the Allied cause while he encouraged rumours among young officers regarding his supposed sympathies for the Axis.[24] He was intelligent enough not to be audacious at a time when he was barely allowed to go through the motions of being king. The scars left on his psyche by those early years remained with him all his life. Years later he felt strong enough to vent his anger and resentment and pledge to practise a scorched earth policy if and when Iran was, once again, invaded by the major powers. 'You are lucky,' he told a journalist in October 1976. 'You have not heard the sound of foreign tanks in Tehran.'[25]

The Shah and his prime minister spent the rest of 1941 negotiating the legal basis of the Allied occupation of Iran. On 29 January 1942, the Tripartite Treaty of Alliance was signed by Great Britain, the USSR and

Iran. Most of the credit went to Foroughi, a seasoned diplomat who had once chaired a session of the League of Nations. The relationship between the Shah and the prime minister was marked by genuine affection and mutual respect. The two men felt they were on the same side in the service of the country at a crucial time in history. Mohammad-Reza Shah felt 'lucky' in having Foroughi at his side and the prime minister, now in deteriorating health, thought only of history's judgment. Never again did the Shah have such a relationship of complete trust, affection and mutual respect with any of the 29 prime ministers who served during his 37-year reign.

In the Tripartite Treaty the Allies stated that the presence of their forces on Iranian territory did not constitute a military occupation. They were supposed to have entered Iran on the basis of an invitation which had never been issued. What was important from Iran's point of view was that the Allies promised to respect Iran's political independence, territorial integrity and national sovereignty. They also undertook to withdraw their forces from Iran no later than six months after the end of the war with the Axis powers. Further, they pledged a package of economic aid designed to alleviate the burden Iran had been forced to bear as a result of the occupation. In exchange Iran undertook to offer the Allies facilities that they had already begun to use in any case. Having formally joined the Allies, Iran severed diplomatic ties with the Axis powers and, in September 1943, finally declared war on Germany.

The eleven weeks of hard bargaining that had gone into the Tripartite Treaty had exhausted the ailing Foroughi who, once the treaty was signed, asked to step down as prime minister. His task was complete: Iran's independence was guaranteed and the monarchy was saved. The Shah persuaded Foroughi to accept the post of Imperial Court Minister and a few months later he was named Ambassador to Washington but was too ill to travel to his new post. Foroughi's successor as prime minister was Ali Soheili, another seasoned diplomat, who had served as minister for foreign affairs and played a key role in shaping the Tripartite Treaty.

Foroughi and Soheili achieved their success in serving Iran partly thanks to the courage they showed in breaking with a long tradition of demagoguery that virtually paralysed Iranian statesmen. The best politician was supposed to be one who knew how to avoid committing himself, how to shrink from responsibility and how to avoid clear-cut decisions. The Iranian politician always looked to the gallery for a clue to his own behaviour and was prepared to sacrifice virtually everything for the sake of being the darling of the mob. In his early days as prime minister Foroughi was put under heavy pressure by many friends and supposed well-wishers not to commit himself to the sinking ship of the Pahlavi state. One day a close friend advised him: 'You must protect your good name above all else. With the country occupied there is nothing but dirty work to do and you might lose your reputation!' Foroughi rejected the advice, arguing that it was precisely at difficult times that one had to risk all in the service of the nation.

Forughi rendered another important service to the young Shah. As prime minister he convened a meeting of all the elder statesmen who had been disgraced under Reza Shah and asked them to serve as advisers to the young king. This informal council met half a dozen times and played a crucial role in cementing the unity of the ruling elites at a time of crisis.[26] The council was disbanded after Forughi stepped down as Imperial-Court Minister.

Mohammad-Reza Shah did not approve of all Forughi's decisions. While he fully associated the Shah with the process of decision-making, Forughi was, nevertheless, determined to restore to the prime minister and, through his office, to parliament some of the powers that had devolved to the person of the monarch under the founder of the Pahlavi dynasty. Thus in a move the importance of which became clear a decade later, Forughi asked parliament to abrogate the law under which the Shah held the position of Commander-in-Chief of the Armed and Security Forces.

For years Mohammad-Reza Shah had dreamed of what he would do as monarch, but now that he had succeeded his father he was virtually powerless to do anything. He did not even know how to fill in his days. The position of the monarch, for so long the focus of all political and military power in the country, had now become largely ceremonial and, in a country under occupation, there were not enough ribbon-cutting and baby-kissing ceremonies to keep a young and energetic Shah busy. He spent more time with his wife and soon began to feel irritated by her constant nagging and the pleasure she took in criticising Iran and all things Persian.

The Shah's small circle of friends did all they could to keep him busy and amused. Perron had been brought back to Tehran from Ramsar and had assumed greater prominence. Alam was now established as a royal confidant. Fardust retained his special position as the Shah's oldest friend. Ayadi and Sani'i joined the inner circle which included a number of other young army officers.

The Shah's principal political adviser was Princess Ashraf. Through her the Shah maintained contact with senior political figures and leaders of the various parliamentary factions. Ashraf, who suddenly discovered that her appetite for politics was matched only by her hitherto hidden talents in that field, quickly realised that power in Iran had been divided into numerous slices each of which was controlled by a different set of players. She saw that it was essential that the Pahlavi family and, thus, the institution of monarchy, build up its own network of loyal friends. At a time when virtually the whole of the Tehran press had been taken over by the Allies or their pro-German enemies, Ashraf secretly financed the creation of a new daily which was to become Iran's most popular newspaper.*[27] The princess also had a group of young and talented politicians whom she quietly promoted up the ladder of power. Among them were Abdol-Hossein Hazhir and Dr Manuche Eqbal who were both to become prime minister.

Shortly after his accession Mohammad-Reza Shah had ordered a general amnesty. This brought freedom to some 200 political prisoners and almost as many people who served terms of banishment after suffering royal disgrace under Reza Shah. Among those thus rehabilitated were members of the Teymurtash family, including Mehrpur and Hushang who had both been the Shah's boyhood friends. Princess Ashraf had had a crush on Hushang Teymurtash and now that he was back in Tehran she had already seized the opportunity provided by the confusion of her father's exile to secure a divorce from Qavam Shirazi, a man she had married on Reza Shah's orders. 'I hated the man from the first day,' she later recalled. 'But what could I do? My father wanted the marriage when I was barely fifteen. I even had to produce a son which I dutifully did.'[28] Shirazi was asked to agree to a divorce under pressure from Mohammad-Reza Shah. He complied just as he had obeyed Reza Shah's order to marry Ashraf. The affair between Ashraf and Hushang Teymurtash soon blossomed into a real passion and the Shah began to fear that he might lose his sister. Thanks to Perron, the Shah learned that Ashraf and Hushang had worked out a plan to elope. The Shah called in Hushang and ordered him to disappear without letting Ashraf know and he obeyed. On the appointed day the princess waited in vain for her lover at the rendezvous. She thought Hushang had betrayed her for his own reasons. It was only years later that the Shah told his sister the truth.[29]

With the monarchy substantially weakened, the unicameral National Consultative Assembly, the parliament, soon emerged as the veritable centre of power in the country. The Majlis had the right to nominate the prime minister and had the power of veto on all other nominations to the Cabinet. The Majlis then sitting had been elected under Reza Shah in less than perfect circumstances, but once the old Shah was gone the parliamentarians simply voted to prolong their own term, citing as a pretext the difficulty of conducting fresh elections under wartime conditions. It was back to the good old days of demagoguery that had preceded the imposition of autocratic rule by Reza Shah. Members of the Majlis even began to attack Reza Shah himself, knowing that the old dictator was several thousand miles away. Politicians who had been among the most sycophantic of Reza Shah's courtiers now went to the rostrum to call him a 'tyrant' and even a 'thief'.

The old Shah and his party spent some time in Mauritius after a long journey that had taken them to Bombay and the Maldive Islands. On

* The newspaper was *Kayhan*.

Mauritius, Reza Shah suffered a heart ailment complicated by fatigue and depression. The British refused to honour their earlier promise of taking the royal exiles either to Canada or Argentina, the reason given being their inability to ensure the safety of the royal party at a time when the Atlantic Ocean was the scene of ferocious naval battles. Reza Shah and his family had eventually been taken to South Africa where they settled in Johannesburg. From there the old king wrote to Mohammad-Reza Shah every week. The young Shah responded by writing in his own hand and on one occasion recorded a moving message to his father and sent the record by special courier. The old man wept as he listened and responded by sending a record of his own voice to Mohammad-Reza Shah. Father and son continued to correspond until Reza Shah's death on 26 July 1944.

In his letters and messages to Mohammad-Reza Shah the old king consistently refrained from raising any issue that might appear even remotely political. 'No one should tell a king how to conduct his business,' he once told his exiled companions in Johannesburg.[30] He hammered home two points, however. The first was that Mohammad-Reza Shah should remain resolute and brave in the face of all difficulties. The second was that he should, as head of the family, protect the interest of the dynasty. It is possible that Reza Shah, despite the fact that he read the Tehran newspapers and received regular reports regarding the situation in the country, did not quite appreciate his son's difficulties in defining a new role for the monarchy in a land where central authority had broken down. Reza Shah had forgotten the old Persian adage that being born the son of a king represented only half of the conditions needed for becoming king oneself – and the easier half, too. Persian kings throughout history had had to reconquer their thrones on taking over from their fathers. Mohammad-Reza Shah was no exception to that 2500-year-old rule. He had to win the proverbial crown that was guarded by two raging lions. For the time being, however, no one gave him the slightest chance of even starting his campaign in anything but name. His portraits were everywhere and the new banknotes issued in 1943 carried his insignia; he also signed and sealed the many laws that the Parliament passed: but he could not appoint a single official, nor could he dismiss anyone. For the time being he was merely playing king.

In time Mohammad-Reza Shah's powerlessness began to emerge as a source of strength. Disgruntled people started to indulge in numerous fantasies about how the young Shah would solve the nation's problems if only he would be given the chance. Selfish politicians were blamed for the ills of the nation, together with Russia and Britain, Iran's two traditional foreign enemies. The Shah was seen as the victim of a conspiracy aimed at keeping the nation divided and weak by undermining the monarchy which had always served as the symbol of Persian nationhood. The young Shah was seen almost as a martyr in a country where martyrdom is often preferred to heroism.

The Shah himself was uncomfortable in the role of the martyr. His character favoured acts of heroism. He wanted to be a winner, as he had been at the school sports tournaments in Lucerne. He wanted to be admired and applauded, not wept over. His European education prevented him from understanding the psychology of his own people. He did not know that the Persians instinctively suspected and disliked the strong, the winner and the hero. They obeyed Reza Shah but never loved him: now they loved Mohammad-Reza Shah but did not wish to obey him. The Shah's almost pathological dislike for what he saw as 'filthy politics' prevented him from understanding the necessity – not to say the legitimacy – of flattering at least a part of popular prejudices. Playing Shah was not a game he enjoyed and he longed for the real thing: the power to reshape Iran. For that he had to wait many long and frustrating years.

4

The Return of the Demons

During his 20-year domination of Iran, first as autocratic prime minister and then as absolute monarch, Reza Shah had defeated virtually all Iran's traditional forces – forces which he described as demons. Within a few months of Reza Shah's abdication the demons were back with a vengeance. Reza Shah's rule now appeared as an exceptional period in Iran's history, a parenthesis in which society had functioned out of its time-honoured norms.

For more than a century before Reza Shah imposed his rule, a pattern of political life had been established that included the presence of a weak, virtually ineffective central government, at the head of which the monarch performed a largely symbolic role. Real power was divided among aristocrats, landowners, tribal chiefs, the shi'ite clergy and – last but not least – Britain and Russia. The first of the demons to return after Reza Shah's exile were the Qajar aristocrats, many of whom had been sent into internal banishment or forced to flee abroad as voluntary exiles. Within a few months they had recaptured their posts and privileges. Some of them even began to use the Qajar aristocratic titles that Reza Shah had abolished.

The aristocratic network was known as 'the thousand families'. In reality it consisted of no more than 50 extended clans. Together they owned something like 70 per cent of all land under cultivation. They also acted as a channel for the distribution of privilege. Through a series of interlinked dowrehs (circles) they were also kept informed about the mood of the public and regulated the political process. In 1941 they wanted to forget Reza Shah as a bad dream. The outsider, the 'alien' who had upset the nation's normal life was now gone: it was important to make sure that his son, already perceived as weak and indecisive, should be kept under strict control.

The second group of demons to return were the mullahs. Many shi'ite clerics had gone into exile to escape persecution under Reza Shah. They now came back to their native towns and re-established their seminaries and reopened their mosques. The young Shah, who had been persuaded that the mullahs had always been supported by Britain, saw the return of the clerics as a British move.[1] The mullahs also regained control of endowment lands and properties (awqaf) and revived the network of 'khoms' through which they received substantial sums of money from the merchant classes of the bazaar. Within a few weeks they had not only revived their nationwide organisation but had also restored the sources of their economic and financial power. The principal shi'ite cleric of the time, Grand Ayatollah Abol-Qassem Esfahani, sent the new Shah a brief cable on one of the religious occasions in December 1941. He received a warm, almost flattering, reply from the monarch. Relations between the Shah and the mullahs were also back to normal. Rules about the enforced shaving of beards and the ban on the wearing of turbans and other traditional headgear were simply ignored without being formally repealed. The mullahs could now reappear in public in their traditional clothes and wear their white or black turbans in peace.[2] Others abandoned their western-style hats and resumed wearing old-style Persian caps made of rolled felt.

By September 1942 the mullahs felt strong enough to present the Shah with a formal list of five demands. Top of the list was the demand that the wearing of the veil (hijab) no longer be regarded as an illegal act. Reza Shah had regarded the abolition of the veil as one of his key achievements and during his very last days in Iran he expressed the wish that women would never again be allowed to return to the Islamic hijab.[3] The mullahs' second demand was that income from endowments be exclusively used for the stated purpose of the donation. That, in practice, meant control by the mullahs: people who bequeathed parts of their wealth as a religious endowment always stipulated that a mullah should supervise the management of the property concerned. A third demand was for the government to ensure adequate supplies of basic foodstuffs, an attempt to portray the theologians as defenders of the poor. The two final demands were more specific: the Shah was asked to restore the teaching of Islamic doctrine in all government schools and to 'compel' the Saudi government to allow shi'ites to repair the tombs of their saints at Medina.[4]

The young Shah immediately set to work to fulfil the wishes of the mullahs presented to him by Ayatollah Mohammad-Hossein Borujerdi. Many reasons have been cited for Mohammad-Reza Shah's apparent keenness to cancel a major part of his father's reforms regarding the role of religion in society, one being his own religious temperament. Unknown to his father he had always performed at least one of the five daily prayers of Islam. Moreover, he carried a miniature copy of the Qur'an in his pocket and would go nowhere without it. On one occasion, many years later, he waited an hour at the airport until someone could bring him his Qur'an; on a state visit abroad he always kept the sacred object in his pocket. 'It was his credit card,' observed one courtier. 'He would not leave home without it.'[5] The Shah's willingness to please the mullahs had other causes. For one thing he was convinced that the mullahs belonged to the 'British' party. In pleasing them he felt he would win good marks from one of the two occupying powers. But, perhaps, the most important reason for the Shah's enthusiastic response to the mullahs' demands was that the list had been addressed to him and not to the prime minister. Someone had, at long last, asked him for something! And that provided the largely unemployed monarch, hungry for action as he was, with something to do – something to get his teeth into.

On orders from the Shah a High Council of Religious Affairs came into being with the prime minister, two other high-ranking cabinet ministers, the speaker, the Chief Justice and three senior mullahs as members. The unity of the mosque and the state, broken under Reza Shah, was thus restored at the highest level. Shi'ite mourning ceremonies, banned under the old king, were now allowed and even encouraged by the government. The young Shah himself made a point of appearing at one ceremony at Sepahsalar Mosque in Tehran. Dressed in full uniform the Shah sat on the floor and cried, or feigned to cry, as a mullah narrated the tragedy of Hossein, the Third Imam.

The Shah also restored the post of Friday Prayer Leader (Imam Jum'ah) of Tehran and invited Sayyed Hassan Emami, the holder of the post, to his palace. The two became close friends until the very end. Religious education was restored in all schools and the Shah ordered a new programme of restoration and renovation for the holy shrines to be financed by himself. He also went to pray at the shrine of Ma'ssumah at Qom and held a number of meetings with Ayatollah Borujerdi.

In 1943 an incident at Mecca provided a new opportunity for further cementing the recently won alliance of the Shah and the mullahs. An Iranian pilgrim, Abutaleb Yazdi, was accused by the Saudis of having committed a capital sin by vomiting at the holy shrine of Ka'abah. The Iranians had argued that Yazdi had not done so deliberately and that the vomiting had been caused by excessive heat. The Saudis were not convinced and had the pilgrim's head chopped off with a sword in public. News of this caused a sensation in Iran where the mullahs seized the opportunity to whip up public opinion against sunni Muslims in general and the Saudis, followers of the Wahhabi school, in particular. The mullahs wanted the government to declare holy war on Saudi Arabia: the government wanted to let the incident simply fade away. An occupied country was in no position to pursue high profile diplomacy, the prime minister argued. The Shah intervened and helped work out a compromise: relations with Saudi Arabia were suspended and a ban was imposed on travel by Iranians to that country. Once again, the Shah got high marks from the mullahs.

Another group of demons unchained after September 1941 consisted of the tribal khans or chiefs who had spent the preceding decade in prison, in banishment, under house arrest or in exile. Before Reza Shah nearly a third of Iran's population had consisted of nomadic or semi-nomadic tribes. The brutal policy of settlement (takht-e-qapu) had reduced this to nearly a fifth of the population by the time Reza Shah's exile began. The largest tribal group consisted of the Qashqa'i confederation of clans and its warlike satellites, the Boyer-Ahmad in the provinces of Fars and Khuzestan. They numbered probably around 500,000 people but could, given the needed arms and money, raise an army of 10,000 or more. The Qashqa'is regarded Shiraz as their capital.

The next large tribal grouping was that of the Bakhtiaris, also located in the foothills of the Zagross mountain range, and moving from the province of Isfahan to the oilfields of Khuzestan. The Bakhtiaris probably numbered around 300,000, taking into account the various Luri tribes affiliated with them. Their chiefs had a long history of cooperation with Britain and had for years ensured the security of the Iranian oilfields on behalf of the Anglo-Iranian Oil Company in exchange for a share of the royalties. The third major tribal grouping was in Kurdistan. The Kurdish tribes represented a population of some quarter of a million. Unlike the Qashqa'is and Bakhtiaris who were all shi'ites, the Kurds were divided into many different religious sects. The sunnis formed a majority with the duodecimal shi'ites coming second, but there were also large groups of Yazidis, also known as Satan Worshippers,[6] and various sufi-dominated sects.[7]

There were two other tribal regions in Iran: the Turcoman Plain and Baluchistan. The Turcomans did not succeed in reviving their tribal structure after Reza Shah's departure partly because the occupying Soviet forces saw such a development as a potential threat to the stability of Soviet Central Asia where an anti-Soviet revolt, in which Turcomans had played a role, had continued until 1936. Similar reasons prevented the Baluch from restoring their tribal structures and raising local armies of their own. The British did not favour a Baluch revival that might have overspilled into neighbouring Baluchistan, which had been annexed to the British Raj.

The Bakhtiaris were part of the mainstream Persian family, but all the other tribal groups had their own specific identities within the broader Iranian identity. The Qashqu'is spoke a Turkic language. The Kurds and the Baluch, although of ethnic Iranic stock, had their own languages. The Turcomans were the farthest removed from mainstream Persians by ethnic background and language. They were also overwhelmingly sunni.

By the end of 1941 central government authority had all but disappeared in most tribal areas. The chiefs were once again masters of the destiny of more than 2,500,000 Iranians. They expelled the farmers that Reza Shah had settled on tribal lands, destroyed the model villages created to pin down the nomads and, more important, looted the arsenals of weapons left unattended in the wake of the disbanding of the regular armed forces. Within a few months the ever-rebellious tribes had thousands of guns at their disposal with which to challenge what was left of central authority. Worse still, some of the chiefs began to offer their services to anyone who would pay.

While the Bakhtiaris revived their traditional ties with Britain and once again received a generous stipend, the Qashqu'is opened negotiations with Nazi Germany. German influence in Iran had been underestimated by the Allies who did not create an intelligence network in the areas under their occupation until 1943. Nazi agents had long been preparing for the day when Iran would become a major prize in the war.

From 1938 onwards Nazi agents had accumulated vast sums of money, part of it from the sale of goods to Iranian enterprises, in special safe houses in Tehran. By 1940 a pro-German fifth column was in place in Iran, its political wing consisting of a semi-clandestine organisation known as Hezb Kabud (The Violet Party) and led by Habiballah Nobakht, a Majlis deputy from Shiraz. The party had members among army officers, intellectuals, the bazaaris and tribal chiefs. It was assured of religious support through Ayatollah Abol-Qassem Kashani who had a long history of anti-British activities.[8] On the military side, General Fazlallah Zahedi, who commanded the Isfahan garrison, was the crucial figure in the pro-German underground network. A popular soldier, despite his well-advertised weakness for the second sex, he was considered in pro-German circles as an ideal future Führer if and when Iran managed to liberate itself with the help of Nazi armies.

In 1942 the Germans bribed enough Bakhtiari and Qashqu'i chiefs to be able to set up a clandestine radio transmitter near Isfahan and to organise special military training courses for 'volunteers' in mountain hideouts. By the end of the year two mobile transmitters had been smuggled into Iran and began broadcasting from Mianeh, under Soviet occupation, and Kermanshah. The Nazis also recruited a number of Armenian Dashnak militants who had fled to Iran to escape Soviet repression in the 1920s and 1930s. Pro-German groups were present in the Caspian region and the Turcoman Plain. In some areas these groups were led by White Russians who dreamed of returning home after Stalin's defeat by Hitler. The fact that Iranian public opinion was overwhelmingly hostile to the Allies largely facilitated the work of Nazi agents and their local associates.

The Nazi plan was simple: once German forces had broken into the Caucasus and reached the Irano-Soviet frontier at the Aras river, the tribal groups, mostly Qashqu'is and Kurds, would stage an uprising and seize the main highways. At the same time German agents would sabotage the logistic lines of the Allied forces. This would be followed by a military putsch by Iranian officers who would ask the Allies to leave. The Allies, cut off respectively from their backup bases in the USSR, and Iraq, would have no choice but to withdraw. In any case they would be thrown out once the German armies poured south after breaking the barrier of the Caucasus.

Did the Shah know of the German plans? What were the plotters' intentions regarding the future of the Pahlavis? Two officers who were members of the secret organisations have asserted that they were convinced that the Shah was kept well informed of what was going on. They were also under the impression that the whole plan had the tacit approval of the monarch.[9] The movement's documents at no point indicate an anti-Pahlavi or anti-monarchy sentiment. Many leading members of the movement were known to be ultra-monarchists. The list of 173 people, including three major-generals and 30 other officers who were eventually arrested reads like a *Who's Who* of pro-Shah militants. In later years the list produced three prime ministers, 28 ministers, 19 generals, one Chief of the Supreme Commander's Staff, 11 ambassadors and many other high officials. This was no grouping of marginal or deranged individuals. Some of the officers on the list were personally known to the Shah and at least two of them were among his close associates in Officers' Faculty days. In the Kurdish tribal revolt of May 1942, in the Rezaieh region, the German-financed rebels were found in possession of pictures both of Hitler and of the young Shah.

On the other hand there is no evidence of the Shah's direct knowledge of or involvement in the Nazi plans. It is perfectly possible that the Germans exploited the pro-Shah sentiments of the army officers and nationalist intellectuals for their own purposes. One or two leaders of the clandestine movement might have even pretended to be in contact with the Shah as a means of achieving a degree of legitimacy. Most conspirators might have felt that the Shah must be on their side even if he knew nothing of the conspiracy. The objective of the German plan, the expulsion of the Allies from Iran, was in full accord with the wishes of Iranian nationalists at the time. But it is possible to argue that had the Shah known about the German plan he would not have supported it. He was a cautious man, convinced that the only way to deal with Britain and Russia was to grant their demands pending the restoration of Iran's own strength. From 1941 onwards his objective was to keep Iran as far away from the larger conflicts of the war as possible. He could not have endorsed a plan that risked turning the country into a major battleground for warring European powers.

In June 1943 the Qashqa'is, presumably in a dress rehearsal for a later and larger operation against Shiraz, entered the small town of Semirom after inflicting a severe defeat on central government forces. However Hitler's defeat on the Volga in February of the same year had dealt a serious blow to German ambitions in Iran. The Qashqa'is began secret talks with the British who were now prepared to pay more than the Germans. By this time the Shah and the prime minister were convinced that Germany would lose the war. On 9 September 1943 the Shah signed

Iran's declaration of war against the Axis powers. British and Russian forces, meanwhile, proceeded with widespread arrests among suspected pro-German elements throughout the country. General Zahedi was kidnapped from his command centre in Isfahan by Fitzroy MacLean, a British intelligence officer. Ayatollah Kashani was captured while performing prayers at a mosque in Tehran. The 173 principal leaders of the pro-German movement were imprisoned at Arak, west of Tehran, under British guard. The Russians arrested some 200 pro-Nazi activists, including many Armenians and White Russians, and shipped them to Siberia where they perished. Those imprisoned by Britain survived and most were released soon afterwards. Only a few principal ring-leaders, including Zahedi and Kashani, were exiled to Palestine, then under British mandate. Britain and Russia believed the political threat that pro-German sympathies posed to their interests in Iran important enough to try to counter it by methods other than police repression. The Russians had gained a march over their British partners by organising the Tudeh (Masses) Party, attracting large numbers of intellectuals and gaining a foothold among oil industry workers in the south. The party had started as a genuine club for left-leaning children of aristocratic and middle-class families even before Reza Shah's departure. It formally became a party in 1941 and quickly came under direct Comintern control. A Soviet secret agent named Bela Tchapkin was effective leader during its first years.[10] He exercised control over the party through two Comintern contacts: the Armenian Ardashes Ovanessian and Reza Rusta who had served a prison term under Reza Shah on a charge of espionage for the USSR.[11]

Tudeh's original leadership consisted of a curious mixture of Qajar princes, ambitious politicians, romantic idealists, trained terrorists and agents of the NKVD, the forerunner of the Soviet KGB. The party's first president was Prince Suleyman Eskandari, a Qajar and a devout Muslim who had among his associates one Sayyed Ruhollah Khomeini, the future ayatollah and revolutionary.[12] The party's overall policy was worked out by the Comintern's Iran desk headed by Cyrus Akhund-Zadeh, an Azerbaijani militant. Immediately after it came into being the party experienced two purges. In the first purge the so-called Trotskyites, led by one Yussef Eftekhari, the only genuine worker in the leadership, were thrown out. In the second purge the supporters of armed struggle, led by Abol-Qassem Mussavi, were eliminated.[13] As this was the period of 'popular fronts' in Stalin's strategy, the Tudeh Party also sought, and found, allies among various middle-class groups. It established a working relationship with the Iran Party, led by the pro-American Allahyar Saleh and the Edalat (Justice) Party led by Abdol-Qadir Azad.

The British also created a political party of their own. This was known as Eradeh Melli (National Will) and was led by Sayyed Zia-eddin Tabataba'i, Reza Shah's early partner in the 1921 putsch. The 'Sayyed' had fled to Palestine to escape imprisonment or worse under the first

Pahlavi. Now he was back in Tehran and, thanks to his undoubted charm and political acumen, was once again the centre of a powerful political circle.

Iran was beginning to feel the economic effects of the occupation. The Foroughi government had devalued the Iranian currency, the rial, largely for political reasons. This caused inflation that by 1942 threatened to run out of the control of a weak administration with virtually no experience in managing an economic crisis. The Allies spent freely, purchasing whatever food they could find for export to Russia. They commandeered trucks and private cars and virtually monopolised the use of the railways. The rudimentary and fragile supply system that had protected Iran against famine for nearly 15 years quickly broke down. In the winter of 1942 Iranians died of hunger by the thousands. In Baluchistan and Luristan people tried to stay alive by eating the roots and leaves of trees and scenes of children 'grazing' in sheep pastures were reported from several provinces. Famine-stricken people poured into Tehran and other major cities and sparked off a series of bread riots. Peasants could be seen in the centre of cities offering their children for sale. Simultaneously, small numbers of Iranians grew immensely rich thanks to the vast sums of money the Allies spent.

The Shah tried to help by creating a Society for Social Services with his twin sister Princess Ashraf at its head. This remained a largely symbolic gesture. The Russians not only did not try to help but had difficulty restraining their own hungry soldiers from looting the village food stocks they found at the Caspian and in Azerbaijan. The British set up a number of soup kitchens but the Iranians refused the humiliation of being fed by those who had stolen their bread to give it to others. Nationalist groups spread the message that anyone who chose to be fed by the British would die.[14]

The government headed by Ahmad Qavam was held responsible for the nation's plight as much as the Allies. The Tehran rioters attacked Qavam's residence and tried to set it on fire. The Shah dispatched Princess Ashraf to Qavam's house in order to ask him to step down as prime minister. Qavam flatly refused. 'This is not Reza Shah's time,' he commented. 'I am in this post not because your brother put me there but because I have a majority in the Majlis.'[15]

The British Ambassador chose to speak to the Shah about the need to put more Iranian money in circulation to take account of the dramatic increase in trade occasioned by the Allied purchases. The Shah refused to comply as this might have led to confrontation between him and the Majlis. The British diplomat then asked the Shah to dissolve the Parliament. Once again the Shah refused: a general election in those explosive days could lead to bloodshed. The British felt they had no choice but to flex their muscles. They moved some of their troops into Tehran, ostensibly to prevent further rioting. The detachment took up positions near the parliament building. The message was clear. Qavam proposed an increase in the volume of money and the Majlis instantly approved. The parliamentary process was exposed as a charade.

All the Shah could do was to have sleepless nights. Years later he wrote: 'During the occupation I was full of sorrow and had many sleepless nights ... I was revolted by the way in which some wealthy Persians became more bloated, in utter disregard of the welfare of their country.'[16]

By mid-1943 it had become clear that the Majlis no longer represented the political mood in the country. In the absence of organised factions within the Majlis it was difficult to secure a majority for pushing through some of the urgently needed measures as members acted almost purely in accordance with their own personal and regional interests. When the Shah dissolved the Majlis few tears were shed, but holding fresh elections posed a number of problems. The Soviets had sealed off their occupation zone and would not allow anyone to enter it without approval of the Red Army. They also prevented Tehran's newspapers from reaching the occupation zone where more than a third of the nation's population then lived.

As the Shah contemplated the possible outcome of fresh elections he saw no grounds for optimism. The composition of the new parliament was not difficult to forecast. The Tudeh was bound to 'win' in constituencies under Soviet occupation. British intervention would not be so blatant, but it was certain that Anglophiles, under Sayyed Zia-eddin, would end up with a large number of seats. The balance would go to powerful individuals, tribal chiefs and big landowners. Princess Ashraf was also promoting a party of her own and hoped to help some of her friends enter parliament.

The Soviet Ambassador, Smirnov, was determined to help Tudeh and its direct allies win 'at least half of the seats'. His British counterpart, Bullard, was equally adamant about preventing the emergence of a Communist majority. The two fought what was, perhaps, an early version of the future Cold War through the parties and newspapers they controlled. As the elections drew close, however, both men had been recalled and Moscow and London decided to tone down their rivalry. The new Soviet Ambassador, a Georgian NKVD agent called Maximov, was a passionate advocate of alliance with other 'progressive forces'. He called in the Tuduh leaders and ordered them to keep their list of candidates limited to only 10 or 20 per cent of the Majlis seats, and instead try and help non-Communist 'progressives' to win wherever possible.

The Anglo-Russian detente in Iran meant that the elections could take place without major incidents. Tudeh ended up with only eight seats plus five more that were captured by fellow-travellers. The Comintern contact man, Ardashes Ovanessian, was one of the victorious Tudeh candidates. So was Jaafar Pishevari, an Azerbaijani journalist who pursued regional aims of his own on behalf of the leaders of the Soviet Azerbaijan

Communist Party. The British saw their principal champion, Sayyed Zia-eddin, elected together with at least 50 other noted Anglophiles. Princess Ashraf's faction won only nine seats, one more than Tudeh. The elections also produced a new parliamentary force in the shape of a group that began to describe itself as Monfaredin (the loners). The most powerful figure in the group was Dr Mohammad Mossadeq who topped the poll in Tehran. A pro-American faction – a totally new factor in Iranian politics – was represented by Saleh.

The United States had become directly involved in Iran late in 1942 by joining the Persian Gulf command. By the end of 1943 there were more than 30,000 American troops and technicians in Iran and the Gulf region. They played a crucial role in increasing the volume of goods shipped to Russia by achieving a tenfold expansion in the capacity of Iranian road and railway networks. It was with American help that a fleet of 4000 trucks, one of the largest in the world, was created by Iranian private entrepreneurs. The US also sent large quantities of food, medicine and other civilian supplies to Iran.

The excitement of the election had not yet subsided when it was announced that an Allied conference at 'summit' level would be held in Tehran. Most Iranians were secretly flattered that their capital had been chosen as the venue of what was clearly going to be an historic occasion. The Allies, of course, refused to give the Iranian authorities any information about the coming conference. Nor would they respond to a request by the Shah to meet the leaders during their stay in Tehran.

Of the Big Three the Shah had met only Winston Churchill when the latter had made a stopover in Tehran on his way to a meeting with Stalin in Moscow in the summer of 1942. The two had lunched together at the Shah's palace and the Shah had seized the opportunity for impressing Churchill with his knowledge of military affairs. This is how the Shah related his meeting with the British leader:

> We were speaking of the Allied intention of invading Europe to crush Hitler's armies. I suggested to Churchill that the Allies should strike Italy first, consolidate their position there, and then stage a massive invasion of the Balkans. As Churchill sat reflecting upon my proposal, I saw a strange light come into his eyes. At that time he made no comment upon my idea, but it was not far removed from his later well-known plan for invading Europe by way of the 'soft underbelly'.[17]

The Shah remained convinced that had the Allies listened to him 'the subsequent history of central Europe would clearly have been different'.[18] As for Churchill there is no evidence to show that he was impressed by the Shah's strategic vision, but the British leader liked the young monarch and later referred to him as 'Reza Shah's gifted son'.

The Tehran Conference was held in November 1943 at the Soviet Embassy. For security reasons president Franklin D. Roosevelt decided to reside at a special apartment prepared for him within the Soviet Embassy compound. Churchill was put up at the British Ambassador's official residence barely a hundred yards from the Soviet compound. All the meetings and official receptions took place in the Soviet buildings where a hospitable Joseph V. Stalin personally supervised such details as the choice of flowers to decorate the tables. During the conference Churchill also marked his 69th birthday at a party with Roosevelt and Stalin present. The Shah, who had expected to be invited until the last minute, did not get the invitation call. But he sent Churchill a beautiful handwoven rug as a birthday present.

Both Churchill and Roosevelt informed the Shah that they would not be able to call on him at his palace. Once again security was cited as the reason. Tehran was rife with rumours of a Nazi commando's secret arrival with the mission to assassinate the three Allied leaders. The Shah found himself in a 'curious situation' because he had to go to the Soviet Embassy to meet Roosevelt while Stalin duly came to the Royal Palace to call on the monarch. The Shah also had a brief meeting with Churchill with Soheili and the British Foreign Secretary, Sir Anthony Eden, also present.

Each of the Shah's meetings with the three visiting leaders had an atmosphere of its own and left its own mark on the young king. The meeting with Churchill was largely devoted to polite exchanges and generalities. Roosevelt spent a few minutes sizing up his interlocutor and then changed to his own pet subject: gardening. The American president told the Shah that he would love to return to Iran after retiring from politics and work as a gardening and reafforestation adviser. The Shah promptly promised to offer Roosevelt a job as chief reafforestation expert with the Iranian government. The Shah was pleased with Roosevelt's informal approach which he construed as a sign of friendship. The monarch did not realise at the time that the American leader had simply wanted to avoid discussing politics with a man he considered as only the titular head of the Iranian state and devoid of executive powers.

The meeting with Stalin was more substantial. The Soviet leader had come to Tehran with a carefully prepared dossier. He opened by recalling the unchangeable fact of geography that made Iran and the USSR neighbours. The two nations were almost condemned to live and work in peace together. The Soviet dictator then proceeded to offer Iran help in rebuilding its shattered armed forces with the supply of a regiment of T34 tanks and a squadron of fighter aircraft. The Shah was 'most tempted'. He was also seduced by Stalin's politeness and the fact that the Soviet leader had come to call on him at the Royal Palace. When details of the Soviet offer were studied, however, the Shah changed his mind. The Soviets wanted to keep the tanks and the planes they offered to sell to Iran under their own command for an unspecified period. They also wanted to have the final say in the location of Iran's future tank and aircraft bases.

Although Iran was not represented at the Tehran Conference its fate was extensively discussed by the participants. The result was a declaration that came as a pleasant surprise to most Iranians. Issued on 1 December 1943 the declaration said, in part:

> The Governments of the United States of America, the USSR, and the United Kingdom are at one with the Government of Iran in their desire for the maintenance of the independence, sovereignty, and territorial integrity of Iran. They count upon the participation of Iran, together with all the other peace-loving nations, in the establishment of international peace, security, and prosperity after the war, in accordance with the principles of the Atlantic Charter, to which all four Governments have continued to subscribe.

This major victory for Iran was achieved, at least in part, thanks to the efforts of Soheili and his close colleagues.

One direct result of the Tehran Conference was a sharp increase in US interest in Iran. In 1941 Roosevelt had received a report regarding the growing importance of the Persian Gulf as a source of energy for the United States. In 1942, Wallace Murray, head of the Near East Division in the State Department, had given the president another report that suggested participation by American companies in exploiting Iran's oil resources. What finally persuaded Roosevelt to 'adopt' Iran as a model of what American assistance could achieve in a poor and backward country was a report by his special envoy to the Middle East, General Patrick Hurley. The envoy proposed American help for the establishment of a democratic system of government complete with a free enterprise economy.

Roosevelt acted quickly. The American military mission to Iran was expanded and the Iranian government was supplied with over 100 military and civilian experts and advisers. In 1944 the American legation was upgraded to embassy status shortly after Britain had announced a similar measure.[19] The United States had not been involved in the initial invasion and occupation of Iran and was not regarded as a colonial power with territorial ambitions in Iran. The Shah and a number of senior politicians, including Ahmad Qavam, had already decided that the US could be brought into Iran as a force capable of counterbalancing both Britain and the USSR. What Germany had failed to offer Iran was now sought from America. It was not surprising that many members of the clandestine pro-German movement became strong advocates of an Irano-American alliance in later years.

Another important result of the Tehran Conference was the easing of tension between the Anglophile and Russophile parties in Iran. Shortly after the conference, Mostafa Fateh, a well-known Anglo-Iranian Oil Company agent contacted Iraj Eskandari, a member of the Tudeh leadership who had won a seat in the Majlis. Fateh suggested the creation of an anti-fascist newspaper as a joint venture. The proposal was quickly approved by the Tudeh leadership and *Mardom* (People) began publication with British money. A semi-literate factory worker named Safar Now'ee was put up as the new daily's director. The editorial board consisted of five people, two of whom, Ehsan Tabari and Bozorg Alavi, also worked for the propaganda section of the British Embassy under Miss Ann Lambton.[20] This curious partnership between pro-Soviet activists on the one hand and the British oil company on the other remained a well-kept secret until 1944 when Mossadeq invented the celebrated expression 'Tudeh-Nafti' (Oil Communists) to describe some of his opponents.

The year 1944 was marked by an almost continuous government crisis. Three successive prime ministers kept constantly reshuffling their cabinet and modifying their policies in order to hold on to fragile majorities in the Majlis. One of the three, Morteza Bayat, offered a programme of socio-economic reforms that was warmly supported by Tudeh. This caused concern among the Anglophiles who promptly voted the government out of office. It was clear that the new Majlis was no more able to tackle the burning issue of reform than its predecessor had been. The spectacle of greedy politicians pursuing their own interests or serving their foreign masters persuaded the Shah to question his 'Swiss illusions' regarding the desirability of a parliamentary system of government for Iran. 'But what do they want?' he angrily asked a visitor. 'Don't they see that the country is on fire?'[21]

Meanwhile the press did not help reassure the Shah about the merits of Western-style democracy. Where only four or five newspapers had existed under Reza Shah, the period of foreign occupation saw the emergence of scores of new dailies and weeklies. Some were directly or indirectly financed by Britain and Russia. Many lived through blackmail and extortion. Together, however, the press as a whole presented a more accurate picture of Iranian life than it had done under the old Shah. The royal family remained a favourite target of both the Tudeh papers and the yellow press of the Right. The Shah was almost never attacked in person and no one questioned the institution of monarchy as such, but the vitriol poured on other members of the Pahlavi family, including Reza Shah himself, was so strong that the Shah constantly brought up the subject of some form of press control with the prime minister.

One day the Shah received the government's propaganda chief in his office. 'These newspapers!' he exclaimed. 'They have robbed me of my sleep. Can we not do something about them?'

'Yes, Your Majesty,' the propaganda chief replied. 'We can take them to court. But I advise against it as Your Majesty will not win. Even the courts are afraid of the newspapers.'[22]

Because the Shah's anger at the behaviour of the press was widely known, it was no surprise that the murder of a prominent journalist at the time was quickly blamed on the Pahlavis. It was not until 1983 that it was fully established that the journalist in question, Mohammad Massud, had, in fact, been assassinated by the Tudeh Party.

On 26 July 1944 Reza Shah died in Johannesburg. The news had a profound effect on the Shah who could not restrain his grief. 'Did you see what they did to my father?' he asked a confidant.[23] It was not clear whom he blamed and what precisely for. This kind of vague remark was to become part of the Shah's style of mystification. There is, however, no doubt that he was deeply aggrieved by his father's demise. Reza Shah had always remained at the centre of his son's thoughts and the old Shah's hold on Mohammad-Reza's mind remained strong until the 1970s. In a book he wrote in 1960, Mohammad-Reza Shah mentioned his father no fewer than 180 times in just over 300 pages. To him Reza Shah was the ultimate point of reference, the supreme measure of all values. He constantly asked himself what his father would have done in this or that situation. This sentimental attachment to his father was a result both of Reza Shah's own extraordinary personality and of Persian patriarchal tradition. A survey of Persian boys in urban areas showed that the vast majority had two principal fears: losing their fathers, and being castrated.[24]

The Shah's increasingly difficult relations with his wife made him even more despondent. Queen Fawziah had apparently received the news of Reza Shah's death with real or feigned indifference. She was bored in Tehran which had virtually no leisure facilities to offer a queen. In her first year she had made a half-hearted attempt at learning Persian but by 1942 she had stopped trying. She spoke to her husband and members of the royal entourage in French. In any case she did not have much to say except for the brief declaration: '*Je m'ennuie!*' which she repeated in a variety of tones throughout the day. To reduce her boredom the Queen stayed in bed until just before noon. This in itself was considered a scandal in a country where most people were up and at work by 7 am. She then spent a couple of hours dressing with the help of her Egyptian maids (she would not trust Iranian ladies-in-waiting). After lunch – which she often took alone – she would go for a drive in the foothills of Shemiran. Afternoons and evenings were spent playing cards with a few attendants. Dinner was reserved for the Shah, but the couple, who had lived in separate apartments since 1942, seldom spent the night together. Fawziah always found an excuse to shirk what the Shah later called 'her marital responsibility'. Members of the court had already began to describe the beautiful Queen as 'the frigid Venus'.

Queen Fawziah was the nominal head of a number of charity foundations and semi-public organisations, but she constantly refused to attend any of the board meetings. She referred to the Pahlavis in less than flattering terms and manifested little enthusiasm for the weekly visits she had to pay to her mother-in-law in the company of the Shah. Worse still the Queen did not seem to take much interest in her own daughter,

Princess Shahnaz. For years Fawziah lived on nervous tension, weakened by periodical attacks of fever due to malaria. From 1944 onwards she felt that there was a campaign to force her out of Iran. She received anonymous letters signed 'well-wishers' in which she was told of her husband's real or imagined amorous sorties. She heard rumours that she might be poisoned and interpreted the cold manner of the Dowager Queen towards her as a repudiation. Princess Ashraf was also critical of Fawziah's 'incorrect behaviour' and believed that the Queen did not do enough to help the Shah in those difficult days. Fawziah had other opponents too. The mullahs did not consider her a 'complete Muslim' because of her sunni background. More than a dozen prominent Iranian families with daughters of marriageable age wished to evict Fawziah and persuade the Shah to take a Persian queen. Some of these families were, apparently, prepared to go to some lengths in their anti-Fawziah campaign, including the sending of anonymous letters and other intrigues.

In December 1944 Ernest Perron, who had continued to be the only person with the right to enter the Shah's private apartment without prior permission, joined the anti-Fawziah camp. The reasons for this are obscure. Some contemporaries have claimed that Perron, a 'British agent' right from the start, was charged with the mission of destroying the marriage and thus killing the possibilities of a Muslim alliance based on an Irano-Egyptian axis after the war.[25] Others have suggested that Perron received a large bribe from one of the families who wished to give the Shah a bride. Yet another theory is that Fawziah herself paid Perron to help bring to an end a marriage that had failed. Others have suggested that Prince Gholam-Reza, the Shah's half-brother who was rumoured to be in love with Fawziah, had engineered the plot in which Perron played a key role.[26] It is, of course, also possible that Perron acted on behalf of the Shah himself. Perron made two important moves. First he informed the Shah that the Queen had started a liaison with a local tennis instructor who had been employed by the Royal Court a few months earlier. The man in question was Taqi Emami. Witnesses swore that they had seen the Queen and Emami together alone in the foothills of north Tehran. The Shah himself, apparently, believed the story and banished Emami from the court. (Emami also had his passport withdrawn and could not travel abroad until the 1960s). The Shah did not bring up the Emami affair with Fawziah directly and behaved as if he had forgiven and forgotten. Then came Perron's next move. He invited the Queen to what he described as 'hunting for the truth.' One evening Fawziah, guided by Perron, arrived at a small villa inside the palace compound that the Shah often used for private meetings. At the villa she discovered the Shah with a certain Pari Khanom, a society beauty, in a situation that was difficult to explain away, although the Shah made a feeble attempt at offering an innocent account of the scene. Back in her apartments Fawziah locked herself in and cried for several hours. That was the end of her marital relationship with the Shah. Every evening the Shah would come and knock at her door. The answer was always the same: '*Pour l'amour de Dieu partez!*'

Meanwhile relations between Iran and Egypt had suffered a setback for a completely different reason. The mortal remains of Reza Shah had been transferred from Johannesburg to Cairo en route to Tehran. The Allies, however, had informed the Iranian government that they would not let Reza Shah's corpse into Iran until after the war. As a result the old Shah's corpse had been mummified and placed in a temporary grave within the Rifa'i Mosque in the centre of the Egyptian capital. Because mummification and temporary burial are against Islamic principle, the move led to a chorus of criticism from Egyptian fundamentalists. Tehran wrongly believed that the campaign had been orchestrated by King Farouk. The Shah was also angry at Farouk's decision to appropriate a number of valuable objects belonging to Reza Shah, including a jewel-studded sword estimated to be worth £6000.

Farouk had been involved in yet another strange incident. Princess Ashraf was on a visit to Cairo to pray at the tomb of Reza Shah. She had been housed in the Qubbah Palace where the Egyptian monarch himself resided. One evening while the princess was changing for a royal dinner a noise was heard from inside one of the wardrobes. The maid who opened the door of the wardrobe nearly fainted: King Farouk had been hiding in it.[27] An incurable voyeur, Farouk was known for his corrupt lifestyle throughout the world and his attempts at becoming the Caliph of all Muslims caused only derision. The grand Irano-Egyptian alliance that Reza Shah had dreamt of was not to be.

In June 1945 Fawziah, now a shadow of her former self, left Iran for Cairo, never to return. After several weeks of resting at the Muntazah Palace in Alexandria, the Queen settled at her brother's palace in Cairo. She refused to answer any of the Shah's cables, letters and verbal messages. She was, once again, the toast of all Cairo and organised questionable encounters for her brother. On one occasion Farouk gathered nearly 1000 young Egyptian ladies in his palace. He was the only man and Fawziah was at his side. News of this sent a shiver up the spines of Iranian mullahs.

The Shah continued to refuse the divorce Fawziah demanded until 19 November 1948. He wrote a long letter, in French and in his own hand, to Farouk in which he rejected charges of his own infidelity and, instead, indirectly accused Fawziah of having been less than faithful. The Shah nevertheless allowed Princess Shahnaz to travel to Egypt and stay with her mother. Five months after the divorce Fawziah married Esma'il Shirin, the nephew of Farouk's favourite mistress.

The collapse of his marriage with Fawziah was not the most serious problem that Mohammad-Reza Shah faced. Three explosive issues loomed on the horizon, the first being Iran's future oil policy. Everyone agreed that the Anglo-Iranian Oil Company was giving Iran a rough deal.

The Iranian government received less than 10 per cent of the company's profits in real terms. Worse still, the Iranian authorities could not even control the amount of crude oil that the company exported. The United States, Iran's new friend, was showing interest in securing a share of Iranian oil. In 1944, in fact, a number of American oilmen had visited Tehran, much to the chagrin of the British. Russia was also making noises about oil concessions in northern Iran.

The second issue Iran had to face was that of ensuring a full withdrawal of foreign troops after the war. This had been agreed in principle by the Allies in the Tripartite Treaty but no precise timetable or mechanism had been established.

Finally, there was the issue of widespread corruption at all levels of government. The nation's entire administrative structure was threatened by indiscipline, incompetence, disregard for the law and bribery. Dr Millspaugh, an American economist who served as fiscal adviser in 1922, was back in Tehran in the same post in 1943 and found the administration on the verge of collapse. Another American adviser, a General Norman Schwartzkopf* who had been invited to help reorganise the gendarmerie, found that he needed another force to prevent the gendarmes from robbing the peasants.

The Shah's inability to cope with the nation's problems was not understood by the common folk who had been brought up with the idea that a Shah could move heaven and earth if he wanted to. Even passionate monarchists began to see Mohammad-Reza Shah as weak and indecisive and claimed that his twin sister Princess Ashraf was 'the only man among Reza Shah's children'. Ashraf, petite but passionate, manifested a lust for politics and power that her brother evidently lacked.

The Shah himself, however, saw things differently. He blamed the forces of occupation for his unsatisfactory performance, saying:

> The British and the Russians wanted a very weak monarch. And I was very young. So obviously then I was even less than a constitutional monarch, because even that could not be applied exactly because again the British and the Russians wanted a weaker monarch than the Constitution allowed. So obviously in those days I was called a playboy and a weakling, that my twin sister would have been much better than myself.[28]

He also vented his frustration by telling anyone who cared to hear that he saw no 'honour or joy' in being 'the king of a nation of beggars led by a gang of thieves'. Before long, however, Mohammad-Reza Shah's image as a weak and indecisive man was to change as a result of a series of dramatic events that included an attempt on his life.

---

*The father of General 'Stormin' Norman Schwartzkopf of Gulf War fame.

5

Six Bullets

'People who think Iran could not live without its oil should remember that the country also risked death because of its oil resources.' This is how Mohammad Sa'ed Maragheh, one of Iran's leading statesmen, described the complex role that Iran's vast oil reserves played in the nation's foreign and domestic politics.[1] Sa'ed was in a position to know. It was during his first term as prime minister in 1944 that the long Iranian oil crisis began – a crisis that, in one way or another, continued until the very end of Mohammad-Reza Shah's reign in January 1979. Shortly after Sa'ed was sworn in as premier, a report prepared for the American State Department in Washington showed that Iran, with more than 10 million tonnes of crude, had become the world's third major exporter of oil behind the United States and Venezuela. It was also the fourth-largest producer of the valuable fuel.[2]

Iran's oil industry was at the time located exclusively in Khuzestan in the British occupation zone. A number of studies had established the existence of substantial oil reserves in other parts of the country, notably the Caspian and Azerbaijan. Sa'ed, therefore, wanted to prepare an overall policy on oil with the aim of ending the British monopoly and tapping the reserves of the north with help from American companies. It was for this purpose that he invited two American oil experts to come to Tehran and help establish a master plan for the nation's principal natural wealth.

The arrival of the American experts provoked an almost immediate reaction from Moscow. Without even informing Tehran the Soviets had undertaken extensive geological surveys in areas of Iran that their army had occupied since 1941. These surveys indicated the presence of oil in economic quantities in northeast Iran not far from the Soviet frontier. It is not difficult to gauge the importance of the discovery for Soviet planners. With an inexpensive source of energy at their disposal in a strategically located region, Soviet planners could speed up the industrialisation of Central Asia and Kazakhstan. Stalin was determined to get his hands on northern Iranian oil which had, in the 1920s, also tempted a number of Americans, including John D. Rockefeller.

The way Stalin proceeded to pursue his oil plans in Iran was so high-handed, so overtly provocative, that it unleashed a violent Iranian backlash which, in turn, led to the oil nationalisation drama in 1951. In September 1944 the Soviet news agency TASS suddenly announced the arrival of a large delegation of diplomats, lawyers and technical experts from Moscow. Headed by Deputy Commissar for Foreign Affairs Sergei Kaftaradze, the Soviet mission settled at the ambassador's residence without telling the Iranian authorities the purpose of their visit. It was nearly two weeks later that Kaftaradze, in an interview with the daily *Ettelaat*, revealed that he had come to Tehran to ask the Iranian government to sign a treaty under which the USSR would be authorised to exploit Iran's northern oil reserves.

The Soviets claimed a monopoly on exploiting Iran's northern oil resources on the basis of a concession granted by the Qajars to a Georgian businessman known as Khoshtaria. The fact that at the time the concession had been given Georgia had not been part of the USSR was ignored by Kaftaradze. Sa'ed, having learned about Soviet designs largely through newspaper reports, immediately made it clear that he would not negotiate any concession with any foreign power as long as Iran remained under occupation. At an open session of the Majlis, however, Sa'ed had to admit that he had, indeed, been involved in a series of 'informal talks' with American and British oil interests before the Soviet bid was made.

The Soviet propaganda machine, notably the Tudeh Party, was set in motion to force the government to grant 'the legitimate interests of our beloved northern neighbour'.[3] Tudeh Majlis members also began attacking Sa'ed for what they described as his refusal to allow the economic development of the northern provinces thanks to the exploitation of oil. Pro-British factions adopted an ambivalent stance as Britain was not opposed to the granting of oil concessions to the USSR provided this did not affect the Anglo-Iranian's monopoly in the south. In any case, the two main occupying powers had already divided Iran into zones of influence.

Soviet bullying tactics were like an electric shock on Iranian public opinion and led to largely spontaneous demonstrations against any concessions to foreigners. A new mood of nationalism, intensely xenophobic in form and content, began to show itself. One man quickly became the chief representative of this new and militant nationalism: Mohammad Mossadeq. (Because of a law doctorate he had obtained in Paris he insisted that he be called 'Dr' Mossadeq.)

At that time Dr Mossadeq was a member of parliament and the unofficial leader of a group of seven or eight deputies who described themselves as Jebheh Melli (National Front). These deputies had close relations with Tudeh members with whom they shared a dislike of the Anglophile politicians who still largely dominated the nation's politics.

Mossadeq was quick to realise that the oil issue could radically alter the national agenda and propel him into the centre of Iranian public life. He drafted a three-point bill which expressly forbade negotiations with any foreign power, company or agent of foreign interests regarding oil concessions. The government was, however, authorised to negotiate the sale of oil and the methods of exploiting its oil resources with foreigners. The bill envisaged prison terms of between three and eight years, combined with perpetual exclusion from public service, for anyone found guilty of violating the ban.

A master of kitman or dissimulation, Mossadeq at first presented his move as one aimed exclusively against the British. He called in Iraj Eskandari, a member of the Tudeh leadership, and asked him to relay a simple message to the Soviet Embassy: the Iranian people hate the word 'concession' and associate it with colonialism; we are trying to present the USSR as a friendly power and not as a colonial one; support us in imposing a ban on all concessions and we will later arrange for the sale of oil to the USSR. Mossadeq also made it clear to Eskandari that he would present his bill at the Majlis the following day only if the Russians gave him the green light.[4] Eskandari took the message to the embassy where, despite the fact that he was a member of parliament, Ambassador Maximov refused to see him in person. Eskandari relayed the message through the embassy's interpreter, Aliev, and waited for half an hour before he received a reply. Moscow had given the 'green light' that Mossadeq had asked for. Eskandari went directly to Mossadeq's home and gave him the good news. The master of kitman warmly embraced the Tudeh leader and said: 'Today you have rendered a great service to your country.'[5]

The following day at the Majlis, however, Mossadeq made a vitriolic attack on all foreign powers seeking to force Iran into granting them oil concessions. The text of the bill he presented was also much more radical than he had promised Eskandari.[6] The Tudeh parliamentary faction, no doubt after consulting the embassy, decided to oppose the bill and three Tudeh deputies spoke against it, one of them Eskandari himself. 'Mossadeq had tricked us,' Eskandari said many years later.[7]

Maximov must have been outraged when he read the actual text of a bill which he had recommended to Moscow as a pro-Soviet move. Kaftaradze was so annoyed that he left Tehran the following day. Two days later Pravda, the daily organ of the Soviet Communist Party in Moscow, criticised the bill and its architect, Mossadeq. In Tehran the Tudeh press launched an anti-Mossadeq campaign. The old fox, feigning surprise at the Soviet reaction, wrote a letter to Maximov in which he accused the Soviets of bad faith.[8]

Relations between Mossedeq and Tudeh took a turn for the worse when, accompanied by Eskandari, the party secretary, Dr Morteza Yazdi visited the nationalist leader at his home in the hope of convincing him of the justice of the Soviet oil demands. Eskandari opened the discussions by saying that northern Iran was the natural 'security perimeter' of the USSR and Iran had better recognise that reality. On hearing this Mossadeq took a knife out of his pocket and waved it at his Tudeh guests. 'If I hear you speak like that again I shall cut out your tongues with this!' He added: 'If the north is a Russian perimeter then the south is a British zone. And where do we, Iranians, come in?'[9]

The Shah supported Mossadeq's bill and the Royal Assent was given instantly. Furthermore, the monarch sent for the Doctor and invited him to assume the premiership. At the time the Shah did not have the power to nominate anyone as prime minister without the prior approval of the Majlis and the invitation was, in itself, no more than a gesture of support. Mossadeq, however, said he would accept the premiership on two conditions. The first was that he be given a personal bodyguard. The Shah immediately agreed. The second was that the British should endorse his premiership before going to the Majlis. A surprised Shah asked: 'What about the Russians?' Mossadeq replied: 'Oh, they don't count. It is the British who decide everything in this country.'[10] A few days later the Shah informed Mossadeq that the British would not approve of his premiership.

This episode was related by the Shah many years later in a bid to cast doubt on Mossadeq's patriotism. But Mossadeq's view at the time reflected only the reality of the situation. The British controlled a majority of the Majlis deputies and could easily have blocked his nomination as prime minister. The Shah's own faction, secretly led by Princess Ashraf, could mobilise at most only a dozen votes. It was not the Shah but British power that decided who should lead the government of Iran.

The Shah was soon confronted with far more serious problems than arranging a hypothetical Mossadeq premiership. The failure of the Kaftaradze mission and the passage of the Mossadeq bill on oil led to an almost immediate and dramatic change in Moscow's policy towards Iran. A few days after the bill was passed, the creation of the Azerbaijan Dimokrat Firgahsi (Azerbaijan Democratic Sect) was announced in Tabriz with a programme that aimed at virtually eliminating all central governmental authority in the province. The Firqah (Sect) immediately set up an autonomous government with Mir-Ja'afar Pishevari, a veteran journalist, as prime minister. Armed guards mobilised by the Firqah and protected by Soviet troops attacked army and police bases and disarmed central government forces. A number of pro-Tehran personalities were shot and their homes looted. The Soviet embassy in Tehran ordered Tudeh to merge its Azerbaijan branch into the Firqah. The Tudeh leaders were taken by surprise at what appeared to them as a bid to detach Azerbaijan from Iran, but nevertheless dutifully complied with Moscow's instructions. Soon afterwards a secessionist movement was launched in Kurdistan too, where a Soviet-inspired 'Democratic' Party, led by Qazi

Mohammad, moved to eliminate central government authority and declared the creation of an autonomous 'republic' at Mahabad.

Until the autumn of 1944, Soviet policy in Iran had been aimed at scoring political gains without antagonising either Britain or the United States. It now seems certain that Stalin and his principal foreign policy aides had no plans for dismembering Iran. They were convinced that post-war Iran would be too weak to pursue an independent foreign policy and would, inevitably, fall into the Soviet orbit. It is of course not easy to persuade the supporters of conspiracy theories that the USSR under Stalin did not have a detailed grand design with regard to Iran. Soviet policy-making was less monolithic than the apparent domination of all life by Stalin might suggest. In the case of Iran it now appears that two competing policies existed side by side. One was that supported by Foreign Commissar Wychieslav Molotov in Moscow whose principal goal was the eventual 'Finlandisation' of Iran. The other was a policy propagated by the Soviet Azerbaijan Communist Party chief, Mir-Ja'afar Baqerov, with support from the secret police boss Lavrenti Beria. Baqerov, who was executed on a charge of high treason on Khrushchev's orders after Stalin's death, had his own dream of a unified 'grand Azerbaijan' under his own leadership. The annexation of Iranian Azerbaijan and Kurdistan would have made Baqerov a veritable power in his own right.

By the end of 1944 Baqerov's plan had won Stalin's reluctant support. Molotov still hoped to harmonise Soviet policy in Iran, however, with policies pursued by Britain and the United States. Accordingly, when the Yalta Conference brought Stalin, Churchill and Roosevelt together in February 1945, Molotov tried to narrow down the issue of Iran's future to one of oil concessions. Both the British Foreign Secretary, Sir Anthony Eden, and the American Secretary of State, Edward Stetinius, tried to persuade Molotov that the USSR should seek no oil concessions in Iran until after the full withdrawal of Allied troops from that country. Molotov was not convinced and Baqerov's adventurous policy, with Stalin's blessing, was pursued with greater vigour in Azerbaijan.

The Tehran government, virtually paralysed by successive changes of cabinet, nevertheless tried to reassert its authority in Azerbaijan by dispatching a column of the regular army to the province. The column's journey came to an end at Sharifabad, 80 miles west of the capital, after being denied free passage by a superior Soviet force. This was followed by the defection of a number of regular army officers to the autonomous 'states' of Azerbaijan and Kurdistan. Taking a leaf out of Stalin's book, Pishevari, who had been a calm and even sweet man all his life, was suddenly transformed into a revolutionary monster demanding more and more blood. The Firqah's paramilitary forces, known as the Fedayeen (those who are ready to sacrifice their lives for the cause) initiated a reign of terror that witnessed the execution of hundreds of people and the murder of many more throughout the province.

In February 1945, Prime Minister Ebrahim Hakimi resigned after three months of desperate attempts to negotiate a way out of the impasse created by the Soviet stance on Azerbaijan. The Shah, acting through Princess Ashraf, tried to mobilise parliamentary support for Motamen al-Molk Pirnia, a veteran statesman who had long served as speaker. The court's candidate was opposed by Ahmad Qavam who had briefly served as premier in 1942.

The Shah disliked Qavam for a number of reasons. The old politician, a Qajar by birth, had plotted against Reza Shah in the 1920s. Later, in 1942, he had run the government without bothering to inform the Shah of what was going on, against the requirements of the Constitution. When the Majlis voted to support the new prime minister, Ahmad Qavam beat Pirnia by only one vote. Qavam's success was achieved with support from Tudeh and the National Front faction led by Mossadeq.

Then aged 69, Qavam was sick in bed when he was chosen as premier. The 'perfume of power', as he later noted, revived him and gave him an intellectual and physical energy that surprised friend and foe. He formed a rather indifferent cabinet and announced that his first move would be to go to Moscow for talks with Stalin.

A Qajar aristocrat, Qavam had served as prime minister in the 1920s with the Shah's father – then known as Reza Khan – as a member of the cabinet. Immensely wealthy – he was one of Iran's largest landowners – Qavam had an inordinate hunger for political power. He remained a bachelor until the very last years of his life and, unencumbered by family responsibilities, he focused his energies on a constant quest for authority. At a time when the Shah's court counted less than half a dozen permanent staff, Qavam's household included more than 100 hangers-on whose principal task was to create an aura of power and prestige around their master.

As prime minister he chose Mozzafar Firuz, an ambitious and highly volatile Qajar prince, as his principal henchman. Firuz if anything had even more lust for power than Qavam himself. The difference was that Firuz wanted to play the Russian card while Qavam, as always, looked further afield towards the United States.

Qavam's strategy in his trip to Moscow was based on the Persian proverb that says: when your choice is between fever and death, choose fever! Contrary to the analysis provided by the Tudeh leadership regarding Moscow's ideological commitment to revolutionary movements, Qavam was convinced that the USSR was just another big power seeking to take unfair advantage of a weaker state. He was thus prepared to offer Stalin oil in exchange for the withdrawal of Soviet troops from Iran. Such a withdrawal, everyone knew, would mean the instant collapse of the puppet governments that Baqerov had set up in Tabriz and

Mahabad. To circumvent the Majlis act that banned any negotiations on oil concessions, Qavam proposed the creation of a joint Irano-Soviet oil company that would sell Moscow crude oil on favourable terms.

Qavam had another card in his hand: support from the United States. He was convinced that Russia and the United States would emerge as the two major world powers after the end of the war. He also believed that Roosevelt and Stalin had established a personal understanding that would, at least in part, counter-balance America's traditional support for British positions in the Middle East. In other words, the United States would not necessarily oppose a legitimate Soviet presence in Iran, simply because this might displease Britain. Qavam summed up the most effective foreign policy for Iran in these terms: 'Turn your back to the British and your face to the Russians but extend your hand towards the Americans!'[10]

Hiding behind his thick, dark spectacles, Qavam was not only a master tactician, but also a fine connoisseur of human nature. Within a few days he had the Tudeh leadership eating from his hand.*

Qavam took a small delegation of Majlis deputies, lawyers and journalists with him to Moscow and at first pretended to have no preset package to offer. His first engagement in the Russian capital was a tête-à-tête with Stalin at the Kremlin. This went very badly. The Soviet dictator ignored the Persian statesman's attempt at creating a relaxed atmosphere by starting with polite conversation and immediately began a litany of complaints against 'Persian craftiness'. 'You Persians have always tricked us,' Stalin said. 'But I warn you that we have no hopes about your ability to solve our problems.'[12]

The same evening, at a party in Qavam's honour hosted by Molotov, the commissar for Foreign Affairs expanded on Stalin's bitter remarks. Molotov singled out Sayyed Zia-eddin for attack and described him as 'our number one enemy in Iran'. He went on to say that 'reactionary circles' – meaning Anglophiles – controlled the Iranian parliament and press.

The Soviets seemed uninterested in substantive negotiations but Qavam persisted. He stayed in Moscow for three weeks and obtained two more meetings with Stalin. The atmosphere at both sessions remained acrimonious as Stalin tried to pressure the Iranian prime minister into virtually accepting a Soviet diktat on all issues. The Soviet plan seemed aimed at forcing the Iranians to break up the talks and take the blame for the consequences. Qavam, however, managed to keep the talks going, while insisting on only two points: Azerbaijan remained an inalienable part of Iran and Soviet troops must withdraw in accordance with the Tripartite Treaty. Neither Stalin nor Molotov seemed to want Azerbaijan detached

---

*Pishevari, however, was not seduced; he had known Qavam for more than 30 years. In a cable to Baqerov in Baku, Pishevari warned that 'the old trickster' might double-cross even Stalin 'whose feet know what our heads cannot even dream of'.[11]

from Iran, although both insisted that Iranian military action against the rebels would be resisted.

At the end of the talks a brief, grim statement described the situation: the two sides had disagreed on practically all issues. Qavam was packing his luggage to return home when he was informed that Stalin was offering a banquet in his honour the following evening. At the banquet Qavam expressed Iran's deep resentment at the Soviets' dilatory tactics with regard to ending the occupation of Iranian territory. It turned out, however, that they had begun to change their minds about Qavam. They had observed him closely during his three week stay in Moscow and had concluded that he was sincere. They agreed to continue negotiating with him in Tehran. Maximov, the Soviet Ambassador who had been too closely identified with the Firqah, was replaced by Sadchikov, who proved a more accommodating partner, and Qavam's formula for the creation of an Irano-Soviet oil company to exploit Iran's northern resources was soon accepted by the Soviets. The company, formed for an initial period of 50 years, was to be jointly owned by the two governments, with the USSR having a majority of the shares.

While Moscow accepted the plan with evident satisfaction, Qavam could not immediately deliver. Unable to even negotiate the terms of the final agreement because this was banned by the famous Mossadeq Act of 1944, the prime minister told the Russians that they would have to wait until fresh elections produced a new Majlis majority that would repeal the Mossadeq Act and approve the Irano-Soviet accord. In the meantime Soviet troops would have to be withdrawn to make the holding of elections possible throughout the country.

On his return home, Qavam began to negotiate with the Firqah regarding their demands for autonomy. This was partly intended to reassure the Russians that their satellite regime in Tabriz would end up with some concessions from Tehran. He also had a large number of leading Anglophiles, notably Sayyed Zia-eddin, arrested on a charge of conspiracy. At least some of the conspirators were known to have contacts with Princess Ashraf and the dowager Queen, who had not ceased plotting to overthrow the Qavam government. They were convinced that Qavam was an enemy of the Pahlavis and had personal ambitions that could endanger the monarchy.

Pahlavi suspicion of Qavam's motives were not totally groundless. The prime minister had created a party of his own, Hezb Democrat (Democratic Party) with a programme copied almost completely from its American namesake. Qavam was convinced that the United States would emerge as the world's dominant non-Communist power and was determined to be head of the pro-American party in Iran. The Democratic Party did not achieve a mass following but became influential through the extensive use – and abuse – of government favours. The party also hired organised gangs of thugs to bully political opponents. On one occasion the party's hired mob attacked the Shah's car as the monarch was driving from the airport to his palace. The mob was in lynching mood and the Shah, in those days, did not have a personal bodyguard. The monarch manoeuvred his car into the garden of the Municipal Café where he persuaded the guardian to close the iron gate and call the police. The incident was soon ended but the Shah's confidence in Qavam was severely shaken.

Qavam's friends referred to him as Hazrat Ashraf (The Noblest Presence) and described him as Shakhs Avval Mamlekat (The First Personality of the Kingdom). The Shah resented these titles as attempts at reducing the authority of the monarchy. For nearly five years the Shah had tried to secure a place of his own on the carousel of Iranian politics and each time had been pushed away. No one was prepared to give him a share of real power and now Qavam was trying to chip at the monarch's honorific position also.

Iranian politics at the time was dominated by two dozen men, all in their 60s, who shared the key posts among themselves. Between them and the Shah – still in his early 20s – existed a wide generation gap. Moreover, they all belonged to a handful of influential families who regarded the Pahlavis as upstarts and outsiders. Older politicians such as Sayyed Zia-eddin and Karim Khan Rashti who supported the Shah did so for their own reasons. They wanted to use the monarch's popular prestige as a weapon in their own fights, on the one hand against Qavam and against the Soviet-backed factions on the other.

The Shah had seen the Azerbaijan crisis as an opportunity for proving both his patriotic zeal and his statesmanship. Accordingly, he had tried to pursue his own plan for the liberation of the usurped province. Qavam had acted his pro-Soviet role so well that many senior politicians, as well as the Shah, were convinced that the prime minister was sincere in his efforts to meet Stalin's demands. There were even those who believed that Qavam symbolised a Russo-American policy aimed at reducing British influence in the country. This impression was strengthened when the Americans formally informed the Shah that, while they supported Tehran's demand for a Soviet troop withdrawal, they would not go to war with Russia over Azerbaijan.[13]

The Shah, advised by Iran's representative at the United Nations, Hossein Ala, tried to play the card of international pressure on Moscow. The matter was, therefore, raised at the Security Council and provoked Stalin's anger. Qavam, once again playing his favourite game of dissimulation, acted as if he disapproved of Ala's move but did nothing to withdraw Iran's case from the United Nations.

Another bone of contention between the Shah and the prime minister was Qavam's decision to reshuffle his cabinet to bring in three Tudeh and one National Front ministers. The deputy premier, Muzzafar Firuz, was already regarded as pro-Russian and the reshuffled cabinet appeared to the Shah as a sign that Qavam really wanted to play the Soviet card. The prime minister, however, gave one concession to the monarchists: Abdol-Hossein Hazhir, a protégé of Princess Ashraf, was named Finance Minister. During the presentation ceremony at the palace the three Tudeh ministers refused to bow to the Shah as protocol required. So the monarch turned his face away while shaking their hands.[14] Allahyar Saleh, the National Front deputy who now became Minister of Justice, had also joined the Tudeh ministers in his less than cordial attitude during the presentation to the Shah.

The most serious clash between the Shah and Qavam came over the issue of granting regular army ranks to a number of Firqah militia leaders. The measure had been part of a package negotiated between Pishevari and Firuz with the prime minister's final approval. The agreement consisted of 15 points some of which – such as the granting of voting rights to women and the teaching of the Azari language at primary schools – might have enjoyed a measure of popular support. Firuz had agreed that three Firqah militia commanders be recognised as brigadier-generals of the Iranian army while around 200 other rebels would obtain lower ranks. He had also promised that all army officers who had defected to the Firqah would be granted a royal pardon and readmitted into the regular forces.

Firuz's imprudent, not to say provocative, undertakings led to a veritable explosion of anger among the Iranian top brass. General Haj-Ali Razm-Ara, the Chief of Staff, was the first to reject any idea of admitting rebels into the regular army. The matter was taken to the Shah, first by Firuz and then by Qavam himself, but the monarch was not prepared to go against the wishes of his own army commanders. 'I would rather cut off my hand than sign such an act of treason,' he told Qavam. Firuz then suggested that the Firqah militiamen be given army ranks on the basis of a cabinet decree, but this was manifestly illegal and even the Firqah commanders would not be a party to it. The matter had to be dropped and the Shah scored his first major gain on the Iranian political chessboard.

Firuz, however could not stop plotting. He began to describe himself as 'the Red Prince' and went from circle to circle talking about the need for a 'social revolution' in Iran. He even created a secret organisation, known as Spantum, its mission to assassinate a number of key personalities, including the Shah, as part of a revolutionary takeover of government.[15] Firuz tried to win over Razm-Ara and invited the general to join 'the winning side'. He told the general that Iran needed a new reforming leadership capable of saving the country from both the Anglophile reactionaries and the pro-Soviet Tudeh and Firqah. The Shah had to go and in the new government Qavam would be named head of state. Razm-Ara would become prime minister with Firuz at his side.

Rumours regarding Firuz's almost open plotting soon reached the Shah and he ordered an investigation, but Qavam moved first by dispatching

Firuz to Moscow as Ambassador. 'The Red Prince' never returned to Iran. After a brief spell in the Soviet capital he settled in Paris. From there he remained in contact with the Tudeh leadership through his aunt, Maryam Firuz, who was mistress of two members of the Tudeh Central Committee at the same time.[16]

The coalition government over which Qavam presided was too divided to tackle the urgent problem of social and economic reform. It was also unable to cope with the growing mood of rebellion in provinces outside Azerbaijan and Kurdistan. In Fars the Qashqu'is, encouraged and heavily bribed by the British, were once again on the warpath. Their chiefs threatened that they would not recognise the authority of the central government until and unless the rebel regimes in Tabriz and Mahabad were destroyed, giving themselves an aura of patriotism that appealed to the regular army which was supposed to crush the Fars rebellion. In oil-rich Khuzestan the so-called Hezb Sa'adat (Well-being Party) also threatened to seek autonomy unless Azerbaijan and Kurdistan were brought back under central government authority.

Qavam's careful courting of the Soviets combined with a vast mobilisation of public opinion in Iran against the provinces' secession finally persuaded Stalin to withdraw his forces from Iranian territory. In the meantime the death of President Roosevelt and the accession of Harry S. Truman to the presidency ended the wartime entente between Moscow and Washington. The US enjoyed a monopoly of nuclear weapons at the time and Truman, through his Secretary of State who visited Stalin in Moscow, had made it clear that the USSR would not be allowed to swallow Iran with impunity. Stalin, busy consolidating his gains in Eastern and Central Europe, though he would do better to avoid military confrontation with the United States over Iran. President Truman later wrote in his memoirs that he had sent ultimatums to Stalin over Azerbaijan, but researchers have now established that no such ultimatums were ever issued by Washington.[17]

Another factor that persuaded Stalin to end his Iranian adventure was his fear that the pro-Soviet militia might not be able to withstand a major attack by Iran's regular forces. The Firqah and its counterpart in Kurdistan lacked popular support and were regarded by a majority of the local population as agents of Russia and enemies of Islam. This meant that Stalin would have to maintain his forces inside Iran indefinitely without any guarantee of securing an oil concession from Tehran.

The Shah began to advocate military action to liberate Azerbaijan after his first major political clash with Princess Ashraf. One day the angry princess arrived at the palace where the Shah was taking his dogs for their afternoon stroll. 'Are you a real man? Or am I the man of this family?' the princess demanded. 'Do you mean to allow the kingdom to fall apart?'[18] On the strength of reports from both Razm-Ara and General Hassan 'Arfa, another senior commander, the Shah was convinced that Iranian forces would be able to defeat the rebels. Qavam, however, was not so sure and derided the Iranian army as a force whose commanders had disguised themselves as women and run into hiding at the start of the Allied invasion.

The Soviets eventually announced that they would withdraw their forces from Iran in the hope that a future Majlis would ratify the oil deal within seven months. After a series of other manoeuvres the Soviets finally left on 9 May 1946, taking with them almost all the heavy weapons they had supplied to the Firqah and Kurdish rebels. More than 3000 Soviet Azerbaijani agents who had provided the Firqah with its administrative and military backbone also left with the withdrawing troops. It was obvious that Moscow wanted to jettison its cumbersome allies in Iran.

The Soviet withdrawal meant that general elections could be held throughout the country. Tudeh, whose ministers had now resigned from the Cabinet, tried to employ extra-parliamentary methods; the Central Committee knew that the party would win no more than a few seats in any free elections.[19]

The Interior Ministry fixed a date for general elections in December and called on the armed forces to make sure that law and order was fully established in all constituencies. This routine reference to the role of the army provided the Shah with an opportunity to involve the armed forces in what was later described as 'the saving of Azerbaijan and Kurdistan'. By 6 December the army had concentrated several units at Zanjan and was ready for action. The Shah, accompanied by Razm-Ara, arrived at Zanjan airport aboard a military aircraft piloted by himself – he had used part of his spare time learning to fly. After a short session with the local commanders he read a short but passionate message to the armed forces and ordered the start of operation liberation. He described the rebels as 'adventure-seeking satans' and 'stateless troublemakers'. He then flew over the Iranian columns in a gesture of personal support for the operation.

News of the Iranian advance left the Firqah and its Kurdish allies in a state of disarray. The Firqah leaders wanted to resist but were ordered by the Soviet Consul in Tabriz, Quoliev, to remain calm. News of the army's advance, however, soon provoked anti-Firqah riots in which scores of people were killed in acts of revenge and counter-revenge. The advancing army began to disarm Firqah forces and occupy rebel bases in contravention of verbal assurances given to the Soviet Ambassador, Vassili Sadchikov. On 12 December, the day Iranian forces arrived in Tabriz to a tumultuous welcome, Sadchikov asked for and was granted an urgent audience with the Shah. The Soviet diplomat had come to ask the Shah to stop all military action against the Firqah or risk intervention by Soviet forces, but before the audience was over a cable arrived from Tabriz announcing that all operations had ended and that the last Firqah leaders and activists were under arrest. The Shah informed the Ambassador about the cable and Sadchikov left without a word.

The top Firqah leaders escaped across the border into the USSR, but the Kurdish rebel chiefs were all captured by the army as well as 45,000 rifles, 3000 submachine-guns and 8,000,000 bullets. The 'liberation' of Tabriz and Mahabad marked the start of a massive crackdown in the three provinces. Within a few weeks military tribunals issued 2500 death sentences and condemned a further 8000 people to lengthy prison terms. Finally, some 36,000 people were sentenced to various lengths of banishment but the sentences were not fully carried out. The new Majlis passed a special amnesty act under which the vast majority of those associated with the secessionists were pardoned and released. In Mahabad 9 leaders, including Qazi Mohammad who had been proclaimed 'President of the Republic', were publicly hanged. In Azerbaijan a total of 33 executions was finally recorded.

The restoration of central authority to Azerbaijan and Kurdistan put the Shah at the centre of the Iranian political map. Most people were unaware of the clever role played by Qavam and also ignored the intricate combination of power politics and international diplomacy that had made the Soviet withdrawal possible. All the people saw was pictures of the Shah giving the order to attack from Zanjan. The crowds that poured onto the streets of Tabriz, Rezaieh and Mahabad to greet the army also carried his portrait.

At the end of December the new Majlis was inaugurated by the Shah. Qavam was confirmed as premier, but the Majlis rejected his oil agreement with Stalin and Qavam was forced to resign. Ibrahim Hakimi, the new premier, declared that the agreement was dead. Qavam made no attempt at defending the agreement. Within a few weeks his party collapsed and the old statesman retired to his estates on the Caspian. The Shah had survived the first challenge to his position by a strong prime minister, but Qavam was not the last politician to try to restrict the monarch to largely ceremonial duties.

The Shah's first objective became the restoration to the monarchy of at least part of the power and prestige that the institution had lost since his father's abdication. He was firmly convinced by now that Swiss-style democracy was a luxury Iran could not afford. As long as 99 per cent of the people remained illiterate and poor the country would do best with a benevolent dictatorship. There is no evidence that the Shah ever objectively analysed the reasons for his father's tragic end which had also landed Iran in a crisis from which she never fully recovered. To Mohammad-Reza Shah it was the result only of foreign aggression. Thus he began trying to protect himself from the dangers of foreign conspiracy.

Determined to play the American card at the first possible opportunity, the Shah strengthened his ties with the United States. He established a personal relationship with the American Ambassador, George Allen, who was the only foreign envoy to be received at the palace once a week. They discussed not only politics but also the Shah's personal problems. Allen was meant to feel that he was a friend of the family.

Regular contact with the British was maintained through Sayyed Zia-eddin who, now that he was out of the prison where Qavam had put him, acted as elder statesman. The Sayyed was a regular visitor to the palace and it was understood that the Shah was keeping him in reserve as a potential prime minister.

The Shah did not abandon the possibility of good relations with Russia either. He had first established contact with Stalin in 1944 when Princess Ashraf was dispatched to Moscow on a scouting mission. The cover for the visit was an Iranian Red Lion and Sun (the equivalent of the Red Cross) mission to Moscow. Once in the Soviet capital, Ashraf demanded an audience with Stalin and two days later she was at the Kremlin. The princess met the Soviet dictator alone in his vast office. Her message on behalf of her brother was simple: the USSR could trust the Pahlavis whose only desire was to maintain Iran's independence free of international rivalries; and the Soviet Union should not exploit Iran's weakness by encouraging secessionist movements in the northern provinces. The meeting lasted nearly two and a half hours (during which Josip Broz Tito, the future Marshal, was kept waiting) and went extremely well. Stalin assured the princess that all Moscow was after in Iran was a reduction in the influence of reactionary forces linked with 'foreign circles'. The following day the princess was invited to sit next to Stalin during celebrations marking the Republics' Day in Moscow. Before Ashraf left Moscow she received a zibeline coat as Stalin's gift, and the Soviet dictator ordered his official artist to paint two portraits of the princess.[20] After this successful initial contact, Ashraf became one of the Shah's principal messengers to Moscow and visited the USSR nine times.

The Shah also pursued his efforts to win the support of the shi'ite clergy. He made a large donation for the restoration of Imam Ali's shrine in Najaf and himself became a regular pilgrim to the holy city of Mashhad. The Tehran Friday Prayer Leader was now a member of the Shah's close circle of advisers. Another religious personality, Haj Agha Reza Raf'i, maintained contact between the Shah and the grand ayatollahs. Finally, one tragic incident was to convince the mullahs that the Shah was truly on their side.

In March 1945 a leading intellectual and jurist named Ahmad Kasravi was assassinated by a Muslim fundamentalist called Hossein Emami. Kasravi had for years waged a campaign against the mullahs and written extensively on the need for an Islamic reformation and the 'de-Arabisation' of Iran. During his trial Emami said he had acted on the basis of a *fatwa* issued by a shi'ite authority. The un-named authority had sentenced Kasravi to death as 'an enemy of Allah'.[21] Emami argued that he had performed his religious duty and should not be punished for the 'elimination' of someone who had been declared 'mahdur ad-damm' (he whose blood must be shed). The court, however, sentenced him to death. A week later a demand for pardon was put to Qavam, then prime minister, on behalf of Grand Ayatollah Borujerdi. Though Hazhir, Princess Ashraf's friend in the Cabinet, strongly supported Emami's release, the cabinet as a whole opposed the idea of allowing a self-confessed assassin to go free.

Borujerdi then sent a six-man delegation to meet the Shah, led by Hojat al-Islam Khomeini who had actually issued the *fatwa* that had led to Kasravi's murder. The Shah agreed to do what he could. He pressed the matter through Hazhir and the cabinet in the end, applied for a Royal Pardon. Emami was instantly pardoned.*

The biggest demonstration of the Shah's desire to win the mullahs' favour came in the shape of his donation for gilding the dome of the shrine of Ma'assumah in Qom, the Iranian stronghold of the shi'ite clergy. The monarch also offered land and money for the construction of a cathedral mosque in the holy city, the first to be built there since the seventeenth century. All these donations were made in response to a demand put by Borujerdi through a six-mullah delegation once again including Khomeini. At the same time the Shah wanted to promote Borujerdi as *primus inter pares* of the grand ayatollahs as a means of shifting the centre of shi'ite clerical power from Najaf, in Iraq, to Qom, south of Tehran.

Those who met the Shah frequently in those days recall that he seemed to suffer from a feeling of permanent unease. He was often tense and manifestly unhappy. The occasional European ladies of pleasure – all blondes of course – who paid brief visits to the palace seemed unable to fully dispel the young monarch's angst. He tried to escape from his unhappiness by indulging in sports and games and went horseback riding every afternoon and was, by 1949, a veritable expert in equestrian matters. His stables included a growing number of expensive mounts purchased in Europe by his stable master Abol-Fath Atabay. The Shah believed that the only thing he was capable of, apart from ruling Iran and, later, the whole world, was to train horses.[22]

His passion for sports cars also continued unabated and by 1949 he had no fewer than 27 cars, including six Rolls-Royces. He had also acquired another passion, flying. He began training to be a pilot in 1944 and by 1946 had received his military pilot's licence from the air force. A year later he purchased a Beachcroft and also learned to pilot civilian aircraft. Later, an American bomber pilot, Dick Colburn, taught the Shah how to fly a B17. Once airborne, he always wanted to test the limits of the aircraft's performance and the American instructor thought it prudent to ignore his contract and left Iran after only a few weeks.

One incident in 1948 persuaded the Shah that he was protected by

*A few years later the same Emami murdered Hazhir, once again on the basis of a fatwa that had sentenced the politician to death as a 'heretic'.

metaphysical forces or, as the monarch put it, by God himself. He was piloting his aircraft over Kuhrang, near Isfahan, with one officer aboard. Shortly after takeoff the plane's single engine went dead and the Shah had to make a forced landing in a rocky ravine. The aircraft finally came to a stop after hitting a large boulder and the collision had torn off the undercarriage and turned the plane upside down. The Shah and his companion were unhurt, as he later recalled: 'There we were, hanging by our seatbelts in the open cockpit. Neither of us had suffered as much as a scratch. . . I burst out laughing, but my upside-down companion didn't think it was so funny. Was that narrow escape good luck, or was it good luck bolstered by something else?'[23]

A year later, on 4 February 1949, the Shah experienced yet another 'miracle' in the series that began with his vision of the Imams in the 1920s. The Shah, wearing a military uniform, arrived at Tehran University to preside over a ceremony marking the foundation of the institution. He was just about to enter the Law Faculty when shots suddenly rang out and bullets flew in his direction. Three bullets passed through his military cap without touching his head. A fourth bullet penetrated his cheekbone and came out under his nose. The gunman was within six feet of his target, aiming his revolver at his heart. Thoughts flashed through the Shah's mind. 'How could he miss? What should I do? Shall I jump on him? But if I approach him I shall become a better target. Shall I run away? Then I shall be a perfect target to be shot in the back.'[24] Still facing the gunman, the Shah began shadow-dancing or feinting. He had recognised the gun and knew it held two more bullets. The gunman fired again and this time wounded the Shah in the shoulder. His last shot stuck in the revolver, which he threw down as he tried to run. The Shah had 'the queer and not unpleasant sensation of knowing' that he was still alive.[25]

The whole drama was over within less than two minutes. The Shah's entourage, including the army officers who escorted him, had run for cover, but once they realised that the gunman was no longer armed they rushed towards him and put him to death in a hail of bullets followed by bayonet attacks. The Shah, meanwhile, was 'bleeding like a young bull whose throat had been slit'.[26] He was rushed to hospital where doctors quickly realised that he had suffered only superficial wounds. The monarch's bloodstained uniform, now a relic, was placed on display at the Officers' Club in Tehran where it remained, something of an ikon, until 1979.

The Shah's escape from death had certainly been miraculous and he had no doubt that God had, once again, intervened to protect him. The same evening he told Princess Ashraf that the whole incident had been designed by the Almighty to show everyone that Mohammad-Reza Shah was under divine protection.[27]

The would-be assassin was Nasser Hossein Fakhr-Ara'i, who had gained entrance to the ceremony as a photographer for a weekly called

Parcham Eslam (The Banner of Islam). Police investigations showed that Fakhr-Ara'i had a highly religious family background. He was also found to have had a long and intimate relationship with Mahin Eslami, a woman of less than perfect reputation whose father worked as chief gardener at the British Embassy in Tehran. The Shah had wanted his assailant alive and had shouted to his entourage not to kill Fakhr-Ara'i. In the heat of the moment, however, no one had listened.

It was with similar haste that the government announced that Fakhr-Ara'i had been a member of the Tudeh Party and had acted on orders from the Communist leadership. Exploiting the mood of anger created by the assassination attempt throughout the country, the government, headed by Mohammad Sa'ed, announced Tudeh's dissolution and issued arrest warrants for its leaders. A bill to ban Tudeh was presented to the Majlis by Interior Minister Manuchehr Eqbal, a protégé of Princess Ashraf. Within a few days hundreds of Tudeh activists were seized and Tudeh offices throughout the country occupied by police. With the help of the Soviet embassy the principal Tudeh leaders escaped the net. Several of them stayed in the embassy for months before they were smuggled out of Iran into the USSR. The entire Tudeh case was based on documents allegedly found at Fakhr-Ara'i's flat that showed he had joined the party. There was no independent inquiry, however, and a number of alternative theories regarding the provenance of the plot were never studied. Forty years later, however, Princess Ashraf was categorical: 'We knew that Fakhr-Ara'i had fired his gun on orders from religious fanatics.'[28]

The Government used the incident as a pretext for smashing Tudeh once and for all. Tudeh did have a terror organisation at the time under the command of Nureddin Kianuri and had already murdered a number of opponents including the journalists Mohammad Massud and Ahmad Dehqan. But killing the Shah does not seem to have ever been discussed even within the terror committee.

The Islamic terror network known as Fedayian Eslam (Islam's Fedayeen) was already responsible for the murder of a dozen prominent personalities including two ministers.[29] It had several reasons for detesting the Shah to the point of desiring his death, if only because he was the son of his father. To the Fedayeen Reza Shah represented absolute evil that had to be 'eliminated for seven generations after him'.[30] Unlike the traditional mullahs who were by now convinced that Mohammad-Reza Shah was fully acceptable as a good Muslim, the fundamentalists wanted his blood for the alleged sins of his father.

There was another – and more immediate – reason for suspecting the fundamentalist terror gang rather than Tudeh. The Iranian government had angered fanatical Muslims by allowing large number of Iraqi Jews to come to Iran on their way to Palestine. Many of these new arrivals had stayed in Iran and created a network of support for the emerging state of Israel. Iranian Jews, at first indifferent to Zionist aspirations, were dragged into the pro-Israel movement under pressure from their Iraqi coreligionists. In some provinces, fundamentalist Muslims became involved in violent clashes with Zionist propagandists. Even the traditional mullahs were angered by pro-Israeli activity and sent a number of cables to the Shah and the prime minister to seek support for the Palestinians. Ayatollah Sayyed Abol-Qassem Mussavi Kashani, a personal friend of the Mufti of Jerusalem, Haj Amin al-Hussaini, had even created a register of Iranian volunteers for jihad in Palestine. The government, however, had refused to stop the Zionists as they did not violate Iranian law. The fundamentalists – and a majority of ordinary Muslims as well – were further enraged when the Sa'ed government extended *de facto* recognition to the newly-proclaimed state of Israel.

The creation of Israel was a particularly painful event for most Muslims who saw it as a Judeo-Christian plot against Islam. Israel came into being at a time when Islam was, for the first time in centuries, developing self confidence, fostered by the accession of several Muslim nations to full independence and the creation of two large Muslim states: Indonesia and Pakistan.

After 1979 the attempt on the Shah's life was officially claimed by the fundamentalists as part of their own 'treasury of heroic deeds', and Fakhr-Ara'i was named a hero-martyr of Islam. In 1949, however, the Shah regarded the Communists as his deadliest enemies and did not believe that his throne might one day be threatened by fundamentalist Muslims.

The Man from Ashtian

When the Shah left the hospital where he had been treated for superficial wounds received in the abortive attempt on his life in February 1949 he was, by all accounts, a changed man. This was not because he was wearing a moustache, grown to hide the scar left above his mouth by the passage of a bullet. He told confidants that God had given him a second life in which to achieve 'something'. The drama of the assassination had made of the Shah a 'living martyr', a highly-admired and enviable position in the eyes of most Iranians at the time. He was the Shah of the shi'ites and had survived a plot by atheist Communists.

The moustache the Shah now sported made him look older – he had just passed his 29th birthday – and added to his authority in a society that associated facial hair with manliness. With the exception of the eunuch king Agha Mohammad Shah Qajar, Mohammad-Reza had been the first clean-shaven Iranian monarch. To most Iranians, a man's moustache was the supreme gauge of his honour. Men would take oaths on their moustache. A hair from a moustache could be used as surety for a loan or the honouring of a commercial contract. Mohammad-Reza's earlier decision to lift the ban that his father had imposed on the wearing of beards had brought him much popularity. Now his new moustache moved him closer to the hearts of his people.

Seizing this opportunity the Shah moved to expand his constitutional powers. A senate was established as an upper chamber of parliament. It was to have 60 members with the Shah appointing half. The politicians who secured a majority in the lower chamber, the Majlis, would no longer be able to do practically as they pleased.

The Shah had disagreed with Ahmad Qavam on most points, but he fully shared Qavam's view that the United States should be invited to Iran as a power capable of counterbalancing both Great Britain and Russia. The only difference was that the Shah wanted to handle the American connection himself. One of the Shah's principal aims at the time was to revive the Iranian armed forces and help them achieve the level of strength they enjoyed under his father. With Germany no longer a potential source of weapons, the Shah had little choice but to turn to the United States. The choice of either Russia or Britain as partners in rebuilding Iran's army would have revived the international rivalries and intrigues of pre-Pahlavi times.

As early as 1946 the American Ambassador, George Allen, had become a personal friend. Rather than pursuing American policy in Iran – at that time Washington had no clear political goals in the country – Allen began to act as the Shah's advocate with decision-makers in the United States. It was Allen who persuaded Washington to jettison Qavam and side with the Shah. It was to keep contacts with the United States under his own control that the Shah dispatched Princess Ashraf to New York and Washington in the summer of 1947 where she was welcomed by major American political figures including President Truman and Secretary of State George Marshall. Soon after that visit the small American technical group in Tehran was expanded into a full-scale military mission known as ARMISH.[1]

By November 1949 when the Shah arrived in the United States on his first state visit – after a brief stay in London, no doubt to reassure the British – a growing number of American private businesses had already established a foothold in Iran. The Shah had also sent two of his half-brothers to study at Harvard.

Before leaving on his state visit the Shah, acting on the advice of the American Ambassador, shaved his moustache. He was made to understand that most Americans associated the moustache with dictatorship and that his best bet was to appear as a democratic and reforming sovereign. The initial purpose of the moustache had, in any case, disappeared – a simple surgical operation had removed the scar left by Fakhr-Ara'i's bullet. The state visit to America lasted nearly two months and was conducted by Washington as an initiation programme for the Iranian monarch, the State Department having hired a private public relations company to handle it.

During his stay in the United States the Shah had fairly extensive meetings with leading Americans including Truman and almost all key members of his administration. He also travelled to eight states, including California and Arizona. He spoke at more than a dozen public meetings and met scores of Americans from all walks of life. He was greeted with 21-gun salutes at West Point and Annapolis, the American naval academy, and was feted by arms manufacturers on more than one occasion. He found America fascinating and believed that he had learned how to deal with the Americans.

In his talks with Truman and Secretary of State Dean Acheson the Shah formally asked for American financial aid. Both men politely refused. Instead, they gave the Shah mini-lectures on the advantages of reform and liberalisation. The Shah, with the Azerbaijan experience still fresh in his mind, wanted money and arms to resist any further Communist threat. The Americans told him that improving the living conditions of the poor and opening the decision-making process to participation by new political forces constituted better defences against Communism. More important, they reminded the Shah that Iran was not a poor country and, thanks to its vast oil resources, could well pay for its own economic and social transformation. Indirectly – and probably without even meaning to do so – the Americans focused the Shah's attention on the necessity of getting a better deal for Iran's oil from Britain.

While in California the Shah was seen escorting a local beauty named Ruth Stevens and American magazines were soon full of pictures and reports about the American 'girl next door' who would become the queen of fabulous Persia. Rumours that the Shah would announce his engagement to Miss Stevens soon reached Tehran and caused a sensation. The Dowager Queen and Princess Ashraf had to dispatch a joint emissary to California to warn the Shah that his American flirtation, already damaging enough, should be taken no further. It seems unlikely that the Shah had ever seriously envisaged taking an American bride. While in the United States he was seen in the company of several other beautiful women, including film stars such as Gene Tierney and Yvonne de Carlo who subsequently visited Tehran as private guests of the Shah.

The Ruth Stevens episode persuaded the Pahlavis back in Tehran that a new and more suitable bride should be found for the Shah. Several leading families began to promote their marriageable daughters as possible candidates. The Court Minister Hossein Ala's ambitious wife was especially active on behalf of their daughter, Irandokht. On his return to Tehran the Shah was presented with a series of photos of suitable would-be queens. He studied them with the help of Ernest Perron who proved extremely difficult to please. He would find one girl too fat and another too thin. The Shah laughed at his friend's comments.

Finding a new wife was not the Shah's main preoccupation on his return from the United States. He was determined to do what Truman and Acheson had advised him and fired a number of notoriously corrupt officials. The move could not go very far, however: the entire Iranian administration was steeped in corruption. The Imperial Corruption-fighting Committee that the Shah created, therefore, soon faded into oblivion; some of its own members would have had to go to jail had the much-vaunted campaign been further pursued.

The Shah was, nevertheless, able to take two important decisions. The first was to begin distributing some of the land he had inherited from his father among the peasants who worked it. The distribution, carried out through the Pahlavi Estates Office, enraged the traditional ruling elites who were, themselves, large land-owners. At an audience at the palace a prominent politician even went as far as telling the Shah that 'some rumours exist about His Majesty having secretly converted to Communism'.[2] The Shah's second important decision was to strengthen the department of economic planning. Independent from the existing governmental structure the department was supervised by Prince Abdul-Reza, one of the Shah's half-brothers and a graduate of Harvard Business School. With the help of a number of American consultants the department had come up with a Seven-Year Development Plan in the first half of 1949 but it had quickly been pushed into the background by the cabinet who saw it as a potential rival.

The Shah's reforms did not lead to the arrival of substantial financial aid from Washington and the American message remained virtually unchanged: Iran should use her oil resources more profitably. All that Washington was prepared to do was to offer token technical aid through the Point IV programme plus a $25,000,000 loan from the Export-Import Bank. The Shah was bitter. This was 'a small fraction of the minimum necessary to rehabilitate our occupation-devastated economy. Such a serious setback convinced many of my people that the United States had deserted them, and anti-American feelings developed.'[3]

The idea of getting a better deal from the Anglo-Iranian Oil Company had for long been an attractive one on political and emotional grounds. Now it became attractive on economic grounds also. The end of the war and foreign occupation had resulted in no improvement in the lives of the masses and the government was even unable to pay its own employees regularly. The nation's financial situation was so desperate that no annual budget could be worked out even on paper and successive governments could do no more than present their budgets to parliament on a monthly basis. By 1950 it had become clear that the occupying powers were not prepared to help Iran repair the damage done to its economy by their presence during the war. Only Russia, in a bid to make Iranians forgive the Azerbaijan episode, offered a £10,000,000 credit line to Iran for the purchase of essential commodities.[4]

Negotiations with the Anglo-Iranian had dragged on inconclusively since 1946 and the company showed a surprising lack of tact and understanding in its relations with Iranians. Because it had bribed large numbers of influential politicians, mullahs, tribal chiefs, journalists and even Communist leaders, the company was convinced that it could always buy its way out of a tight corner in Iran. Anglo-Iranian constantly refused to send its senior directors for talks with Iranian ministers. When an American banker suggested that the Anglo-Iranian Chairman, Sir William Fraser, go personally to Tehran for talks, the British businessman sneered at the very idea. 'Good heavens, no!' he told his American visitor. 'Persians are like children and should not be taken seriously.'[5] Iran's income from oil at the time was just over $120,000,000, a fraction of what the Anglo-Iranian paid in taxes to the British Government.

News of Western oil companies offering better deals – including fifty-fifty agreements – to Saudi Arabia and Venezuela was widely publicised in Iran where public opinion could not understand why similar terms were not forthcoming from Anglo-Iranian. The British management also refused to offer an 'Iranisation' plan to enable more Iranian nationals to obtain better jobs within the oil industry. Iranian politicians became angered by reports that Anglo-Iranian used its profits in Iran for the purpose of developing new oilfields elsewhere in the Middle East.

Hoping to persuade Anglo-Iranian to adopt a more reasonable attitude, the Shah nominated Ali Mansur, a well-known Anglophile, as prime minister in March 1950. But the Majlis withheld its support for Mansur pending some evidence of his success in modifying the rigid Anglo-Iranian position. Within a few weeks, unable to report progress, Mansur was forced to resign. In June the Shah asked the Chief of Staff, General Haj-Ali Razm Ara, to form a new government.

Razm-Ara, a graduate of the French military school Saint-Cyr, had distinguished himself in the Azerbaijan and Kurdistan campaigns where he supervised operations against secessionist forces. Brave and brimming with energy, he was also known for his lack of scruples. In Mahabad he had promised to spare the life of the Kurdish leader Qazi Mohammad in exchange for the latter's surrender but had ordered the man to be hanged nonetheless. Always at his work at 5 am, never betraying the slightest emotion, Razm-Ara, despite the fact that he was short and of slight build, began to appear like a new Reza Khan. People had already started to wonder about his real ambitions. Did he want to push out the young and indecisive Shah and claim the crown for himself? Or did he harbour republican dreams? Razm-Ara had even been suspected of an indirect role in the failed attempt on the Shah's life.

Why did the Shah choose Razm-Ara as prime minister? The standard reasons cited at the time and later were the monarch's need for a strong man to cope with the wily politicians, and his belief that by associating the armed forces with national politics he would enhance the influence of the monarchy. A simpler explanation, however, might seem more plausible: with Razm-Ara as Chief of Staff the Shah would not have been able to take full control of the army for himself. Razm-Ara was a tough soldier with a following of his own among army officers and might have stood up to a young monarch with virtually no military experience. Also, the Shah knew that prime ministers did not stay long in office. Thus Razm-Ara, aged 49, would be pushed out of both Iranian political life and his military career too after a few months. He would be rendered harmless. It is also possible that the Shah's American friends encouraged him in the choice.

Within three months of his accession to the premiership, Razm-Ara was identified by both Princess Ashraf and the Dowager Queen as an enemy. The new prime minister stopped government funds that had been allocated to a charity headed by Ashraf. More important, Razm-Ara had launched a reform programme of his own and also conducted the oil negotiations in the utmost secrecy. The Shah had to read the Tehran newspapers for information regarding his prime minister's policies and programmes. Taj al-Moluk went to the holy shrine at Rey, near Tehran, to ask the saint buried there to remove Razm-Ara, and Princess Ashraf, who had no firm religious beliefs, went to a Roman Catholic church to light six candles and make the same wish.[6]

Razm-Ara certainly tried to act as an independent prime minister, in accordance with the Constitution. He also multiplied his contacts with the US embassy and encouraged rumours about his own special relations with the Americans. The *New York Times* ran an editorial praising Razm-Ara and the US embassy in Tehran was promoted to the level of a first class diplomatic mission on Truman's order. When it came to actual financial aid, however, Washington proved unforthcoming. A team sent to survey Iran's demands rejected Razm-Ara's application for an aid package worth $100,000,000 and instead recommended a $25,000,000 loan on far from attractive terms. The US thus continued to push Iran towards confrontation with Britain over oil revenues.

Whether or not he sought supreme power for himself, Razm-Ara did nothing that could be interpreted as hostile to the Shah or his family. On the contrary, it was Razm-Ara who, in the teeth of opposition from many quarters, organised the return to Tehran of Reza Shah's mortal remains. For more than five years the Shah had tried to achieve this without success. The sumptuous mausoleum built to house the mummified corpse of the first of the Pahlavi kings in south Tehran had remained empty. Razm-Ara not only brought 'the greatest son of Iran in many centuries' back home from Cairo but also organised a hero's burial for the man who had founded the nation's modern armed forces. The prime minister also asked the Majlis to grant Reza Shah the title of 'Great', a title given to only three other Iranian Shahs during 2500 years of monarchy.[7] This was a slap in the face for Britain and Russia who had forced Reza Shah into abdication and exile.

Razm-Ara conducted his negotiations with Anglo-Iranian in utmost secrecy. Early on he was convinced by the company's technical experts that Iran was in no position to run her oil industry without British help for a long time yet. Thus he began to aim at securing for Iran the best deal possible short of full nationalisation of oil. By this time, however, the idea of nationalisation, first put into circulation in Tehran by a number of American oil executives and experts, had captured the imagination of many Iranians.

Since 1944 Mossadeq had consistently spoken about the necessity of getting a better oil contract but had never raised the possibility of nationalisation. Then in 1950 he began to advocate nationalisation, apparently persuaded by his younger and more militant associates, notably the journalist Hossein Fatemi. As a popular and highly-respected senior politician, Mossadeq was a powerful voice in favour of a policy that Razm-Ara was determined to oppose and the prime minister was clearly trying to swim against the tide. When the issue of nationalisation was raised at the Majlis, Razm-Ara committed the fatal mistake of reading a text prepared by Anglo-Iranian with the aim of refuting nationalisation without having taken the trouble to edit it to make it sound like the speech of a prime minister. It appeared as if the prime minister had been recruited by Anglo-Iranian's public relations office.

The Shah, never adequately informed about what was going on behind the scenes, followed the unfolding of the oil drama with a mixture of satisfaction at Razm-Ara's ineptitude as a politician and concern about the growing mood of xenophobia in the country. At the same time the monarch's mind was focused on another important topic: the choice of a new wife capable of producing an heir.

For more than a year several members of the Pahlavi family had been scouting in Iran and abroad for a suitable bride for Mohammad-Reza Shah. Princess Shams, the Shah's elder sister, and Princess Fatemeh, a half-sister, were especially active in this field. Shams had been banished by the Shah after she had divorced her husband, Fereidun Jam, and married Ezzat-Allah Minbashian, the son of an army musician.[8] She now wanted to regain at least part of her lost status within the family by engineering a suitable marriage for the Shah. Fatemeh's motive was almost the same. She had married an American adventurer named Patrick Hilliyer against the express orders of the Shah. She, too, wanted to persuade her brother to accept Hilliyer, now converted to Islam and going around under the name of Ali Agha.

The girl that Shams and Fatemeh chose as their candidate for the position of future queen was an 18-year-old mixed race named Soraya Esfandiari. The Shah, advised by Perron, had just rejected Ashraf's candidate, a mixed race girl named Nina Bakhtiar, and was open to new suggestions. When photos of Soraya arrived in Tehran the Shah and Perron instantly agreed that the girl was worth a closer look. Shams was given the mission of bringing Soraya to the court.

Soraya was at that time in London, living in a bedsitter in Kensington and attending a private English language school. Soraya was the daughter of Khalil Esfandiari, a minor tribal chief with links with the Bakhtiari confederation of clans; his wife was Eva Karl, born in Moscow but of German and Baltic extraction. The Karls had fled Russia after the revolution and settled in Berlin where Khalil met Eva in 1926. Khalil was a student at Berlin University and Eva worked in a restaurant to earn a living. They married in 1926 and two years later Khalil took his bride to Isfahan. It was there that Soraya was born on 22 June 1932.

When the idea of making Soraya queen was first raised Khalil Esfandiari was in great financial difficulties, partly as a result of his gambling excesses during frequent visits to European casinos. The

Esfandiaris had returned to Europe and settled in Switzerland in 1947 and Soraya had finished her schooling in Montreux and Lausanne.

In September 1950 a triumphant Shams arrived in Tehran with Soraya and a few days later the Dowager Queen organised a dinner party, ostensibly to present Soraya to the Shah's sisters and brothers. In the course of the dinner, however, the Shah himself appeared, wearing his favourite Air Force uniform, clearly determined to win Soraya's heart. Soraya, unprepared for a meeting with the Shah, did not recover from her surprise for the rest of the evening. The Shah, however, was immediately convinced that Soraya was the girl he wanted.

The party continued with a series of society games in which the Shah took an active part. Shams and Fatemeh had seized the opportunity for smuggling their respective husbands into the family reunion and the family had not been so happy since 1940. Before leaving the party the Shah asked Shams to seek the hand of Soraya on his behalf. The question was put to Soraya soon after she had returned to her uncle's home where she was staying and she asked to think the matter over. She was told the Shah had demanded an answer that same night. 'Well,' she said. 'In that case my answer is yes.' She then burst out laughing before retreating to her room.[9] The following day the date of the wedding was fixed for 26 December.

The brief period of courting was, by all accounts, one of the happiest moments in the Shah's life. He tried to impress his bride-to-be with his dexterity in piloting a variety of military and civilian aircraft. He took her riding in the foot-hills of Shemiran and taught her to play tennis. The couple inspected the various royal palaces so that Soraya could choose the one she would want to use as their future home. She was 'horrified' by the sad state of the palaces. The largest, the Marble Palace, was rejected because Soraya felt suffocated by so much marble and so many mirrors in a building that delighted the *nouveaux riches* but symbolised bad taste for most Iranians. Saadbad, north of Tehran, had a pleasant garden but offered only one bathroom for the whole of the palace, used not only by the royals but also by the 300-strong army of domestic servants and guards.

Soraya finally chose a fairly modest villa on Pasteur Avenue and decided to refurbish it as the future royal residence. A French decorator offered to do the work for £35,000. The Shah said he could not afford this and arranged for an Iranian contractor to tidy up the villa. One day at lunch he offered his fiancée a lengthy explanation of her future duties as queen. 'Do not believe that I can offer you an easy life,' he told her. 'I hope you have no illusions on that score.'[10]

The couple's idyll was brutally interrupted when, three weeks after her arrival in Tehran, Soraya fell seriously ill with typhoid of which there was an epidemic in the capital. As various doctors failed to stop Soraya's fever, it was announced that the wedding would no longer take place at the announced date. It was in some desperation that the Shah agreed to let Lieutenant-Colonel Karim Ayadi, a veterinary surgeon with the army, try where others had failed: to save Soraya from what looked like certain death.

Ayadi was a personal friend of the Shah from Military Faculty days then engaged as veterinarian attached to the royal stables. At the same time he attended the Tehran Medical School on a part-time basis with a view to obtaining a medical degree. Ayadi administered what Soraya later described as a miracle drug and the future queen soon began to recover. 'Ayadi saved my life,' Soraya later told everyone, but what the veterinarian had done was no more than a clever gamble with aureomycin, a new drug about which he had read in a French medical journal. The miracle medicine had been flown to Tehran from the United States. Ayadi, now strongly supported by Soraya, was named Chief Royal Physician four years before he obtained his doctorate.

The wedding finally took place on 12 February 1951. Soraya was still too weak to wear the massive bridal gown designed and made for her by Christian Dior. To reduce the weight of the gown, the Shah and Ayadi, each using a pair of scissors, cut off the 10-yard train as the French *couturiers* watched in horror. Ayadi also ordered his grateful patient to wear a woollen jumper over her wedding dress until the very last moment and under no circumstances to take off the woollen army socks that she had put on before getting dressed. February in Tehran is extremely cold and the bride was further protected with a heavy fur coat. When the Iranians saw pictures of their new queen, they felt reassured: unlike Fawziah who had been considered too bony for Persian tastes, Soraya appeared well-built and wholesome. Only evil tongues described her as 'positively fat.'

At the wedding the Shah wore a uniform designed on his own instructions and looked like a lift-boy in an old-fashioned hotel. He had never paid much attention to his clothes since becoming king and it was not until the 1970s that he began to order his suits and uniforms from French designers.

The wedding lacked much of the glitter of the Shah's marriage to Fawziah nearly 12 years earlier. There were no foreign guests and no seven day and seven nights festivities in accordance with Persian tradition. Times were hard and the Shah did not wish to appear extravagant. The day after the wedding the couple left for the Caspian resort of Babolsar for a two-week stay during which Soraya would complete her convalesence. A full honeymoon was to come later in the spring when the royal couple planned to make a round-the-world trip.

When they returned from Babolsar the atmosphere in the capital had already changed to one of intrigue and agitation. Despite its official dissolution, Tudeh had resumed activity as the United Anti-Colonial Front. Islam's Fedayeen, now openly supported by Ayatollah Kashani, had joined forces with Mossadeq and his National Front supporters in an anti-British campaign of growing popularity. Despite rising political tension the Shah was determined to take his bride on a real honeymoon and the local Dutch airline agent was charged with the task of establishing an itinerary for their round-the-world tour. On 7 March 1951, however, the honeymoon plan had to be dropped.

Early that morning Razm-Ara had gone to the main mosque in Tehran to attend a memorial service organised for Grand Ayatollah Fayz who had died a few days earlier. A few minutes after entering the courtyard of the mosque the prime minister was shot and killed by a young man who immediately gave himself up. The prime minister was dead before he could receive any medical attention. The assassin at first introduced himself with his *nom de guerre* of Abdallah Mowahed Rastegar, but he was quickly identified as one Khalil Tahmassebi, a carpenter working in the Tehran bazaar. It was also established that Tahmassebi was a member of the clandestine terror network whose hatred of Reza Shah extended to his son: Islam's Fedayeen. The network was led by a charismatic militant named Mostafa Mir-Lowhi who used the *nom de guerre* of Mohammad Navab Safavi. Mir-Lowhi had for years worked for the Anglo-Iranian Company in the southwest and despite his black turban and mullah's gear, was not a regular member of the shi'ite clergy. He had not completed any theological course and might have been accused of posturing in his newly-acquired identity as a mullah. The first rumours in a city where rumour was always preferred even to verifiable facts, linked Razm-Ara's murder to a British plot. Razm-Ara, so the rumour went, was America's man who therefore had been eliminated by the British through Mir-Lowhi's organisation. (Mir-Lowhi, of course, had been a British agent since early boyhood, the rumour-mongers insisted.) Another theory was that Razm-Ara had been murdered on the Shah's orders, through Princess Ashraf's shadier contacts. Recent research, however, has fully established that Razm-Ara was killed by the fundamentalists with at least the tacit approval of Ayatollah Kashani.

In the heat of the drama two men appeared as potential beneficiaries from Razm-Ara's death: the Shah and Mossadeq. Razm-Ara, a strong contender for power, was a major obstacle on the separate paths of both the Shah and Mossadeq, both of whom sought supreme power for themselves. The Shah was, naturally, in a better position to seize the opportunity offered by Razm-Ara's sudden removal, but once again proved hesitant and indecisive, appointing Hossein Ala prime minister.

Ala, a highly-skilled diplomat, was too much of a gentleman to be a central player in the rough game played by Majlis politicians in their savage struggle for power. By choosing Ala the Shah had, in fact, asked for a time out in a game where none was allowed. Unknown to the Shah – and to almost everyone else – Razm-Ara had obtained a major concession from Anglo-Iranian: the British company had agreed to offer

Iran a new contract with a fifty-fifty division on the profits plus concessions on the employment of Iranian personnel. Razm-Ara had kept the good news to himself in the hope of using it as his gift to the nation on 21 March, the start of the Iranian New Year. Had the Shah immediately appointed a stronger personality to succeed Razm-Ara, the Anglo-Iranian offer might have pushed Mossadeq's bitterenders into the background, at least for a time. But while the Shah hesitated, Mossadeq, aware of the potential popularity of the fifty-fifty idea, moved quickly to raise the stakes to a level at which the Shah would cease to be an effective player.

Before the confusion caused by Razm-Ara's murder could be dispelled Mossadeq propelled a bill through the Majlis which nationalised the Iranian oil industry. This meant that whoever became prime minister would have his hands tied in advance. The Shah gave the bill royal assent within a couple of days. Ala, isolated in the Majlis and openly defied by Tudeh and Mossadeqist demonstrators in Tehran, was threatened with assassination by Kashani who declared the new prime minister 'undesirable for Islam'.

The Majlis Anglophile majority that had panicked into passing the oil nationalisation bill now tried to regain the initiative by putting forward Sayyed Zia-eddin as the new prime minister. The Shah seemed favourable but would not take the first step: the Sayyed was too closely identified with British interests in Iran and the Shah did not wish to be seen openly on his side. A Machiavellian scheme was then worked out by the Majlis majority leaders, Jamal Emami and Hadi Teheri, to make the Sayyed appear as the only possible premier without involving the Shah in a dirty political game. At the session of the Majlis convened to support the new prime minister, Emami suddenly turned to Mossadeq and asked: 'Well, sir, why don't you become prime minister yourself so that you can carry out your nationalisation scheme?' The assumption was that Mossadeq, who had refused a previous offer of the premiership from the Shah, would refuse. Emami and Taheri believed that Mossadeq was a demagogue with no other objective in life except making trouble for the government of the day in order to become the darling of the mob and all the discontented strata of society. Mossadeq, the two politicians were certain, would never accept responsibility. To everyone's surprise, however, Mossadeq accepted Emami's offer that same day and put his name forward for the straw poll organised to appoint the new premier. The confused majority, unaware of Emami's original scheme, believed that the Shah and the British had endorsed Mossadeq and voted him in.

While all this was going on at the Majlis, Sayyed Zia-eddin was sipping tea with the Shah at the palace, waiting for a call from Emami to tell him that the scheme had worked and that the Anglophile leader would lead the next government. Then the Sayyed would have immediately kissed the Shah's hand and begun work. That afternoon, however, it was Mossadeq

THE 'GIANT' AND HIS CHILDREN. Reza Khan, who later became Reza Shah and founded the Pahlavi Dynasty, is seen in his Cossack uniform with three of his children in 1923. From left to right: Muhammad Reza, Shams, and Ashraf (*photo Henri Cartier-Bresson/Magnum*).

FROM THE FAMILY ALBUM. Queen Taj al-Moluk poses for a family picture with four of her children. From left to right: Princess Shams, Crown Prince Muhammad Reza, Queen Taj al-Moluk, Prince Ali Reza and Princess Ashraf (*photo Camera Press*).

A SWISS EDUCATION. Crown Prince Muhammad Reza with other members of the football team at Le Rosey School in Switzerland. The prince was captain of the team that won the 1935 football cup in the Swiss schools championship (*photo Popperfoto*).

Above: LEARNING THE CRAFT. Crown Prince Muhammad Reza accompanies his father Reza Shah during a tour of the provinces. Reza Shah took his son with him everywhere and tried to prepare him for assuming the leadership of a turbulent country (*photo Rex Features*).

Left: THE CHOSEN BRIDE. Queen Fawzia, the Shah's first bride, in an amateur dramatic performance at the Palace in Tehran. Fawzia was chosen as Crown Prince Muhammad Reza's bride by his father Reza Shah (*photo Popperfoto*).

Right: THE NEW SHAH. Prime Minister Muhammad Ali-Furughi greets Crown Prince Muhammad Reza at the entrance of the Parliament building in Tehran in September 1941. Minutes later the Crown Prince took the oath as the new Shahanshah of Iran (*photo Popperfoto*).

Left: THE MAN FROM ASHTIAN. Dr Muhammad Mossadeq, who led the movement for the nationalisation of oil in Iran. He was appointed Prime Minister by the Shah but quarrelled with him over the exercise of executive power (*photo Fabian Bachrach/Camera Press*).

Right: A POWERLESS SHAH. The Shah relaxes with one of his dogs. The picture was taken in 1950 when the monarch lacked any real power (*photo Henri Cartier-Bresson/Magnum*).

Below: THE RETURN OF THE EXILE. The Shah takes the salute at a military parade in Tehran in 1953, shortly after his return from a brief exile in Baghdad and Rome. On the left is General Zahedi who became Prime Minister in 1953. On the right is Colonel Nassiri, later head of the SAVAK (*photo Popperfoto*).

Left: THE ROYAL PILGRIM. The Shah, dressed in a
pilgrim's apparel, prays at the central mosque in
Mecca during a state visit to Saudi Arabia
(*photo Popperfoto*).

Below: A PEASANT'S GRATITUDE. The Shah tries
to restrain a peasant trying to kiss the royal feet.
The Shah's land reform project led to the
distribution of rural farms among more than three
million peasants (*photo Thomas Hoepker/
Magnum*).

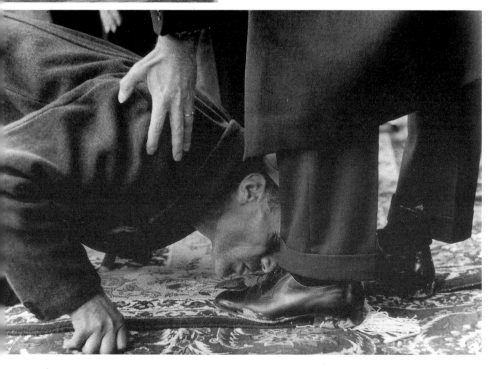

THIRD TIME LUCKY. The Shah with his third wife Queen Farah at a state occasion in Tehran after the birth of their first son in 1960 (*photo Popperfoto*).

AN AMERICAN IN TEHRAN. The Shah greets President Dwight D. Eisenhower at Mehrabad Airport in September 1958. Eisenhower was the first US President to pay a state visit to Iran (*photo Sergio Larrain/Magnum*).

Left: ON THE PEACOCK THRONE. Twenty-six years after his accession to the throne, Muhammad Reza Shah crowned himself in a state ceremony. The crown he wore had 3,380 diamonds, 378 pearls, five emeralds and two sapphires (*photo Popperfoto*).

Below: THE HEIR. A nervous young Prince Reza at the coronation (*photo Sygma*).

Left: ROYAL BANQUET. The Shah greets Queen Elizabeth II on her arrival for a Persian banquet at the Iranian Embassy in London during a state visit he paid to Great Britain in 1961 (*photo Popperfoto*).

Right: COMMANDER IN CHIEF. The Shah arrives for a military parade in Tehran in November 1977. In his later years the monarch spent much more time on building up his armed forces than any other task of government (*photo Abbas/Magnum*).

Below: LOYAL FRIENDS. The Shah and Empress Farah with President and Mrs Nixon during a state banquet at the Niavaran Palace in Tehran in 1972 (*photo Associated Press*).

THE BIGGEST PARTY IN HISTORY. The Shah reads his speech during a formal ceremony at Persepolis marking the 25th centenary of the foundation of the Persian Empire. Some of the Shah's royal guests are seated in the front row to his left (*photo Associated Press*).

who came to the palace for the traditional hand-kissing ceremony before starting work on the composition of his new cabinet.

Why did Mossadeq accept the premiership? One reason was that he was afraid of being thrown into prison in the event of Sayyed Zia-eddin forming the new government:

> If Sayyed Zia al-Din [sic] had become prime minister, there would have been no Majlis left for me to be able to pursue the matter [of oil nationalisation]. He would have had me arrested or sent into exile along with others, and, in one word fenced up the country so there would not be the slightest noise from anyone or anywhere to distract him from finishing his task.'[11]

A parliament dominated by a pro-British majority had chosen as prime minister a man who had made it his life's mission to end the British domination of Iranian oil and politics. On 8 May Mossadeq's cabinet, now formally nominated by the Shah, received the Majlis's vote of confidence. Of the 102 deputies who voted, only three were against.

Mossadeq owed his unexpected success to many different factors. The Shah's tergiversation had disorganised the old politician's opponents. Sayyed Zia-eddin's scruples regarding the Shah's constitutional prerogatives led to additional delays that strengthened the pro-Mossadeq groups. Teheri and Emami had proved to be too clever for their own good. Tudeh gave Mossadeq a helping hand through propaganda and strikes. Mossadeq also owed the fundamentalists a special debt of gratitude, not only for Razm-Ara's murder but for the subsequent campaign of violence that destabilised Ala's shaky government.* Mossadeq paid his debt to the fundamentalists by preventing Khalil Tahmassebi's trial. Razm-Ara's assassin was given the title of 'national hero' and returned to his carpenter's shop, announcing that he would be ready to kill again for the glory of Islam.

The Shah had first heard of Mossadeq through Ernest Perron. In 1939 the enigmatic Swiss had asked Crown Prince Mohammad-Reza, the future-Shah, to help save the life of 'a distinguished personality'. The personality was Mossadeq who had been banished to the remote eastern city of Birjand on the Afghan border. Mossadeq's relatives who contacted Perron claimed that the old man's youngest daughter had even gone insane because of her father's exile.[12] The Crown Prince raised the matter with Reza Shah and obtained an unconditional pardon for Mossadeq who soon returned to Tehran. Mohammad-Reza Shah was persuaded that he had thus saved Mossadeq's life. Mossadeq himself partially endorsed this view. He wrote: 'I missed no opportunity to thank the Shah for his intervention at the time, and until the last day of my office I did not take a single step against him.'[13]

*The campaign led to 17 deaths, including three Britons, in a series of riots in Tehran and the provinces. Meanwhile, most Majlis deputies received death threats from Islam's Fedayeen.

Mossadeq was, perhaps, just over 70 years old when he became prime minister. The exact date of his birth was never known as he was widely suspected of having changed the date at least once in order to qualify for membership of the Majlis. The electoral law made it clear that those aged below 30 and above 70 could not be elected to the Majlis and Mossadeq, who loved being a parliamentarian above all else, knew that he could not keep changing his date of birth for ever. When he became prime minister he was, in fact, bidding a final farewell to his parliamentary career.

Mossadeq's family originated from the small town of Ashtian, west of Tehran. His father, Mirza Hedayat, had been a successful bureaucrat who had married a Qajar princess and subsequently become a considerable landowner. Mossadeq's official biographies claimed that he had been appointed Chief Treasurer for the Province of Khorassan at the age of 15. The uncertainty about Mossadeq's exact dates makes that claim difficult to support. Nevertheless, Mossadeq must have been a precocious political genius for he was not yet 20 when he was discovered plotting against the Qajar Mozaffareddin Shah in or around 1901. He was sent into exile to Paris where, for a brief moment, he flirted with local socialist groups. He also tried to study at university but was soon too ill to pursue a serious academic career having developed a stomach ulcer and a mysterious 'nervous disease' which he continued to claim he was suffering from until the end of his life. That 'mysterious disease' often caused him to faint, at times in the middle of a speech or at a cabinet meeting. Was this a form of epilepsy or just a Mossadeq gimmick to win sympathy in a society where most people, because they were themselves victims of a variety of diseases, almost distrusted anyone who was in robust health. Mossadeq died at the respectable age of 86 and yet for 60 years he acted as if his next breath would be his last.

Mozaffareddin Shah had allowed Mossadeq to return home from exile in Paris because his mother claimed he was about to die far from home. Back in Tehran, Mossadeq married Lady Zia Saltaneh whose highly respected family background – she was born into a clan of religious leaders linked by marriage to the Qajars – gave the young politician additional political connections. The couple had five children and remained deeply in love until the end. Judging by Mossadeq's own private papers the two individuals who influenced him most were his mother and his wife. Mossadeq claimed that his main motto in life came from his mother who taught him that 'the weight of an individual in society is determined by the degree of hardship he endures for the sake of his people'.[14]

Mossadeq actively participated in the Constitutional Revolution of 1906, which briefly ended absolute monarchy, and was elected to the very first parliament in Iran's history as a representative of the aristocracy. In 1911 he returned to Europe in the company of his wife and first two children as well as his ever-anxious mother. He enrolled as a law student at Neuchâtel University in Switzerland and did research into the Islamic law of inheritance. He was 31 years old. After obtaining his bachelor's degree, Mossadeq wrote a thesis on the subject with the help of Ayatollah Muhammad-Ali Kashani. He obtained his doctorate of law and returned home in the summer of 1914 when his mother began to refer to him as Aghay-e-Doktor (Mister Doctor) and everyone around took the hint. From then on he was known as Dr Mossadeq as-Saltaneh.[15]

Mossadeq spent the next five years after his return to Iran teaching at a local law school. He also served in the ministry of finance. An active member of a political club known as 'anti-establishment democrats', he refused an offer to become Finance Minister in 1919. The excuse he cited was that he wished to return to Switzerland and personally supervise the education of two of his children who had stayed behind in Neuchâtel. Back in Switzerland he applied for Swiss citizenship in the hope of starting a new career as a legal expert. Swiss naturalisation laws, however, proved too complicated and required many years of continued residence before a demand for citizenship could be granted. Accordingly, he applied for permission to settle as a permanent resident and, prevented from practising law which was reserved for Swiss citizens only, registered as an import-export agent. Towards the end of the year he returned to Iran to sell his lands, wind up his financial affairs and say goodbye to his motherland, probably for ever.

During his initial stay in Paris Mossadeq had joined the Freemason's lodge of the Grand Orient. In Tehran he had been an active member of a local lodge headed by Moshir Dowleh and in 1919 that same Moshir Dowleh had been appointed prime minister and expected Mossadeq to help him. He asked Mossadeq to become governor of the province of Fars and Mossadeq accepted, thinking he would stay in the job just long enough for his financial affairs to be sorted out before leaving for Switzerland.

While in Shiraz, the capital of Fars, Mossadeq established cordial ties with resident British diplomats and military officers, especially a Major Meade, who served as Consul, and a General Fraser, who commanded the South Persia Rifles, a force of Indian and Baluch colonial soldiers. More than 40 years later Mohammad-Reza Shah used that episode as evidence that Mossadeq had, all along, been a British agent.[16]

There was no reason for Mossadeq to quarrel with local British officials who were mere executants of policies decided in London and New Delhi. In any case, as governor, Mossadeq had instructions from Tehran to maintain close relations with representatives of Britain, then the dominant foreign power in Iran. Furthermore Mossadeq was still thinking of one day obtaining Swiss nationality and did not even dream he would become the symbol of Iranian nationalism in an anti-British movement.

After Reza Khan's 1921 putsch Mossadeq decided to stay in Iran and served in a number of official positions. He supported Reza Khan's policy of reform but opposed his bid to become Shah.[17] This meant a period of disgrace that, with brief exceptions, Mossadeq spent out of office until Reza Shah's abdication in 1941. In the 1940s Mossadeq consolidated his popular base and was elected to the Majlis from Tehran. He maintained contact with Mohammad-Reza Shah through a number of channels, including the ever-obliging Perron. In 1949 Mossadeq and the Shah were unofficial allies in their separate efforts to end Qavam's premiership.*

During the 1949 election campaign, when Qavam was trying to fill the Majlis with members of his own Democratic Party, the objective alliance between Mossadeq and the Shah came into the open on at least one important occasion. As de facto leader of a disparate coalition of candidates opposed to Qavam's obvious plan to rig the election, Mossadeq encouraged his supporters to organise a series of demonstrations which the police dispersed with little difficulty. The organisers then decided to involve the Shah on their side and led a crowd of several thousand to the royal palace with the stated aim of seeking sanctuary there. Against Qavam's wishes the Shah decided to let the sanctuary-seekers stay in the Palace grounds and hold their meeting. Later, the Court Minister also received a delegation of 20 leaders of the demonstrators. When the group left the palace they declared the formation of a National Front (Jebheh-Melli) to fight in the election.[20]

Thus when Mossadeq assumed the premiership there was no apparent cause of dispute between him and the Shah. Mossadeq was no rabid revolutionary as far as the nation's political structure and economic system were concerned. An aristocrat and a major landowner, he could not have been a champion of radical socio-political reform. As a man with more than 40 years of parliamentary experience he could not have been the enemy of the monarchist 1906 Constitution. His basic aim at the time was to force the British to swallow the bitter pill of Iranian oil nationalisation and to this end he formed a broadly based government in which his National Front friends did not have a majority. The important post of Interior Minister was entrusted to General Fazlallah Zahedi and the first few weeks of Mossadeq's premiership were marked by the warmth of relations between him and the Shah. Mossadeq reassured the Shah by recalling a long-forgotten incident. In the 1930s Mossadeq, elected to the Majlis, had refused to take the oath of loyalty to Reza Shah before taking his seat. In the 1940s, however, Mossadeq regularly took the oath of loyalty to Mohammad-Reza Shah at the start of the Majlis sessions.

* Mossadeq and Qavam were cousins but had always remained political opponents. Their hatred of each other was to lead them to unpardonable excesses in later years. Qavam ridiculed Mossadeq's use of 'Dr' as part of his signature. 'What is he a doctor of?' Qavam liked to joke. 'Can he cure my ancient piles?'[18] Mossadeq in turn, described Qavam as 'semi-literate'.[19]

Meanwhile the idyll the Shah had enjoyed with his new wife began to be disturbed by a number of incidents. Soraya, who spoke Persian with a mixture of German and Isfahani accents, never quite mastered the intricacies of the language despite the efforts made by a number of eminent teachers. On New Year's Day the new Queen embarrassed everyone by suddenly stopping in the middle of a message to the nation during a live radio broadcast. Soraya had simply hit a word she did not remember how to pronounce — hours spent rehearsing the simple text had proved ineffective. Soraya burst out laughing as the whole nation listened.

Two weeks after that incident the Shah asked Soraya to banish her aunt, Mrs Forugh Zafar, from the royal court. Soraya was devastated: Mrs Zafar was her closest friend and confidante. A marital scene ensued during which the Shah accused Mrs Zafar of working as a secret agent for an unnamed foreign power and Soraya agreed to send her aunt and confidante into disgrace. The two women continued to have periodical secret meetings which, later, were discovered by the Shah's agents.

Soraya tried to even the score with the Shah and suddenly demanded that Perron be excluded from the court. The Shah immediately refused; this was the last thing he was prepared to do. His refusal came with such force that Soraya simply retreated.

The Queen, barely 19 years old, exasperated the court with her childish ways. She had a dolphin imported from the United States and a vast pool built. She then bought a water-softener to make sure that the creature suffered no hardship. At that time even the royal couple themselves did not enjoy purified water in Tehran. The dolphin followed the Queen everywhere in the palace, knocking down expensive furniture and drying itself on exquisite Persian carpets.

The Shah, however, loved his wife's childish ways and ignored mounting criticism from several different sources, including the Dowager Queen Taj al-Moluk who had never warmed to Soraya. The Shah was even prepared to understand Soraya's frequently demonstrated dislike of Princess Shahnaz and as a result, reduced the number of visits he made to his only child. The Shah had strongly criticised Fawziah's lack of interest in social welfare and other activities of public interest, but Soraya proved even less prepared to play the role of a benevolent queen. For the first time in his life, however, he was in love; and Soraya knew it.

A Prisoner of the Marble Palace

When he took over as prime minister in May 1951, Dr Mohammad Mossadeq was regarded by most Iranians as the ideal choice at an exceptionally difficult time. His age, family background and personal fortune reassured the ruling classes. His long and consistent campaign in defence of constitutional rule, combined with his militant anti-foreigner discourse, appealed to the still small but influential middle class. The poorer masses liked Mossadeq's promise of a better life thanks to oil revenues that would, once the British were beaten, begin to pour into Iranian coffers.

Mossadeq offered other attractive features as a politician. He had never been involved in any form of corruption at a time bribery, bakhshish and embezzlement were widespread at virtually all levels of the administration. Even his cousin Qavam, several times wealthier than Mossadeq, had not escaped the temptation of using the premiership for self-enrichment and offering illegal gains to his political allies and cronies. The traditional Iranian politicians – and Qavam was an excellent specimen of the breed – were firmly convinced that 'the populace' should be kept out of politics for the good of society. One of their favourite sayings was: 'The masses are like beasts!'[1] To them politics was one of the fine arts that had to be practised with great care by the chosen few in a complex, chess-like game of intrigue and counter-intrigue. Getting the ordinary, illiterate and hungry people involved would be a prelude to chaos. To get elected to the parliament, they saw no need for electoral rallies, public speeches and canvassing. All that was needed was to win the prior approval of the central authorities and then get the influential people in each constituency – the mullahs, the leading merchants, the landowners, the tribal chiefs and the military commanders – to send the 'beasts' to the polling stations with the desired instructions. The game was played according to strict rules observed by everyone regardless of personal rivalries.

Mossadeq, however, was a born actor and needed the largest audience he could get. He loved being loved by the crowds and was not comfortable with behind the scenes politics among only a few players. He enjoyed the open space, took pleasure in exercising his fine oratorial talents, and basked in the adoration of the crowds. In short, he was a populist, a lone wolf among oligarchs who totally ignored the well-established function of politics as a form of public entertainment. They enjoyed playing the game but shuddered at the thought of offering the populace a share of the excitement.

Mossadeq wanted to bring everyone in. He would tell excited mobs about details of his supposedly secret talks with, say, the British Ambassador. He would describe the populace as 'true makers of history'. On one occasion, addressing a street-corner crowd, he said: 'Here is the true Parliament! For the Parliament is where the masses are!' Mossadeq would change his tone of voice, gesticulate, wave his fist and, to take the drama to its crescendo, would simply faint amid the well-rehearsed lamentations of his aides: 'O, our hero is dying! The enemies of the people have killed him!' At a time when the majority of Iranians went either half-naked or dressed in nondescript rags, the oligarchs wore finely-cut suits complete with neckties. Mossadeq, on the other hand, wore open-collar shirts and suits made of rough Iranian cloth. After he became prime minister he often appeared in his pyjamas plus his woollen dressing gown which he wore when he went out to address rallies of his supporters.

Mossadeq made the crowds laugh and cry. He confirmed their prejudices and superstitions and flattered their vanities – they were, in most cases, all they had left. They loved him, but did he love them? No one could know for sure.

The old politician spent most of his political career in opposition yet when he finally acceded to power he lacked a coherent programme. Even his decision to accept the premiership was taken on the spur of the moment for purely short-term, tactical considerations. When Mossadeq led the Majlis into passing the 9-point oil nationalisation bill on 20 March 1951, he gave the impression that it was the result of years of long and sober reflection. In fact, Mossadeq had been converted to the idea of nationalisation only 10 days before by the journalist Hossein Fatemi who later became Mossadeq's Foreign Minister and Abbas Eskandari, a Majlis member who, rightly or wrongly, was considered a British secret agent.[2] It was Eskandari who offered Mossadeq an exposé about the post-war Labour Government in Britain and its policy of nationalisation and Eskandari and Fatemi asked Mossadeq to study the nationalisation option for Iranian oil. The old politician said he would think the matter over and a few days later he surprised everyone by tabling the historic bill which immediately gained immense popularity among all sections of the population.

It is possible that Mossadeq believed that the Labour government in London which had organised the decolonisation of India and carried out a massive policy of nationalisation at home would be sympathetic to Iranian grievances over oil. Here was a perfect example of using a socialist technique to change a colonial situation in a backward country that had long suffered from imperialism. How could British socialists deny the legitimacy of the Iranian move? The answer to this question came very quickly. The British government led by Clement Attlee would not recognise the legality of Iran's move despite offers of compensation to Anglo-Iranian. The left-wing members of the Attlee cabinet, at first prepared to study Iran's case, quickly rallied to the jingoistic policy championed by Emanuel (Manny) Shinwell, who wanted 'Old Mossy', as Mossadeq was now described by Fleet Street, crushed and punished.

Mossadeq had no contingency plan and asked Washington to mediate. This came in the shape of a visit to Tehran, in July 1951, by Averell Harriman, President Truman's special envoy, but Mossadeq could not simply cancel the nationalisation law that he himself had fathered. And Britain would not negotiate on the basis of that law as a *fait accompli*. The American intervention was seized upon by Tudeh – now acting through a number of cover organisations – as an excuse for an anti-Mossadeq demonstration. Tudeh mobs clashed with the police and eight people were killed. Everyone expected Mossadeq to resign but, encouraged by Fatemi, he stood fast. Instead, he dismissed Zahedi as Interior Minister and referred the police chief to the state tribunal on a charge of misconduct.

The American Ambassador in Tehran, Henry F. Grady, continued to urge Washington not to abandon the mediation effort and it was partly thanks to his perseverance that Harriman stayed in the game. In August a British team, led by Richard Stokes, Lord Privy Seal in the Attlee cabinet, arrived in Tehran for talks. Stokes offered a face-saving formula: Iran's oil industry would be put under the 'umbrella' of a national company – thus preserving the principle of nationalisation – while a new fifty-fifty contract was drawn up with Anglo-Iranian who would receive a renewed concession.

Mossadeq, of course, could not accept the idea of a new concession. More than anyone else he had been responsible for rendering the very word concession (emtiaz in Persian) unacceptable to a majority of Iranians. Stokes understood Mossadeq's position and subsequently tried to convince the Labour government to further soften its stance on the issue, but the British Ambassador in Tehran, Sir Francis Shepherd, regarded Mossadeq as a charlatan who could not be trusted, even reporting to the Foreign Office that Mossadeq was an opium-addict and presumably acting under the influence of the drug. Sir Francis's tough talk was music to the ears of the Anglo-Iranian directors who had decided that 'Old Mossy' had to be taught a lesson. Within a few months British public opinion, led by the anti-Mossadeq campaign in Fleet Street, was so hostile to the Iranian position that any talk of a compromise with Tehran became an electoral liability for the now fragile Labour government.

Things were no better on the Iranian side. Mossadeq himself had fallen victim to a classical example of 'overkill' in his anti-British propaganda. He had so demonised the British that nothing short of a full and dramatic confrontation with Britain now satisfied the growing crowds that demagogues of differing shades continued to drag into Tehran's streets. Iran needed a major fight with one of the two powers that had traditionally humiliated and exploited her. The oil nationalisation issue quickly became an excuse for pursuing that fight to the bitter end. Mossadeq was intelligent enough to understand that, but he was not wise enough – not to say unselfish enough – to risk his own popularity by preventing the temperature of the nation from rising to fever pitch. At first, he had been the radical among radicals; soon he became a relative moderate compared to others who began to preach an all-out holy war against the entire outside world. The Tudeh propaganda machine and Hossein Fatemi must share the blame for constantly radicalising the popular mood in the country.

Had Iran been in a position to win a clear victory over Britain she might have benefited from the confrontation. Humiliating the former oppressor might have given the Iranian nation the self-confidence it so badly needed, but anyone with an understanding of the reality of the balance of power at the time might have known that Iran had little chance of inflicting the desired crushing defeat on Britain. The nation's economy was simply too weak and too dependent on oil income to withstand a long embargo imposed by Britain. Iran's armed forces were in no position to stand up to British sabre-rattling from bases in Iraq and Bahrain. The option of playing the Russian card, which in later years became a standard game in many Third World countries, was simply not available to Iran at the time: Russia remained as hated as Britain in the eyes of most Iranians, especially the religious groups who disliked Communism. Also Russia pursued its own selfish designs in Iran, notably with regard to oil, and could not be considered a disinterested ally. The presence of Tudeh made the Russian option still less attractive to Mossadeq and most Iranians.

Mossadeq had never visited Iran's oilfields in Khuzestan and had a less than perfect understanding of how the industry operated. Soon he was left with an idle industry that produced no revenue but demanded vast sums of public money to pay its employees. Rashly – once again motivated by a desire to remain popular – Mossadeq had agreed to keep all the 60,000 employees of the industry on the government payroll even though they no longer even went to work. The redundant workers spent their time either attending political rallies – where they found the Tudeh's programme attractive – or simply pocketed the government wage but took on other jobs as well.

The prime minister tried to sell some oil to non-British companies but the policy never got off the ground. The British Royal Navy simply seized the tankers carrying Iranian crude – described by London as 'stolen property' – and imposed an effective embargo. Iranian oil exports came to a complete halt for the first time since 1908. Mossadeq, always an excellent 100-metres contestant in the field of politics, found himself caught in a marathon competition for which neither he nor Iran had been adequately prepared.

Mossadeq's objective was, of course, right from the Iranian point of view. The presence of Anglo-Iranian had always been an impediment to the normal development of Iran's political and economic life. The company frequently interfered in domestic policies by financing its own candidates at elections and subsiding newspapers that served its interests. Large numbers of tribal chiefs and influential politicians, including some mullahs, had been among the beneficiaries of the company's secret funds for years and the company's decisions on such matters as oil offtake and price had a direct impact on Iran's overall economy. And yet the Iranian government had absolutely no say in either production quotas or pricing its crude.

The company could bring the government to its knees by reducing either production or price or both. In short, it acted as a state within the Iranian state. Even a strong and highly-centralised government under Reza Shah had not quite succeeded in gaining control of the company's activities and with post-war Iran apparently condemned to a series of weak governments, the company's potential for acting as a law unto itself was even greater. Mossadeq's contention that Iran would not achieve full and real independence unless she controlled her own oil was correct. The trouble was that he did not know how to achieve such a goal.

When the Stokes talks were broken off the British government and Anglo-Iranian filed separate suits against Iran at the International Court at The Hague. The basis for both suits was the 1933 contract signed between Reza Shah and Anglo-Iranian. Iran, however, could not accept the court's jurisdiction because this was a case of dispute between a country and a private company and thus was not covered by the court's authority. Britain then referred the matter to the Security Council of the United Nations. Mossadeq seized the opportunity and decided to present Iran's case in New York personally. In October 1951 he arrived in the United States – his only visit to the country – and made a passionate speech at a session of the Security Council. When the council decided to postpone a decision until the International Court had ruled on the issue of its own competence, the result was seen in Iran as a personal victory for Mossadeq. Britain retaliated by freezing Iran's assets.[3]

The prime minister went to Washington and held a number of meetings with President Truman and Secretary of State Acheson. But it was Deputy Secretary of State George McGhee, a sincere admirer of Mossadeq, who had been charged with the task of conducting the more substantive talks with the visiting Iranian delegation. Both Mossadeq and McGhee wrongly believed that the advent of the new Conservative government in Britain after general elections that saw Attlee defeated might offer a fresh opportunity for an amicable solution to the oil dispute.

The Americans offered what they thought was a way out of the impasse: Iran would agree to sell Britain oil at a discount – a figure of 65 cents per barrel was mentioned at one stage – in lieu of compensation to Anglo-Iranian. Acheson, persuaded by McGhee that Mossadeq was the only credible alternative to a Communist takeover in Iran, apparently believed that the new, and more militantly anti-Communist government of Sir Winston Churchill in London would see the wisdom of accepting the nationalisation of Iranian oil as a barrier to Soviet expansion. Mossadeq was asked to prolong his stay in the United States to give Acheson time to discuss the McGhee formula personally with Sir Anthony Eden, the new British Foreign Secretary. Acheson was disappointed.

The American politician met Eden in Paris for a series of tête-à-tête talks. Eden immediately rejected the basic American contention that Mossadeq was the best man to keep Communism out of Iran. Iranian society contained other strong forces capable of resisting Russian expansionism. There were, in fact, grounds for arguing that Mossadeq was already a Tudeh fellow-traveller and, unwittingly, was paving the way for Communist takeover. Eden referred to Britain's long experience in the country and advised Acheson to let London handle the oil crisis. The best America could do was to send Mossadeq home empty handed.[4]

The British position had, if anything, hardened under the Conservatives. Eden now wanted not only compensation for Anglo-Iranian's physical assets – including the world's largest oil refinery at Abadan – that had been seized by Iran, but also for the company's loss of revenue until 1990, i.e. until the end of the 1933 contract. There was, of course, no way for Iran to meet such extravagant demands without undermining the principle of nationalisation itself.

Mossadeq returned home after a briefing from Acheson. It is possible that McGhee gave Mossadeq a fuller account of the British analysis, including Eden's belief that alternative forces could be built up against both Mossadeq and the Communists. This meant that Mossadeq was now in danger of being toppled. He lost no time in trying to forestall such an eventuality, ordering the closure of the British consulates in January 1952 and strengthened the state of emergency rules that he had imposed right from the start of his premiership. He also carried out a highly-criticised general election in which he prevented some of his opponents from returning to the Majlis. The election process was simply suspended in many constituencies. In Tehran and several other major cities, however, the National Front and its allies won major victories that confirmed Mossadeq's popularity. As always in Iran, the prime minister's enemies began to look to the Shah as a potential ally and gave him apocalyptic prophecies about the nation's future under Mossadeq.

Mossadeq had had two influential personal enemies within the Pahlavi family since the mid-1940s. The first was the Dowager Queen who referred to Mossadeq as 'Khorus Jangi' (Fighting Cock) and disliked him for his frequent personal attacks on Reza Shah after the latter had gone into exile. Mossadeq's other enemy was Princess Ashraf who had quarrelled with the old man in 1949 during their first meeting. Ashraf had invited Mossadeq to join the board of trustees of her charity organisation and the politician had accepted. But the discussion had somehow been diverted to the issue of the Trans-Iranian Railway and Mossadeq had repeated his well-known position that the construction of the line had been Reza Shah's 'greatest act of treason against Iran'.[5] The meeting had ended with an angry Ashraf demanding a butler show Mossadeq out of the palace.[6] A few days after Mossadeq became prime minister, Taj al-Moluk warned the Shah to be on his guard. 'This man wants to end our dynasty,' she told her son. The Shah perhaps to placate the formidable Taj al-Moluk, raised the matter with Mossadeq through Court Minister Ala. Mossadeq responded by reasserting his loyalty to the monarchy and the person of Mohammad-Reza Shah.[7]

Early in 1952 the International Bank for Reconstruction and Development, no doubt encouraged by Washington, came up with a new formula for settling the Iranian oil crisis. The IBRD, a part of the World Bank, proposed to manage the Iranian oil industry for an initial period of two years, selling the crude it produced in Iran at $1.75 per barrel. Of this Britain would receive 58 cents, to cover compensation, and Iran 37 cents, the remainder being spent on production costs. Mossadeq at first agreed to work on the formula but quickly changed his mind and asked the bank to withdraw. The British government that by now did not want any settlement without Mossadeq's overthrow had scored a major point in their effort to persuade Washington that 'Old Mossy' would never accept any deal.

Why did Mossadeq reject the plan? The answer must be sought in the old man's psychology. He was more comfortable saying no than saying yes, as all his life he had opposed whatever accords successive governments made with foreign countries or companies. He was also vulnerable to pressure from his aides and confidants who had learned to manipulate him. 'Mister Doctor!' they would tell him, 'you represent the people's only hope. The people will not accept a compromise from you!' Mossadeq loved that sort of talk.

On his return from New York Mossadeq made a stopover in Cairo where King Farouk had been overthrown and colonel Gamal Abdul Nasser established as the new leader. Large crowds of Egyptians had given Mossadeq a hero's reception. Pro-Mossadeq papers in Tehran now described their champion as the 'beloved leader of the entire suffering humanity'. Mossadeq's special adviser on oil, Kazem Hassibi, and his Finance Minister, Ali Shayegan, played major roles in pushing Mossadeq towards an inflexible stance. But Mossadeq's 'evil genius' was, by all accounts, his Foreign Minister Hossein Fatemi. Mossadeq had no clear idea of where he was going or, indeed, where he wanted to go – he was a tactician and lacked the more complex strategic vision. Fatemi, on the other hand, had his own secret agenda: he dreamed of Iran as a republic in which he himself would exercise real power behind a facade provided by Mossadeq.[8]

The prime minister never discussed any long term policy on oil. He had never visited Iran's oil installations and did not want to know about the technical and economic issues involved. He made his policy on oil as on most other matters, on a case by case basis. Cabinet meetings were often devoted only to routine matters. Mossadeq feared that one or more of his ministers might be informers for the Shah or the British and seldom raised sensitive issues at cabinet meetings which often took place in his bedroom. Dressed in his pyjamas the prime minister would stay in bed while the ministers read their reports. Occasionally, he would fall asleep and ministers would have to wait until he reopened his eyes.

The new but incomplete Majlis renewed Mossadeq's premiership but in July 1952 he announced that he was unable to govern without extraordinary powers. He also sent one of his ministers, Baqer Kazemi, to tell the Shah that the prime minister would personally assume the post of Minister of Defence. The Shah, who had regained the position of Commander-in-Chief after years of effort and intrigue, was not prepared to let Mossadeq seize control of the armed forces through the back door by controlling the military budget as well as appointments. He told Soraya: 'It seems that we might soon have to leave this country.'[9] That night the Shah did not sleep.

When the Shah rejected Mossadeq's demands the latter promptly tendered his resignation. The Majlis nominated Qavam as new prime minister on 17 July. The Shah – who did not like Qavam – reluctantly agreed. His two choices, Allahyar Saleh of the National Front and Abdallah Mo'azzami, an independent parliamentarian with cordial ties with Mossadeq, could not have obtained a majority.

The returning Qavam, now 75 years old, was a pale shadow of his former self, lacking the mental and physical energy to cope with the situation. Years of exclusion from political power had destroyed much of his network of clients and supporters. His éminence grise was the journalist Hassan Arsanjani who was made his assistant. Arsanjani wrote a provocative statement on behalf of the prime minister in which he threatened opponents with the use of force and more than hinted that oil nationalisation might be scrapped. This was a fatal mistake. Despite the hardship suffered by most Iranians, nationalisation was still popular among virtually all classes of society. The match Arsanjani had dropped in the powderkeg produced the inevitable explosion. Tens of thousands of people poured into the streets of Tehran in defiance of martial law and demanded Qavam's departure. After four days of rioting in which some 30 people were killed, Qavam tendered his resignation and went into hiding. Violent mobs attacked and burned his home and would have lynched him had he been captured. The American Embassy offered Qavam its protection but the old statesman refused.

Not surprisingly there were no candidates for Qavam's succession – none except Mossadeq, of course. On 22 July he was reappointed prime minister with all his demands satisfied. On the same day the International Court of Justice rejected Britain's application against Iran. The British judge had voted for Iran while his Russian counterpart had abstained. This was to be Mossadeq's finest – and final – moment of triumph.

At the end of August 1952 Truman and Churchill sent Mossadeq a joint note to invite him to a fresh round of talks on a new formula. Mossadeq rejected the note outright. He must have known that by doing so he would cement an Anglo-American alliance against himself. Later, in October, he severed diplomatic ties with Britain and announced that his policy of 'cutting off the hands of the thief' (Khal'e Yadd) would be pursued with increased vigour. Psychologically he began to prepare himself for a fight to the bitter end. Unencumbered by complex, tedious and unglamorous negotiations that threatened to sully his good name, he began to rehearse the role of the pure hero who fights a host of native and foreign villains and falls, sword in hand, on the field of honour.

Iran needed a settlement of the crisis more than Britain. Mossadeq's prediction that Britain – and the West in general – would be unable to do without Iranian oil proved wrong. Oil companies developed new production centres. Saudi and Iraqi exports rose sharply and Kuwait was put on the world petroleum map. Oil prices steadied, then began to show a downward trend. At the same time Iran was feeling the effects of the economic embargo imposed by Britain. The nation's ruling elite, of which Mossadeq and his friends formed an important part, was badly divided. In the provinces law and order was breaking down despite martial law. Clearly the nation needed a leader who would bite the bullet and bring the dispute to a negotiated end. This had been the role that Foroughi had played after Iran's invasion by the Allies in 1941. Foroughi had been attacked by all and sundry and accused of betrayal and collaboration with the invaders, but he had been prepared to sacrifice his good name and, ultimately, his life in order to make the best of a bad situation for Iran. He had saved the country's independence and territorial integrity by bowing to the short-term demands of the Allies. Mossadeq, however, was not that kind of man. He liked to say: 'All I have is my good name' or 'I'll not exchange my good name for anything under the sun!'[10]

Once he had decided to fight to the bitter end, Mossadeq, much like a chess-player, began to remove all the pawns that he thought might threaten him when the inevitable showdown with Britain came. His objective – a correct one from his own point of view – was to deny 'foreign enemies' any credible base inside Iranian society. With no local allies, the 'foreign enemies' would either have to accept his terms or opt for full-scale military invasion. In the first case Mossadeq would become a victorious hero; in the second, he would attain the exalted status of a national martyr.

The first pawn that he took out was the Senate, which he abolished two weeks after the Shah had inaugurated it. Mossadeq could never obtain a majority in a chamber where half of the members were the unelected appointees of the monarch. Next, the prime minister disbanded the Supreme Court which might have questioned the legality of some of the decisions taken by his government. The Majlis, he controlled in two ways: by preventing the filling of seats left vacant and by asking his supporters to walk out whenever the going got rough for the government and thus leave the house without a quorum.*

Mossadeq then proceeded to purge the armed forces of senior officers loyal to the Shah and promoted his own supporters to positions of command. At the same time he put into effect a new Security Law under which many opponents of the government, including a number of newspaper editors were imprisoned. To teach other potential rivals a lesson Mossadeq also ordered the confiscation of Qavam's property and banished the dying man to Lahijan on the Caspian Sea.

Opposition to Mossadeq's increasingly dictatorial methods continued to grow. By the end of 1952 such prominent former supporters as Hossein Makki and Mozaffar Baqa'i had broken with him. Even Ayatollah Kashani now joined the opposition. Tudeh, on the other hand, began to throw its support behind Mossadeq through its many front organisations such as the Peace Movement, the Anti-Colonial Youth and the Central Trades Union. Then came a long overdue clash with the Majlis.

Mossadeq demanded the Majlis divest the Shah of his position as Commander-in-Chief and entrust military responsibility to himself as prime minister. The Majlis refused to include the issue in its agenda despite a favourable report from a seven-man parliamentary commission. Mossadeq had not yet absorbed this shock when the Majlis decided to name Makki, a Tehran deputy, as member of a watchdog committee that regulated the volume of money put into circulation by the government.

While the row with the Majlis was brewing, Mossadeq tried to persuade the Shah to leave the country. Through a number of Majlis deputies he put it to the Shah that matters might be helped if His Majesty were to take a much-needed holiday abroad. The Shah might have himself begun to think of jumping without being pushed. He was now virtually

---

*This tactic was known as 'obstrooksiyoon' from the French 'obstruction'.

powerless, a prisoner in his palace. He could not go on official visits even inside Iran without prior authorisation from the prime minister. People were increasingly afraid of calling on him and he could not even indulge in his favourite pastimes, riding, speed-driving and flying, for fear of being censured by the pro-Mossadeq and Tudeh press who now began to attack him in person. Soraya's constant nagging about how boring life was in Tehran added to the Shah's unhappiness. He became almost a chain-smoker and spent long hours playing cards with Perron and a few other friends. Rather than fighting back, he waited for events to unfurl, apparently resigned to his eventual dethronement by Mossadeq.

The Shah remembered those days in these terms: 'Mossadeq had relatives of Qajar blood and he himself had bitterly resented my father's coming to power. His policy was clearly to do everything possible to discredit the Pahlavi dynasty and to advance slowly, millimetre by millimetre a day, towards exterminating it.'[11]

This, of course, is an exaggeration. Mossadeq had no long term or carefully designed plan on any issue. And it would be difficult to prove, in a court of law, that he had taken any specific actions to end the Pahlavi dynasty. In 1953 he wanted to get the Shah out of the way so that the latter could not be used as a focus for opponents of the government.

Mossadeq's reading of the Iranian Constitution was original and unusual, but it would be difficult to prove it strictly illegal on all counts. The vague text of the Constitution could be read in two ways. One reading gave virtually all powers to the Majlis and the prime minister and regarded the Shah's role as largely symbolic. An alternative reading gave the Shah extensive authority as the head of all three powers – the legislative, the judiciary and the executive – as well as the commander-in-chief of the armed forces. Needless to say Mossadeq and the Shah read the Constitution in different ways and never bothered to compare notes or to seek a compromise. Supreme power is one of those things that simply cannot be shared.

Mossadeq might have treated the Shah as a son and helped him learn the intricacies of statecraft. The Shah was no less anti-British than Mossadeq had been. He had not forgotten how the British had driven his father out of the country and nearly sabotaged his own accession to power. As a young man the Shah also thirsted for action but Mossadeq would not give him even the tiniest piece of it. Forughi had used exactly the opposite method in dealing with the Shah with positive results for both men and for the nation. The Shah might have looked to Mossadeq as a father figure. He could have won Mossadeq's trust and even friendship by flattering the old man's inflated ego. Mossadeq took the initiative of shutting the Shah out of the nation's business and treating him as no more than a rubber stamp, but the Shah might have taken the initiative of reopening the dialogue with Mossadeq. He did not. The two men lived and worked on the same street; only a five-minute walk, even at

Mossadeq's slow pace, separated their homes. Yet in three years during which their fates, and that of the nation, remained interlocked, the two men never met alone. Leaving aside official ceremonies which Mossadeq had reduced to a bare minimum, the prime minister called on the king only once: on 28 February 1953. On that day Mossadeq had taken the trouble of going to the palace because he had been informed by the Court Minister that the Shah and Queen Soraya planned to leave the country the following day.

Mossadeq came to say goodbye before attending a farewell lunch for the royal couple in the presence of the full cabinet. Lunch had been fixed for 1.30 pm but the Shah had asked Mossadeq to come at noon so that there would be enough time for a substantive discussion regarding issues of national interest. The Shah received Mossadeq alone but, after a brief moment, asked the Queen to join him for a pre-lunch drink of tea with the prime minister. Mossadeq had no intention of talking politics with the Shah. All he wanted was to make sure that the royal couple left with a minimum of noise. He suggested that the Shah and his wife travel by road and almost incognito to the border with Iraq in order to avoid public demonstrations.[12] The Shah agreed.

The Shah and the Queen were by now the only prominent members of the royal family still in Iran, all others had been exiled on Mossadeq's orders. The Dowager Queen had been asked to leave for Switzerland and Princess Ashraf had been sent to Paris where, unable to receive money from Iran, she soon found herself in financial difficulties and had to borrow from the businessman Jamshid Jahangiri.

As the royal couple sipped tea with Mossadeq a large crowd began to form at the palace gates. The ministers who had been invited to lunch were telephoned and told that the rendezvous was off. Soon the prime minister heard the mob shout 'Death to Mossadeq!' He was badly shaken and concluded that there was a plot either to force him to resign there and then or to have him murdered by the mob. The crowd at the gate of the palace had been brought together by Tehran's leading cleric, Ayatollah Mohammad Behbehani. Ayatollah Kashani had given a helping hand by issuing a statement opposing the Shah's departure. As the crowd shouted louder and louder a messenger came to inform Mossadeq that he had received an urgent telephone call from the American Ambassador. Mossadeq immediately asked to be excused and said he would return to his office. At the gate of the palace the prime minister quickly realised that he would have to face a lynching mob so he returned and, with Soraya's help, sneaked out of the palace through a backdoor. On foot and half running, he reached his home before the mob could catch him. The police stopped the mob from attacking his home for a few minutes, giving him time to climb the wall and escape to the safety of the neighbouring American aid office. With the help of American technicians he managed to get away and reached the Majlis where a plenary session was in progress. At the session he told his own version of events, even claiming that he, too, was opposed to the Shah's departure.

Meanwhile, Ayatollah Behbehani's henchmen attacked Mossadeq's home and caused much damage. Later, a pro-Mossadeq mob arrived on the scene and the two camps fought a pitched battle in the street before being chased away by the police. Once calm was restored and Mossadeq was able to return home he struck back. He appointed a new Chief of Staff and a new Police Chief and asked Court Minister Ala to resign which the latter promptly did. A Mossadeq associate, Abol-Qassem Amini, was named Court Minister without the Shah's prior accord. The prime minister also ordered the early retirement of 136 senior army officers. Through Amini, Mossadeq informed the Shah that he was ending all personal contacts with the monarch. Even official contacts were reduced to the bare minimum. The Shah tried to make Mossadeq review his position but failed. Several attempts by the monarch to meet the prime minister at the home of the latter's son – Dr Gholam-Hossein Mossadeq – bore no fruit. The old man would not forget the humiliation he had suffered and was fully convinced that the Shah had planned the entire episode to force him out of office or even have him killed.

The newly created Security Committee, set up to by-pass ordinary courts, was ordered to meet every day to pass speedy sentence on government opponents. At the same time the new Chief of Police, Brigadier-General Afshar Tus, distinguished himself by his brutality in suppressing opposition rallies and sending his men to smash the printing presses of newspapers unfriendly to the government. He became the target of a counter-attack planned by Baqa'i and his friends who were now determined enemies of Mossadeq.

Baqa'i was the leader of the Toilers' Party of Iran and a Majlis deputy, as well as a formidable speaker and a highly talented practitioner of political intrigue. It was he who, with the help of a number of army officers, had the Chief of Police kidnapped and held hostage in Tehran. When it became clear that detectives would soon discover the whereabouts of the hostage the kidnappers had him murdered. The murder of Afshar Tus created a sensation and exposed the government as vulnerable. Mossadeq retaliated by ordering a series of indiscriminate arrests.

General Fazlallah Zahedi, meanwhile, President of the Retired Officers' Club in Tehran, had emerged as an outspoken critic of the government and Mossadeq wanted him arrested. To escape arrest Zahedi sought sanctuary at the Majlis, a right respected by tradition though not fully recognised under law. Zahedi's sit-in at the Majlis provided a focus for opposition. Every day thousands of people came to express their support for his cause while opposition deputies sharpened their attacks on Mossadeq. By June 1953 it had become clear that the Majlis was now a bastion of opposition to the prime minister and Mossadeq began to think of dissolving parliament.

His mind on this subject was made up when the Majlis chose Hossein Makki as member of a watchdog committee responsible for regulating the volume of new banknotes issued by the government. Makki, once described as Mossadeq's 'spiritual son', had become an outspoken critic of the prime minister because of the latter's indulgence in building up a personality cult. Mossadeq was now called Pishva (Führer) and described as 'The Father of the Nation' by his more sycophantic supporters. On these and other grounds Makki had opposed the extension of Mossadeq's extraordinary powers for a further six months.

Mossadeq had ordered the printing of 3.1 billion rials (about £30,000,000) in new banknotes without authorisation for paying civil servants and oil industry workers. The watchdog committee, made up of Mossadeq loyalists, had kept the secret. Now it was obvious that Makki, once he discovered the truth, would tell the whole world. On strictly legal terms Mossadeq might have been able to justify the extra notes he had put into circulation, but the immediate effect of the revelation would have been a sharp rise in the rate of inflation which had already eroded standards of living and created armies of new paupers throughout the country.

Since only the Shah had legal power to dissolve the Majlis, Mossadeq thought of a new stratagem for achieving his objective without risking a royal rebuff. Had the Shah been asked to dissolve he might have refused and thus appeared as the champion of democracy against a dictatorial old man. Mossadeq therefore decided to have 'the people' dissolve the parliament and organised a referendum – a measure not provided for under the Constitution – to send the deputies home, and have his own extraordinary powers extended. Only Tudeh enthusiastically supported the referendum idea. To speed up things Mossadeq decided that rural areas, where 70 per cent of the population lived at the time, should be excluded from voting. In cities, where polling did take place, people were invited to cast their ballots in distinctly marked 'yes' or 'no' booths. It was made abundantly clear that those who emerged from the 'no' booths would receive unwelcome attention from pro-Mossadeq and Tudeh tough guys who supervised the making of history by 'the people'.

With the Majlis thus disbanded the Shah was the only pawn still left on the opposite side of the chessboard. Mossadeq intensified his war of nerves against the monarch by having the tanks that guarded the royal palace removed and most of the soldiers attached to the person of the monarch sent to their barracks. He vetoed a plan for an official visit by the Shah and the Queen to Azerbaijan, and foreign ambassadors who wanted to call on the monarch were invited to clear the matter with the prime minister beforehand.

Mossadeq was totally mistaken in seeing the Shah as the central figure in a growing conspiracy against the government. The Shah was simply not the type and had rejected a series of approaches by a variety of groups who, by the end of 1952, were plotting against Mossadeq. These included retired army officers, the mullahs, members of the Majlis and leaders of the trade and professional guilds. More important, Britain had started to create a network of contacts that could, when the time came, be used against Mossadeq. The Shah was involved in none of these activities and almost certainly did not even learn about them in any great detail. Sulking in his palace, he was simply waiting for the worst to happen. His belief that only what is 'written' will come to pass rendered him largely inactive at a time of acute danger.

The network the British had created — and financed — to the tune of £5000 a month — was headed by three brothers of established Anglophile credentials.[13] Seyf-Allah, Assad-Allah and Qodrat-Allah Rashidian had begun working with the British during the war when their family had made a fortune by providing ancillary services for the Allied forces of occupation in Tehran and Isfahan.

Although they received a stipend from the British, the three brothers were not pure mercenaries. They were convinced that Iran needed to stay in the western orbit in order to escape a Communist takeover. In 1952 they believed that Mossadeq was paving the way for a *coup de force* by the underground Tudeh organisation. From November 1952 onwards the Rashidians and their political allies had began recruiting elements who specialised in mobilising the mobs that had always played a crucial role in Iranian politics. Mossadeq owed much of his power and prestige to massive mob support and the Rashidians began to fish in waters previously reserved for Mossadeq and Ayatollah Kashani. The fact that Kashani and other mullahs had now turned against Mossadeq facilitated the Rashidian brothers' task.

At the time no one had any precise idea about how Mossadeq could be dislodged. In any case, Britain would not move without first securing at least tacit support from the United States as the risk of a direct confrontation with Russia had to be taken into account.

Washington remained unwilling to move against Mossadeq until January 1953 when the new Republican Administration of President Dwight D. Eisenhower began work with John Foster Dulles as Secretary of State. Under Allen W. Dulles, a brother of John Foster, the CIA had long sympathised with the British view that Mossadeq had to be pushed out of office.

When Eisenhower's Administration took over from Truman's it lost no time in throwing America's support behind the British plan which received its final shape at the end of April 1953. The CIA code-named the plan Operation Ajax, from the name of a brand of detergent. The idea was that the 'red' of Communism would be washed out of Iran. The British chose the code-name Operation Boot: the aim was to boot 'Old Mossy' out of power. The American operational chief was Kermit Roosevelt, a loose cannon and adventurer who was put in charge of the entire scheme. The British, with their embassy in Tehran closed, could not play a direct role in the actual events planned.

The scenario, worked out by the British and supported by the Americans, was fairly simple: the Shah, exercising his constitutional right, would dismiss Mossadeq and appoint a new prime minister. Then, if Mossadeq or his friends tried to hang on to power nonetheless, the monarch's decision would be enforced by a pincer movement in which loyalist army officers would act in support of Tehran mobs. The religious leaders would provide the moral backing that the new prime minister might at first need. On the advice of the Rashidians it was agreed that the new prime minister should be a military officer. Professional politicians could not be trusted and the armed forces needed to be reassured. Informal canvassing in Tehran produced the names of three generals: Amir Ahmadi, Yazdan Panah and Zahedi, as most likely to enjoy the support of the officers' corps. Zahedi was chosen for two important reasons. First he was already active in opposition to Mossadeq and, second, he had impeccable anti-British credentials.[14] The swash-buckling, skirt-chasing Zahedi was also the youngest of the three and therefore best able to face the physical strain of what might have turned into a long politico-military crisis.

One important problem remained: how to persuade the Shah to play the role assigned to him in the scenario? First he had to be informed about the plan, and as a virtual prisoner in his Marble Palace at the time, the Shah could not be easily approached without Mossadeq learning about it.

8

Back from the Brink

Early in June 1953, Princess Ashraf, then an exile in Paris, received a surprise visit from Assad-Allah Rashidian. He told the princess that the stage was set for Mossadeq's overthrow with the help of 'strong forces at home and friendly foreign powers'.[1] He asked whether the princess would agree to meet with two emissaries of Washington and London to discuss further plans. She agreed and the meeting took place in the Bois de Boulogne, a public park west of Paris. The two emissaries were a British intelligence operative named Colonel C.M. Woodehouse and Brigadier-General Norman H. Schwartzkopf, who had served as commander of the Iranian gendarmerie for a number of years.[2]

The two men, with Rashidian acting as interpreter, informed the princess that 'a beneficial change' could come about in Iran provided the Shah agreed to cooperate. After a brief discussion they asked the princess whether she could deliver a top secret letter to the Shah in Tehran. The princess agreed provided she was informed about its contents. She was told that the letter assured the Shah of 'full support from the United States and Great Britain' if he decided to dismiss Mossadeq as prime minister and appoint Zahedi instead.

The princess agreed to go although her passport had been confiscated by the Iranian embassy in Paris on orders from Mossadeq. She boarded a regular KLM flight and arrived in Tehran on the morning of 25 June. At the airport she was whisked away from the runway by Mrs Khojasteh Hedayat, a personal friend who had bribed a few airport officials to look the other way. The princess went into hiding at the home of her half-brother, Prince Gholam-Reza. The prince's wife, Homa Alam, was a friend and often acted as informant for Ashraf.

News of the princess's return to Tehran was quickly leaked to Mossadeq and the old man sent a general to ask Ashraf to leave immediately. The prime minister also doubled the guards around the Shah's palace with strict orders that Ashraf should not be let in. Under pressure from Mossadeq the Royal Court issued a statement expressing the Shah's displeasure at his sister's return and called on her to go back into exile. As the war of nerves continued it became clear that Ashraf would not be allowed to see her brother. She was not even allowed to receive her own husband, Ahmad Shafiq, who had stayed behind in Tehran.[3] The princess finally decided to get the letter to the Shah through the Queen. She met Soraya in the garden of the Saadabad Palace for a few minutes only and the two women hid behind a row of rose bushes as Ashraf handed over the letter. The princess left Tehran for Paris the following day.

Mossadeq, meanwhile, issued an arrest warrant for General Zahedi, who had gone into hiding, and also imprisoned large numbers of potential troublemakers. Still hopeful of playing the American card, the prime minister extended his negotiations with the Soviet Union as part of his 'negative balance' policy. This was supposed to frighten the Americans and rally them to his side in order to prevent the domination of Iran by Russia.

The opposition, however, was daily gaining ground. A mass rally addressed by Ayatollah Kashani earlier that month had brought together more than 100,000 people – the largest crowd ever in the nation's crowd-dominated politics. It was becoming more and more clear that Mossadeq's organised support was mainly provided by the Tudeh Party and its splinter group, Niruy-e-Sevvom (Third Force), led by Khalil Maleki.

The Shah's procrastination was not ended by the letter that Soraya brought him. How could he be sure that he was not being led into a trap? Who would guarantee his own safety if the plan backfired? The Shah was not a man to take risks without a fifty-fifty chance of winning. In any case wasn't Mossadeq digging his own grave by turning virtually all powerful groups against himself?

In their brief meeting Soraya had told Ashraf that the Shah was thinking of leaving Iran, 'at least for some time'. The Queen herself kept complaining about the fact that she had not been to Europe for more than two years. Life at the palace was hard as Mossadeq had cut the royal lists to a bare minimum and on the rare occasions when a state banquet was organised at the palace the Queen had to sign for every item of jewellery she borrowed for the occasion from the crown jewels. A detective would be present at the banquet to watch over the jewels, which were immediately returned in exchange for a receipt. Mossadeq, who had earlier stopped the Shah from distributing his own lands among peasants, also decided to 'repossess for the nation' the wealth the monarch had inherited from Reza Shah. The value of the Shah's estate was put at around £7.5 million in February 1953. To forestall further pressure from Mossadeq the Shah transferred all his property to the government in exchange for an annual payment of 60,000,000 rials (nearly £300,000) to the Pahlavi Foundation, a charity the Shah set up at the time.

As the Shah failed to act the Anglo-American plotters decided to make yet another attempt at reassuring him about the chances of success against Mossadeq. In July Schwarzkopf arrived in Tehran for a 48-hour visit. His cover was a round-the-world tour that he had supposedly won in a lottery organised by an air company. Neither Mossadeq nor Tudeh were fooled and instantly called for the American's expulsion. Schwarzkopf nevertheless succeeded in calling on the Shah – a 'personal friend of many years' – and assured him of full American support for a policy safeguarding Iran's constitutional monarchy and combating Communism.

Even then the Shah refused to move. He asked Schwarzkopf to ask Washington to ascertain Britain's real intentions. This was done and two weeks later Roy Henderson, the American Ambassador, relayed a message from Churchill: Great Britain would support the Shah if – and when – he exercised his constitutional powers! Chief among these powers, of course, was that of dismissing the prime minister.

The success of 'Operation Boot' partly depended on its timing. On 10 August the Majlis term would officially come to an end, after which the Shah would become virtually the sole source of constitutional legitimacy in the country. His inaction, however, could leave Tudeh enough time to organise revolutionary committees at various levels and make its own bid for power. It had also become clear that Tudeh had succeeded in infiltrating the armed forces and might well oppose a coup against Mossadeq.

Kermit Roosevelt meanwhile had entered Iran illegally through Iraq. He managed to organise a secret meeting with the Shah on 4 August. The Shah said he would agree to the plan provided clear signals came from both Churchill and Eisenhower. He also said that he and Soraya would leave the country if and when the plan suffered the slightest setback. The Shah's rationale for this suggestion was that his dramatic departure would mobilise patriotic forces against Mossadeq and force a dénouement to a conflict that had continued for too long. The American agent agreed to relay the messages. The signals the Shah had asked for came in the form of two agreed sentences that were included in a speech by Eisenhower and in a programme broadcast by the BBC's Persian service.

On 10 August, the day the Majlis dissolution was to come into effect, the Shah and his Queen left Tehran for the Caspian coast in their car. Ernest Perron was left behind to mind the store, so to speak, and report to the Shah by phone. The Shah was supposed to sign the edicts (farman) dismissing Mossadeq and appointing Zahedi before leaving Tehran but the papers were not ready in time and it was agreed that he should sign them later at Kelardasht, the Caspian resort he was headed for. By the time the edicts had been sent to the north and duly signed before being brought back to Tehran it was 14 August and to keep anything secret for 48 hours in those chaotic days was well-nigh impossible. News that something unusual was afoot was given to Mossadeq by one of his clansmen, Mohammad-Hossein Ashtiani, who at the time worked at the Court Ministry.[4]

The task of delivering the two edicts was assigned to Lieutenant-Colonel Nematallah Nassiri, the commander of the Shah's personal bodyguard. Nassiri arrived in Tehran with the edicts late at night on 15 August. By the time he arrived at Mossadeq's residence it was 1 am on 16 August. The Lieutenant-Colonel, known for his brutality and courage but never for his intelligence, was not surprised to see the prime minister's residence had been turned into a fortress guarded by several tanks and an unusually large number of soldiers. Nor did he stop to ask why it was that the Chief of Staff, Brigadier-General Riahi, was at Mossadeq's side at such an unusual hour. Mossadeq received Nassiri, read the edict and then ordered the Shah's messenger's arrest. The old comedian had found a clever line: the edict brought by Nassiri was a forgery and thus a conspiracy against the head of state – that is against the Shah! Mossadeq, a loyal prime minister, had no option but to defend the monarch!

Nassiri, as delicate as a bull in a china shop, had made yet another gaffe before calling on Mossadeq. He had delivered Zahedi's appointment edict in the presence of several other officers, at least one of them with Tudeh connections. They promptly informed Mossadeq of Zahedi's whereabouts and the newly-appointed prime minister had to run for his life. Clearly, the Anglo-American venture had failed.

News of the failure was telephoned to the Shah by Perron before Mossadeq's men came to pick him up. The Shah had never really believed in the plan and now he clearly panicked. He and Soraya, accompanied by Mohammad Khatami, a junior Air Force officer and a pilot, drove to Ramsar where one of the monarch's light aircraft was parked on the local airport runway. It was aboard that plane that the Shah, Soraya and a couple of attendants flew to Baghdad. Soraya had taken the precaution of bringing her box of personal jewels with her. But the couple had only one change of clothes, shoved into a plastic bag, and no clear idea where they wanted to go. For months the Shah had thought of flying away but, as always, he had done nothing to plan his eventual departure. In Baghdad they were housed in a royal palace on orders from King Faisal, but the Iraqi king did not call personally on his uninvited guests. The Iranian Ambassador in Baghdad, on instructions from Foreign Minister Fatemi in Tehran, had instantly demanded the extradition of the royal couple from the Iraqi authorities.

Soraya was happy. The very fact of getting away from it all had ended her sombre mood and restored her lovely smile. The couple went to the holy shrines of Najaf and Karbala where the Shah may have looked for a sign from the saints who had appeared to him in his childhood. There was no sign and, back in Baghdad, they were given to understand that their prolonged stay in the city would not be welcome to the Iraqi authorities.

The Shah had for years promised Soraya a Roman holiday and now decided to make that dream come true. The next day the couple arrived in Rome. Soraya, convinced that they would never return to Tehran, began looking for a possible home in Italy. An offer of hospitality from King Farouk, himself now in exile in Capri, was politely declined by the Shah. Soraya also went on a shopping spree using 'a humble gift' of cash provided by a local Iranian businessman. A few hours later Princess Ashraf also arrived in Rome and immediately began pressurising her brother not to give up the fight.

Meanwhile, Tehran was in turmoil. The Tudeh had posted slogans on the walls of the city calling for the creation of a 'people's democratic republic'. The call had been indirectly endorsed by Fatemi. Ayatollah Kashani, now convinced that Mossadeq had definitely won, tried to renew ties with him in the hope of stopping Tudeh. Kermit Roosevelt was hiding in a safe house provided by the Rashidian brothers and already thinking of how best to escape with his life. Washington had ordered its Ambassador, Henderson, to leave Tehran to avoid complications if and when Mossadeq discovered the role of the US in the failed plot. The Rashidian brothers fled and were hiding in Isfahan. Riahi, the Chief of Staff, had decided that from 19 August onwards there would be no prayers for the good health of the Shah at army barracks and that he would reveal the new text of daily prayers for the army on that day at a ceremony at the Military Faculty in Tehran.

Mossadeq, for his part, was left with a complex situation. Although he had long desired the elimination of the Shah from the power game he had not foreseen the event as it actually happened. He had hoped that the Shah would leave the country in perfectly normal circumstances, as Ahmad Shah, the last of the Qajars, had done three decades earlier. But now the Shah had left after appointing a new prime minister. Technically, because he had not abdicated, the Shah was still the head of state. Should Mossadeq officially depose the king? If yes, how? There were no constitutional formulae. Theoretically, a constituent assembly could be elected to choose a new king or a new dynasty – or even a new system of government altogether. But who could hold elections under those circumstances? And what guarantee was there that the Shah's supporters would not win an election? For a day or two Mossadeq toyed with the idea of creating a Regency Council and the scholar Ali-Akbar Dehkhoda was even mentioned as a possible head of such an organ. Tudeh proceeded to destroy the statues of the Shah and his father in Tehran and provincial cities. The party also printed hundreds of thousands of new postage stamps carrying its own insignia in the name of 'the people's democratic republic' of Iran. The party also distributed thousands of photos of the exiled poet Abol-Qassem Lahuti, who had become a member of the Cheka, a forerunner of the Soviet KGB, and lived in Soviet Tajikestan. The party wanted to promote Lahuti as the first 'president' of a republic it was now certain would be created in Iran within a few weeks at most. On 18 August a *Times* editorial predicted that Iran was lost first to chaos and then to Communism.

Convinced that the royalist camp was defeated, Mossadeq began to think of building up his defences against a possible challenge from Tudeh. The Shah and many of his supporters claimed in later years that Mossadeq had reached a secret accord with the Tudeh leadership and was, in fact, a Communist fellow-traveller, but the latest research shows such allegations to be untrue. Mossadeq was as anti-Communist as any wealthy landowner with long experience of Freemasonry could be. He wanted all power for himself and certainly did not relish the thought of becoming an Iranian Kerensky. Mossadeq did delude himself with the thought that the West would not move against him for fear of pushing Iran into the arms of Russia. In his memoirs he says that the death of Stalin, in March 1953, had left his own government in Tehran fully exposed to plotting by Britain. At any rate it was to prevent Tudeh from gaining control of the streets of the capital that Mossadeq imposed a curfew that banned all demonstrations. He brought in a detachment of the army to help keep order and put his relative, Brigadier-General Mohammad Daftari, at the head of the National Police with orders to enforce the strict curfew.

Mossadeq did not know that Daftari was a passionate monarchist and placed his loyalty to the Crown above family relations with his kinsman. Then Mossadeq made another fatal mistake: he telephoned his leading supporters to ask that they keep their troops off the streets for a few days until law and order was restored. Pro-Mossadeq organisations thus received instructions to fully cooperate with the police and the army and the streets of Tehran were, thus, cleared for the pro-Shah crowds who were now also assured of police and army protection. The royalist leaders immediately understood that the balance of forces had changed in their favour and a group of military cadets decided to murder Riahi, the Chief of Staff, on 19 August if and when the latter made any anti-Shah move within the armed forces.

The crowds that had been mobilised to pour onto the streets of Tehran on 16 August had not been given a chance to do so because of the plot's failure. On 19 August, however, they began to march. They came from the city's poorest districts in the south and moved towards the centre where Mossadeq's residence and most government buildings were situated. These were versatile crowds: among them were professional, rent-a-mob figures and local tough guys such as Tayyeb Haj Reza'i. There were also a number of 'professional ladies' from Tehran's red light district. Mrs Malekeh Etezadi, a formidable lady with a particular reputation, was present with her own contingent as were members of Tehran's body-building clubs known as *zur-khaneh* (houses of force). Peasants were brought in from nearby villages in dozens of vans and trucks. Ayatollah Kashani's crowd of bazaar merchants and apprentices were also there. But the backbone of what soon became a popular riot was provided by workers at the Tehran cigarette factory, the railway and the army's various arsenals and arms manufacturing units inside the capital. These were different crowds from those Mossadeq attracted. The old statesman brought together civil servants, teachers, students and other middle-class strata. Gangs of thugs were often used by Mossadeq to defend his crowds, and tactical alliances with the mullahs at times added a religious colouring to demonstrations in his support. But when the chips were down he could only really count on support from sections of the urban middle classes. And his supporters, fairly prosperous and educated people, would be no match for the type of crowds that poured out to support the Shah on 19 August.

News of the unexpected uprising and the support given to it by the police unnerved Mossadeq. He sat at home, dressed in his pyjamas, surrounded by ministers and advisers and wondered aloud about what was to be done. His Interior Minister, Gholam-Hossein Saddiqi, a much-respected figure, has given a graphic account of Mossadeq's total loss of nerve on that fateful day. The prime minister, told that the crowds were shouting 'We want the Shah!', suggested that he should publish a statement saying that he, too, supported the departed monarch. He then changed his mind and ordered Saddiqi to remove the Chief of Police from office. It was soon clear that the soldiers had joined the crowds and were approaching the prime minister's residence.

When bullets began to fly into the residence, he suggested that everyone present in the room commit suicide as a gesture of protest against what was happening. Nevertheless, he moved his bed to a safer position away from the trajectory of the bullets that continued to be fired at the residence. The commander of his personal bodyguard, Captain Davar Panah, at first promised to fight the invading mobs to the last drop of his blood, then a few minutes later advised the prime minister to leave the house and go into hiding.

For the second time in six months, Mossadeq, still in his pyjamas, had to climb the wall into a neighbour's house and remained in hiding for the rest of that fateful day. Incredibly he made no serious attempt at rallying his supporters nor had he thought of offering them leadership at a moment of crisis. For some still mysterious reasons he had concluded that the game was up. It is possible that Mossadeq was by then so thoroughly exhausted, morally and physically, that, perhaps, he welcomed the chance to get out of the dead-end he had largely led himself into during the previous six months. After all, he was at least 73 years old and, although his frequent shows of falling ill might have been so many hoaxes, could not have been in robust health. He worked at least 12 hours a day at one of the most difficult and nerve-shattering periods in Iran's turbulent history. On 19 August 1953, therefore, he had little fight left in him and might have been unconsciously glad that he was being forced to leave the stage without having sullied his name by making a compromise with the hated *ajnabi* (foreigners). He would become a martyr and would still be loved by 'the people'.

It is also possible that Mossadeq quickly realised that resistance on his part would be credible only with support from Tudeh. And he would, the Shah's protestations to the contrary notwithstanding, always prefer monarchy to a Communist regime.

Much mystery surrounds the role that Tudeh played – or rather did not play – on 19 August 1953. The party had at least 50,000 members and active sympathisers in Tehran alone. As it became clear later, Tudeh also controlled a network of 600 officers, including a general, and, perhaps, thousands of NCOs within the armed forces.[4] It had at least two well-organised terrorist groups, respectively led by Major Khosrow Ruzbeh and Central Committee member Nureddin Kianuri and could have carried out a series of assassinations. In later years, Kianuri claimed that Tudeh did not move because Mossadeq asked the party to stay quiet. He claims that he personally telephoned Mossadeq to ask for permission to stage an uprising in support of the government.[5] This may or may not be an accurate account of what Kianuri did on that day, but in 1953 he was not senior enough to contact Mossadeq directly. In any case Mossadeq could not have agreed to a plan that kept him in power only thanks to the Tudeh network.

There were at least two certain reasons why the formidable Tudeh machine failed to move on that fateful day. The first was the rigidity of decision-making within the party's Leninist structure based on 'democratic centralism'. This prevented local sections of the party from taking immediate action and, by the time the central leadership met to discuss the situation, it was too late. The second reason was Tudeh's abject dependence on Russia. Moscow had dispatched Anatoli Lavrentiev, the man who orchestrated Czechoslovakia's takeover by the Communists, as Soviet Ambassador to Tehran only a few months before the August 1953 events. Lavrentiev, a protégé of the Soviet police chief Beria, lost much of his influence in Moscow after Stalin's death and the subsequent disgrace of Beria himself. The Russian leadership, at the time locked in a power struggle that opposed Khrushchev's faction to the group led by Malenkov, was in no position to use Tudeh in a bid to seize control of Iran. Moscow had other matters of more urgency to worry about at the time.

The crowds that moved towards the centre of Tehran on 19 August 1953 quickly understood that the police and the army were on their side, but this was no military *coup d'état*. Zahedi remained in hiding outside Tehran until the fight was over. The 400 military cadets who had begun a hunger strike in support of the Shah two days earlier joined the crowds but took no specifically military action. The police helped by releasing hundreds of pro-Shah militants who had been thrown into prison on 16 August. The crowd attacked and burned Tudeh and pro-Mossadeq headquarters and indulged itself in many acts of violence. At least 100 people lost their lives, many of them Mossadeq and Tudeh supporters who fell victim to revenge killing.

In later years many extravagant claims were made by the CIA with regard to its own role in the events that led to the fall of Mossadeq. CIA agents, such as Kermit Roosevelt, portrayed themselves as heroes of an oriental adventure. The fact, however, was that they had badly failed in their part in a plan that, worked out by the British, represented no more than a wild gamble. That plan failed on 16 August and all the Iranians who were supposed to put it into effect were either arrested or went into hiding. The 19 August uprising was caused by Mossadeq's own mistakes and the fear of wide sections of Iranian society that the country might fall under Russian domination. The Americans were startled at the turn of events on 19 August as they had already decided that Mossadeq had won. Ambassador Henderson had rushed back to Tehran precisely in an effort to contact Mossadeq and minimise the damage caused by the failure of 'Operation Ajax'. On 20 August the American Embassy reported to Washington that the crowds that had overthrown Mossadeq the previous day were the most genuinely popular witnessed in the Iranian capital for more than two years.[6]

Legends have also been spread about the supposedly fantastic sums of money that the CIA spent in Tehran. Some have even claimed that $10,000,000 in Iranian 10-rial banknotes were distributed in south Tehran on 18th August.[7] All records show that the funds allocated for 'Operation Ajax' did not exceed $1,000,000. Of this less than $100,000 had been spent when it was assumed that the entire plan had collapsed. The remaining sums were, later, presented to General Zahedi when he assumed the premiership.[8]

On the morning of 19 August a despondent Shah and a sparklingly happy Soraya were out shopping on via Condotti, oblivious of the fact that the tide had turned in Tehran. The Shah wanted to buy himself some sports gear and tennis rackets. Soraya tried a few dresses at a designer shop but decided not to buy. She was now sure that she and her husband would have all their lives in which to visit every *haut couturier* in Europe. Back at the Hotel Excelsior, where they had settled in a vast suite, the couple went to the dining room and ordered lunch. They had just begun sipping their coffee when an American reporter rushed in with a dispatch from Tehran that announced the fall of Mossadeq and the constitution of a new government by Zahedi. Soraya burst into tears and, as a number of people gathered around the royal couple, the Shah, waving the news agency dispatch in his hand, said: 'I knew they loved me. I knew it!' He then took Soraya's hand and said: 'We are going home!' A couple of hours later the Shah gave his first press conference after 'victory'. He praised the courage of his people and claimed that he had left the country in order to prevent bloodshed.

The Shah's decision to leave the country, taken largely for personal reasons, proved a politically wise move. Had he stayed in Tehran he might have bowed to Mossadeq's diktat after the failure of the 16 August move. His absence gave the crowds something concrete to demand: the Shah must return! Had he stayed, a prisoner in his palace and unable to communicate with the outside world, Mossadeq could easily have claimed that the edicts brought by Nassiri were forgeries and that the Shah had never dismissed the government.

The Shah and Queen Soraya spent a sleepless night on 19 August, waiting for direct news from Zahedi, but the new prime minister had other more urgent tasks to attend to. Hundreds of Tudeh activists and Mossadeq supporters were rounded up but Mossadeq and his foreign minister Fatemi still remained in hiding. By dawn on 20 August, Zahedi, with his son Ardeshir at his side, had completed the task of putting his new government in place and establishing his authority. He then sent a brief cable to the Shah: the entire nation is impatiently waiting for the return of Their Majesties![9] With this invitation in hand the Shah ordered Princess Ashraf to find an aircraft to charter for his return journey to Tehran. He then took Soraya shopping again and presented her with a set of diamond jewellery. Still uncertain about the actual situation in Tehran, he asked the Queen to spend some more time in Europe; she would return home in a few weeks' time.

With his chartered aircraft filled with reporters the Shah flew out of Rome. But he did not go directly to Tehran. The aircraft landed at Baghdad where the entire Iraqi royal family had now gathered to welcome the fugitive king of only three days earlier. The Shah, after further brief visits to the shi'ite shrines of Najaf and Karbala, spent the night in Baghdad. Overnight Zahedi rushed the Shah's military uniforms and decorations from Tehran to the Iraqi capital and the Shah, dressed in his uniform of Commander of the Imperial Iranian Air Force and piloting his own Beachcroft plane which had been flown to Baghdad overnight, arrived in Tehran before noon on 21 August. At the airport several generals fell to his feet and kissed his boots, a scene that no one had seen in Iran since Reza Shah's time. Zahedi, however, simply saluted and then, acting like a father, embraced the Shah. Perron was also at the airport, tears in his eyes.

In a message to the nation later that day the Shah said that he felt that he was only just beginning his reign. 'Up to now I was Shah only because I had inherited the crown from my father. With your glorious uprising you have now made me an elected Shah!' He ordered 19 August, 28 Mordad on the Persian calendar, to be named National Uprising Day. Thus 28 Mordad became the framework within which a new mythology was gradually developed with its own heroes and villains. The uprising was presented as a fine symbol of the unity of the Shah and the Nation against local and foreign demons. Every year until 1979, 28 Mordad was celebrated throughout the country in the style of a solemn political mass with the image of a virtually deified Shah at the centre of all ceremonies.

Before the week had ended Tehran was struck by two sensational items of news. The first was Mossadeq's decision to come out of hiding and surrender himself to Zahedi who, although prime minister, continued to work from his old office at the Retired Officers' Club. Zahedi had sent his own son, Ardeshir, to escort Mossadeq to the club where the former prime minister was confined before being transferred to a military prison. The second came from the Soviet Embassy which had sealed itself off since the evening of 19 August. Having learned that the monarchists had won on 19 August, Ambassador Lavrentiev had tried to commit suicide and the embassy staff awaited the arrival of a new man to take charge from Moscow. There were also rumours that Lavrentiev had tried to defect to the Americans but had been arrested by his own people before leaving the embassy.[10]

Whatever the truth of the matter, Lavrentiev, once considered a star of Soviet diplomacy, simply disappeared for ever.

The Zahedi government imposed a new martial law with a little-known officer, Brigadier-General Teymur Bakhtiar, a relative of Queen Soraya, as Martial Law Administrator. Between 1500 and 3000 people were arrested throughout the country and nearly 50 newspapers were closed down. The army, which had played a supporting role in the uprising, claimed a much larger share of the spoils than its actual contribution could justify and more than 100 senior officers divided the top posts among themselves. The political prisoners, including Mossadeq himself, were judged by military tribunals, in violation of the laws and practices then in force in Iran. The new government was anxious to do away with the political trials as quickly as possible, and this meant by-passing the civilian courts that might have spent years deciding all the cases. The military prosecutors made a habit of almost automatically demanding the death penalty for those accused of having 'conspired against the state' and no fewer than 800 such demands were made, including one for Mossadeq. Ayatollah Kashani also came out in support of the death sentence for Mossadeq.

After a long trial during which Mossadeq found ample opportunity to indulge in his favourite oratorical and theatrical numbers, the former prime minister was sentenced to death, immediately commuted to three years imprisonment on the Shah's orders. In any case, Mossadeq, could not have been sent to his death as an old law prohibited the execution of people aged over 60. Of the military tribunal's death sentences against 32 Tudeh officers, however, only nine were carried out. A few other opponents such as Fatemi, the journalist Karimpur Shirazi, and the Tudeh terror commander Ruzbeh were murdered by General Bakhtiar's operatives in sordid circumstances. These political murders more than offset the generally moderate policy that the new government had adopted towards Tudeh and pro-Mossadeq militants.

The Shah–Mossadeq duel had been a confrontation within the ruling elite of Iran. In a sense even the Tudeh Party, at least as far as its leadership and middle-rank cadres were concerned, constituted part of the ruling elite. The family trees of Mossadeq, Zahedi and several Tudeh leaders met at more than one branch. The events of August 1953 and their immediate aftermath, however, divided the ruling elite and created wounds that were never fully healed. Different members of the elite began to see the nation's immediate past in diametrically opposed terms: to the Mossadeqists he had always been right and just – indeed, he was the infallible Pishva' (Führer); to the royalists, Mossadeq was nothing but a traitor while the Shah was a great national hero. As always, the split in the ruling elite was, in time, extended to divide the whole nation. Different views of the past automatically led to different visions of the future also. The Shah was back on his throne, but he no longer had the chance of setting an agenda that would be wholeheartedly adopted by his people. A section of the ruling elite would never forgive him, no matter what he did.

The new Zahedi government had hoped to get the economy off the ground with massive aid from the United States, but American aid was slow in coming. After months of haggling the Americans agreed to provide $51,000,000 instead of the $250,000,000 that Zahedi had asked for. Washington's stringency was intended to force Iran to settle the oil dispute quickly. This was done and Iran began exporting oil again in 1954. Under the new agreement, the principle of nationalisation was retained. The National Iranian Oil Company (NIOC) retained the title to all oil found in the country and the tasks of exploration, production and exporting were contracted to two companies owned by western oil corporations. British Petroleum, as Anglo-Iranian was now known, received a 40 per cent share with a further 14 per cent going to Royal Dutch Shell. The five major American companies received 8 per cent each and the remaining 6 per cent of the shares went to CFP, the French oil company. Iran's income from oil sales was fixed at 12.5 per cent of the posted price and the foreign companies, now known as 'the Consortium', promised to increase production to meet Iran's growing foreign exchange requirements.

With the oil issue out of the way the Shah moved quickly to get rid of Zahedi. The general had a strong personality of his own and could communicate directly with the Americans, now emerging as Iran's leading foreign partners. Moreover the Shah, who never liked to feel obligated to anyone, was not comfortable with a prime minister who had been instrumental in putting him back on the throne. 'His Majesty is grateful by nature,' Princess Ashraf recalled. 'But he was, somehow, never able to say thank you!'[11]

Too shy to tell any high official – let alone a prime minister – that he was being fired, the Shah was even more reluctant to face Zahedi in person at the time of the latter's dismissal. His Majesty's desire to dismiss Zahedi was communicated to the general through the Court Minister. Zahedi then asked for an audience which was instantly granted. 'I have come to ask Your Majesty's permission to retire,' the prime minister said. 'Well,' the Shah replied, 'how could we decline a request from so loyal a servant such as Your Excellency?' After this little comedy had been played out, Zahedi was named Iran's Ambassador to the UN in Geneva and was, in fact, sent into exile. Given that many prime ministers of Iran, during more than a century, had ended their term of service in imprisonment and death, Zahedi was, in a sense, among the lucky ones.

Soraya had returned to Tehran after a prolonged stay in Switzerland. For the first time since her marriage she felt she was being treated like a Queen. More important – and also for the first time – her husband appeared relaxed and genuinely happy and had stopped 'glueing his ears' to the wireless set in expectation of the latest bad news.[12]

Soraya, however, did not share his happiness. She had not yet produced a child and remained so jealous of Princess Shahnaz that the Shah had to call on his only daughter in secret.

Partly in the hope of soothing Soraya the Shah asked her to go to Europe on a mission to find a husband for Shahnaz. The Shah had two candidates in mind: King Faisal of Iraq and Prince Sadruddin, the younger son of the Agha Khan. Shahnaz was staying on the French Riviera and it was decided that she should meet the two potential suitors there in the presence of Soraya and Princess Shams. The meetings were arranged but Shahnaz, who by now had developed a crush on Ardeshir, General Zahedi's only son, was not interested. An angry Soraya returned to Tehran, convinced that Shahnaz wanted to stay in Iran only to be a thorn in the side of the woman who had replaced her mother as Queen.

Savouring his victory, the Shah was determined to make of his thirty-fifth birthday on 26 October 1954 a truly grand occasion. Massive celebrations were planned throughout the country and hundreds of prisoners, including many Tudeh activists were set free. The Dowager Queen, back from the exile into which Mossadeq had dispatched her, was reigning over a happy clan of Pahlavis. Her contribution to the celebrations was a large party that she organised at her palace in the hope of bringing the entire family together for the first time since Reza Shah's abdication and exile. Mohammad-Reza Shah, also hoped to be able to announce the good news that Soraya's doctors had hinted at a few days earlier. But when the birthday party began at Taj al-Moluk's palace, it was instantly clear that there was chill in the air. The Shah, who had already been given the news that Soraya was not to be a mother in the near future, was in sombre mood. He became positively angry when he was told that his younger brother, Prince Ali-Reza, had not yet returned from a hunting trip to the Caspian forests. The party could not begin without the prince, the Shah's favourite brother. The champagne bottles remained unopened and the sumptuous dinner prepared by chefs flown in from Paris went cold. Ernest Perron was almost in tears.

Ali-Reza, the Shah's only full brother, was the family's joker. He did a bit of everything and was not good at anything in particular – except hunting wild bears in the province of Mazandaran. Boisterous and full of energy, he might have resented the fact that the crown had gone to his shy, withdrawn and, apparently, indifferent brother. But Ali-Reza felt no resentment; he loved and adored his brother and, having been a witness to the ordeal of kingship in Iran, did not covet the crown. Nevertheless, he was the only other member of the Pahlavi family at the time who could, legally, succeed Mohammad-Reza as Shah. The Shah's five half-brothers were automatically barred from succession because of their connection with the Qajars through their respective mothers. And the Shah's only child, Princess Shahnaz, could not ascend the throne because the Constitution clearly demanded a male heir.*

When it was discovered that Ali-Reza had died in a plane crash in the mountains of Mazandaran, the family was plunged into a major crisis. The need for the Shah to have an heir became an urgent political issue. With Ali-Reza gone, a single bullet from an assassin's gun could end the Pahlavi dynasty. Under the Constitution, monarchy was a 'divine gift' to the Iranian nation as a whole and only its exercise was transferred to a particular family. If that family were no longer able to exercise the function of the monarch for whatever reason, the 'divine gift' would simply revert to its original owner: the nation. That meant the convening of a new Constituent Assembly and the election of a new reigning family.

The fact that the Shah had not yet fathered a son was beginning to become a topic of conversation and speculation at many tea-houses and family gatherings throughout the country. The more enthusiastic monarchists felt despondent about the fact that their King of Kings was not blessed with a son – God's supreme gift to any man. The Shah's detractors used the topic for weaving yarns about the monarch's alleged 'unmanliness' – a charge that could devastate a man's reputation in macho Persian society. Soraya's failure to produce the required heir combined with her aloofness made her increasingly unpopular. People admired her beauty, especially her deep, green almond-shaped eyes, but found her cold and selfish. Evil tongues began to refer to the Queen as 'the German cow' or 'the barren one'.

The Shah, however, loved his wife more than ever before. Whenever he could – and that was quite often in those days when nothing much

---

*In the mid-1940s Ali-Reza had fathered a son, Patrick, through a controversial liaison with a Polish divorcee he had met in Paris. But the half-Polish, illegitimate Patrick, who was eventually adopted as a member of the family, would not have been acceptable as a Crown Prince of Iran.

happened in Iran – he would take her to secret hideaways in the mountains or on the Caspian or go driving with her in the great Iranian desert that resembles a lunar landscape. On the fifth anniversary of their marriage the Shah offered Soraya an exquisite coronet, designed by the American, Harry Winston, which she was supposed to wear at a future coronation ceremony. The Shah had not yet been crowned and, now that he was the real master of the country, planned to do so as soon as possible.

Partly to gain international status and partly to fulfil the promise of a world tour made to Soraya, the Shah organised a series of state visits that took the royal couple to India, Turkey, the USSR, Spain and the United States. While in New York the couple underwent a series of medical tests to find out why they had so far failed to have a child together. No anomalies were found and the couple were told to wait: there was no reason to despair.

Capricious and coquettish as she was, Soraya was not easy to live with. She would seize upon the flimsiest of pretexts for provoking a scene of conjugal discord. She would then begin to shout as she threw everything she could get hold of through the windows. The Shah would only laugh and try to cajole her: 'Allons! Allons!' he would say,' Soyons sérieux!'

One major row occurred over Dr Karim Ayadi, the Special Royal Physician. Ayadi was an adept of the Baha'i faith, considered heretical by the shi'ite's. After the fall of Mossadeq, a massive anti-Baha'i campaign was launched at the initiative of Ayatollah Kashani. One of Kashani's demands was that there should be no Baha'is in the Shah's entourage. The Shah agreed and banished several personal friends. He also turned a blind eye as hoodlums, supported by the police, attacked and partly destroyed the Baha'i temple (Hazirat al-Qods) in Tehran. Soraya, however, could not understand why the Baha'is should be persecuted and insisted that Ayadi remain at the palace. In the end Ayadi himself convinced the queen that it was better for everyone not to provoke the mullahs. He disappeared for a few months but later returned to become one of the Shah's closest confidants.

Another row between Soraya and the Shah centred on her mother's excessive taste for alcoholic drinks. The aging Mrs Esfandiari had a habit of withdrawing to her quarters in the palace with a bottle of whisky after sunset. She would re-emerge at night, singing German lieder.

Pressure on the Shah to tackle the succession problem began to mount from the beginning of 1957 and even Grand Ayatollah Borujerdi had a message relayed to the Shah on the subject. The Shah did his best to keep the issue on the backburner as long as he could. He discussed the possibility of amending the Constitution to enable Princess Shahnaz to be named heir-apparent, but this was strongly opposed by the ayatollahs. Prophet Mohammad had said that a country led by a woman would experience only misery and decline! The idea of lifting the ban on the Qajars was also briefly mentioned to enable the Shah to name his half-brother Gholam-Reza as Crown Prince. The mullahs suggested that the Shah take a second wife, a perfectly legitimate act under Islamic law. In fact, Mohammad-Reza Shah was the only monogamous king in Iran's history and there seemed no reason why he should complicate his life by refusing a perfectly legal solution with the full backing of the religious establishment. But Mohammad-Reza was not a typical Persian monarch; his foreign education had distanced him from the mass of his subjects. He would not even discuss bigamy as a solution to his problems.

In July 1957 Dr Manuchehr Eqbal, who had succeeded Ala as prime minister, told the Shah that the problem of succession could no longer be avoided. The country needed major reforms that might provoke violent reaction from many sections of society. It was necessary that the dynasty be assured of continuity before the reform projects could be put into effect.

The Shah, who was also under pressure from Taj al-Moluk, knew that he could no longer postpone a decision. He discussed the matter with Soraya and the two agreed that the matter be referred to an informal 'council of wise men'.[13] The solution offered by the council was the one the Shah had already rejected: a second marriage. The matter was, nevertheless, put to the couple again. Soraya, wrongly, believed that her husband had changed his mind on the issue of bigamy and created a scene, refusing to speak to the Shah for a few days. All along she was, somehow, convinced that Mohammad-Reza would never leave her.

One evening in February 1958 the royal couple went to a nearby ball after a private dinner at the palace. As they danced Soraya asked the Shah whether or not he would be prepared to abdicate and follow her into a life of anonymity and happiness. The Shah apparently ignored the suggestion, which she had put to him several times before, and Soraya withdrew to an adjacent restroom, apparently in tears. When she returned she saw the Shah dancing with a beautiful blonde. Later that night, as the furniture flew in the royal suite at the palace, Soraya announced that she was leaving Iran 'for good'. She gave the Shah an ultimatum: he must either abdicate and follow her into exile, or keep his crown and lose her. On 13 February 1957 Soraya flew out of Tehran and soon settled at St Moritz in Switzerland where the Shah had acquired some property. She agreed to talk to the Shah on the telephone only to repeat her decision not to return. A few days later a delegation of dignitaries arrived to persuade Soraya to come home. She refused. 'This is fate,' she said. 'Please send my personal belongings from Tehran.'[14]

On 14 March Princess Ashraf called on the Shah. She found her brother in his indoor swiming pool. Before she could say anything the Shah, coming out of the pool, said: 'It's finished. Soraya is gone and will not return. We will be separated with mutual consent.'[15] A few hours later an official communiqué announced the divorce. Soraya never returned to Iran. She received the equivalent of $80,000 as mahrieyh, the money that husbands have to pay to a wife they wish to repudiate in accordance with Islamic law.[16] She was also allowed to keep the collection of jewels that the Shah had given her over the years. In addition, the Shah bestowed on her the title of Imperial Highness. After their divorce the Shah and Soraya exchanged a few letters. On at least one occasion they almost agreed to meet informally again, but they finally both resisted the temptation. Their life together had lasted almost exactly seven years. Less than a year after the divorce, Soraya's name had been all but effaced from the thousands of public places named after her in Iran and everyone had forgotten the unlucky queen — everyone except the Shah.

9

Playing Revolutionary

In later years the Shah liked to describe the 1950s as 'the era of groping in the dark.' Mossadeq was gone, banished to his estate at Ahmad-Abad and hardly allowed contact with the outside world. The Shah, however, never forgot or forgave the man who nearly ended the Pahlavi dynasty. In 1954 the Shah told his confidants that his task was easy: All we have to do is to go in the opposite direction from Mossadeq and we shall get everything right![1]

Mossadeq based his foreign policy on 'negative balance': the Shah named his 'positive nationalism'. In 1954 he opened negotiations with Moscow with a view to settling a number of border disputes and other problems. This was done and the USSR returned to Iran the gold reserves that the Red Army had taken away during the war. The Shah visited Moscow and established cordial relations with the post-Stalin leadership. Trade between the two neighbours rose to its highest level ever. The Shah gave his 'word of honour as a soldier' to Khrushchev that Iranian territory would never be used as a base for aggression against Russia.

As the cold war entered a new phase in the wake of the Korean war. Iran was also determined to become a member of the Western camp. In 1955 the Shah took Iran into the Baghdad pact, a British-sponsored alliance, that also included Iraq and Turkey. Zahedi, then still prime minister, opposed this and saw the pact as an attempt by Great Britain to regain her predominant position in the Middle East.[2] The general had tried in vain to establish the United States as Iran's principal foreign partner. (It was long after Zahedi had left office that Iran signed a bilateral mutual aid agreement with the United States in December 1959.)

Having reversed Mossadeq's foreign policy, the Shah adopted a new economic strategy for the nation. He adopted an interventionist attitude towards economic development and in 1954 he revived the Plan Organisation which Mossadeq had scrapped. Within a few months, a new seven-year development plan was unveiled.

The Shah described his economic philosophy in these terms: 'The state must play a vital role in the coordination and control of national production. I reject(ed) pure capitalism.'[3]

The plan was reduced to a five-year term and approved by the Majlis in March 1956. It envisaged investments of more than $1.2 billion. This was a massive figure, bearing in mind that Iran's per capita GNP at the time was estimated at below $100 per annum. In addition to its rising oil income, Iran used American aid and foreign loans to finance the ambitious plan and meet the needs of the ordinary budget. For the first time in 15 years the civil servants were, once again, paid on time and the whiff of corruption that had disappeared from government offices under Mossadeq was back, hanging heavy in the air. Rumours began to fly around that the Shah received a cut of every investment made with the help of his Director of Plan, the colourful and controversial Abol-Hassan Ebtehaj.

The Shah responded by creating the first of many Anti-Corruption Commissions to cleanse the administration. Later, he created the Imperial Inspectorate which reported exclusively to the monarch. As part of the anti-corruption drive several army generals were put in front of tribunals.

General Ahmad Ajudani provoked the monarch's anger because of technical difficulties in a power station built by the French in west Tehran that the general had supervised. On the day of inauguration in the presence of the Shah, the power station simply went dead after the monarch had pushed a button to establish the electrical current. The brief current, however, had been enough to kill the swans who had made their home in a nearby pond. General Haj-Ali Kia, a former army intelligence chief, was discovered to have embezzled around $1,200,000 through a non-existent intelligence network. He had spent part of the money for building a high-rise block of flats and offices which everyone referred to as 'where-did-you-get-it-from?' General Morteza Hedayat, the country's only four-star general at the time, was accused of having received bribes worth a few thousand dollars from an importer of batteries. General Farzanegan was accused of embezzlement at the post office.

The launch of big development projects, such as the dams on the rivers Karaj, Sefidrud and Dez, created ample opportunities for kickbacks and commissions. New rich families appeared in Tehran and other major cities, bringing with them lifestyles hitherto unknown to most Iranians. They were ostentatious and superficial and to many Iranians appeared vulgar. Pepsi Cola, hamburgers and French-style breads were introduced in Tehran where new cinemas, restaurants and shopping centres opened almost every other month. The government had become an instrument for channelling much of the nation's wealth into the pockets of a small minority of the population.

As always, corruption quickly created its twin demon of repression. In 1957, using a decree issued under Mossadeq as an excuse, the government created the State Security and Intelligence Organisation, which soon

became known by its acronym, SAVAK. General Teymur Bakhtiar who
had served as Martial Law Administrator in Tehran since August 1953
was named its first chief.

With SAVAK firmly installed martial law was lifted. At the same time
the Shah ordered the creation of two political parties in the hope of
developing a controlled parliamentary system in Iran. One party was
known as 'Melliyun' (The Nationalists) and the other chose the name of
'Mardom' (The People). Melliyun was led by Dr Eqbal while Assadollah
Alam – who was by now established as one of the Shah's closest
confidants – assumed the Mardom leadership. The twin parties never
really got off the ground and soon degenerated into mere instruments for
the distribution of government favours.

Although the Shah now stood at the centre of the new power structure,
he was by no means the demi-god he later became. The mullahs still
remained powerful despite the setback they suffered when nine leading
members of the Islam Fedayeen, including the two terrorists who had
killed prime minister Razm-Ara and the intellectual Ahmad Kasravi, were
hanged in Tehran. This time the Shah felt strong enough to refuse a
demand for pardon from the ayatollahs. The older politicians also
retained part of their former prestige and power thanks to their
nationwide connections and vast experience in public service. The Shah
had not yet found a new team of his own and had to rely on the ruling elite
that had taken shape under Reza Shah.

In 1957 Dr Eqbal underlined the Shah's supremacy with a speech in
which he described himself as 'a born slave' of His Majesty. The older
politicians listened in horror as the new prime minister told the Majlis
that he would be no more than the executant of the Shah's orders. Reza
Khan, the Shah's father, had been a prime minister who plotted to capture
the kingship. Mohammad-Reza Shah was a king who had dreamed of
capturing the premiership. With Dr Eqbal he achieved his aim.

One man, however, was still in a position to represent a threat to the
Shah: General Bakhtiar, the ruthless SAVAK chief. Tall, good-looking
and charismatic, this graduate of Saint-Cyr had moved up the ladder
partly because of his family ties with Queen Soraya. But he had soon
distinguished himself by his talents for political intrigue. Under Bakhtiar,
SAVAK, while still in its infancy, welcomed instructors from the CIA as
well as the Israeli intelligence service, MOSSAD. Most of the organisation's initial recruits, though, were repenting Tudeh militants who had
grouped themselves into the informal Ebrat (Repentance) circle with
Bakhtiar as their protector. It was under their influence that Bakhtiar
tried for a while to give himself the image of a man of the people. Bakhtiar
maintained contact with former Mossadeqists partly through his
cousin, Shahpour Bakhtiar. The general also tried to present himself to
Washington as a potential 'strongman' for Iran. During a visit to
Washington he called on Allen W. Dulles, the CIA director, and aired his

ambitions in broad but unmistakable terms. Dulles took the precaution of immediately informing the Shah[4] who waited nearly two more years before he felt strong enough to remove Bakhtiar.

In the meantime Bakhtiar emerged as his own worst enemy. Anxious to become as rich as he could, as fast as he could, he entered into a variety of shady deals ranging from illegal imports to the export of opium. He also accepted substantial bribes in exchange for releasing political prisoners. In 1953 Bakhtiar's entire personal fortune had consisted of a brick house in Tehran. Six years later he had built himself a sumptuous palace just opposite the Shah's summer palace at Saadabad. In addition he owned five villas, a palace on the Caspian, 11 farms, 3 homes in Europe and impressive bank accounts in France and Switzerland. After 1956 the general began to smoke opium and developed a drinking problem. His weakness for women also undermined his prestige. In one incident he threatened a famous composer with death unless the latter would abandon his wife, a popular singer.

The Iraqi *coup d'état* of 1958 in which King Faisal and most members of his family were brutally murdered, came as a deep shock to the Shah. The Iraqi monarchy was generally regarded as the centrepiece of British power in the Middle East, yet it was destroyed with a single blow. Were the British no longer capable of protecting their friends? Or, worse still, had they decided to replace tired dynastic regimes with new military ones capable of better resisting the lure of Communism? Wouldn't someone like General Bakhtiar be tempted to repeat what General Abdul-Karim Qassem had done in Iraq?

In the meantime the Eqbal government went from one failure to another. The prime minister, a hard-working man with virtually no imagination, never succeeded in giving his government a coherent policy and was content with following the Shah's sporadic and often contradictory orders. In August 1960, Eqbal took his role as 'born slave of the Shah' one step further and asked His Majesty to approve the full list of future members of the Majlis which was due for election in August. The Shah, who never refused to issue an order whenever he was asked for one, agreed. Two weeks before polling day the list of would-be MPs was published and widely circulated in Tehran. When the results were officially announced Eqbal had won 80 per cent of the seats with the rest going to Alam's Mardom exactly as the list had envisaged. Only two politicians whose names had not figured on the list were elected. Eqbal had taken the liberty of attributing all the 15 seats for Tehran to his own party in violation of the list that had reserved 5 for Mardom and 3 for independents.

The Majlis, whose term had been increased from two to four years in 1956, was no longer the powerhouse it had been until the end of the Mossadeq era, but it retained enough prestige and influence to attract a large number of ambitious politicians. Eqbal's brazen cheating at the election, therefore, provoked many angry cries. The Shah, anxious lest his own name be dragged into the scandal, acted quickly by dismissing Eqbal. A few days later a number of law suits were filed against the former prime minister who was also manhandled on the campus of Tehran University where he had resumed his teaching career at the Faculty of Medicine.

The Shah's troubles with Bakhtiar and Eqbal between 1958 and 1959 only helped underline the need for settling the problem of his succession. Several friends and well-wishers were again charged with the task of scouting for a suitable bride. Taj al-Moluk received a stream of eligible debutantes every week. Especially active in the search for a future queen was Ardeshir Zahedi, who had married Princess Shahnaz in October 1957. Each week a new list of possible brides for the Shah would be revealed in Tehran. Some families even paid the Persian yellow press to mention the name of their daughters as candidates for marriage to His Imperial Majesty.

While looking for a wife the Shah went through a series of brief liaisons: the 22-year-old Dokhi, the 19-year-old Safieh and the German actress Helga Andersen were seen in His Majesty's company on different occasions. One liaison that began to look serious concerned Princess Maria-Gabriella of Savoy, the daughter of ex-King Umberto of Italy. The Shah met the princess in Switzerland and, after a while, apparently began to consider taking her as his wife. The princess was neither Persian nor Muslim, as the Constitution required, but the problem of nationality could be solved, as it had been in Fawziah's case, by an act of Parliament. The issue of religion was trickier and Maria-Gabriella would have to convert to Islam or force the Shah into a dangerous clash with the ayatollahs. A committee of French genealogists, meanwhile, came out with the results of its research into the roots of Maria-Gabriella's family. It had traced the ancestry of the Italian princess to one Princess Zelidah, daughter of Muhammad II, the eleventh century Muslim ruler of Seville.[5] The Iranian press gave prominence to this very useful discovery – which had cost the Iranian embassy in Paris a pretty penny – and told their readers that the Shah was, in fact, planning to marry a girl with an impeccable Muslim background.

Ex-King Umberto, Maria-Gabriella's father, however, prided himself as a good Catholic and would under no circumstances agree to his daughter's conversion to Islam. After lengthy negotiations in which attractive sums of money were mentioned, Umberto's intermediaries said that their master would keep quiet if the Pope gave his benediction to the marriage. In February 1959 the Shah paid a brief visit to Pope John XXIII during which the Pontiff said he could not sanction the marriage unless the Iranian Sovereign converted to Catholicism.[5] In May the Iranian government announced that rumours regarding His Majesty's marriage with 'a foreign subject' were unfounded and that the Shah would not take a non-Muslim as a wife.[6]

A few months later Princess Shahnaz and her husband Ardeshir Zahedi found a new candidate, an 18-year-old student of architecture named Farah Diba. She had returned home from Paris, where she had spent the previous 18 months at the Ecole des Beaux Arts, for the summer holidays. She was recommended to Zahedi by her uncle, Dr Esfandiar Diba, the royal dentist. Zahedi and Shahnaz found Farah simple but charming and decided to present her to the Shah. The Shah had already seen Farah at the Iranian Embassy in Paris during an official reception for Iranian students in 1957 but the Shah had forgotten the encounter. In later years he was teased by Farah who asked him: How could you forget having met me? Was it not love at first sight?

Farah was the only daughter of Sohrab Diba, a Saint-Cyr graduate who had died in 1948. Diba hailed from an old Azerbaijani family with distant ties with the Qajars. Farah's mother, Farideh Khanom, was from the Qotbi family of Gilan. Farah herself was born on 15 October 1938 in the Romanian capital Bucharest where her father served with the Iranian mission. Through her father, Farah also traced her roots to a descendant of the Prophet Muhammad and was, therefore, entitled to the title of sayyedeh (lady).[7] She was brought up by her maternal uncle whose son, Reza, she considered as a brother and friend. Both the Diba and Qotbi families had strong nationalist and monarchist credentials and it was only normal that Farah and Reza Qotbi became active members of the Pan-Iranist youth movement in the 1950s.

After graduating from two Tehran French schools – Jeanne d'Arc and Razi – Farah went to Paris in 1957 and took residence at the Dutch Students' Hostel. In Paris she had no political activity although the Iranian student community in Europe was beginning to discover the excitement of defying the established order in society. Two of Farah's closest friends at the time, Vida Hajebi-Tabrizi and Mina Rostami, were Marxist-Leninist militants. Both of them boycotted the embassy reception during which a number of students were presented to the Shah. Farah went along but during the reception she was quickly pushed to one side by more enthusiastic students who virtually mobbed the King of Kings. When order was restored the students present were briefly introduced one by one. When Farah's turn came the Shah expressed surprise at the fact that a girl wanted to become an architect.

The following day Farah related the encounter at the embassy in a letter to her mother. 'I saw the Shah, mother,' she wrote. 'And he had such sad eyes, beautiful and sad eyes. His voice was warm but I hardly remember what he said.'[8] Farah went on to express mild criticism of the fact that the Shah had taken time off in Paris to go to an expensive restaurant: 'Is it right for the Shah to go to a restaurant at such a sensitive time in our country?' she wrote to her mother.

It was also in Paris that Farah heard the news of the Shah's separation from Soraya. She wrote to her mother: 'I have just heard that His Majesty and Soraya have parted. *Dommage!*[9] The Shah's search for a wife, a favourite topic of the French press in those days, was discussed at the hostel and the school of architecture, mostly by students who wanted to tease Farah. At one student party Farah was presented with a cardboard crown and hailed as the Queen of Persia. At another party all those present signed a paper declaring that Farah should become queen. '*La chatte pour le Chah!*' they shouted as they presented her with the image of a cat.[10]

When she arrived in Tehran for her summer holidays in July 1959 Farah did not imagine that she would be the Shah's wife before the end of the year. She agreed to go to Hessarak, Zahedi's residence, at the urging of her uncle and other family members. There she was presented to Princess Shahnaz. The two women met a number of times and it soon became clear that Farah was under scrutiny. At one tea party at Hessarak the Shah suddenly appeared. After a few moments of shock, Farah recovered her composure. She reminded the Shah of their previous encounter and he asked her about the Iranian student community in Paris. There was no hint that the Shah was interested in Farah beyond a mere polite exchange. Shahnaz, however, was an enthusiastic campaigner. She took the shy student to various royal palaces and introduced her to Taj al-Moluk and Princess Ashraf. Later a more formal presentation ceremony was held at Taj al-Moluk's palace with all the family members – except the Shah – present. Several further meetings then took place with the Shah at Hessarak where Farah, the Shah, Zahedi and Shahnaz spent time playing society games and sipping tea or coffee. On two or three occasions Farah was also invited to fly in the Shah's special aircraft with Zahedi and Shahnaz, but still no one was willing to mention a possible engagement.

In September Farah was preparing to return to Paris to work on a project she had proposed as part of her university examinations when she was advised by Shahnaz to postpone her return for a few more days. Finally, one day in October, the Hessarak session of society games suddenly developed into a solemn ceremony. The Shah motioned all those present to leave except for Farah. 'I wish to have a private talk with you,' he said. 'I hope you don't mind.' He then related at some length how his two first marriages had ended in divorce. He also gave a brief account of his responsibilities as the King of Kings and the hardship he had suffered before 1953. After a brief silence the Shah suddenly asked: 'Will you accept to become my wife?'

This was the first time in his life that he had proposed. Fawziah had been chosen by his father and the proposal to Soraya had been relayed to her by her uncle. Farah lost no time in replying: 'I will be honoured, Your Majesty.' The Shah then held her hand, for the first time, and said: 'You will become the Queen of Iran and shall have to shoulder great responsibilities. You must work hard and be prepared for self sacrifice in the way I have chosen for the nation. You will face many dangers. Are you still prepared to say: yes?' The answer came without delay: 'Yes, Your Majesty! I am prepared.' Years later when she asked the Shah why he had chosen her he replied: 'I liked your simplicity, your purity.'[11]

Why did Farah accept to marry the Shah? She was not quite 19 years old, a full 20 years younger than the Shah. Was she fascinated by the man or by his position as monarch?' 'The two were one,' she said, many years later. 'And I knew that I loved the man who was asking me to marry him.'[12]

Once the engagement was formalised Farah was isolated from the rest of the world and asked to observe a strict and detailed timetable. After a month-long stay in Paris, during which she ordered her wedding dress, purchased the two wedding rings and had her hairstyle changed, Farah returned to Tehran. The wedding took place on 21 December. As the wedding date approached and the country prepared for seven days and seven nights of celebrations in accordance with Persian tradition, clouds began to gather on the political horizon. A series of industrial strikes, first started by south Tehran bricklayers, threatened to spread to other more crucial sectors. More important, the new Iraqi dictator, General Qassem, suddenly decided to order a massive military build-up on the Shatt al-Arab, the river that forms part of the frontier between Iran and Iraq. For two critical days the two neighbours stood on the brink of war. In the end, the wedding went ahead as planned but the royal couple had to postpone and then shorten their honeymoon on the Caspian.

As queen, Farah achieved almost immediate popularity. She had several features that pleased the Iranians: she was 'fully Iranian' and also worthy of honour because she descended from the family of the Prophet. She was a brunette with deep black eyes of the kind most Persians cherish. (The Shah's outlandish taste for blondes was not shared by his compatriots.) Farah appeared to be slightly taller than the Shah, but this could not be held against her. The new queen's athletic physique and her well-publicised love of sports disconcerted some religious circles, but even the more conservative Iranians now understood that times were changing.

Ten months after the marriage, the Shah personally drove his wife to a maternity hospital in south Tehran. After nearly three hours of suspense, during which the Shah broke his rule about smoking no more than 10 cigarettes a day, an excited Atabay barged into the waiting room to announce the birth of the Shah's first son and heir.

To mark the birth of the Crown Prince on 31 October 1960 the Shah ordered the release of the last 98 political prisoners and a reduction of 20 per cent in that year's income tax. The French press, which had adopted Farah almost as a French export to Iran, instantly chose a name for the new-born prince: Cyrus! The Tehran newspapers, however, had another idea: they wanted the boy to be named Reza. They won.

While the Shah was getting married and fathering a son the nation's political situation deteriorated sharply. With the Eqbal government destroyed by corruption and ineptitude, the Shah hastily created a new government under Jaafar Sharif-Emami. The new prime minister began work on 22 September 1960 but was quickly overwhelmed. Lacking political experience, Sharif-Emami tried to buy his way out of the crisis by promising wage and salary increases, but with a budget deficit that had continued to grow throughout the previous six years, he had little room for manoeuvre in that direction. People began to speak of a power vacuum at the centre of the government. Bakhtiar, backed by his network of SAVAK agents and informers, began to act as a law unto himself.

Technically, Bakhtiar was an assistant to the prime minister and had to report to Sharif-Emami on all his activities. In practice, Bakhtiar ignored the prime minister and, at times, would not even take telephone calls from him. Touring the country, Bakhtiar openly campaigned for changes that, in time, would turn him into the real ruler of the country. Bakhtiar also claimed to enjoy US support.

In February 1961 Bakhtiar made a brief visit to Washington and met the newly-elected President John F. Kennedy and members of the new Democratic administration. At the White House, Bakhtiar played a dirty trick. He told Kennedy that the Shah regretted the mistake of giving financial support to the Republicans during the American presidential campaign. That 'mistake' had been made on the advice of 'ill-meaning individuals who surrounded the Shah'.[13]

The Shah had established a personal relationship with Richard Nixon during the latter's term as vice-president. In the 1960 campaign, the Shah might have made a symbolic contribution to the Nixon campaign, but various sources spoke of his '$12,000,000 gift' to the Republican Party. Thus, when Kennedy won against the Shah's expectations, it was clear that relations between Tehran and Washington would soon enter a stormy passage. Matters were made worse by Kennedy's penchant for messianic activism. The new president saw himself as a knight in shining armour with a mission to make the world a better place. Iran was the very last country that Eisenhower visited as President and his successor wanted to know why. He concluded that the Iranian government was inefficient and corrupt and had to accept the painful medicine of reform.[14] But was Bakhtiar a man capable of offering reform?

The Shah, always a cautious player, was fully aware of the weakness of his position in any direct confrontation with the United States. At that particular time Iran badly needed US support to face another threat from radical Arab regimes with President Gamal Abdul-Nasser of Egypt as their most vociferous spokesman. Early in 1961 Iran decided to allow Israel, which she had given de facto recognition, to open an 'interests section' in Tehran. This was used by Nasser as an excuse for launching a massive campaign of propaganda and sabotage against Iran and Iranian interests in the Middle East. Egypt's policy against Iran was strongly supported by Syria, Iraq and the newly-created republic in Yemen. Nasser ordered the Arabs to change the name of the Persian Gulf to the Arabian Gulf and called for the detachment of the province of Khuzestan (which he called Arabistan) from Iran. Egyptian secret agents also tried to contact old Mossadeq and encourage him to resume his struggle against the Shah.

In the meantime relations with Moscow had also soured, apparently because Russian analysts had concluded that Iran was in a pre-revolutionary phase. In his first 'summit' meeting with Kennedy in Vienna, Khrushchev told the American leader that Iran would 'fall like a ripe plum'. Two clandestine radio transmitters from Baku, in Soviet Azerbaijan, and East Berlin beamed violent anti-Shah propaganda into Iran.

The Shah's internal and external problems encouraged the Mossadeqists to attempt a comeback on the Iranian political scene. As always they based their analysis on the assumption that, provided they could show enough strength inside Iran, they would win support from the reform-minded Kennedy administration in Washington. And the Shah, so it was assumed, could not last long without American support.

In May 1961 a series of strikes, spearheaded by schoolteachers, led to clashes with the police. A teacher named Yussef Khan-Ali was killed at one of the demonstrations. A nervous Sharif-Emami instantly offered his resignation. It seemed as if all that the Shah had created in nearly seven years of hard work was falling apart. He decided to cover his most vulnerable flank by neutralising the Americans. His device was the choice of Ali Amini as the new prime minister. Amini had served as ambassador to Washington and claimed to have established a close friendship with Kennedy during the latter's term as a member of the US Senate in the 1950s. As usual in Iranian politics, everything proceeded on the basis of vague assumptions and suppositions. Amini never said he was a friend of Kennedy or that he enjoyed American support, but when others said this, he would not deny it either. And since it was deemed impossible for an Iranian politician not to have some connection with at least one foreign power, Amini was quickly accepted as the man that Kennedy wanted as prime minister in Tehran. Years later even the Shah repeated this view. There is, nevertheless, no evidence that the Americans had any special views regarding who should form the new government in Iran. What was sure was that Kennedy championed a programme of reform in all so-called developing countries.

Amini was to prove to be the last of the old-style politicians to head a government in Iran. He loved making speeches, using excessive language that pleased the crowds, and was a master of the fine art of Persian political intrigue. Within days of taking over the premiership he was in contact with the mullahs, the Mossadeqists, the tribal chiefs and the bazaar leaders. The most immediate threat to his government came from Bakhtiar who, by using excessive force to disperse a student demonstration on the university campus, had provoked a vast anti-government movement among the urban youths. The SAVAK chief then tried to blame Amini and sent signals of his own to the Mossadeqists through his cousin Shapur. The Mossadeqists, under a revived National Front, had manifested their strength by organising a rally in which some 100,000 people participated with cries of 'Mossadeq back to power!'

Amini invited the National Front to join the cabinet but the latter, locked in the absurd belief that Mossadeq was still 'the legal prime minister', refused to take part in an 'illegal government'. This naive and sentimental attitude to politics quickly neutralised the National Front, and in effect, deprived an important section of the urban middle classes from a direct role in the unfolding drama. Mossadeq's heirs proved very much like him: they attached more importance to preserving their own 'good name' than to contributing to the solution of the nation's problems. They acted in the maximalist tradition that had prevented the development of a normal political life in Iran for more than half a century. They either had to have everything they demanded or they would rather settle for nothing at all – nothing plus the sacred 'good name' of 'unsullied men'.

Once the National Front had worked its own way into the background, Amini could no longer threaten the Shah as the new prime minister lacked a constituency of his own. This left the Shah free to strike against Bakhtiar.

Early in June Bakhtiar had paid a controversial visit to his tribal region in the vicinity of Isfahan amid rumours that he was distributing arms among the Bakhtiaris. On his return to Tehran, the general was called to the palace for tea. When Bakhtiar entered the Shah's office he noticed that General Hassan Pakravan was also present. Before Bakhtiar could speak, Pakravan informed him that 'a change' had been decided with regard to SAVAK: 'His Majesty has ordered me to relieve Your Excellency of your burden as director of SAVAK.'[15]

Bakhtiar's dismissal was part of a larger purge planned by the Shah. Bakhtiar was not arrested and was allowed to stay in the army, albeit without any specific assignment. Other victims of the purge were not so lucky. General Kia, director of the army's counter-intelligence bureau, General Alavi Moqaddam, who had served as Interior Minister, and General Ruhallah Navisi, who headed the Iranian fisheries, were sent to jail together with 31 other generals and 270 colonels. Amini, who supported the Shah in the purge of army officers, had his own list of those who had to be dismissed or jailed and the 'cleansing' of the Ministry of Education led to the dismissal of 643 high officials and the banishment of a further 370. In the rest of the government service more than 500 civil servants of all ranks were thrown in prison. To show that the 'cleansing campaign' did not spare the Royal Court, Amini also ordered the arrest of Mrs Ehsan Davalloo, the wife of Amir-Hushang Davalloo who had established himself as one of the Shah's closest confidants. In fact, with Ernest Perron already dead and buried, Davalloo was generally regarded as the successor to the mysterious Swiss who had been the monarch's companion for nearly a quarter of a century. Those who knew the Shah's illogical, or in any case inexplicable, affection for Davalloo, understood the pain that the monarch must have felt at the time.

The principal item on Amini's agenda was his land reform project. This was worked out by Hassan Arsanjani, who served as Minister for Agriculture, and partly inspired by the Shah's own earlier sale of his land to the peasants. The sale of royal land at nominal prices had continued on and off since 1949, but the Shah's efforts to get an overall land reform bill through parliament produced no results because the very landowners who risked losing their property held a majority in the Majlis. Amini therefore dissolved the Majlis in order to proceed.

The charismatic Arsanjani, a former journalist and speech-writer for Qavam, toured the country to mobilise the peasants in support of the government. This was a clever political move: the regime as a whole was by then isolated in the urban areas and threatened by internal dissent. It was necessary to enlarge the scope of Iranian politics by bringing new forces into the picture: the peasants, who still formed some 70 per cent of the population, offered an important source of potential support.

Amini's anti-corruption drive and land reform programme succeeded in confusing the Shah's opponents and reassuring Washington that Kennedy's desired 'changes' were well under way. Amini had played his role and the Shah could now get rid of him with a minimum of risk. Arsanjani had to go also: the minister was beginning to emerge as a national figure with a following of his own. Before he could dismiss Amini, however, the Shah had to push Bakhtiar definitely out of the game.

On 26 January 1962 Bakhtiar was invited to the palace. The general had just returned from the United States where he had been unable to meet any high officials. (He had resumed his intrigues only a few days earlier.) At the palace, instead of being shown into the Shah's office he was met by Pakravan. 'General,' Pakravan said, 'we have reports regarding your need for medical treatment abroad. His Majesty has agreed that you should have the facilities needed in Switzerland.'[16] Bakhtiar immediately realised that he was under arrest. A few hours later he was on board a plane for Geneva. A SAVAK agent had brought him a small suitcase with his clothes in it.

In April 1962 the Shah and Queen Farah paid their first state visit to Washington. The first meeting between the Shah and President Kennedy was marked by a distinct lack of warmth. Kennedy received the Shah at the Oval Office and talked to him from across the presidential desk. The American leader began by giving his guest a lecture about the desirability of combating Communism through reform and clean government. The Shah felt humiliated but, as always, controlled his emotions. When his turn came he reminded Kennedy of Iran's tumultuous history and spelled out his plans for the future of the country. The Shah probably never won Kennedy's friendship, but before the Washington visit ended, Kennedy had learned to respect him. The Iranian visitor had not been the playboy king that Kennedy had apparently expected: he had spoken as an experienced politician with a good grasp of the international situation. The Shah achieved the two objectives he had fixed for himself: he became convinced that Kennedy was not particularly attached to Amini and he persuaded the American president to increase US financial support for Iran and a request for $800,000,000 in civilian and military aid was presented.

A few weeks after his return to Tehran the Shah completed his plans for Amini's dismissal and on 16 July 1962 Amini tendered his resignation. The Shah, once again had a free hand to appoint the prime minister of his choice. The man he picked was his personal friend and confidant Amir-Assadollah Alam.

Alam might have appeared an odd choice as prime minister at a time when the Shah was promising the nation 'a true social and economic revolution'. The new prime minister was a considerable landowner and represented the old establishment that the Shah wanted to combat. Alam, nevertheless, offered a number of crucial advantages: he was trusted by the Shah as a friend and was known for the long-established relations between his family and Great Britain. He would therefore not think of plotting with the Americans against the monarchy. Lacking a serious formal education, Alam also pretended to be a simple, if not naive, country gentleman. He also affected laziness and always made a point of having a siesta. Very soon, however, Alam proved himself a consummate politician with the gift of leadership. He often had difficulty with the more complex theoretical concepts, but when it came to taking decisions and implementing them he was first rate.

On 9 January 1963 the Shah addressed the first national congress of rural cooperatives in Tehran. There, with Alam at his side, the monarch announced a six-point reform programme to be put to a national referendum. The points were:

1   Land reform through the distribution of farmlands to those who worked them;
2   Nationalisation of forests and grasslands;
3   Sale of shares in government-owned factories to the public. Proceeds to be used for financing land reform;
4   Profit-sharing for workers employed by industrial and service companies;
5   Reform of the electoral laws to give women the right to vote and be elected to parliament';

6   Creation of a Literacy Corps in which army conscripts with higher
    education would serve as teachers and be dispatched to rural areas.[17]

On 27 January 1963 the referendum produced the desired results: 99
per cent of the votes approved the Shah's reform project which was to
become known as the White Revolution. To launch his 'revolution' the
Shah had recourse to political methods which he deeply disliked and with
which he could never feel comfortable. He had harangued a congress of
peasants and used some of the demagogic terms that Mossadeq had
specialised in. The very idea of a referendum was also copied from
Mossadeq as was the policy of governing without parliament. Was the
Shah being dragged into politics which he regarded as the province of
charlatans and cynics?

The Shah's vision of the ideal form of government was not so far
removed from that of Mossadeq. In that ideal model one man, the king,
prime minister or Pishva* would act as the guardian of the nation's
highest interests. The Pishva, because he loves his people, could never do
anything that might not be good for the people and the country. He might
sacrifice the interests of the few for the benefit of the many. But he would
never harm 'the people' or 'the nation' as a whole. Mossadeq's version of
the same model envisaged a role for crowds, political groups – though not
for formal political parties – and religious associations whose task was to
support the Pishva by fighting his opponents and making him feel loved
and cherished. In the Shah's model, the Pishva's decisions were to be
carried out exclusively through the bureaucracy with the armed forces
always ready to crush any opposition. All that was left for 'the nation' to
do was to applaud the Pishva and make him feel good. Mossadeq and the
Shah advanced exactly the same argument in defence of their respective
models: Iran, being constantly prey to the devilish appetite of rapacious
foreign powers, the influence of the ajnabi (foreigners), multiplying the
centres of political power would allow the ajnabi to infiltrate the nation's
structures. Neither man could envisage a situation in which different
sections of the Iranian society might, for reasons of their own, oppose the
Leader. They could conceive of no circumstances in which an opposition
movement could emerge without foreign backing and intrigue.

The Shah's – and Mossadeq's – model was, in turn, based on the
concept of 'Ismah' (Infallibility) that is at the heart of the shi'ite theory of
the state. The true ruler of the community is the Imam who represents the
Will of Allah on earth. In the absence of the Imam, his nayebs (deputies)
could rule in his name. After the seventeenth century the Shahs of Persia
were formally recognised as heads of the shi'ite community and, thus,
legitimised as rulers with the support of a clerical hierarchy that they
themselves developed.

*The title given Mossadeq by his supporters, meaning Führer.

The Shah's reform project generated some enthusiasm in the country-side where living conditions had remained unchanged for centuries. The peasants who became landowners felt that they were being admitted into a society which had previously treated them as mere serfs. The measures announced by the Shah were also supported by the growing urban middle class that saw in them the possibility of a further extension of the national market. Many landowners also found the reform project attractive: farming was no longer as profitable as it had once been and the land distribution law envisaged fair compensation for those dispossessed. The proceeds could then be invested in more-profitable industrial activities or the always-lucrative field of urban real estate. The sixth point of the reform plan, which allowed young men and, later, young women to spend their national service as teachers in the villages rather than in the armed forces, was warmly received by the student community both at home and abroad. The idea had, in fact, been put to the Shah by a group of Iranian students in London during His Majesty's official visit the previous year.

The only important group that had immediate reservations about the six-point programme consisted of the mullahs and their more fanatically minded supporters in the bazaars and among landowners. First they thought that the electoral law reform envisaging voting rights for women and opening the way for the election of women to local councils and the Majlis was in contravention of the Shari'ah (canon law) under which a woman was considered as 'half a man' in judicial terms, receiving half of a man's share under Islamic laws of inheritance. The electoral reform, however, was not limited to the issue of women's rights. It also extended full voting rights to all religious minorities. The main minorities – Christians, Jews and Zoroastrians – already had the right to choose their own deputies for the Majlis, but when it came to local elections they were effectively disenfranchised. The reform project ended that anomaly.

The second reason for the mullahs's opposition to the six-point programme was that, under the proposed land distribution schemes, the clergy would lose control once more of endowment lands (awqaf). With awqaf lands distributed among the peasants, the mullahs risked losing an important source of income and, thus, of economic power.

The reform programme was, nevertheless, popular enough to persuade the grand ayatollahs of Qom, Najaf and Mashhad that a protest movement launched at that time might lead to their defeat. The shi'ite clergy does not have an organised structure and can act with authority only if it is supported by a substantial section of the population. In 1963 it could not mobilise mass support in opposition to the Shah's proposed reforms and as a result did not venture beyond vague expressions of dissent.

There was another reason for the grand ayatollahs's mild reaction to the reform programme. With the death of Grand Ayatollah Borujerdi in 1969, the shi'ite hierarchy had lost a paramount leader capable of

commanding universal respect. Mohsen Hakim Tabataba'i, the most
senior of the grand ayatollahs, was not yet fully established as *primus
inter pares*. Hakim also suffered from another handicap: he lived in
Najaf, Iraq, and needed the Shah's support in order to counter growing
anti-Shi'ite moves by the pan-Arab Ba'athist regime then in power in
Baghdad. Ayatollah Kashani, who might have opposed the Shah's
reforms, was dead and had not yet been succeeded by another political
mullah. One mullah, however aspired to filling the gap left by
Kashani's death: Ruhollah Mussavi Khomeini.

In 1963 Khomeini was a Hojat al-Islam teaching at a seminary in Qom.
In the 1940s he attempted to enter parliament as a member for the holy
city but failed because of opposition from Borujerdi. Khomeini also
associated with the Islam's Fedayeen terrorist group and, for a while,
tried to attach himself to Kashani. He was the writer of a number of
incendiary pamphlets against modernising intellectuals and was also
known for his poems, including a satire he wrote against Borujerdi. In
1949 Khomeini tried to win publicity by writing an open letter to
Borujerdi in which the grand ayatollah was asked to oppose amendments
to the Constitution. The amendments then discussed were aimed at
augmenting the Shah's powers and providing for the creation of a senate.
Nevertheless Khomeini, in his usual radical style, spoke of 'a plot to harm
Islam and the shi'ite faith'. Borujerdi, who described Khomeini as a
sharur (trouble-maker), ignored the letter.[18]

In 1963, supported by a number of dispossessed landowners,
Khomeini once again posed as the champion of Islam against a
government accused of 'plotting to destroy the Faith of Muhammad'. The
Hojat al-Islam became spokesman for the Shah's many opponents,
including Bakhtiar who, now in exile, had begun his own campaign
against the monarch. Khomeini presented the reform programme as one
aimed at handing over the government of the country to religious
minorities, notably the Baha'is, and also declared the land reform to be
contrary to Islamic law.

Khomeini's message captured the imagination of enough people to
provoke a number of riots in Tehran and other big cities in June 1963.
Rioting was particularly intense in the capital as hundreds of jahel (tough
guys) led crowds of pauperised former peasants and well-to-do bazaaris
on a rampage through the centre of the capital, burning, smashing and
looting many government offices and forcing the police to retreat. The
army had to be called in. Alam, the prime minister, wanted immediate
and strong action but the Shah hesitated. From his palace north of Tehran
he kept telephoning the prime minister to make sure 'that there is no
bloodshed'. He wanted Alam to settle the trouble through negotiations,
although no one could be sure who the leader of the mobs was at the
time.[19] Alam had not forgotten that the Shah had dismissed
Sharif-Emami as prime minister after only one demonstrator died in

Tehran in 1961 and was determined not to suffer the same fate. He decided to order the troops to fire on the crowds without consulting the Shah. Then, having given the order, he asked his cabinet director not to disturb him until after the sacrosanct siesta.[20] By the time the prime minister had ended his siesta, the capital was calm again and the army was in control. Hundreds of people were killed as troops, led by Colonel Gholam-Ali Oveissi, fired indiscriminately on the feverish crowds. Many rioters had already put on their shrouds and had come to seek martyrdom in the service of Islam. They would rather die than see women enjoying the same rights as men and non-Muslims being promised the same treatment as Muslims.

The riots failed because they did not develop a coherent pattern of leadership. At the same time the political platform presented by Khomeini, with indirect support from General Bakhtiar, was a thoroughly reactionary one that repelled large sections of the urban population, notably the strategically important student community. Within a few days the troubles were over and Khomeini was taken to a prison in Tehran. Scores of other mullahs were banished to remote provinces. The Shah emerged from the challenge with his position substantially strengthened. A few weeks later several leaders of the Tehran riots were hanged. Among them was Tayyeb Haj-Reza'i, the man who had led the mob in the pro-Shah uprising of August 1953. At his trial he was charged with collusion with General Bakhtiar. In later years, however, he became a 'martyr-hero' of the Khomeinist movement with a special place in the Islamic revolutionary iconography.

Alam wanted to have Khomeini hanged along with other trouble-makers but this was opposed by the SAVAK chief, General Pakravan, a pipe-smoking intellectual who believed that 'reasonable dialogue' was the best answer to all political problems. Pakravan visited Khomeini in the latter's place of detention and left with the belief that the rebellious mullah had modified his 'unreasonable' position. Khomeini, however, had merely practised taqiyeh or kitman (dissimulation) in order to mislead and confuse Pakravan. The French-educated general, more at home with Saint Augustine than shi'ite theology, had simply been led up the garden path by the crafty cleric from Qom.

Back in the holy city Khomeini basked in his enhanced status. He had established himself as a national figure without much suffering. Others had died in the streets or were hanged in public in his name, but he was alive and could wait for another opportunity to challenge the government.

Throughout the entire episode Khomeini had been careful not to burn all his bridges with the government. He even sent a well-wisher's telegramme to Alam to warn the prime minister against 'machinations by enemies of Islam'. In his addresses at the Qom seminary, the Hojat al-Islam also pretended that he was anxious to save the Shah from being

misled by Baha'is, Jews and other enemies of the faith. The Shah himself
was not to blame and the fault was with his entourage.

The Shah saw the defeat of the riots as a fresh popular endorsement of
his person and programme. In a message to the nation he said that since
his White Revolution was now stained by blood as a result of plots by
'Red-and-Black Reaction', a term he used to describe Communist and
religious opponents, the reform movement had better be renamed: the
Revolution of the Shah and the People. In time the entire episode was
rewritten to make it appear as if the toiling masses of Tehran had
themselves acted to crush a counter-revolutionary revolt led by feudal
barons and mercenary mullahs. The stage was set for a new mythology of
power to be shaped with the 'revolutionary' Shah as its central figure.

10

On the Peacock Throne

Until the 1930s few Iranians had ever heard of Cyrus the Great, the Persian king who had created the first empire in history more than 25 centuries ago. The once glorious city of Pasargadae (Pazargad) where Cyrus was buried had shrunk to a ghost village with only a handful of inhabitants. Cyrus's tomb, which had once stood at the centre of an imperial mausoleum, was now a mass of ruins in the middle of a lunar landscape: the nomadic tribes who pastured their sheep in the vicinity believed that it was the resting place of King Solomon's mother. Even the locality's original name had disappeared and Pasargadae was referred to as 'Mashhad Morghab' (The Place of Morghab's martyrdom).[1]

Not far from Pasargadae were the ruins of Persepolis, the Achaemenian capital. A scene of desolation, Persepolis had been renamed Takht Jamshid (The Throne of Jamshid) after a mythological king. Only a handful of Iranians who could read the scholarly papers of European Orientalists knew that the 'Throne of Jamshid' was, in fact, a city which had once boasted it was the centre of the universe. During 14 centuries of slow but steady conversion to Islam, Iran had forgotten its ancient past. Even the tiny Zoroastrian minority had not succeeded in keeping the memory alive beyond a mass of incoherent mythological beliefs.

Reza Shah's belief that most of Iran's ills stemmed from its 'Arab-zadehgi' (literally: being hit by Arabisation) had brought ancient Iran back into official political discourse as the cornerstone of a new national identity. With Reza Shah forced into exile, the re-Iranisation effort had been abandoned in the chaos and confusion of war and political crisis. Mohammad-Reza Shah's own Islamic beliefs made him a far less enthusiastic 're-Iraniser' than his father had been. But in the 1960s Mohammad-Reza Shah rediscovered Persian nationalism as a potentially attractive alternative to two ideologies that, he was convinced, threatened Iran's well-being and independence: mullah-dominated shi'ism and Soviet-sponsored Communism.

The Shah had at first benefited from the influence of the mullahs in his own fight against Mossadeq. In 1963, however, the revolts inspired by Ayatollah Khomeini symbolised the return of the mullahs to their traditional aim of acting as a state within the state. The Shah, recast in the role of a revolutionary, needed a strong, highly-centralised and increasingly authoritarian state apparatus in order to impose his reforms on a reluctant society. He could not allow the mullahs to dictate the nation's agenda, and to combat the mullahs he needed an ideology capable of rivalling militant shi'ism.

In the 1950s and the 1960s the Iranian state also faced the challenge of Communist revolutionary ideas. The pseudoscientific terminology of Marxism-Leninism and its messianic message of redemption through revolution appealed to many recently-urbanised and hastily-educated youths in Iran and other Middle-Eastern societies. The rising prestige of the USSR as a superpower capable of achieving impressive economic and technological results in a relatively short period of time added to the appeal of the leftwing ideologies among the urban middle classes. Soon after he launched his 'revolution', the Shah realised that the ideological ground was almost fully occupied by his opponents.

The vast majority of the people, peasants or paupers in urban areas, would not easily abandon the imagined security of ancestral beliefs. They were too vulnerable, too weak to take risks with new ideas – even ideas that might promise them a better life. Resigned to the fact that this world had nothing to offer them except humiliation and terror, they invested their meagre hopes in the promised paradise of the Prophet. And they were convinced that the mullahs held the keys to that eternal life of peace and plenty. In the bigger cities and among the middle classes, the ideological ground was occupied either by the left or by an assortment of vague concepts collectively known as 'Mossadeqism'.[2]

In this context it was almost inevitable that the Shah should try to play the card of Persian nationalism. The political climate in the region further encouraged the Shah in making that choice. Arab nationalism, symbolised by Nasser, was still in the ascendancy, prior to Egypt's military defeat by Israel in the 1967 war, and directly threatened Iran's position in the Persian Gulf. Partly to counter that and partly in the hope of mobilising support at home, the Shah revived the issue of Iran's sovereignty over the Bahrain archipelago in the Persian Gulf. In 1944 the Majlis had passed a resolution ordering the government to restore Iranian rule to Bahrain and the archipelago had been declared an Iranian province and assigned two seats in the Majlis. At the time, however, Bahrain was a British protectorate under an Arab ruling family and there was little that Iran could do to recover it. The issue failed to capture the imagination of the people and was gradually allowed to fade. In any case, the Shah was the last person to take the risk of provoking an international conflict in order to work his way out of a tight corner at home.

With the nationalist discourse established as part of state policy, the

Shah introduced a second element in the ideological cocktail he hoped to create. This was the idea of 'modernisation'.

In 1964, in a review of the nation's performance during the decade that had followed the fall of Mossadeq, the Shah startled even his admirers by promising to 'change this country beyond recognition in a decade'. Addressing the nation, he said:

My ultimate goal is to take Iran to the level of civilisation and progress that the most developed countries have achieved. This we shall do in 20 years. Compared to 10 years ago we have reduced the gap that separated us [from the advanced nations] by half. But it is the second half of the gap that will be most difficult to cover.[3]

At the time the Shah was portraying that future, Iran was still one of the poorest countries in the world. Despite its rising oil revenue and the undoubted increase in economic activity since 1953, the Iran of 1964 still had a annual per capita GNP that was lower than that of Portugal and Greece, Europe's poorest nations at that time. More than 70 per cent of the people were still illiterate and the country, almost as large as the whole of Western Europe, had only 5000 kilometres of paved roads. There were fewer than 4000 doctors of medicine for a population of nearly 25 million.

A programme of national renaissance and modernisation might well have captured the imagination of large sections of society had it been espoused by a charismatic political leader capable of mobilising the forces necessary for the task ahead. Because of his position as monarch, the Shah could not become the effective leader of a political movement, his task being to stand above all classes; to be, in the words of Kavus Voshmgir, the 'sun who shines equally brightly on everyone, rich or poor, powerful or powerless'.[4] As a 'revolutionary leader', on the other hand, he was forced to take sides, to be for one group and against another. An Iranian king had never entered the political arena himself and even Reza Shah, who had ruled Iran more like a military dictator than a traditional Shah, had somehow managed to retain a certain distance from political quarrels. He had not espoused any particular ideology and would not have dreamed of setting grandiose goals either for himself as ruler or for the nation. He told his son that his only aim was to create a government machine that would continue to function even after he had gone.

Mohammad-Reza Shah believed that nothing was too good for Iran and had persuaded himself that, provided the nation followed him with conviction, the sky was the limit of what could be achieved. His idealism, his activism, his thirst for achievement and his belief that the machinery of government could be employed as an instrument of radical change reflected his Western education and outlook. Traditionally, however the Iranian Shahs, with a few exceptions, saw their task as one of managing society, not changing it. They represented society's inertia. What is known as 'constructivism' – the idea that a society can be reshaped in accordance with plans worked out by its leaders – was alien to them. They shared the belief of the common folk that government was, at best, a necessary evil. All that most Iranians had traditionally wanted from their government was that they be left alone to go about their business in peace. The government was a monster that took from them without ever giving anything back. It could not be trusted and was to be cheated at every available opportunity.

The more traditional politicians, far better informed about how things worked in Iran, had grave reservations about the Shah's new policies. In 1963 a groups of senior statesmen led by Hossein Ala demanded an audience with His Majesty to express their misgivings about the royal 'revolution'.[5] They tried to explain that a society organised its life on the basis of countless decisions taken by countless individuals every day, and that it was impossible for any group of men to try and enforce dramatic change. The group also advised the Shah not to enter into direct confrontation with the shi'ite clergy. The Shah, his morale boosted by the crushing of the June revolt, attacked the elderly advisers with terms of abuse. 'You must all be thrown into a toilet bowl and flushed away,' he told them. One of those present, Abdallah Entezam, summoned enough courage to say: 'Majesty! No one dared tell lies to your father. But now no one dares tell you the truth.' Entezam, who had served as Foreign Minister and Chairman of the National Iranian Oil Company, fell into royal disgrace until 1978.

Another traditional politician who tried to warn the Shah against 'playing with revolution' was Hassan Ha'eri-Zadeh, a veteran member of the Majlis, but he too was rudely rebuked and sent home. Before leaving his audience with the Shah he took the risk of uttering his celebrated verdict: 'Your Majesty! Your father was a prime minister who became Shah. But you are a Shah who tries to become prime minister. Why?'[6]

The Shah was convinced that no one loved Iran as much as he did and that unless he himself stepped in to save the nation from backwardness no one would. In 1976 he explained this view at some length:

> Look at all that has been done. We have destroyed the big landowners and the tribal khans who exploited the people, in just over a decade. Would this have been possible without the Shah leading the revolution by putting his position, his prestige and, indeed, his life on the line? Passing a land reform bill through parliament, under ordinary circumstances and without my intervention, could have taken twenty years or more. Does Iran have so much time to waste?[7]

The Shah used similar arguments to justify the growing role of the state in the nation's economic life. He asserted that the Iranian private sector would never have the necessary financial strength to create a steel industry or compete with western multinationals in such fields as petrochemicals and machine tools. The state also had to assume a number of social and cultural responsibilities that, in the more established societies of the West, are performed by the middle classes.

Are you against state intervention? Very well. But remember that if the state does not build schools in the villages no one will. And if the state does not subsidise higher education only few people will be able to go to university in this country. And how can we distribute the nation's income when, in many areas of the country, we do not have a middle class apart from government employees?'[8]

The launch of the reform programme marked the start of a massive expansion in the size and role of the government in Iran. As the few derelict factories that had been inherited from the Reza Shah era were sold to the private sector, new state enterprises came into being. The catchword was industrialisation, which the Shah hoped to achieve with help from the USSR and the Eastern bloc states. Along with most other Iranians, he was persuaded that the capitalist West would not allow the emergence of new industrial rivals and Iran was, therefore, left with no choice but to take its first steps towards an industrial society with the help of its ideological enemies.

The idea of creating a steel plant had captured the imagination of urban Iranians since the 1930s. Reza Shah had ordered a foundry from Nazi Germany in 1939 but the plant was not ready for delivery before 1941, by which time Reza Shah was already in exile. During his state visit to America in 1949 the new Shah invited several US companies to revive the project. Most firms contacted politely declined. A couple of smaller concerns sent their engineers to Tehran to have a look but they were unanimous in pronouncing such a project 'wasteful and economically unjustifiable' for Iran at the time. This was, of course, immediately seen as an American plot: The 'selfish' United States did not want to run the risk of creating new competitors!

Next, Iran approached West Germany and the steel mill issue was discussed by the Shah and Federal German Economy Minister Ludwig Erhard during the latter's visit to Tehran in 1956. Erhard advised the Shah to concentrate his efforts on turning Iran into an agricultural power first and then use the surplus created by the rural sector for the purpose of industrialisation. The Shah was deeply hurt: he felt as if the West wanted to keep him out of the 'club of the rich'.[9]

The Shah's concept of modernisation was essentially a physical one symbolised by factory chimneys, electrical pylons, high-rise apartment blocks and plentiful supermarkets. He believed that no country would be fully respected without first creating a steel industry. In the mid-1960s he read a report in an American magazine regarding the future of the world which prophesied that by the end of the century there would be three categories of nations: the first-class industrialised countries, the second-class rural countries and the third-class nations that would 'never catch up with civilisation'. He was determined to lead Iran into the top league and the steel mill was finally created with Soviet financial and technical help near Isfahan. By the time it began production in the late 1960s it was already technologically outmoded and operated at above average costs.

In 1964 the radical mullahs made one more attempt at stopping the Shah's reform movement through mass protest. Once again, Khomeini, now recognised by many as an ayatollah and thus enjoying greater moral authority, raised the banner of revolt. This time his excuse was an act passed by the Majlis under which certain categories of American servicemen seconded to the Iranian armed forces would enjoy extra-territorial capitulary rights. The passage of the act coincided with news that Washington had granted Iran a new $200,000,000 loan. These accords with Washington had been concluded during Alam's premiership but came to a conclusion after he had left office.

Alam resigned as prime minister after holding a general election in which, for the first time since 1941, not a single politician who might have dreamed of defying the Shah was elected. The election was dominated by a new group called the Progressive Centre led by Hassan-Ali Mansur, the 43-year-old son of Rajab-Ali Mansur, the veteran politician and former prime minister. Mansur, a shrewd observer of the political scene, recognised the existence of a leadership gap in the country. The older politicians were fading from the scene: many had suffered royal disgrace but most were simply too old and, often, too sick to seek office and influence. The Shah was visibly looking for new recruits and Mansur offered the Shah access to a new and expanding source of support: the pool of technocrats educated at home and abroad. Mansur's group, openly supported by the Shah, was allowed to win a large number of seats in the new Majlis.

The majority of the new deputies, however, came from peasant and working-class families. The Shah wanted a parliament that reflected the actual composition of the population. The landowners who had dominated the Iranian parliament for more than half a century were totally absent. There were also no mullahs and the number of bazaaris was kept to a strict minimum. From a demographic point of view the new Majlis was, indeed, an accurate representation of male Iranian society – it also included a number of women members, elected for the first time –and might well have symbolised the nation's unity in support of the reform movement. The trouble was that the members knew that they owed their election not to the voters but to the government, so instead of acting as spokesmen for the people they quickly became government spokesmen in their constituencies.

By all accounts there was no need for the government to manipulate the election process. In any free election at the time supporters of the reform project would almost certainly have won a majority even though the Majlis would have also included many mullahs – who would have ferociously opposed the reforms – and a few nostalgics of the Mossadeq era. As it was the Majlis elected under Alam's premiership did not reflect the full reality of the political mood in Iran. It was, therefore, not difficult for Khomeini to defy its decisions.

This time Khomeini appeared not only as a champion of Islam but also as a defender of Iranian nationalism, a very strange role for a pan-Islamist. Other leading Qom ayatollahs, notably Ayatollah Mohammad-Kazem Shariatmadari, also condemned both the 'capitulation' act and the loan from the United States. Khomeini made his own the anti-Israel slogan that was nightly beamed to Iran by radical Arab radios. In a speech in Qom he criticised the Mansur government in these terms:

> The source of all our troubles is America. The source of all of our troubles is Israel. And Israel also belongs to America. Our MPs belong to America. Our ministers belong to America. America has bought them all . . . The American president should know that he is the most hated man in Iran.[10]

The ayatollah also expressed the resentment felt by many members of the military with regard to the 'capitulation' act:

> They have dishonoured our army by setting an American sergeant above our four-star generals. The [military] have no prestige left in Iran. . . If I were an army officer I would resign. If I were a member of the Majlis I would resign. . . If the country is under American occupation, tell us. In that case, seize us and throw us out of the country.[11]

This was precisely what Mansur decided to do. Abducted from his Qom residence in the middle of the night, the ayatollah was brought to Tehran and forced into exile in Turkey. The new SAVAK chief, General Nematallah Nasiri, had suggested that Khomeini be disposed of in a little 'unfortunate' accident, but Mansur chose the more classical punishment of exile and by the end of November 1964 the whole episode was forgotten by most people.

But not by all. Militant fundamentalists began to reorganise in clandestine groups, having concluded that the age of open protest in the form of demonstrations and the closing of the bazaars had come to an end and that other methods of struggle had to be found.

The vast majority of the mullahs, however, quickly reached an understanding with the government. The Shah withdrew his earlier threat of a direct and open confrontation with the religious establishment. In exchange the leading ayatollahs agreed to mind their own business. Soon the government began to sweeten the bitter pill by channelling large sums of money to the shi'ite seminaries through hundreds of mullahs. In time no fewer than 3000 mullahs, of all ranks, became SAVAK informers.[12]

Just over two months after Khomeini was pushed into exile, the 'punishment' that he had promised Mansur on behalf of Allah was meted out. On 21 January 1965 Mansur was shot while stepping out of his car at the gate of the Majlis building. He had been scheduled to introduce a new bill on oil agreements. His assailant was a 20-year-old theology student named Mohammad Bokhara'i, a member of Islam's Fedayeen terrorist group that SAVAK had written off as long disbanded.

Mansur was transferred to Pars Hospital, run by his friend Dr Manuchehr Shahqoli. For five days he fought for life but died without regaining consciousness. News of the terrorist act had reached the Shah and Queen Farah at a ski resort north of Tehran where the Shah was 'deeply moved' and immediately flew to the hospital in a helicopter. 'They have not yet become fully quiet,' he told Farah, enigmatically. Whom did he mean? The fundamentalists, probably. A state funeral was organised for Mansur, who was buried in a graveyard reserved for members of the royal family. To make it abundantly clear that the assassination would not change the government's policies, the Shah chose Amir Abbas Hoveyda, Mansur's life-long friend, and Finance Minister at the time, to assume the premiership.

Hoveyda, then aged 45, had not yet had a chance to emerge from Mansur's shadow and design a political image of his own. Most people were convinced that he would be no more than a stop-gap prime minister, but he stayed in the job for nearly 13 years.

Born in Tehran, Hoveyda was the elder son of Ayn al-Molk, a career diplomat who had served as Iran's envoy to Iraq and Saudi Arabia. At one stage Ayn al-Molk had converted to the Baha'i faith and become active as a missionary for what the shi'ites saw as 'a deadly heresy'. Ayn al-Molk's wife, however, had not converted to her husband's faith and remained a devout shi'ite. Closely related to an old family of mullahs, Hoveyda's mother tried to inject her own beliefs into the minds of her two sons. Ayn al-Molk's death when Hoveyda was in his teens meant that the future prime minister was brought up more as a shi'ite than as an adept of Baha'ism. He spent his boyhood in Beirut where his father had served as Iranian Consul-General and, after studying politics and economics in France and Belgium, Hoveyda started a diplomatic career which took him to West Germany in the immediate post-war period and, later, to Turkey, where he became a friend of Mansur who also served at the embassy in Ankara. The two friends returned to Tehran together and married two sisters. Mansur became an economic adviser for the government and Hoveyda was appointed a member of the National Iranian Oil Company's board of directors.

Hoveyda lacked Mansur's charisma and seething ambition for political power. Had it not been for his friend, Hoveyda might never even have envisaged a political career. A polyglot – he was fluent in Persian, Arabic, French and English and had a good command of German and Turkish – Hoveyda was an intellectual. Where Mansur's energy was more physical, Hoveyda's was essentially cerebral. His chief assets as a politician proved to be his ability to listen to everyone and his seemingly boundless patience in an impatient society. Very quickly he established himself as the new type of politician that the Shah had, perhaps unconsciously, looked for since the late 1950s. In time, Hoveyda proved to be the only prime minister with whom the Shah was almost always comfortable. Mansur had, at times, appeared too gripped by his own personal ambition to be fully trustworthy on a long-term basis. Even Alam, a confidant of the monarch for a quarter of a century, had not succeeded in putting the Shah completely at ease.

Hoveyda won the Shah's confidence because he quickly understood the monarch's psychology. The Shah was basically a shy person who would adopt an aggressive attitude if and when he felt threatened. He wanted to be treated as a 'boss' and consulted on all matters. He did not realise that he who is consulted on all matters might end up with no proper understanding of any particular issue.

Hoveyda was a passionate student of semiology and an avid reader of Barthes and Lacan. 'We live in a universe of signs,' he liked to say. 'People fight and die for signs.'[13] It was in semiological vein that he designed his own political image as 'a square man in a round body'. His pipe, the orchid he wore in his buttonhole – a different colour each day to accord with the pattern of his necktie – and his walking stick defined his difference and shaped his image as a reassuring, almost grandfatherly figure of innate benevolence.

Part of the quarrel that many prime ministers – including Mossadeq and Qavam – had had with the Shah was rooted in petty personal jealousies and consideration of form and protocol. Hoveyda couldn't care less about appearances. He did not want to appear a 'big cheese' and was almost incapable of political jealousy and envy. He had never sought political power and seemed to have no difficulty returning to a private life whenever necessary. In time, however, precisely because he appeared not to want personal power, he became the first truly powerful prime minister in Iran's contemporary history.

Hoveyda presided over the expenditure of fabulous sums – more than $200 billion during his premiership. Under him the government machinery expanded into a veritable giant that employed nearly a million people. Four successive general elections produced parliaments filled with his friends. Ignoring appearances he emerged as the real power behind the throne and played a crucial role in reshaping Iranian society in the 1960s and 1970s.

Hoveyda's quiet appearance at the centre of Iranian political life coincided with the emergence of another powerful figure at the Shah's side: Queen Farah. The shy girl who had at first been awed by the sight of 'those massive salons of marble and mirror' in the Golestan Palace, quickly realised that power – which she likes to refer to as 'responsibility' – was there to be seized by anyone who dared reach for it. This is how she remembered her early days as queen:

A most boring experience, on the whole. I had nothing to do. At times I just drove my car around Shemiran to kill time. The royal palaces at first impressed me because I had not seen anything better. But after our first state visits to foreign countries, I realised that the Iranian royal palaces were, in fact, semi-derelict and underequipped houses. The Shah's Special Residence, for example, had only two bedrooms and we had to leave it as soon as the family grew. We took over the Niavaran Palace which had been built as a guest house for foreign dignitaries. It had no air-conditioning system. At Saadabad, the summer residence, the electrical system kept breaking down, especially at the height of the hot season.[14]

To keep herself busy, Farah began 'sticking my nose' into the basement of the various palaces. These she found 'as full of an assortment of objects as Ali Baba's cave'. Wearing a pair of old jeans she would spend hours in 'those caves'. She discovered veritable treasures: old Qajar paintings, a table service presented by President Mitterrand of France, handwoven carpets and traditional items of furniture.

But cleaning the palace basements was not Farah's sole idea of her role as queen. She tackled the seemingly impossible task of equipping the palaces with 'a minimum of basic necessities'. These included the construction of additional bathrooms, new kitchens and special quarters for guards and servants. With Hoveyda's help, the queen also succeeded in replacing the old furniture of some of the palaces with new. Until 1965 the palace used to rent furniture, as well as table services, whenever a state banquet was given and the royal table was always decorated with 'horrible plastic tulips from the bazaar'. Her first major victory as queen was to get rid of 'those horrors'.[15]

Farah had received 'no special training for my role as queen'. They did not even send me on a course in etiquette and protocol. I did not know how I should behave. Should I sit or stand up when an ambassador came for a courtesy call? Whom could I ask for guidance? In the end I received my training on the job'.[16] One day she brought the issue of her role up with the Shah. 'Well,' he said. 'I will make sure that you are kept informed about all that is going on in the country. There are, of course, topics that you had better not get involved with. You are a woman and might reveal secrets under torture.' Under torture? Farah was shocked. The Shah apparently had prepared himself for the very worst. But what were the forbidden topics? Farah never found out for certain, but she guessed that the Shah referred to petroleum policy and military affairs as well as some 'sensitive areas of foreign relations'. [17]

It took Farah more than five years and the birth of three children before she felt her position as the Shah's wife was unassailable. In the first years of the marriage she had continued to receive anonymous letters warning her about the Shah's alleged inability to remain faithful to a single woman. Evil tongues continued to wag: Farah's sole function was to mother the royal children while the Shah turned to other women for true carnal pleasure. None of this, of course, was true. The Shah was maturing – growing old in fact – and was beginning to be more interested in reviving the Empire of Cyrus the Great than the harem of Fath-Ali Shah which was reputed to contain 365 women at any given time.

One day the Queen brought up the Shah's widely reported desire to find a foreign bride before he met Farah. 'I can tell you that the only reason was that I thought I would have fewer problems with a foreign wife: to begin with her family would not be breathing down my neck all the time,' the Shah explained.

In 1965 the couple discussed the Shah's plans for a coronation. Unlike his father, who had crowned himself shortly after becoming king, the Shah remained uncrowned 25 years after his accession to the Peacock Throne. Before he could fix the date, however, the Shah went through another attempt on his life.

Just over two months after Mansur's death, the Shah and Queen Farah were preparing for a long trip abroad that would take them to Africa, South America and Canada. Under the Constitution, a Regency Council had the task of exercising the Shah's powers during the latter's absence or illness. According to tradition the Council was composed of two of the Shah's half-brothers, the speakers of the two houses of parliament, the Chief Justice and the prime minister. In April 1965 the Shah had decided to go ahead with his long foreign tour despite initial doubts about the ability of the new prime minister, Hoveyda, to handle a crisis if and when necessary. After six weeks of close collaboration with the new prime minister the Shah had concluded that Hoveyda, with his cool nerve, could be safely left in charge.

For several months the Shah had made a habit of walking his eldest son Reza to a kindergarten organised for the royal children inside the Marble Palace. The building where the kindergarten was situated was a few hundred yards away from the Shah's own office where he would go after delivering Prince Reza. Virtually every inch of the short walk was protected by heavily armed Imperial Guardsmen. On 10 April 1965 the Shah suddenly changed his daily routine because he was told that Prince Reza was that day expecting to welcome a new child who was just joining the kindergarten: the prince and his new friend would leave the palace later in the company of their teachers. The Shah, therefore, decided to drive to his office. The decision almost certainly saved his life.

As the Shah stepped out of his blue Cadillac he felt that a commotion had almost simultaneously broken out just over 50 metres away. Paying no attention to what was going on and accompanied by his Protocol Chief Logham Adham, the Shah entered the palace building. Once there, he heard shots being fired. Within seconds, a guardsman, with a machine gun firing in all directions forced his way into the palace. The two officers guarding the entrance ran for cover. Inside the entrance hall another guardsman, Lieutenant Ali Babayan, fired at the assailant and wounded him in the knee but the assailant was faster and killed Babayan with a shot to the head. A second guardsman, Lieutenant Ayat Lashkari, rushed to stop the assailant as he headed for the Shah's office. Lashkari, too, was shot dead, but before falling he had had time to empty his machine gun into the attacker's body. Dripping with blood, the assailant continued his advance towards the Shah's office, firing all the time. One of his bullets hit the wall a few inches away from the desk behind which the Shah was sitting. Now there was no one to stop the gunman who pushed open the door of the royal office in a mass of metal and blood. He had no strength left and instantly collapsed in front of the monarch's desk.

This is how the Shah related what he instantly saw as 'another miracle':

The firing seemed to come from everywhere and, for a while, I thought a general armed uprising had broken out. We remained in the office without moving as the sound of shooting came closer. I had no arms in my office at the time, not even a revolver. The sound of machine guns was terrifying. A bullet came in through the door and hissed by my ear.[18]

Within seconds the court officials and the guardsmen who had run into hiding reappeared and rushed towards the monarch's office, certain he had been hit. The Shah, however, met them with a grim face. 'Clean up here,' he ordered. 'We are expecting a foreign guest.'[19] The foreign guest was the commander of the French navy who had come on an official visit to Iran. When the Frenchman entered the Shah's office barely 20 minutes after the assassination attempt, everything was calm and orderly. There was nothing in the Shah's attitude to show that he had just escaped a violent death. It was only an hour later, when the French officer returned to the embassy, that he learned about the drama he had just missed at the palace.

The man who had tried to kill the Shah was a conscript named Reza Shams-Abadi who had, apparently, planned to murder the monarch and Prince Reza during their morning walk. The Shah was spending vast sums of money on security and yet he had nearly been murdered in his own palace. The entire episode was bad publicity for SAVAK and the half a dozen other intelligence outfits that worked more or less outside legal control. The Western news agencies that reported the incident at first spoke of a lone gunman suddenly going berserk, but this was a theory that appealed to western minds. Iranians wanted something more substantial to chew on. They would never believe that anyone would do anything in the realm of power and politics without being involved in a complex conspiracy.

Accordingly a variety of stories began to fly around, one of which said that Khomeini, now in exile, had signed a fatwa sentencing the Shah and his son to death. The government, however, did not encourage this version – it would have given too much importance to Khomeini who was already being blamed for having organised the prime minister's murder in January.

Another story spoke of a conspiracy by army officers working on behalf of the exiled General Bakhtiar, now in Switzerland and feverishly plotting against the Shah. The Shah always tried to portray the army as an absolutely loyal force, but he had subjected the same loyal force to no fewer than five successive purges in less than a decade. In one purge the director of the army's counter-intelligence, General Wali-Allah Qarani, had been accused of involvement in an American-sponsored plot against the Shah and excluded from the armed forces.[20] In 1965, however, it was hard for the Shah to accept the humiliating suggestion that his own beloved army, which consumed more than a quarter of the national budget, might have plotted to kill him. It was necessary to find others to blame. SAVAK, anxious to justify its existence, obligingly came up with a marketable story.

Ever since 1961 SAVAK had identified Iranian student communities abroad as important centres of opposition to the regime. In that year Iranian students abroad, estimated to number around 10,000 at the time, had created a confederation with headquarters in London. Thus students attending British universities were more carefully watched by SAVAK agents. One student who received special attention was a Manchester University physics student named Parviz Nik-Khah. A passionate idealist, Nik-Khah had quickly decided that only Marxism-Leninism could create a just and prosperous society in Iran but had found the Tudeh party in exile too conservative, too corrupt, for his taste. In 1963 he visited Moscow where he was tricked by SAVAK agents into a supposedly 'private encounter' during which he was filmed and taped. He found the USSR nothing like the socialist paradise he had dreamed of. On his return to London he took a leading role in splitting Tudeh in the name of Maoist militancy. In 1964 he returned to Iran to study the modalities of starting a proletarian revolution based on the Maoist model. There, because of his charm and the sheer purity of his idealism, he established himself as the de facto leader of a circle most of whose members were graduates from Manchester and other British universities. A member of that circle, Ahmad Mansuri, had been in contact with one Samad Kamrani, a mechanics apprentice at a garage in Kashan. Kamrani, in turn, had once known Shams-Abadi, the Shah's would-be assassin, who was also a native of Kashan.

SAVAK moulded these pieces of information together and came up with the story of a vast conspiracy to kill the Shah and create a Communist state in Iran. The alleged conspirators were also accused of having established contact with the fugitive Bakhtiar. SAVAK did not say so in so many words, although newspaper accounts it inspired did, but it tried to give a British dimension to the entire incident. Nik-Khah and eight of his fellow 'conspirators' had all graduated from British universities and simply could not have acted without a nod from London! The theory SAVAK put into circulation was simple: Britain, jealous that Iran was getting closer to the United States, had tried to have the Shah killed by Communists who had their own reasons for hating the Pahlavi regime. Logically, the Shah could not have taken the SAVAK story seriously. Perhaps he did not, but there were signs that he liked to believe it.

The SAVAK story took into account some of the myths and fantasies that the Shah, against his own better judgment, could not quite set aside: Britain had always been an enemy of the Pahlavis. No Iranian would dream of treason except under foreign influence. The Iranian people could not have legitimate grievances of their own and acted violently only when duped by foreign enemies of the nation. While Britain was an enemy of the Pahlavis, Communism remained the enemy of the country as a whole. Opposition intellectuals, in the end, were nothing but vulgar terrorists plotting to murder a father who was taking his son to kindergarten. The Shah, however, was protected by metaphysical powers – in short, God – and emerged with greater authority after every cowardly attempt on his life!

The military tribunal that judged the alleged conspirators sentenced Ahmad Mansuri and Samad Kamrani to death. Nik-Khah, who had held the tribunal spellbound with his passionate oratory for several days, was given a life sentence. Others received terms of imprisonment ranging between three and nine years. The military prosecutor had demanded the death sentence for all the accused except two but the SAVAK story was so hard to sell even in an Iranian military court that the whole episode eventually ended without tragedy. The Shah commuted the death sentences and within five years none of the conspirators was left in prison.

After being sentenced to death Mansuri demanded to see the Shah. 'This is my last wish before I die,' he said in melodramatic tones. Mansuri who had been presented as the ringleader of the plot, was a graduate of Leeds University. He looked more like a second-hand car salesman than a Narodnik terrorist. When he found himself in the Shah's presence at the palace he broke into tears and tried to kiss the monarch's foot. Queen Farah watched the early part of the proceedings from the balcony that overlooked the central hall of the palace. Once Mansuri had stopped crying, the Shah motioned Farah to come down the stairs and join the bizarre encounter.[21]

Mansuri's audience was quickly exploited as the basis of a series of stories about the Shah's magnanimity towards those who wished to harm him. It was reported that all the conspirators had demanded to see the monarch only to kiss his feet and thank God that His Majesty was still alive and well to lead the nation. The Communist agents of perfidious Albion had suddenly seen the light.

Later the same year 53 people, among them several mullahs, were arrested and tried on a charge of 'plotting to create an Islamic government'. Almost at the same time 14 Tudeh leaders, all living in the Soviet bloc, were sentenced to various prison terms in absentia. SAVAK meanwhile began increasingly to regard its own former chief, Bakhtiar, as the regime's 'most dangerous enemy'.

Bakhtiar had moved to France and was openly trying to forge a coalition against the Shah. The French secret service informed the Iranians that Bakhtiar had contacted some of his former Saint Cyr contemporaries who had joined the underground Organisation de l'Armée Secrète (OAS), a terrorist group that had fought and lost a bloody battle against General de Gaulle over the issue of Algerian independence.

On 19 May 1967 another attempt to kill the Shah was discovered: 40 soldiers opened fire on the monarch's limousine on its way to the palace. The Shah, however, was not in the car. SAVAK investigations quickly established Bakhtiar as the man behind the plot.

Once again this latest attack had come only days before the Shah and the Queen were due to start a state visit. Two weeks later came yet another attempt to assassinate the monarch, this time with the Queen: a Volkswagen laden with explosives was to be driven by remote control into a head-on crash with the limousine that carried the royal couple in West Berlin. Once again the Shah and the Queen were saved by the fact that they were not in the car they were supposed to be in at the time. A German student was killed in the explosion and provided the then rising student protest movement with a martyr.

It is possible to argue that this constituted a watershed for the student movement in western Europe, sparking off a series of strikes and demonstrations that gripped most German campuses and then spilled over into Britain and France.

Involved in the attempt to kill the Shah and Queen Farah were a number of radical German students who, later, created the Baader and Meinhof terrorist groups that, after their merger, plagued German political life for more than a decade. The West Berlin police, however, quickly released most plotters without charging them. Only one Iranian student, Aliqoli Namdar, was brought to trial. He informed the court that he had worked on behalf of General Bakhtiar who had provided both the idea and the money needed to carry out the plot. Namdar was sentenced to eight months imprisonment. The lightness of the sentence and the fact that most members of the plotting group had been set free, persuaded the Shah that some foreign powers had been behind the plot to kill him. Iran's relations with West Germany remained tense until 1971.

In August 1967 the Military Prosecutor in Tehran issued an arrest warrant against Bakhtiar. The former SAVAK chief was about to fall into a French police net in Nice when, informed by his OAS associates, he fled to Beirut. From the Lebanese capital Bakhtiar began to contact the Shah's various opponents, including Khomeini and the Tudeh chiefs, with a view to creating a broad alliance against the regime. He was also in touch with

Nasser and Khosrow Qashqa'i, two brothers who had once led the warlike tribes of Fars before being forced into exile by the Shah. Also through the OAS network, Bakhtiar began smuggling guns into Lebanon for future trans-shipment to Iran. (One of Bakhtiar's aides, Shapur Zandnia, was arrested by the Lebanese police while trying to bring in a shipment of illicit arms.)

Despite all this, when they were asked to hand Bakhtiar over to Iran, the Lebanese authorities refused. Iran offered to pay the wife of the Lebanese president a cash 'gift' of £1,200,000 in exchange for Bakhtiar's extradition. The deal was agreed and Iran paid the money into a numbered Swiss account before the Lebanese president, Charles Hélou, suddenly changed his mind. There were reports that Bakhtiar had paid him a greater sum to be allowed to stay in Beirut.[22] To save Bakhtiar from assassination Hélou had him imprisoned with the understanding that he would be set free soon afterwards. Iran retaliated by breaking diplomatic relations with Lebanon.

Bakhtiar eventually arrived in Baghdad where the Iraqi authorities, then involved in a campaign against the Shah, rolled out the red carpet. Bakhtiar met Khomeini but failed to enlist the ayatollah among his own supporters. The former SAVAK chief then contacted the Tudeh leadership and the remnants of the secessionist Azerbaijan Democratic Sect. The Tudeh secretary general, Reza Radmanesh, and the leader of the Democratic Sect, 'General' Panahian, travelled to Baghdad and entered into an alliance with Bakhtiar. A 'united democratic movement' with Bakhtiar as paramount leader was put together and a formal announcement regarding the start of 'the liberation struggle' against the Shah was scheduled for 30 August 1970.

Early in August an Iran Air jet was hijacked by two men describing themselves as Bakhtiar supporters, who ordered the pilot to fly to Baghdad. The two men appeared to be ordinary farmers. The 13-year-old brother of one of them was with them during the flight and there was no reason why their word should not be trusted. The hijack appeared all the more genuine because the Shah's nephew, Captain Shahryar Shafiq, also happened to be aboard the aircraft. SAVAK could not have endangered the life of the Shah's nephew, Bakhtiar's associates argued. Furthermore, the Shah and the Queen were at the time in Switzerland and Bahktiar, judging by his own experience, thought that SAVAK would not launch any important operation with the Shah out of the country. The two hijackers, however, were SAVAK agents who had undergone special training with the help of MOSSAD, the Israeli security service, for several months. The young boy who travelled with them was returned to Iran together with the aircraft and all its passengers and crew and the two men immediately joined Bakhtiar's entourage. Three weeks later they persuaded Bakhtiar to accompany them to a spot near the Iranian border where they claimed they had created an operational base. Bakhtiar,

blinded by his ambition, followed them. He was killed in that remote
corner of the Irano-Iraqi border and his body thrown into a ditch. The
two assassins crossed back into Iran where their SAVAK controllers
awaited them.[23]

With Bakhtiar definitely out of the way, the Shah had only one
prominent enemy left: Ayatollah Khomeini. The SAVAK chief, General
Nasiri, had wanted Khomeini eliminated in 1965 but had failed to get the
Shah to agree. After Bakhtiar's murder Nasiri once again brought up the
subject of 'doing away' with Khomeini. Once again the Shah refused.
Khomeini was a sayyed, a descendant of the Prophet, and should not be
hurt. In any case the ayatollah was over 70 years old and could soon be
expected to die a natural death.

The Shah though that he could look forward to what he regarded as
'the zenith of his reign' with greater confidence.[24] The 'zenith' was the
celebration that he had decided to hold to mark the twenty-fifth centenary
of the foundation of the Persian Empire by Cyrus the Great.

The idea of the ceremony had first been put to the Shah by his cultural
adviser and speechwriter Shojaeddin Shafa in 1960. Shafa himself had
first heard about this from Soviet Iranologists during a bilateral cultural
conference in Leningrad. No one was quite sure about the exact date of
the anniversary and when the Shah suggested that this be fixed in a way to
coincide with his own coronation Shafa promptly agreed. The coronation
was set for 1967 but by 1965 it had become clear that the government
would not be able to finance the massive celebrations that Shafa had
envisaged for the twenty-fifth centenary of Cyrus the Great. At his
suggestion, the monarch agreed to postpone the celebrations until a time
when 'the nation can pay full tribute to its founder'.[25]

By 1965 the Shah had already begun to think of himself as Cyrus's true
heir: it was to him that History had assigned the task of reviving Iran's
ancient glory. He agreed to postpone the celebrations but went ahead
with the more modest coronation ceremonies, preceded by the convening
of the Constituent Assembly which was called to revise the Constitution
at the Shah's demand. The assembly modified three articles of the
constitution that dealt with the question of the king's succession. The
Shah himself was given the power to designate any one person or group of
persons as Regent or Regents pending the coming of age of the Crown
Prince. Under the Constitution the Crown Prince could not be sworn in as
Shah before reaching the age of 21.

It was generally assumed that the constitutional amendments decided
by the Assembly were meant to enable the Shah to name Queen Farah as
Regent. The assembly heard a series of laudatory speeches regarding the
queen and applauded a genealogical report that traced Farah's ancestry to
Imam Hassan, the second Imam of shi'ism. There were newspaper reports
that Farah, once crowned as Queen alongside the Shah, would automatically become Regent, but for reasons that were never fully explained the

complicated legal process of naming Farah as Regent was never completed. The Shah, who had initiated the project, somehow failed to sign the necessary documents and have the legal formalities attended to.

The Queen herself was never quite sure what her status was on that score: 'His Majesty never told me what my duties as Regent were,' Farah remembered many years later. 'And I could not, of course, bring the subject up on my own. How could I envisage my husband's death? That seemed like the end of the world to me.'[26]

The New Achaemenians

For more than 25 centuries monarchy provided the central element in Iran's national identity. A monarch, Cyrus the Great, and his Achaemenid successors had created the Iranian nation as a blend of numerous tribal and ethnic groups that inhabited the West Asian Plateau. The Shahanshah (King of Kings) ruled over the nation thanks to the Farah-e-Izadi (Divine Grace) bestowed on him by Ahura-Mazda (the God of Good). When a king was led astray by his pride or cruelty the Divine Grace would be withdrawn. Then would follow a period of corruption and chaos, destruction and death. The same tragic fate would strike the country if the nation betrayed its king or defied his authority in an act of rebellion. The Shahanshah was the nation's father, teacher, judge, general and architect.

The Arab conquest of Iran and the advent of Islam only momentarily interrupted the mythologised relationship between Iranians and their kings. The ancient Iranian theories regarding the role of the monarchy were adopted by the Muslim caliphs, albeit with cosmetic modifications, and the Persian model of government continued to be applied with the help of an Islamicised political vocabulary and the various Turkic and Mongol dynasties which subsequently ruled Iran also adopted the Persian way of life.

The Safavid dynasty (1502–1736) gave the Persian monarchy fresh vigour by making it the champion of shi'ism, and thus of 'True Islam', at a time when the Ottoman Empire, dominated by Turkic ruling elites, represented mainstream sunnism. Under the Safavids the role of the monarch as chief priest and warlord was emphasised at the expense of his status as father and teacher.

The Constitutional Revolution (1906–11) brought about a fundamental change in the perception of monarchy and its role in Iranian society. It has been argued that those intellectuals who wrote the text of the Constitution, largely based on the Belgian model, did not quite understand what they were doing. And Mozaffareddin Shah, the Qajar monarch who granted the Constitution, certainly did not fully appreciate the consequences of his assent. That constitution redefined both the origin and the function of monarchy. It continued to regard monarchy as Mohebat-e-Elahi (a Divine Gift) but made it clear that the recipient was the Iranian nation as a whole and not any particular king or dynasty. Since the nation as a whole could not exercise the powers and responsibilities of the institution, a man could be designated as monarch for the purpose. The 'gift' thus given to an individual or a dynasty by the nation could also be taken back by the nation. (In 1911 the parliament dethroned Mohammad-Ali Shah because the latter had tried to ignore the Constitution and in 1925 a Constituent Assembly took the 'Divine Gift' back from the Qajars and presented it to the Pahlavis.)

The 1906 Constitution was full of contradictions. Its basic principle was supposed to be national sovereignty, but it excluded any possibility of using that sovereignty for the purpose of carrying out reforms that might contradict Islamic laws, either in form or in substance. A five-man committee of theologians was, in effect, given a veto over all legislation. (This provision was, however, never applied.) Reza Khan, who had understood the inherent contradictions of the Constitution, tried to resolve these by seeking the establishment of a republic before abandoning the idea under pressure from the mullahs. In practice, however, even after he became king Reza Khan acted as a reforming autocrat and not as a constitutional monarch, with his own specific political and economic programmes. While managing to preserve some distance from the squalid political arena, he could not stand above politics as the 1906 Constitution required the king to do. It is possible to argue that traditional Iranian monarchy really came to an end with the demise of the Qajars.

Both Pahlavi kings tried, at different times and with different methods, to de-emphasise the Islamic character of Iran. To achieve this they both encouraged the revival of Iran's pre-Islamic 'Aryan' past. During the 1930s Nazi Germany, acting through Iranians who had studied in Berlin, played a crucial role in portraying Iran as an 'Aryan nation' humiliated by successive waves of invasion. In 1936 the Reich formally recognised Iran as 'the homeland of the Aryan race' and Iranians as 'Aryans by blood and culture'. This meant that Germans were free to marry Iranians and many did.

Reza Shah was naturally influenced by the apparent popularity of autocratic rule in countries as diverse as Turkey and Italy and greatly admired Germany's rising power which he regarded as the direct result of the strong leadership offered by Hitler. Although he consistently respected the 1906 Constitution in form, Reza Shah never felt himself bound by it. He would not become a mere figurehead and constantly advised his son and heir not to do so either.

Between 1941 and 1953, however, Mohammad-Reza Shah tried, at times reluctantly, to play the role of the figurehead monarch. Some years later he wrote, with evident pride, that he was the first in the history of Iranian kingship to have 'fully used his constitutional powers'.[1] His willingness to reign but not to rule was, to a large extent, due to the fact that he had no other choice at the time: senior and older politicians never took him seriously and would not allow him any autonomy. Nevertheless, it is fair to say that Mohammad-Reza Shah's European education may have contributed to his initial readiness to accept the Constitution's essentially Western view of the role of the monarchy in Iran.

By the end of the 1960s the Shah seemed to have lost whatever faith he might initially have had in the efficacy of Western democratic methods in transforming Iran into a modern nation state. His favourite title of 'the democratic Shah' was quietly dropped by his publicity office. A new image of the Shah was that of 'the new Cyrus', destined to revive Iran's ancient grandeur.

This new image was specially underlined during the Persepolis ceremonies that marked the 25th centenary of the foundation of the Persian Empire. Facing the tomb of Cyrus the Great, the Shah had taken the solemn oath of remaining faithful to the eternal values of 'Aryan Iran'. 'O Cyrus,' the Shah had declared, in a voice choked by emotion, 'rest in peace. For we are awake.' The Shah's eulogy at the tomb of Cyrus quickly developed into the core of what the regime's publicists presented as the new 'national renaissance ideology'.

The Shah, pragmatic by temperament and conviction, never presented a coherent vision of Iran and its place in history. This task was largely assumed by his cultural adviser, Shojaeddin Shafa, who was convinced that Islam was 'the root cause of many of this country's ills'.[2] This was a far more radical position than that of the Shah himself who was never prepared to fully reject Islam as a religion and often posed as a defender of the faith. His objection was to the influence of the mullahs and not to that of religion as such. In an interview in 1976 he said:

> I know full well that as long as the mullahs are around there will be no possibility of (lasting) reform. My father and I have both suffered at the hands of these religious fanatics ... The first step towards (lasting) reform is the elimination of the mullahs.[3]

The mullahs, however, were not the only ones that the Shah blamed for Iran's misfortunes. In 1972 he wrote: 'For Iran's decline we must, of course, blame the nation's poverty and ignorance as well as the treachery of native politicians. But the main culprits were foreign powers.'[4]

Despite its many contradictions the Shah's new 'philosophy' developed a certain inner logic and a measure of thematic consistency during the 1970s. 'We don't need foreign ideologies,' the Shah told the nation. 'We have our own national ideology which began with the history of our race over three thousand years ago.'[5] (Actually there was never full agreement on an exact starting date for Iranian history which was vaguely believed to have taken shape with the arrival of 'Aryan tribes' on the Iranian Plateu circa 2000 BC.)

The new ideology was never given a clear label. At one point the term 'Pahlavism' was suggested, apparently to rhyme with Western 'isms which the Shah saw as 'poisonous foreign beliefs'.[6] The label 'Aryamehrism' fared no better and the term 'positive nationalism', popular in the 1960s, was all but forgotten by 1971. Nor was there any attempt at codifying His Majesty's 'philosophical thoughts' until 1975 when the Shah appointed a committee chaired by prime minister Hoveyda to 'write down the philosophy of our Revolution'. The committee, whose membership varied between 30 and 50, brought together a number of professional philosophers and teachers of philosophy as well as ministers and high-ranking civil servants and military commanders.[7] After weeks of deliberation the commission produced two different reports, both written by former Communists who had become high-ranking members of the bureaucracy. The Shah read both reports and rejected them without comment. Later he said that he rejected the reports because their authors had 'missed the essential dialectics of our philosophical system'.[8]

The Shah's system of thought could in no way be considered as philosophy, although he liked to see himself as 'a philosopher king'. It was based on a number of simple – not to say simplistic – assertions and offered a number of equally straightforward, though perhaps naive, promises. Iran had had a golden past and could aim at a golden future. Because Iran had once been a world power and a shaper of history there was no reason why she would not become a leading actor on the international scene again. Iran was one of the 15 largest countries in the world and situated in a region of great strategic importance. The fact that Iran enjoyed a high rate of population growth meant that she would become one of the world's 15 most populated countries within a decade or two.[9] Iran's oil reserves, the third largest in the world, meant that the nation would continue to have a ready source of cash at least for another half a century or so. The discovery of the world's second largest reserves of natural gas in Iran in the 1970s added to the country's importance as a source of energy for the industrialised nations. The road ahead was, therefore, clear: Iran had to use its income from energy exports to create industries whose future income would cover the loss of oil and gas revenues when those reserves became exhausted. In other words, Iran had to become an industrial power.

To become an industrial power, the Shah's analysis continued, Iran needed a long period of stability. There could be no capital accumulation, no long-term investments and virtually no serious educational system without a stable political system. Political stability, in turn, was achievable only through strong and dedicated leadership at home combined with an adequate degree of military spending to dissuade potential foreign aggressors. To regain her place as a world power Iran had first to become a regional power.[10] This meant that Iran must build itself up as an oil power, a military power and an economic power all in one. The deadline set by the Shah for achieving this goal was 1980, after which Iran, so he hoped, would continue its ascent towards becoming a world power. Prime minister Hoveyda explained the Shah's vision thus:

> His Majesty believes that there is a bus that will leave for a marvellous destination at the end of this century. A few nations, the first class ones, will be on board that bus when it leaves. A few others, the second class ones, will be taken for part of the trip only. Others, the third class nations, will simply miss the bus and get buried in the dust left behind. His Majesty wants Iran to be on that bus, among the first class nations.[11]

The Shah himself put it slightly differently in a number of speeches, interviews and public messages. He maintained that an exclusive club of 'first class nations' dominated the globe thanks to their economic, political, cultural, military and diplomatic power. Jealous of their privileges, these nations would not readily admit new additions to their club. The original members were the United States, Great Britain and the 'White Commonwealth' nations and France. West Germany, Japan and Italy had been admitted after their defeat in the Second World War while Holland was a junior member. The USSR could become a member when and if it abandoned Communism. Potential future members were Brazil, South Africa, China and, of course, Iran. The demand for 'equal treatment from the big powers' became one of the main themes in the Shah's discourse both at home and abroad.

In the 1970s Iran furthered her relations with the developing nations and took part in various attempts at securing a better economic deal for the Third World, a term the Shah disliked intensely. Despite having convinced himself that Iran was a natural member of the Western camp, the Shah would, on occasions, direct his fire and fury against the West which he accused of 'greed, selfishness, corruption and arrogance'. When the chips were down, however, he was almost always on the side of his 'Western allies'.

The Shah's attempt to turn Iran into a leading oil power created a great deal of tension in his relations with the West. The Shah saw oil as 'a gift from God' to the Iranian nation and a symbol of Iran's 'eternal greatness'. Iranians had discovered oil – some of it on the surface – together with natural gas more than a thousand years before Christ. They had built fire temples using oil and natural gas. They also used oil and tar for the purpose of lining the *qanats* (underground water canals). Mortar and bitumen from oil was used for building dams, such as the one on the River Susa, as well as for surfacing roads such as the 'Imperial Highway' that linked Susa to Athens during the reign of Darius the Great. In the royal palaces of Persepolis oil was used for lighting. In the Shah's phrase 'a noble substance', oil had, by the end of the 1960s, been established as one of three areas – the others were defence and foreign policy – in which His Majesty insisted on having the last word.

The 1954 agreement with the oil companies had been accepted by the Shah as the least of all evils under the circumstances, but this did not mean that he had forsaken the ultimate goal of securing for Iran the full control of her most important industry. The Mossadeq episode persuaded the Shah that Iran was in no position to rid herself of the multinational oil companies in a single dramatic blow. Instead a gradual approach was adopted, under which Iran would exploit her growing power and influence over the years to reassert her full sovereignty and control over her oil. Thus in 1957 a Petroleum (Exploration and Exploitation) Act was passed under which the National Iranian Oil Company (NIOC) was granted full control of all Iranian oil reserves outside the area assigned to the Consortium. Within months, the NIOC concluded two agreements with two minor oil companies – one Italian and one American – under which Iran was to receive 50 and 75 per cent of the profits after tax, a distinct improvement over terms agreed with the Consortium.

In 1960 the Shah gave his enthusiastic support to a Venezuelan initiative aimed at the creation of an association of oil exporting nations. The result was the creation of the Organisation of Petroleum Exporting Countries (OPEC). A distinguished Iranian oil expert, Fuad Rouhani, was chosen as OPEC's first secretary-general.

The creation of OPEC was prompted by the sudden decision of major multinational oil companies to reduce the price of Venezuelan and Persian Gulf crude by up to 35 cents a barrel. Since all royalties and taxes paid by the companies were calculated on the basis of the posted price for crude, the new reductions meant a major loss of revenue for all the governments concerned.[12]

OPEC's declared policy of progress through negotiations fitted the Shah's strategy of slow but steady nibbling at the monopolistic powers of the Western oil cartel, the notorious Seven Sisters. Nevertheless, by 1966 Iran's revenue from each barrel of oil sold through the Consortium was still lower than in 1958 and it was by nearly tripling her exports than Iran managed to finance the modest development projects of the 1960s. Unwilling to take on the Seven Sisters in a direct confrontation, the Shah tried to diversify Iran's oil markets. A number of barter agreements were concluded with the USSR and her Eastern and Central European allies. Joint ventures were launched with India and a number of small and medium-size Western oil companies.

The 1967 Arab-Israeli war dramatically increased Iran's status as an oil exporter. Iran refused to join the Arab oil boycott against the West, even allowing production to increase to make up for part of any possible shortfall in world markets. The Consortium rewarded Iran by agreeing to return 25 per cent of the territory allotted to it under the 1954 agreement.

Iran, as a leading member of OPEC, began to emerge as an oil power

Left: THE OPEC HAWK. The Shah at a press conference on oil prices. In the early part of the 1970s he led the OPEC in seeking dramatic increases in prices of crude oil (*photo Gamma/Frank Spooner Pictures*).

Below: A FRATERNAL BOND. The Shah with President Muhammad Anwar Sadat of Egypt. Each addressed the other as 'My brother' (*photo Rex Features*).

Above: THE END OF A FRIENDSHIP. The Shah
and Empress Farah with President and Mrs
Carter on the balcony of the White House in
Washington in 1977. Carter's Presidency marked
the start of the breakdown in traditional ties of
friendship between Iran and the United States
(*photo Associated Press*).

Right: THE MAN FROM KHOMEIN. Ayatollah
Ruhollah Khomeini, the Shi'ite cleric and
politician, who led the revolution against the
Shah (*photo Gamma/Frank Spooner Pictures*).

Below: THE END OF A DREAM. Revolutionary
crowds march in the streets of Tehran with cries
of "Death to the Shah" in 1978 (*photo Camera
Press*).

THE FRIEND WHO WAS LEFT BEHIND. Amir Abbas Hoveyda, the Shah's Prime Minister for nearly 13 years, squares up to leading mullahs. Later he faced an Islamic revolutionary tribunal in Tehran, and he was executed on 7 April 1979 (*photo Camera Press*).

IN EXILE AGAIN. The Shah with his eldest son Reza in Panama in 1980. Crown Prince Reza later declared himself Shah of Iran during a ceremony in Cairo, Egypt (*photo Camera Press*).

Right: THE SOLITUDE OF A REFUGEE. The Shah, deep in thought, in his exile home on the island of Contadora in 1980 a few months before his death (*photo Camera Press*).

Below: A BRIEF MOMENT OF JOY. The Shah, in his exile refuge, takes a moment off with the youngest of his children Princess Leila Pahlavi (*photo Camera Press*).

Below: THE FUNERAL IN CAIRO. President Nixon escorts Empress Farah during the Shah's funeral in Cairo in July 1980 (*photo Associated Press*).

from the beginning of the 1970s. The major oil companies had badly miscalculated demand for oil and imposed production cutbacks on Iran and other major producers. During the 1960s, however, world demand for oil had risen by almost 300 per cent. Oil imports rose from just over 9,000,000 barrels a day in 1960 to more than 25,700,000 barrels in 1970. OPEC's total production of just over 7,800,000 barrels a day in 1960 exceeded 22,000,000 barrels a day in 1970. Of this more than 80 per cent was accounted for by Saudi Arabia, Iran, Iraq and Kuwait. Persian Gulf oil cost less than a third of the production cost of United States crude and the companies made unprecedented profits.

In June 1968, a year after the Arab oil boycott, OPEC's sixteenth ministerial meeting approved a joint statement which to many observers marked the start of the 'OPEC revolution'. The document clearly stated that OPEC members should aim at gaining control over both prices and levels of production while also keeping the companies under close surveillance with regard to their marketing and other policies. These objectives were to be pursued through negotiations – not confrontation – with the companies concerned.

The next two years were spent on largely fruitless efforts by various OPEC nations, including Iran, to entice the major companies into accepting a new deal on prices and production. The companies continued to treat OPEC governments as 'immature children' who should be dealt with firmly[13] and confrontation became inevitable.

It came in September and October of 1970 when Libya's maverick leader Colonel Muammar al-Qaddhafi ordered a cut in production, an increase in prices and a number of punitive measures against recalcitrant companies. The Shah, despite his intense personal dislike of the Libyan leader – once described by His Majesty as 'a mad dog' – fully backed the Libyan decisions. Once he was sure that Qaddhafi had succeeded, the Shah came forward to demand equal treatment for Iran. The companies had no choice but to grant him what they had grudgingly given Libya.

In subsequent years the Shah used the tactic of hiding behind supposedly radical Arab regimes within OPEC on a number of occasions. This enabled him to maintain his reputation as a moderate and an ally of the West while squeezing more revenue out of the companies. Iran's studied moderation made her the pivotal power within OPEC, especially between 1965 and 1975 when she was the world's largest exporter. Iran's objective interests, however, dictated a far more radical policy on oil prices and production levels than was the case with Saudi Arabia and other moderate members of OPEC. Iran's known oil reserves at the time represented less than a fifth of Saudi Arabia's,[14] while Iran's population of 35,000,000* required greater capital resources than did Saudi Arabia's 4,000,000 inhabitants. Iran had every interest in selling its limited oil at

*In 1970.

the highest price possible while the Saudis wished to keep the price of oil down in order to prevent the emergence of alternative sources of energy that could lose them much of the Western market in a few decades.

OPEC's twenty-first conference in Caracas, Venezuela, in December 1970 adopted a series of measures designed to increase the revenues of member states at the expense of Western companies. Iran lost no time in announcing an increase in posted prices and the abolition of most discounts granted to the Consortium since 1955. The tax base for the companies was also increased from 50 to 55 per cent. Then in a speech on the occasion of the seventh anniversary of the White Revolution the Shah told an audience of workers and peasants that for a long time the companies had 'cheated and robbed Iran'. 'Today we are putting an end to all that,' he announced. He informed his audience that Iran's oil revenue had lost more than 28 per cent of its real purchasing power in ten years as a result of the fall in the value of the dollar and the sterling currencies used for payment to OPEC members. Later, at a press conference, the Shah raised the possibility of a global deal to prevent 'leapfrogging'.* He suggested that the price of crude oil – and later other raw materials – be index-linked to prices of industrial goods so as to end a situation in which 'the poorer nations become constantly leaner and the richer ones fatter'. Addressing the West he said: 'Well, one day you are going to explode.'[15] this was the first time that the Shah had cast himself in the role of the defender of the developing nations against the West as a whole and not merely against Western oil companies.

Calling their attention to OPEC's Caracas Resolution, the Iranian government invited the Consortium plus 12 smaller oil companies to attend a conference in Tehran with the purpose of negotiating a new 'framework for cooperation'. The oil ministers of Saudi Arabia and Iraq together with Iran's Finance Minister formed a team on behalf of Persian Gulf OPEC members. The companies accepted the invitation and the conference was inaugurated on 12 January, only to reach a deadlock the same day: the companies refused to recognise OPEC as a negotiating partner. The Consortium's representatives claimed that they had come to Tehran only to obtain information with regard to recent OPEC decisions.

The Shah's reaction was to threaten the companies with unspecified reprisals. He also called for an extraordinary OPEC session in Tehran.

The talks were eventually resumed only to break down once again and this time the companies called on the US and British governments for help. The US acted swiftly by sending an undersecretary of state to Tehran and Riyadh on a fact-finding mission. The move angered the Shah who telephoned President Nixon to seek clarification. Later, at a press conference, he warned the West against taking the side of the oil companies and for the first time threatened the United States and Europe with an OPEC oil embargo:

*Whereby the prices of individual goods and raw materials continually jump ahead of one another, never achieving parity or stability.

There would be a crisis if the companies thought they could bluff us or put pressure on us to make us surrender. It would be a still more dangerous crisis if the big industrial countries tried to back the companies and defend their interests. There would then be a confrontation between what we will call the economic imperialists or imperial powers, or the new manifestations of neo-colonialism, . . . and countries that are not yet fully developed. Then anything could happen: not only the stoppage of oil flow but, maybe, a much more dangerous crisis. It would be the rising of the have-nots against the haves.[16]

Despite the Shah's warnings the companies once again walked out. Iran reacted by convening a special OPEC ministerial conference in Tehran. The Shah addressed the conference and suggested that producer governments add a straight $1 to their total receipts from each barrel of oil sold to the companies. The conference passed a resolution endorsing the Shah's view and also threatened the blacklisting of any company that might fail to fall into line.

The companies eventually agreed to negotiate and in mid-February they concluded an agreement with the six Persian Gulf members of OPEC. Posted prices were increased by 35 cents to an average of $2.15 and a standard 55 per cent tax, similar to the Venezuelan system, was accepted. The agreement raised the oil income of the six countries concerned by over $1.2 billion in 1971 and marked the start of a steady increase in Iran's oil income which continued until 1977.*

The Shah considered the Tehran agreement as the fruit of his own steadfastness in the face of thinly-veiled threats from companies that had long interfered with Iran's domestic politics. The agreement marked a watershed. From then on it was OPEC, not the companies, that took the major decisions on production levels and prices.

The Shah spent the next two years lending his support to various measures taken by Venezuela, Algeria, Iraq, Saudi Arabia, Kuwait and Libya against various Western oil companies. In January 1973 he drew the companies into a showdown he must have been preparing for some time. Accusing the Consortium of having failed to fully protect Iran's interests in accordance with the 1954 agreement, he claimed that Iran had 'ample grounds' for not renewing that agreement beyond 1979. He suggested the choice of an alternative to the companies: either they should immediately return to Iran all areas of decision-making and operations not yet in Iranian hands, or continue operations beyond 1979 on the basis of an undertaking to raise Iranian exports to 8 million barrels a day and make sure that Iran received the same price for her oil as other regional producers. Having thus opened hostilities the Shah, accompanied by Queen Farah and the royal children, withdrew to the Swiss ski resort of St Moritz where he had acquired a property in 1956. St Moritz was quickly transformed into a scene of hectic diplomatic activity as company

*Iran's oil revenue amounted to more than $4 billion in 1973, more than twice what it had been two years earlier.

presidents and special emissaries from various Western governments came to discuss the Shah's demands and the implications of growing Iranian militancy within OPEC.

The Shah conducted the negotiations personally, often in the absence of his ministers, oil advisers and other governmental figures. He was out to make Iran's dream of nationalising her oil come true and he did not want to share the credit. On 16 March he announced the 'total surrender' of the companies and 'our full victory'. What was to become known as the St Moritz Agreement was signed the following day. Under it the Consortium handed over to Iran total control over all aspects of the oil industry as well as full ownership of installations that had been managed by them since 1954, including the Abadan refinery, then the world's largest. Thus the 1954 agreement which the Shah had never liked was cancelled six years before it had run its full course. Members of the Consortium became 'simple clients of Iran's oil' who would, because of their long association with the country, enjoy the first right of refusal on a major part of Iranian production.

Next, the Shah turned his attention to the question of fixing oil prices. The relative ease with which he had 'defeated' the Consortium had persuaded the Shah that the oil companies were no longer in a position to make or break governments. The NIOC was ordered to put part of Iranian crude production on auction in world markets. Prices offered, mostly by Japanese customers, reached the then incredible figure of $17.80 per barrel. Iran and other Persian Gulf producers were persuaded that a great deal more could be squeezed out of the companies, but when Iran and her partners demanded that posted prices be raised from $3 per barrel to $4.20, the companies rejected this out of hand.

A few weeks later the balance of power dramatically changed in favour of Iran and her OPEC partners. The outbreak of a new Arab-Israeli war on 6 October 1973 created a mood of panic in world markets as the Arab members of OPEC decreed a new oil boycott against the West. Iraq meanwhile seized the opportunity to nationalise the Western-owned Basrah Petroleum Company. The Shah, faithful to his earlier promises, kept Iran out of the Arab oil embargo despite strong pressure from Egypt which had by then been established as a close friend. At the same time, however, Iran resisted Western pressures to increase production as part of efforts to cover the shortfall in supplies caused by the Arab boycott. On 16 October the Persian Gulf members of OPEC, led by Iran, announced that they had increased the posted price of their crude from $3 to $5 per barrel. At the next full OPEC meeting in Vienna on 20 December the Iranian Minister of Finance, Jamshid Amuzegar, dropped a bombshell by announcing that Iran wanted crude prices raised to between $12 and $15 per barrel, according to quality. The conference ended by approving a minimum price of $11.65 per barrel, a fourfold increase over 1970 prices. What was immediately described as 'a new oil shock' by the Western media was thus unleashed in the face of largely symbolic protestations by the companies. Iran's oil revenues increased to nearly $20 billion a year.

The Shah was still far from satisfied. He described the new price, labelled as 'extortion' by the Western media, as a sign of 'our kindness and generosity' and claimed that the real market price for oil was more then $75 per barrel, i.e. the minimum cost of producing an equivalent amount of alternative energy. Furthermore oil was 'a noble element' and it was almost a crime to burn it when one knew that it could be used for the production of no fewer than 70,000 derivatives. Oil was a non-renewable gift from God and ought to be 'treated with respect and love', the Shah said in one of his more lyrical moments.

What was the Shah going to do with so much money? It was clear that the Iranian economy simply could not absorb the injection of billions of extra dollars without suffering double-digit inflation. Also, the Shah had no interest in throwing the Western economies into recession: indeed the West and Japan remained the main markets for OPEC oil and it was essential to help them avoid a slump. Having secured the dramatic price increase he had planned since 1967, the Shah reverted to his traditional policy of moderation in 1974. He advised the Arab states to end their embargo against the West. He also announced that Iran would offer financial aid to any of the Western economies that might need it. A series of aid packages for the developing nations was also introduced. Between 1974 and 1978 Iran allocated more than $11 billion of her oil income to foreign aid projects that included low-interest loans to Britain worth $1.2 billion.

The successive oil price increases, nevertheless, caused some tension in relations between Iran and her main Western ally, the United States. The Shah's close personal relations with President Richard Nixon led some observers, including at least one Arab oil minister, to believe that the sharp increases in oil prices were plotted by Iran with America's tacit approval. The 'conspiracy theory' was that the US, by provoking oil price increases, wished to clip the wings of both Japan and Western Europe, which were emerging as serious economic rivals. Iran's role was to take all those extra dollars from Western Europe and Japan and transfer them to the United States in exchange for American weapons. The fact that Iran's imports of American weapons rose almost fourfold during the 1970s seemed to lend some credence to this convoluted analysis, and this in turn was supported by an examination of the Nixon Doctrine.

President Nixon paid a state visit to Iran in May 1973, the first American president to do so. In Tehran he went out of his way to praise the Shah as one of the outstanding leaders of the twentieth century. The visit helped establish the Nixon Doctrine as a major element in international politics. The United States, humiliated in Vietnam, now wanted to help build up strong regional allies who would be capable of resisting Communist aggression on their own. Applied to the Persian Gulf region, the Nixon Doctrine meant full support for the Shah's policy of expanding the Iranian defence forces. This, in turn, required more money which could come only from oil. In other words the success of the Nixon Doctrine in Iran's part of the world required a dramatic rise in crude prices.

During the state visit Nixon and the Shah only briefly discussed oil at the full formal sessions they held in the presence of officials from both sides, but the two men also had two private sessions about which no official account was published. Cynics believed that the 'oil shock' was planned behind closed doors during those sessions. The 'conspiracy theory' was, as usual, right in drawing attention to circumstances but wrong in its conclusions. The United States could not have hoped to benefit from creating economic difficulties for its own principal trading partners. Also, the US was, by 1973, the world's largest importer of crude oil and Nixon must have known that within a decade nearly half of his country's energy needs would have to be met by imports.

American displeasure at the Shah for his role in the oil price hikes was manifested on a number of occasions. Nixon's Treasury Secretary William Simon called the Shah 'a nut' and refused to withdraw his insult despite private and public demands by Iran. The Tehran media, pointing to the years of personal friendship that tied Nixon and the Shah together, openly hoped that the president would use the first opportunity to sack Simon, but that did not happen. In January 1974 the United States suggested that oil prices be cut by about 50 per cent to help the world economy out of recession. This was firmly rejected by the Shah who warned President Nixon against any attempt at creating a 'consumers' cartel' to challenge OPEC. The Shah also strongly condemned a threat by Secretary of State Henry Kissinger to use force against OPEC members under certain conditions and promised to help beat off any attack on any of the oil-exporting nations.

The sharp rise in Iran's oil income after 1971 removed most of the impediments to the Shah's plan for equipping the armed forces with the massive arsenal of weapons he had dreamed of since he first came to the throne. With the British out of the Persian Gulf, Iran was now the legitimate pretender for the position of regional power. The Persian Gulf contained some two-thirds of the world's known oil reserves which, if they were to fall into Soviet hands – whether directly or through client states – could threaten the very basis of Western economic strength. The Shah, always insisting that Iran was part of the Western world both by choice as well as by necessity, put forward Iran as the regional 'superpower' capable of filling the strategic gap in full accord with the Nixon Doctrine.

Until the 'White Revolution' the Iranian armed forces had been used essentially for keeping order at home. During the 1963 disturbances provoked by Ayatollah Khomeini it was the army that eventually succeeded in restoring law and order. In close consultation with his American allies, the Shah redesigned the Iranian armed forces after 1965 in the hope of preparing them for a regional – rather than a domestic – role. The 1967 Arab-Israeli war, the introduction of supersonic fighter-bombers into the Middle East by Iraq, Syria and Egypt, and the dismemberment of Pakistan as a result of an Indian invasion in 1971 were some of the events that persuaded the Shah that the law of the jungle prevailed in the world. 'Last time we were attacked and occupied because we were weak,' he commented in an interview. 'It was all our own fault. We were guilty of being weak. Next time? There will be no next time. Never, never again'.[17]

Before the British withdrawal from the Persian Gulf, Iran's defence strategy had been entirely geared at facing a possible Soviet invasion from the north. US military planners saw Iran as a mere pawn on the global chessboard of conflict with the USSR. In 1968 a number of American generals and Pentagon officials visited Tehran to discuss the country's role 'in the overall strategy of the West'. Their plans provided for an Iranian defence line along the Zagross mountain range, meaning that in the event of a Soviet attack Iran would abandon virtually all of its northern provinces – including nearly half of its population – in order to concentrate on defending the southern provinces where the oil wells were situated. Worse still, the American plan envisaged the use of nuclear weapons to create a 'death zone' in northern Iran as a means of preventing further Soviet advances.

The plan was discussed at a meeting of Iranian commanders and American officials. The Iranians refused to envisage what they saw as 'a betrayal of half of our population'. For their part the Americans saw any attempt at fighting the Russians north of the Alborz mountain range as 'suicidal'. The matter was finally taken to the Shah who sided with his commanders. 'We are ready for suicide,' he told the meeting.[18]

In 1971, however, Iran's military capabilities were rated as 'largely inadequate' by most experts at home and abroad. Iran spent a lower percentage of its GNP on defence than any of the other major regional powers. At that time Iran's GNP was estimated at around $10,100 million of which under $1,000m was spent on the military. Iran's total forces numbered just over 220,000. The Air Force, virtually non-existent until the mid-1960s, had been built up partly thanks to the enthusiasm of Generam Mohammad Khatam, the Shah's brother-in-law and himself a military pilot. The Navy, however, was in its infancy and was unable to protect Iran's long coastline on the Persian Gulf and the Gulf of Oman.

The Shah was firmly persuaded that nothing except sheer military strength could guarantee a nation's independence and territorial sovereignty. He was proud of the fact that his dynasty, the Pahlavis, was the first in Iran's history since the seventeenth century not to have lost territory to foreign invaders. In private he spoke bitterly of 'Iranian territories gobbled up by Russians' in Central Asia and the Caucasus. He was convinced that Russia was determined to conquer Iran and turn it into 'the Soviet Republic of Iranistan' and hoped to prevent such an eventuality by a combination of diplomacy and military strength. He was prepared to give the Russians a share of Iran's growing prosperity and to recognise Moscow's legitimate interests in the region: until the very end he was careful not to allow important Western economic interests to be developed in northern Iran. At the same time he promoted the creation of a number of Irano-Soviet joint ventures in the northern provinces. Nevertheless, he had persuaded himself that Russia would never settle for anything short of a full takeover and that, he argued, had to be resisted by force with military support from the United States.

By the early 1970s Iranian defence was reorganised to face three types of threat. The Soviet threat remained the major one and the Shah had somehow convinced himself that any Russian attack on Iran would trigger the Third World War. All Iran needed to do in that domain was to be in a position to resist long enough for American forces to arrive. A second and more immediate source of danger for Iran was identified in the shape of radical Arab states. Nasser of Egypt had for years openly called for the overthrow of the Shah and the full control of the Persian Gulf – which he called 'the Arabian Gulf' – by the Arabs. Ba'athist regimes in Syria and Iraq went even further and claimed that the oil-rich Iranian province of Khuzestan – which they called 'Arabistan' – had to be detatched from Iran and 'reunited with the Arab motherland'. The fact that Egypt, Syria and Iraq, at different times and in different degrees, were allies of the USSR made them look even more menacing. All three were heavily armed by the USSR and were ruled by military regimes that espoused socialism and militant Arabism. Of the three Iraq was seen by the Shah as the vanguard of Arab expansionism against Iran while Egypt and Syria were more preoccupied with Israel.

While Iran's position with regard to the USSR was essentially defensive, Iranian military planners envisaged an offensive strategy with regard to the radical Arab states. Thus it was assumed that Iranian forces would immediately move into Iraq at the start of a major conflict leading to war. Iran also had elaborate plans for the destruction of Iraqi and Syrian air forces on the ground.

After 1970 Iraq emerged as the main threat to Iranian security. The Ba'athist regime's increasingly close ties with the USSR – culminating in the Soviet-Iraqi treaty of friendship and cooperation in 1972 – were seen in Tehran as fresh signs of a Soviet strategy for encircling Iran.*

Iranian leaders had always regarded the creation of the Iraqi state by Britain in 1921 as a deliberate act of provocation against Iran's interests.

*By 1973 there were more than 5000 Soviet military and defence-related experts in Iraq and both Moscow and Baghdad gave the impression that Iraq had unlimited access to Soviet weapons systems.[19]

They saw Iraq as a British military base in the Middle East and the British air base at Habaniyah, near Baghdad, was always regarded as a threat to Iran's oilfields in Khuzestan. In 1941 British forces, using Iraq as a springboard, invaded and occupied southern Iran. In 1951–3 the British again used Iraq as a military base against Iran during the oil nationalisation crisis. Iran also saw itself as the natural protector of the shi'ites who formed 60 per cent of Iraq's population, as well as the Kurds who belonged to the larger ethnic Iranic family. As far as Iranian ruling elites were concerned there had been no justification in turning Mesopotamia into a new nation-state.

In 1971 Iraq severed diplomatic relations with Iran in protest against an Iranian-inspired plot to overthrow the Ba'athist regime in Baghdad. The pretext used, however, was the Iranian move to reassert sovereignty over three tiny islands in the Strait of Hormuz. The islands – Abu Musa, Greater Tunb and Lesser Tunb – were all situated in Iran's territorial waters but had fallen under British control in 1919. Later, the British had transferred the administration of Abu Musa to the Shaikh of Sharjah, one of the seven states of the Trucial Coast under British protection. The two Tunbs were handed over to another trucial ruler, the Shaikh of Ras al-Khaimah. The three islands dominated the navigable channels in and out of the Persian Gulf and could not be left in 'weak and irresponsible hands'. Their seizure provoked little military or diplomatic reaction from the Arabs but the entire operation was presented by Iranian propaganda as a personal victory for the Shah who needed such a feat in order to partly offset the effect of his decision to relinquish Iranian claims to the Bahrain archipelago. The 'loss of Bahrain' had undermined the Shah's prestige among the more militant Iranian nationalists who had provided him with a measure of popular support against the mullahs and clandestine left-wing parties.

Iran's relations with Iraq had never been easy. Even when Iraq was still ruled by a monarch, the Shah considered it as a potential enemy. The 1968 *coup d'état* in Baghdad was at first warmly welcomed in Tehran as the pro-Ba'ath Party officers who seized power had been in contact with Iranian security for a number of years and received substantial sums of money. It seemed that Iran's policy of supporting the Iraqi Ba'ath against the Nasserists, at that time considered more dangerous, had paid off. The new Iraqi regime dispatched one of its key members, Air Marshal Hardan Abdul-Ghaffar al-Takriti to Tehran only days after the coup. Al-Takriti made no secret of the Ba'ath's long association with the Iranian embassy in Baghdad.[20] Very soon, however, it became clear that the pro-Iranian faction of the Ba'ath had only served as a smokescreen for more hardline and chauvinistic leaders, among them the party's rising star Saddam Hussein al-Takriti.

It became clear that the new generation of Ba'athist leaders was prepared to abandon the party's strong anti-Communist traditions in order to create a 'popular front' against both Iran and Israel and anti-Iranian propaganda was resumed with greater intensity towards the end of 1969. Iran responded by announcing its intention to repudiate the 1937 treaty that delineated the country's borders with Iraq. The treaty, imposed on Iran by Britain which at the time supported Iraq, gave the Iraqis full sovereignty over the Shatt al-Arab waterway that formed part of the border with Iran, which was manifestly unfair: the Shatt drew some 60 per cent of its waters from Iranian rivers that poured into Meso-potamia. Also, the entire eastern shore of the river over some 90 kilometres consisted of Iranian territory. Successive Iraqi governments had promised to negotiate a new treaty which would provide for joint sovereignty over the Shatt al-Arab without ever honouring their word. The Shah was determined to cancel the 1937 treaty which, in private conversations, he described as 'a black spot on my father's record'.

Nasser's death in 1970 paved the way for a rapid rapprochement between Iran and Egypt. This meant that the Shah could turn the heat on Iraq without risking a united Arab reaction. The Iraqis played into Iranian hands by announcing that all ships passing through the Shatt al-Arab would have to fly the Iraqi flag and pay tolls set by the Basra Port Authority. The Iraqi announcement came while the Shah was away on a state visit to North Africa but the Iranian response came quickly. Tehran announced that any attempt to stop Iranian ships would be considered a casus belli. Meanwhile Acting Foreign Minister Amir-Khosrow Afshar informed parliament that the 1937 treaty had been abrogated. Iranian forces were put on maximum alert as a merchant vessel, flying the Iranian flag and escorted by several gunboats, entered the Shatt al-Arabs from the Persian Gulf and reached the port of Khorramshahr without being challenged. A festive mood dominated the entire operation as hundreds of private boats, filled with cheering Iranians, accompanied the cortège while Iranian fighter-bombers broke the sound barrier above. Saddam Hussein, then established as Baghdad's strongman, shied away from immediate, direct confrontation and began planning for a long struggle against Iran.

Between 1970 and 1974 Iran and Iraq fought an undeclared and largely unreported war. During that period more than 1,500 'exchanges', including full-scale artillery battles, were recorded by the Iranian authorities.[21] Casualties on both sides were in the thousands.

At first the Iraqis had the edge thanks to superior weapons supplied by the USSR. The Soviets further demonstrated their support for Iraq through a number of symbolic gestures. For example, the Soviet prime minister Alexei Kosygin visited Iraq in 1972 and made a point of crossing the Shatt al-Arab in an Iraqi vessel in full view of Iranian gunboats.

Right from the start of the conflict Iran played the Kurdish card against Iraq. Mulla Mostafa Barzani, a veteran Kurdish rebel leader who had been sentenced to death in absentia in Iran during the 1940s, was invited to Tehran and received by the Shah. Barzani had already contacted both Israel and the United States and received promises of financial and diplomatic support. By 1971 his guerrilla army had grown to a maximum strength of 30,000 well-armed men.[22] Iran supplied several pieces of heavy artillery and, after 1973, even offered air cover to Kurdish forces during major engagements with the Iraqi army.

Tehran also played the shi'ite card against the Iraqi Ba'athists. Several grand ayatollahs based in Najaf in southern Iraq had close links with Iran and received financial support from the government in Tehran. In 1973 the shi'ites organised a number of strikes and political demonstrations against the Ba'ath. Saddam Hussein responded by ordering a mass deportation of Iraqi shi'ites into Iran. The first groups were rounded up at their homes at night and taken to the Iranian border in army trucks where they had to walk to Iran. Many of the deportees died on the way because of exposure after losing their way in snow-covered mountain gorges. Early in 1974, when the Shah personally visited the refugee camps on the border, plans had already been prepared for a full-scale war with Iraq and the Iranian high command was confident of victory within one week.[23] The Israeli lobby in Tehran also strongly encouraged an Iranian attack on Iraq with the aim of destroying the Iraqi war machine. The Kurds, for their part, were keen on throwing in all they had in the hope of snatching the north Iraqi towns of Mosul and Kirkuk and setting up the nucleus of an independent Kurdistan.[24]

In the event the Shah refused to embark on full-scale war. Instead he allowed occasional air raids on Iraqi positions by the Iranian Air Force and the Airborne Brigade, commanded by General Manuchehr Khosrowdad, was also ordered to carry out commando attacks in support of Barzani's peshmerga (guerrillas). Iranian surface to air missiles were later used to bring down a number of Iraqi MiGs. At the same time the Shah encouraged efforts aimed at mediating between Iran and Iraq: he was interested solely in imposing a new border treaty and not the conquest of Mesopotamia as some of his generals suggested.[25]

A series of secret talks were held between Foreign Minister Abbas-Ali Khalatbari and his Iraqi counterpart Murtadha Sa'eed Abdul-Baqi in Istanbul and Geneva. In Geneva, the talks were held at Château de Bellrive, the official residence of Sadruddin Aga Khan, then UN High Commissioner for Refugees. The two sides came to an agreement under which Iraq accepted to share its sovereignty over the Shatt al-Arab with Iran. It was evident that Saddam Hussein sought a quick settlement so that he could turn his attention to the Kurds who threatened the very foundation of Iraq as a nation-state. But when Khalatbari reported the result of his negotiations to the Shah over the telephone, His Majesty surprisingly rejected the accord. Why did the Shah veto an agreement that offered him all that he had asked for since 1970? Khalatbari himself believed that the Shah was still distrustful of the Iraqis and did not want to be rushed into a hasty agreement while time was on Iran's side.[26] Others suspected Israeli and American pressure on the Shah not to let the Iraqi regime off the hook just yet.[27] A third view was that the Shah saw Iraq's diplomatic surrender as a major victory for Iran and did not want anyone else to share the credit for it. Eight months later the Shah signed a new agreement with Saddam Hussein under the glare of television lights in almost exactly the same terms already negotiated by Khalatbari. The foreign minister was not seen even in the background.

The final agreement, signed in March 1975, was negotiated with the help of Algerian Foreign Minister Abdul-Aziz Boutfeliqa. It granted Iran's demand of joint sovereignty over the Shatt al-Arab and set the border at the Thalweg point – the deepest point in the navigable channel in the estuary. In exchange Iran agreed to evacuate a number of strategic hills it had captured from Iraq since 1970. More important, Iran agreed to stop all aid to the rebel Iraqi Kurds. The Barzani movement collapsed like a house of cards and more than a quarter of a million Kurds fled into Iran. Barzani himself was brought to Tehran, broken, a virtual prisoner. 'I am finished,' he said at a meeting in the Iranian capital.[28]

The settlement of the border dispute with Iraq meant that Iran became the only country in the region to have no territorial problems with any of its neighbours. The Shah was extremely proud of what he saw as one of his finest achievements. He called Iran 'an island of stability in an ocean of trouble'. The entire region from North Africa – where Morocco was involved in the Western Sahara war – to the Indian subcontinent formed an 'arch of instability'. The Arab-Israeli conflict, the Indo-Pakistani confrontation over Kashmir and the Afghanistan-Pakistan dispute over Pushtunistan were only the most important minefields that threatened the region. In the middle of all this, Iran was a veritable haven of tranquillity with good relations with all of the region's states.

The Soviet threat remained in the background, however, and made itself felt every now and then. Russia's presence in the Horn of Africa, first through Somalia and then through Ethiopia, was regarded by the Shah as part of a Soviet attempt at encircling Iran and the oil resources of the Persian Gulf. Russia was also strongly implanted in South Yemen where the only Communist regime in the Muslim world held power. Russian bases at Aden and on the island of Soccotra were seen by the Shah as just two of the links in a red chain that extended from India to Africa. The 1973 *coup d'état* in Afghanistan, which led to the overthrow of the monarchy, caused great consternation in Tehran where a Soviet plot to encircle Iran was suspected. Very soon, however, Iran moved into Afghanistan in full diplomatic force and established privileged relations with the new diplomatic regime of President Mohammad Daoud. Iran offered to match all Soviet aid to Afghanistan and promised to link the landlocked country to the Persian Gulf through a new railway system between Kabul and Bandar-Abbas.

By 1975 the Shah was confident that Iran, thanks to its military strength and close alliance with the United States, was no longer immediately threatened by either a Russian attack or pressure from radical Arab states. Egypt under President Sadat had become a close friend and ally and, with encouragement from the Shah, was rapidly moving into the Western camp. Iraq was tamed and Syria, now isolated, was put on the list of nations receiving Iranian aid. Only Libya and South Yemen persisted in their propaganda attack against the Shah, but they were too weak and too remote to pose a serious threat to Iran's predominant position in the Persian Gulf.

A third threat remained: terrorism. The Shah's close relations with Israel and his refusal to help any of the various Palestinian guerrilla organisations made him a *bête noire* of Yasser Arafat, George Habash and other guerrilla chiefs who, in any case, detested the Shah's anti-left policies and saw in him 'a reactionary leader linked with Imperialism'. The various guerrilla groups within the Palestine Liberation Organisation began training a number of Iranian volunteers for urban guerrilla operations against Iran. The PLO and, more especially, the People's Front for the Liberation of Palestine (PFLP) led by Habash were also involved in the training and arming of the guerrilla movement in the Omani province of Dhofar.

This movement called itself the Front for the Liberation of the Occupied Arab Gulf and used a number of bases in South Yemen, receiving support from China, the USSR and East Germany. After 1972 Cuban military advisers were attached to the PFLOAG in the Yemeni province of Hadhramaut. Volunteers from two Iranian Marxist-Leninist groups also fought alongside the Dhofari rebels after 1972.

The Shah saw the Dhofar rebellion as part of the Soviet plan to encircle the Persian Gulf and threaten its oil resources. Thus it was with little difficulty that he accepted an invitation by Sultan Qabus of Oman to send Iranian forces into the sultanate for the purpose of helping quell the rebellion. By 1975 there were more than 12,000 Iranian troops fighting in Dhofar who played a key role in ending the rebellion in 1977. A token Iranian force remained in the sultanate until after the Shah had been overthrown.

Iran's victory in Dhofar encouraged the Shah in pushing his policy of 'forward pressure' against his perceived Soviet threat even further. He formulated his new vision of Iran's 'natural defence perimeters' with a view to a global role for his revived Persian empire. He spoke of Iran as an Indian Ocean power and entered into talks aimed at creating a triangle – with Australia and South Africa – for the defence of the region. At the same time he invited India, Pakistan, Bangladesh and Singapore to join Iran in promoting an Indian Ocean Common Market. Iranian diplomacy, meanwhile, promoted international action aimed at declaring the Indian Ocean a nuclear free zone.

As the Shah's interests in international affairs grew he began to find

Iran's own domestic problems rather boring, if not irrelevant. He was genuinely convinced that Iran had no major internal problems and that 'the little bumps on the road' would be ironed out in time. Iran was headed for the 'Great Civilisation' – that is a welfare state in which the government would look after every single member of society from 'the womb to the tomb'.[29] (The seemingly endless oil income would cover the necessary expenses.) Official propaganda about the Shah's promised land of plenty soon produced the inevitable effect of creating expectations that no government could have satisfied within the life of a single generation. And yet the Shah boasted about his determination 'not to ask the present generations to make any sacrifices for the future'.[30] He attacked those who counselled caution in distributing promises as 'mean and envious of the good life that we want to provide for our people'.

The pressure on Iranian financial resources was already great even in 1974, the year in which the nation's oil income increased fourfold. The Shah insisted that the armed forces receive the lion's share in the new five-year development plan unveiled by premier Hoveyda and some $30 billion was earmarked for defence expenditure between 1975 and 1980, nearly 32 per cent of the total plan allocations. The share of defence expenditure was, in fact, even bigger, as a number of high-cost projects presented as purely economic also had military aspects.

The build-up of the nation's military might further encouraged the Shah in his belief that Iran was now a major player on the world stage, but it also put strong pressure on the nation's as yet insufficient human and infrastructural resources. The quadrupling of Iran's oil income marked the beginning of a socio-economic crisis that was to bring down the Pahlavi regime long before the new five-year plan, presented as 'the key to the Great Civilisation', had been completed. The Iranian political, administrative and economic leadership was simply not prepared to cope with the new reality.

12

Empire of Gold and Fear

In 1974 as Iran's oil income quadrupled, the prime minister, Amir Abbas Hoveyda, sent his cabinet colleagues a note in which they were asked to urgently seek new ways and means of spending the nation's unexpected windfall. 'Those who are afraid of spending ought to leave,' he warned in an interview. His government was determined to come up with the biggest budget in Iran's history. 'Money is no longer a problem,' he said again and again. 'What we need is ideas.' At the end of the year, after all budget allocations had been raised drastically, Hoveyda still complained that he had been left with 'millions with which we do not know what to do'.

The prime minister's largesse was not whimsical. He believed that Iranians had to be reassured about the future by being persuaded that they no longer had to put up with a life of poverty and despair. 'I want the people to feel that all they need to do now is to work hard and be patient,' he said. His message, however, was not received the way he had intended. As news of the bonanza spread to the countryside tens of thousands of peasants abandoned their land and poured into cities in search of the proverbial – and non-existent – streets paved with gold. In the second half of the 1970s Tehran's population rose from some 2,800,000 to nearly 5,000,000. The population of Isfahan more than doubled to exceed 1,000,000. Mashhad, Shiraz, Ahvaz, Tabriz and Bandar Abbas also experienced dramatic population increases. A new underclass of seasonal workers came into being and began to threaten the stability of society.

The seasonal workers on the fringes of large cities were later joined by more than a million Afghans who poured into urban Iran in search of a share in the oil boom. The government tried to cope with the problem by imposing rigid urban development laws and regulations that further complicated the situation. The acute shortage of housing from which urban Iran suffered was made worse by zoning laws copied from France and the United States. In some cities, notably Tabriz and Yazd, the old downtown districts were declared part of the national heritage and could, therefore, not be demolished for redevelopment. Shortages of building materials made matters still more difficult. Military projects absorbed large quantities of cement, concrete, bricks and girders and pushed prices through the roof. In just two years rents increased by more than five times in Tehran and other major cities as more than a million foreigners from 30 different nationalities arrived to help build the Shah's 'Great Civilisation'. In some smaller towns Iranians felt as if they were being squeezed out of their own society by the sudden arrival of so many people with so many different cultures.

The Shah had never wanted the Iranian people to vote for him. He believed that he was where he was thanks to divine will – and he had little need of the Iranians to finance his government thanks to the oil revenue. His army had need of only a small number of carefully chosen Iranians as the defence of the realm was entrusted to sophisticated and superior weaponry often maintained and partially commanded by foreign advisers. As the new industrial projects multiplied the importance of native workers also diminished. Iran lacked the technological elites needed for the type of projects that the Shah was interested in. Even those Iranians who did take part in the projects at higher managerial levels were mostly foreign educated and had lost contact with the mass of their countrymen: many of them spoke English, even among themselves. One could see young Iranian couples at Tehran's posh restaurants and dance rooms court each other in English or French. Ministers compared notes in English and the new-rich imitated them.

By the mid-1970s the old traditional elites who had ruled Iran since the end of the eighteenth century had all but disappeared. Their places had been taken by new elites whose provenance determined their social and cultural outlook. The supreme test for joining the new ruling class was that of loyalty to the person of the monarch. The dramatic increase in the number of governmental posts meant that the traditional families could no longer fill even a fraction of the new positions of command. 'There simply are not enough cousins for all the jobs available,' the Shah himself once said in a light mood. He was pleased that he could recruit his men from outside the traditional families who had retained their Qajar links and continued secretly to regard the Pahlavis as upstarts.

Where did the Shah's new men come from? The main field of recruitment remained the bureaucracy itself. In 1975 no fewer than 20 of the 24 cabinet members had civil service backgrounds. Some of the more solid and successful ministers, such as the Foreign Minister Abbas-Ali Khalatbari, had remote Qajar links. The military also provided many ministers. The post of Minister for War was always held by an army officer,[1] but retired generals and colonels could also be called upon to head such departments as agriculture, commerce and interior.[2] A SAVAK connection was also an asset in some cases. In virtually all the cabinets between 1968 and 1978 at least one SAVAK member held a ministerial

post.[3] The business community had surprisingly few direct representatives in the top echelons of the government.[4] The Shah also kept his own
relations and personal friends out of the cabinet after 1968. Here the only
notable exception was Mehrdad Pahlbod, the husband of Princess Shams,
who served as Minister of Culture for nearly 12 years. Another exception
was Reza Qotbi, a cousin of Empress Farah, who headed the state-owned
radio and television networks for over a decade. Princess Ashraf, a maker
of ministers until the mid-1950s, was, by 1970, reduced to a more modest
role: she could no longer propel members of her circle into ministerial
positions but was allowed to influence the choice of a few ambassadors.[5]

An American connection was also an asset: the Shah's policy was firmly
based in close alliance with the United States and the hope that access to
American technology and arms would help Iran speed up her own
development. The American Point IV programme served as a training
centre for Iranian managers, producing a future prime minister, Jamshid
Amuzegar, and a dozen more future ministers.[6] This, of course, did not
mean that those who had an American connection, through education or
marriage, were necessarily more loyal to the Shah or favoured the US role
in Iran. Many were Iranian patriots who did not approve of the Shah's
special relations with Washington which they regarded as ill-advised and
potentially dangerous. In the 1970s, in fact, American universities
produced many of the regime's most determined opponents, especially on
the left. It was on the campus of American universities that Iranian
Communism found its second wind at that time. 'The only place Lenin
still lives today is on the campus of American universities,' prime minister
Hoveyda once observed, only half in jest.[7]

The Soviet-sponsored Tudeh Party had ceased to pose a serious threat
to the Shah's regime after Mossadeq's overthrow in 1953. In the 1970s,
closely following Moscow's lead, Tudeh changed its analysis of the
regime and began to see the Shah as an agent of historical modernisation
in Iran. This change of tactics by the Tudeh leadership lost the clandestine
party a good part of its audience among Iranian students and intellectuals
many of whom continued to be fascinated by the revolutionary ideas of
Marx and Lenin. China and Cuba, before they established friendly ties
with the Shah, were regarded as new and shining examples of successful
popular revolutions. The bulk of the Iranian Left was thus won over by
the Maoist and Castrist discourse. The role of 'US imperialism' in Iran
was seen as the central issue, meaning that the Shah's many reforms, some
of them of genuine importance, could be dismissed as mere window-
dressing 'in the service of Imperialism'. The idea that the regime could be
influenced from within was firmly rejected and, since it was not possible
to have an impact on the regime's overall attitude and policy through
normal political processes, armed struggle was advanced as the only
course open to those who wished to change things in Iran.

Armed struggle, in practice, meant terrorist attacks on selected targets.

The Marxist-Leninist Fedayeen preferred guerrilla operations in the countryside in imitation of Mao Tse-tung. They attacked posts of gendarmerie in remote regions and murdered local government officials. The Mujahedeen guerrillas, on the other hand, favoured action in urban areas. They robbed banks, planted bombs near supermarkets and airline offices and murdered a number of SAVAK and military officers. Among their victims were six American army officers and NCOs seconded to the Iranian forces.

Both the Fedayeen and the Mujahedeen also drafted plans to assassinate the Shah, members of his family and senior civil and military officials. At least one group, linked with the Fedayeen and led by the reporter and poet Khosrow Golsorkhi, had come up with a plan to kidnap Empress Farah and Crown Prince Reza during the annual art festival at Shiraz and Persepolis. A dramatic attempt at kidnapping the American ambassador, the murder of two army generals and a series of daring bank hold-ups propelled the guerrillas onto the front pages with the result that SAVAK's position within the regime was further strengthened.

The various guerrilla groups were all but defeated by 1977. A mixture of sheer brutality on the part of SAVAK – which practised a shoot-to-kill policy – and reckless adventurism by some of the guerrillas themselves managed, in the words of the Shah, to 'burst open the blister'. American, Israeli, West German, South Korean, Iraqi and Egyptian intelligence services helped SAVAK fight the guerrillas at various stages by providing information and, in some cases, special training as well as equipment.[8] Seven years of guerrilla operations affected more than a dozen cities, including the capital itself, as well as scores of villages. In the vast majority of cases the operations undertaken by guerrillas did not go beyond the distribution of tracts and pictures of Mao, Castro, Che Guevara and Lin Biao. In some cases harvests were burned in the hope of creating panic in rural areas. These operations claimed nearly a thousand lives, most of the victims being the guerrillas themselves. SAVAK and the armed forces also suffered over 200 fatalities.

SAVAK's success in crushing the guerrilla movement was, as subsequent events showed, only temporary. Nevertheless it was enough to enhance dramatically the position of the secret police within the structures of the state. SAVAK reports greatly exaggerated the guerrilla threat and pictured a prospect of widespread urban terrorism backed by foreign Communist regimes. Since almost all of those involved in guerrilla activities were students or graduates with middle- and upper-class backgrounds – many of them having returned home after studying in Europe or the United States – SAVAK analysts identified the newly emergent urban social and economic groups as the main sources of threat to the regime. Students, intellectuals and professional people became prime targets for SAVAK repression.

Between 1970 and 1978 an estimated half a million people, almost all of them with urban middle-class or upper-class backgrounds, were 'interviewed' at least once by SAVAK. These 'interviews' sometimes came in the form of raids on private homes in the middle of the night. In most cases, however, the 'interviewee' would be politely invited to present himself at one of SAVAK's many safe houses at a given time. The 'interview' could last an hour or several days. In some cases it could degenerate into a longer drama of imprisonment and torture.[9] The Shah never admitted the presence of any political prisoners in Iran. Instead, he preferred to speak of 'traitors' and 'terrorists'. It is entirely possible that he convinced himself that anyone who questioned his judgment on any major issue was motivated by other than legitimate dissent. The Shah regarded politics in the normal sense of the term as a 'deadly poison' for Iran. He believed that politicians were motivated by greed, love of power and a craving for popularity.

Worse still, the Shah believed that for countries like Iran which still had a long distance to cover before attaining the status of developed nations, politics was a waste of time and historic opportunities. Iran needed firm government, discipline and quick decision-making. The British, for example, spent seventeen years deciding whether or not to build a fourth terminal at Heathrow. In monarchist Iran His Imperial Majesty could approve the building of 50 new airports in one afternoon. The distribution of land among poor peasants could never have taken place through ordinary political channels: the major landowners, in alliance with tribal chiefs and the mullahs, would always control parliament and prevent land reform. A multi-party system could only open the way for foreign powers to gain a direct role in Iranian political processes through their agents and sympathisers. Democracy could be safely practised by the rich, well-organised and, above all, militarily powerful nations. Iran would not reach that stage before the end of the century. The Shah had countless examples of how foreigners manipulated Iranian politics whenever the monarch was weakened.

SAVAK and some members of the Shah's entourage had a vested interest in strengthening his belief that dissent was just another name for treason and one of the first things that SAVAK tried to 'prove' about anyone suspected of harbouring dissident views was the foreign link. Entire dossiers were made up – filled with fake evidence or mere inferences – to show that virtually all of the regime's known critics had, at some time or other been in contact with foreign powers – chiefly the USSR, the United States, Britain, and various radical Arab states. The fact that the Tudeh leaders, for example, were certainly in touch with Moscow and that individuals like Teymur Bakhtiar had cooperated with Iraqi intelligence against Iran, gave credence to the Shah's wild assertions. Through daily confidential reports that could not be independently verified, SAVAK promoted the Shah's mood of suspicion and fear. Writers, artists, businessmen and university teachers who became exceptionally successful or popular were identified by the SAVAK as potential threats if not to the regime at least to the hegemony of the secret police itself. The 'successful ones' were, therefore, gently persuaded, if not actually forced, to declare openly their loyalty to His Imperial Majesty whenever the occasion arose. Those who refused to do so were put on the black list and subjected to harrassment or worse. Some were simply framed and prosecuted on trumped-up charges, often linked to the possession or use of narcotic drugs. One example was the popular crooner Dariush who had dared include in his repertoire a song written by a Communist poet. The popular star was suddenly presented as an opium addict who had been involved in the illegal sale of the narcotic. He spent several weeks in prison and was released after publicly paying homage to the progress Iran had made under His Imperial Majesty.

Many of SAVAK's victims were writers, poets, journalists and other intellectuals. In 1975 the black list of banned books included more than 2000 titles and, to some writers and poets, having trouble with SAVAK became a means of ensuring their own popularity. Some less scrupulous ones disappeared for a few weeks only to spread the rumour that they had been picked up by the secret police. In one celebrated case the novelist Gholam-Hossein Sa'edi was arrested by the police in 1971 after a midnight brawl during which he tried to stab his South African girlfriend in central Tehran.[10] Immediately the rumour was spread that he had been kidnapped and murdered by SAVAK. The fact that he had been arrested by the SAVAK on a previous occasion gave the rumours credibility and sales of his books rose dramatically as a result.

SAVAK was also unhappy about those individuals who for one reason or another were close enough to the Shah not to fear his secret police. SAVAK tried to undermine their position by cooking up stories about their alleged disloyalty, corruption or 'foreign links'. Reza Qotbi, a cousin of the Empress and head of the national radio and TV network, was accused of harbouring Communists and protecting enemies of the regime.[11] Jamshid Amuzegar, a senior minister for many years, was branded 'an American agent' by SAVAK's rumour machine. Other high-ranking personalities were given supposedly sensitive information because of which their names featured on hit lists of anti-regime terrorists. The implication was clear: you are alive because SAVAK protects you. In some cases SAVAK went even further and threatened individuals they could not control with assassination by calling on the person concerned and informing him that a plot to kill him had been uncovered. 'We are ready to protect you,' the SAVAK emissary would say. 'But we cannot do so unless we have your full cooperation.'[12]

The climate of fear engendered by SAVAK led to a gradual distancing of the Shah from the people. The Shah stopped appearing among his subjects without prior arrangement and the number of official visits the monarch paid to various parts of the country was drastically reduced. Until the early 1970s the Shah made a point of changing his prearranged itinerary in provincial tours in order to go among the people. He was seen sitting down to discuss the problem of fishing with fishermen at Bandar-Abbas and the prospects of agriculture with farmers in Dezful. In later years, however, he had become virtually inaccessible. He would travel only by air and even inside the cities would move around aboard his blue and white helicopter. Row after row of civilian dignitaries and military officers would stand to attention for hours before His Imperial Majesty's chopper appeared in the sky. Even high-ranking officials were told to maintain a distance of several metres from His Imperial Majesty. Physical contact between the monarch and the people, so important in the Shah's style until the end of the 1960s, had all but disappeared.

The Shah, who had escaped many attempts on his life, had, over the years, learned to disdain death. He was not afraid of dying as he was convinced that only God knew the day of each man's death. He agreed to distance himself from the people as a means of reducing the risk of assassination because SAVAK and certain of his confidants persuaded him that his physical elimination would lead to the dismemberment of Iran. Court Minister Assadollah Alam lost few opportunities to hammer in that theme. 'Dark forces are determined to eliminate our beloved Shah,' he liked to say. 'And our supreme duty must be the physical protection of His Imperial Majesty.'[13]

The Shah limited his travels inside Iran to visits to major new development projects. In his reign the number of hydroelectric projects in Iran rose from one to 20, including the world's sixth-largest dam. Thousands of new industrial workshops and factories came into being. Land under cultivation more than doubled. New port facilities were built. More than a dozen brand-new towns serving new mines, industrial units, military bases or agri-businesses were born. The number of universities and centres of higher education rose from 5 in 1946 to nearly 200 in 1978. The Shah was always at hand to cut the ribbon and make a speech about Iran's economic and social miracle. Gradually his old vision of Iran as a country of poverty-stricken villages and ill-equipped towns faded away and was replaced by a new image of shining factories and brand-new housing estates. This vision was further strengthened in the Shah's mind as he watched Iranian television or read the local newspapers and magazines. He dearly loved to deceive himself about the reality of Iran's situation and circumstances helped him achieve that goal.

The regime made little effort to improve its image in the eyes of the people. What mattered was the regime's image of itself. The Shah did not want the majority of Iranians, even less the outside world, to recognise the reality of his brave new world of discipline and industry. What mattered was that he should believe that reality and he did. In 1976, during a speech inaugurating a new dam, the Shah spoke in lyrical tones: 'All around us is barren desert. And yet we have created a lake here. This lake will become a source of life. The desert will become a garden. This is the future of our beloved land.'[14]

The Shah forgot that there were more than 60,000 villages in Iran – many of them with fewer than 200 inhabitants. He never visited the shanty-towns that, by the mid-1970s, had thrown lassos around every major Iranian city. Iran's poverty was not his fault – it was the result of more than two centuries of decline, war and sheer bad luck – yet the Shah felt personally ashamed of it and tried to persuade himself that it had all but disappeared. He hated bad news and argued that Iran had had enough of it in the last 200 years. Those who gave him the bad news were told off, shunned or, in a few cases, even thrown into disgrace. In a conversation he recalled that as a child he had always refused to read those pages in his history text book that related Iran's defeat by the Muslim armies in the seventh century. 'I simply could not bear the humiliation,' he said. 'I tore those pages out of the book and threw them away. There is no need for us to focus on the negative aspects of our existence.'[15]

One person who did bring the Shah bad news was Empress Farah. As the Shah travelled to 'future Iran', his wife toured the 'Iran of yesterday'. She visited leper colonies, earthquake-stricken villages in the desert and remote tribal regions where central government had a nominal presence only:

> I saw the problems while His Majesty saw the achievements. In bed we would compare notes. I would report about what was going wrong in the regions I had just toured. His Majesty would try to dismiss my report as exaggerated or one-sided. At times he would tell me that such minor problems were *des accidents de parcours* or the heritage of the past, and that all would be well in a few years time. Sometimes, however, he would get impatient and edgy. 'No more bad news please!' His Majesty would command. And I would, naturally, change the subject.[16]

The Shah was apparently convinced that given another decade or so he would solve all of Iran's basic problems. He pointed to the experience of Japan during the Meiji period and Germany under Bismarck as two examples of feudalistic societies reaching the industrial age under the guidance of an autocratic state structure. Iran would never become a superpower, if only because it lacked the necessary population base. But the Shah had no doubt that by the year 2000 Iran would be one of the world's five or six major powers.

> God is with Iran for the first time in a long time. This is an opportunity that will not come twice. Today we have everything needed to make Iran great again. We have everything – except, perhaps, time.[17]

The political discourse of the regime emphasised the Shah's apocalyptic fears about Iran missing her historic chance. The vocabulary used in the regime's propaganda was partly borrowed from Marxist-Leninists. The Shah was a leader of 'workers and peasants', and his White Revolution had primarily benefited the 'toiling masses'. At a meeting with the Soviet leader Leonid Brezhnev in the Kremlin in Moscow the Shah surprised members of his entourage by boasting about 'the truly socialist nature of Iran's policies'.[18] He specifically referred to one of his reform projects under which urban workers were to be helped in purchasing up to 49 per cent of the shares of the companies that employed them. The measure was never fully implemented but it appeared threatening enough to scare away some foreign investors and persuade some wealthy Iranians to send even more of their money to foreign bank accounts.

SAVAK was partly in charge of conducting the regime's battle against ideological enemies and it too drew heavily on Marxist-Leninist jargon. This was in part due to the fact that many of SAVAK's founding fathers were turncoat Communists who, after worshipping Stalin for years, now turned the Shah into their idol.

SAVAK marked its entrance on the scene of ideological battles by publishing the magazine Ebrat (Bitter Lesson) in which recanting Marxists exposed the inconsistencies of their discarded faith. From the very earliest stages SAVAK theoreticians believed that shi'ite Islam, the nation's main religious faith, could provide an effective weapon in the fight against Communism and the government was thus persuaded to emphasise its religious profile. From 1954 the nation's only radio network in Tehran devoted a minimum of three hours each day to religious programmes written and performed by mullahs. The government – through SAVAK – also began to subsidise a number of ayatollahs. At first modest, the subsidy topped the $40 million mark by 1977. The Shah also personally invested in the dispatch of mullahs to foreign countries to propagate shi'ism. One such mullah was Imam Musa Sadr who later became the leader of Lebanese shi'ites and broke with SAVAk to join Ayatollah Khomeini's struggle against the Shah.[19]

In 1955 SAVAK employed a total of 178 people. By 1975 this had risen to 3225. At the same time the organisation's annual budget exceeded $120 million. Because SAVAK used equipment and, at times, even human resources belonging to other governmental agencies the real cost of its operations was much higher than its own budget might suggest. The regular police and army units often took part in SAVAK-led operations against guerrilla groups. The management of prisons, where some 3000 political prisoners were held at any given time, was in SAVAK's hands, but the cost of the operation was met through the Ministry of Interior. SAVAK agents attached to many Iranian embassies and consulates throughout the world were put on the payroll of the Ministry for Foreign Affairs. Finally, the prime minister's office, using special funds, financed a number of SAVAK operations at home and abroad.[20] It was also through the prime minister's special fund that more than 700 foreign figures in 30 countries received secret financial donations from Iran: those put on the Iranian payroll included senior politicians, journalists and other people regarded as influential. The head of at least one Western intelligence service received cash gifts of $10,000 a month as an Iranian consultant.[21] In Pakistan, Kuwait, Iraq, Turkey, Lebanon, Afghanistan and Jordan secret funds from Iran financed a number of publications and kept several political parties alive. Iranian money also helped the activities of rebellious Kurds in Iraq and enabled the Muslim Brotherhood to continue its operations against the Syrian Ba'athist regime.

Nominally SAVAK was under the direct supervision of the prime minister. The organisation's head had the title of assistant to the prime minister but was not a member of the cabinet. The first SAVAK chief, General Teymur Bakhtiar, had not felt obliged to report either to the Shah or to the prime minister on a regular basis. His successor, General Hassan Pakravan played the game in strict accordance with the law and regularly reported to the prime minister who was his hierarchic superior. Pakravan's successor, General Nasiri, on the other hand, virtually ignored the prime minister and directly reported to the Shah during his weekly audience at the palace. It is possible that the Shah himself indirectly encouraged Nasiri to bypass the prime minister to whom some of SAVAK's confidential reports, especially on leading public figures, were never submitted. But the Shah, always careful to take into account the prime minister's constitutional powers, almost invariably kept him informed.

The cabinet was seldom informed. Some SAVAK reports were read by key ministers – two or three individuals at most – especially with regard to foreign affairs and sensitive economic information. The rest of the cabinet was kept in the dark. This helped increase SAVAK's influence within the upper echelons of the bureaucracy: the possession of information is a source of extraordinary power in societies where virtually everything is regarded as a state secret.

Organisationally SAVAK was divided into eight directorates. Of these only two really mattered in political terms: the Third and Eighth Directorates. The Third dealt with internal security and was modelled on the American Federal Bureau of Investigation (FBI) and the French Direction de la Sécurité du Territoire (DST). The directorate had agents in 157 cities inside the country, and was in contact with some 20,000 'sources' or informers. Most informers collaborated with SAVAK for a variety of personal reasons, including hopes of quicker advancement within the bureaucracy. Very few received regular cash payments, but many did receive occasional gifts that ranged from a bottle of after-shave lotion to a gift voucher for a locally-made automobile.[22]

SAVAK's human base for information gathering was thus extremely narrow. At the same time the organisation was not able to attract the more intelligent and better-educated elements of the urban middle- and upper-classes that might have helped it make better use of modern techniques of intelligence gathering and analysis. Fewer than 100 SAVAK employees had a higher education and only nine held PhDs. This did not prevent many SAVAK agents from using the title of 'Doctor' and over the years the very word 'doctor' became a synonym for 'torturer' in Tehran's intellectual circles.

The other active SAVAK arm, the Eighth Directorate, dealt with counter-espionage and foreign operations. Largely staffed by army officers, the directorate cooperated closely with the CIA, British Intelligence, the South African BOSS, the Turkish MIT, the Israeli MOSSAD and, after 1973, the Egyptian Mukhaberat. The main directorate assignment was to keep an eye on Soviet agents in Tehran and neighbouring countries.

Between 1954 and 1979, however, the directorate scored only two notable successes in that field. An army general, Mostafa Moqarrabi, was identified as an agent of Soviet Military Intelligence (GRU) and sent to the firing squad. The general had worked for the ultra-sensitive Armed Forces Planning Command for years and at the time of his arrest was the chief of that organisation. He was uncovered largely thanks to the CIA which had for years wondered about the route through which the Soviets secured so much information about CENTO. A second Soviet spy, Ali Tehrani, was caught with help from BOSS. The South Africans recruited a KGB spy who had once served in Tehran and their new 'asset' informed them about KGB activities there. The incident brought Tehran and Pretoria closer together and in 1973 General Fraser, the retiring head of BOSS, was named South Africa's ambassador to Iran.

SAVAK's failure to effectively counter Soviet espionage activity in Iran became abundantly clear in 1982 when General Vladimir Kuzishkin, the KGB chief in Tehran, defected to Britain. Kuzishkin revealed that the KGB and GRU had maintained a network of more than 400 agents in Tehran throughout the 1970s. This meant that the Iranian capital had been the second most important centre for Soviet intelligence activity after New York. Kuzishkin also told the West that the Soviets had planned to kill the Shah in 1963, apparently to take advantage of the urban riots fomented by Ayatollah Khomeini.[23] The plot had failed after the agent assigned to the task of setting off a bomb that was to blow up the Shah's car failed to identify the right button. SAVAK had absolutely no idea about the real scope of Soviet clandestine operations in the country.

The United States was partially aware of SAVAK's weakness and inefficiency as an intelligence organisation. The US Embassy in Tehran, for example, noted in a confidential report in 1977 that SAVAK was 'overestimated and inefficient'.[24] The regime's opponents exaggerated SAVAK's effectiveness and described it as an omnipresent secret police with an effective hold on all aspects of Iranian life. Some SAVAK chiefs put this to good use for their own purposes and pretended that the safety of the regime depended entirely on their hard work and diligence. The organisation used a special TV programme to publicise its role in 'protecting the nation against its enemies'. It also encouraged rumours according to which more than a million SAVAK informers watched everyone, everywhere, all the time. Opponents of the regime, naively, helped spread the rumour and thus indirectly helped the SAVAK in fostering a climate of fear.

Because of its basic inefficiency, when put under unusual pressure by the opponents of the regime SAVAK could become exceptionally brutal. SAVAK interrogators often used torture prior to 1977 and practised a shoot-to-kill policy against urban guerrillas fighting the regime.[25] In at least one case, eight Marxist-Leninists who were about to be released from prison after having served their sentences were shot in cold blood. The massacre was presented as 'an accident provoked by prisoners who tried to escape'. At times SAVAK eliminated the regime's opponents and presented this as the work of anti-Shah guerrillas. One case involved the murder of Ahmad Aramesh who had for years served as a high official of the regime. Aramesh, who had played a role in toppling Mossadeq in 1953, had become an opponent of the Shah after 1971. He was shot in a Tehran public park, allegedly quarrelling with unidentified urban guerrillas.

The urban terrorist groups failed to provoke the mass uprising they continued to hope for until their final defeat in 1977, but they did succeed in enhancing SAVAK's prestige and strengthening its hold on the administration. They also indirectly helped provoke a climate of disaffection which led to the growing isolation of the Shah within the country.

Between 1970 and 1977 the Shah's personality cult was systematically built up by the government. Official propaganda emphasised the Shah's role as Commander-in-Chief of the armed forces and presented politics as a branch of war. Premier Hoveyda began to refer to the Shah as Farmandeh (Commander) in direct violation of the Constitution which regarded the monarch as a symbol of national unity set above day-to-day politics. Gradually, a new image of the Shah emerged: His Imperial Majesty was no longer the traditional king who could stay above political factions and act as the last arbiter of national policies. He had become the leader of one political faction among many. Because all the credit for the country's undoubted progress was attributed to him, it was only natural that the Shah should also take the blame for the countless problems that still remained.

In March 1975 the Shah abandoned the last reservations he might have had about abandoning the multiparty system in existence and ordered the creation of the Rastakhiz (Resurgence) as an umbrella organisation to run the government. Under the previous system only four parties had been allowed a legal existence. The governing Iran Novin (New Iran) Party of Premier Hoveyda had, over the years, developed into a powerful organisation with some 50,000 members and branches throughout the country. Used by the prime minister as an effective instrument for distributing jobs and favours, Iran Novin had begun to appear as a potential threat to the supremacy of the royal court in all matters pertaining to individual and group advancement within the civil service. Ambitious civil servants no longer looked to the Shah's immediate entourage for patronage and protection as the Iran Novin Party machine offered what was needed. Leaving aside a few sensitive cabinet seats about which the Shah had views of his own, the prime minister had a virtually free hand in placing his own protégés in all echelons of the administration. Between 1965 and 1977 the number of people directly or indirectly employed by the state nearly quadrupled. This was accompanied by a rise in the government's budget from just over $2 billion to more than $50 billion a year. The government controlled 53 per cent of GDP and dominated all aspects of the economy as the nation's largest employer, the biggest customer for farm products and industrial goods and the source of some 75 per cent of all private sector investment.

By 1975 the Shah might have had the feeling that the government's new powers were no longer under his own full control. The Iran Novin Party held mass rallies and national conferences and while it continued to pay tribute to the Shah's personality cult it was obvious that the party was beginning to build its own networks of loyalty and connection. Many ambitious politicians with impeccable records of loyalty to the Shah were gradually pushed aside as Iran Novin activists occupied more and more sensitive and lucrative posts. Some discontented politicians and civil servants gathered around Hushang Nahavandi, Empress Fara's dynamic private secretary, who had previously served as a minister as well as rector of Tehran University. Another group was formed around Mohammad Baheri, an undersecretary at the Ministry of Court, and a protégé of Alam. Meanwhile, the Mardom (People) Party which for years had served as the loyal opposition tried to resist Iran Novin's irresistible advance in the provinces. The ultranationalist Pan-Iranist Party, for its part, accused Iran Novin and Hoveyda of having 'betrayed the nation' by abandoning traditional Iranian claims over Bahrain.

Iran Novin and its rivals hardly touched the mass of Iranians: their skirmishes were all fought within the narrow sociological stratum of civil servants and politicians. It was this stratum, however, whose voice the Shah heard the loudest. Thus, the decision to merge all the existing parties and groups into one was partly designed to silence complaints about Iran Novin's monopolistic tendencies.

The Shah unveiled his new plan at a meeting of some 20 influential individuals. The leaders of the four legal parties, the prime minister, the speakers of the two houses of parliament, the minister of court and the editors of Tehran's leading newspapers were present at the palace meeting where the Shah made a brief reference to his own lifelong opposition to a one-party system which, in 1960, he had condemned in these terms: 'If I were a dictator rather than a constitutional monarch, then I might be tempted to sponsor a single dominant party such as Hitler organised or such as you find today in Communist countries.'[26]

Rastakhiz, as the Shah described it at that meeting, was not to be a political party but a form of national front within which a wide variety of parties and mass organisations might operate. The 'front' was to insist on loyalty to three basic principles only: the system of monarchy, constitutional government and the 'White Revolution' reforms. Theoretically, there was no reason to prevent people from creating their own political parties and groups on the basis of those principles. Within a few weeks, however, the entire project had been taken over by zealots, many of them former Communists now working for SAVAK, who modelled Rastakhiz on Leninist parties based on democratic centralism. Thus Iran became a one-party system with the Shah regarded as its ultimate leader. After an initial period in which hopes of political reform, notably at the lower levels of decision-making, were encouraged by government propaganda, Rastakhiz became just another branch of the bureaucracy with its entire budget provided by the government. Hoveyda remained in control of the party machine – basically the same as Iran Novin's – and while his rivals described Rastakhiz as an instrument of change, the prime minister emphasised the importance of stability.

The voluntary dissolution of the Iran Novin Party came before it could celebrate its twelfth anniversary. It was the first governing party in Iran to have lasted that long. Hoveyda and other party leaders had hoped that Iran Novin would retain its position as 'the guardian of the Shah-People Revolution' for many more years to come and Hoveyda saw no reason why Iran Novin should not develop into a genuine party of the centre with its own sources of support in the country. In private conversations he expressed the hope that Iran Novin would play a role in ensuring political stability when the Shah was no longer there. He did not, of course, imagine the overthrow of the monarchy. What he wanted to prepare for was the smooth transfer of power to the Crown Prince when the time came. There are no indications that the Shah ever doubted Hoveyda's loyalty to the monarchy, but there were many hints that his Majesty was not quite happy with the rising power of Iran Novin.

The fate of a building designed to house Iran Novin's headquarters in Tehran illustrated the country's basic instability. The site of the building in northern Tehran was earmarked for the Free People's Centre back in 1965, but before building work could begin the centre's founder, Tehran Mayor Ahmad Nafisi, had been found guilty of embezzlement and thrown into prison. The site had then been transferred to Iran Novin, then led by Premier Mansur. Mansur could not break ground for building to start because he was gunned down by an Islamic terrorist. Building work for a 30-storey tower began under Atallah Khosravani, the party's secretary-general until 1969, but he too was removed from power after quarrelling with a cabinet minister during a poker game. Building work was resumed when Manuchehr Kalali took over as party secretary-general but before it was completed Iran Novin itself disappeared on the Shah's orders. The site and the uncompleted building were then transferred to Rastakhiz but Rastakhiz too disappeared before the building was finished. After the 1979 Islamic Revolution the building, still incomplete, was occupied by the Islamic Republic Party. The building was completed in 1983 but by that time the Islamic Republic Party, too, had been disbanded on Khomeini's orders.

The Shah seldom missed an opportunity to emphasise the importance of stability as the basic condition for Iran's economic and social development. At the same time, however, he injected a great deal of instability into the system. Because high officials owed their presence in decision-making positions to His Majesty's pleasure rather than to the political support they commanded in the country they could never be sure about their future and ministers could be dismissed without prior notice. The Chief of Staff of the Armed Forces, General Fereidun Jam, who had generally been regarded as a close friend of the monarch, arrived for his weekly audience at the palace where he was curtly told by a court official that His Majesty would not see him. 'General,' the official said. 'Go back and send your number two. You are relieved.'[27] (Because of his extraordinary shyness the Shah never sacked anyone personally and the task of conveying the bad news was always entrusted to court officials.) Virtually all higher levels of government were gradually trained to focus their activities on one goal only: to please the Shah. Some tried to justify their attitude by arguing that since the Shah worked for the good of the nation, pleasing him meant no more than serving the country.

The Shah provoked instability in another, more important, way. He would announce major policy decisions without the slightest prior notice. High-ranking officials attending a minor ceremony in the presence of the Shah would suddenly learn that their policies had been reversed. One day His Majesty would announce a scheme for giving urban workers a share in profits. Another day he would inform the nation that all private schools and hospitals had been nationalised. It is almost certain that he took the decision to turn Iran into a one-party state without seeking advice from any of his aides or confidants. Even Empress Farah learned about the move only after it had been made public.[28] In 1974 the Shah surprised his own economic advisers by ordering them to increase public spending by 141 per cent to take into account the nation's growing income from oil.

The Shah regularly presided over sessions of the High Council of the Economy, the High Council for the Budget and Plan, and the High Council for Educational Revolution. At these sessions he would listen to ministers' prepared speeches which in most cases had been cleared with him before being made. He would then ask a number of brief questions before issuing his 'commands', often in the presence of reporters and in front of TV cameras. There would be no opportunity for discussing and debating the issues involved. The Shah would tolerate – at times even encourage – discussion only in restricted meetings with no more than one or two high officials at any given time. Senior ministers would be called in to present their views and offer advice. The task of announcing potentially unpopular measures to the country was reserved for the prime minister and his cabinet colleagues: His Majesty only brought the good news.

The Shah had a decisive advantage over the high officials who worked with him. He was the best-informed person in the country. His Majesty received the prime minister, the army Chief-of-Staff, the SAVAK head, the oil company president, senior ministers, provincial governors, ambassadors, leading businessmen, foreign dignitaries; all alone and in private. Since he would never share his information with anyone else his corps of aides and advisers often had to base their judgment on guesswork. Unconsciously, the Shah was exacting revenge. For years authoritarian prime ministers such as Qavam, Razm-Ara, Mossadeq and Zahedi had kept him in the dark about important issues; now it was his turn to become the fount of all knowledge in the country. Did he also continue to doubt the loyalty of his aides? In the case of some: yes. He suspected some of his senior ministers of having 'special ties' with either the United States or Great Britain. Secretly he resented these often-imaginary ties but at the same time, because of the basic contradiction in his own world view, he was more circumspect with those officials who were supposed to enjoy the patronage of the great powers.

In the second half of the 1960s and the early 1970s the Shah succeeded in attracting a large number of highly educated, talented and motivated Iranians. One critical foreign observer paid tribute to the Shah's aides in these terms: 'Never in my career had I encountered such a shining array of talent. With one or two exceptions, the government establishment was composed of men of great skill, high intelligence and expertise and what seemed an infinite capacity for hard work.'[29] And yet the Shah often treated many of his ministers as children needing constant supervision. This is how he described his presence at a cabinet meeting: 'There is no need for me to bring it to order since the ministers are waiting for me to speak. I don't use a gavel and control the meeting merely by the look in my eyes, facial expressions and tone of voice.'[30]

The Shah had an opinion on virtually everything, ranging from the interbreeding of Holstein cows with Persian bovines to nuclear disarmament. Virtually all major public events were inaugurated either in his presence or with a special message read on his behalf by the Empress or a high official. In 1974, for example, the Iranian media published no fewer than 73 special messages from His Majesty. To this must be added more than 20 speeches made by the Shah, plus his statements in the course of two dozen press conferences and interviews given to foreign journalists. From his Olympian solitude the Aryan Sun distilled his rays of wisdom in all directions.

The terminology used to describe the Shah's intervention in the work of government changed over the years. Until the mid-1950s official propaganda spoke of 'royal comments' (nazar molukaneh): this meant that His Majesty's views lacked any executive authority. Between 1956 and 1965 official propaganda referred to the Shah's 'guiding points' (rahnemud). Between 1965 and 1975 there was talk of 'royal instructions' (avamer molukaneh). After that the public was told that His Majesty issued 'auspicious commands' (farman homauyuni).

As the official adulation of the Shah – jokingly referred to as 'Shadulation' in private conversations in Tehrani high society – reached new heights, or rather depths, of sycophancy, His Majesty became increasingly convinced of his own divine mission to revive Iran's ancient grandeur. He wanted everyone to know that he was in full command, that he knew everything and that, as the nation's most ardent patriot, he was the only one to have devoted his entire life to the service of the country. He took an almost childish pleasure in confounding his ministers and generals at official meetings by suddenly revealing information about their field of work of which they were manifestly unaware. 'Well, you didn't know that, did you?' he would then ask with a malicious twinkle in his eye. 'You see, we have to keep an eye on everything.'[31] In the middle of the 1973 Arab-Israeli war the Shah convened a meeting of his top generals at the Supreme Commander's office and gave them a lecture, complete with maps and slides, on the opposing strategies of Egypt and Israel.[32] 'This is really your work that I am doing,' he scolded the generals. 'We ought to know how people fight their wars in our region.'[33]

The Shah had a generally low opinion of his civilian and military aides and was constantly worried that things might go wrong. He insisted on knowing every detail of negotiations with foreign governments or businesses for fear that the Iranian team might simply give the family silver away. 'This world is full of sharks,' he once said. 'We are now in the power game and our officials are sure to make many mistakes. This is why as King I have to be doubly careful.'[34]

A number of incidents helped confirm the Shah in his fear that things might go wrong at any time. In 1969 the Iranian Navy invaded a tiny island in the middle of the Persian Gulf and hoisted the imperial flag on top of an oil rig installed by an American oil company. Iran had learned about the American presence on the atol through the British, whose maps showed it to belong to Iran. The American company, however, had begun prospecting work on the island (and on a neighbouring atol) under Saudi licence. After a miniature diplomatic storm, Washington persuaded Iran and Saudi Arabia to take one atol each and allow the matter to rest. The Iranian atol was named Farsi (Persian) and shown on television as the prize of a new victory by the Imperial Iranian Navy. A naval garrison of nine men was put there but once the TV cameras were withdrawn the atol and its garrison were forgotten. The nine soldiers quickly ran out of provisions and, lacking any means of communication with the mainland, were in a sorry state when a British oil tanker discovered them by pure chance and took them to safety in Abu Dhabi. Reports of the incident drove the Shah into a mood of anger mixed with despondency and he responded by sacking the entire Navy high command. All naval officers ranking above captain were put on an early retirement list.

Two years later another incident, again involving the Navy, re-confirmed the Shah's worse fears of inpending disaster. An Iranian flotilla of two frigates and several escort ships was ordered to make a goodwill visit to the Saudi port of Jeddah. The idea was to show that, with the British now out of the region, the Iranian Navy was capable of keeping the peace in the Persian Gulf and its western approaches right up to East Africa. The Iranian flotilla was scheduled to arrive in Jeddah on the anniversary of the Shah's birth and a massive reception had been organised in their honour. On the appointed day, however, there was no sign of the ships and for a full 24 hours no one knew what had happened to them. Later it was revealed that the main ships had run out of fuel somewhere in the Arabian Sea and were waiting to be relieved.[35]

When angry the Shah would stay in his office and sulk. One sure sign that His Majesty was in a bad mood was that he would seize a strand of his own hair and endlessly weave and unweave it. Unlike his father, who vented his anger by swearing aloud and beating people in his presence with a stick, Mohammad-Reza Shah would interiorise his frustration. At the end of a bad day he would return to his private apartments, his head low and his myopic grey eyes seething with chagrin. He could not understand why, given goodwill and hard work, things could still go wrong on some occasions. With Mossadeq and other mischief-makers and demagogues out of the way, there was no reason why the country should not run like clockwork.

Because there was hardly any public debate on major issues of domestic and foreign policy, the media and, to a lesser extent the parliament, which had virtually no say in shaping governmental decisions, seized upon minor problems to vent their deeper resentment. Tehran's unbearable traffic jams, which the Shah did not experience because he used his helicopter, provided a favourite subject for expression of public dissent against the authorities. Other issues exploited for the same purpose included the rising cost of housing, partly due to speculation, and occasional shortages of certain items of food. One such shortage provoked the Shah's anger. In the late 1960s bananas, previously unknown in Iran, were introduced first as a rare delicacy and, later, as an item of mass consumption. In 1974, however, the country experienced a sudden shortage of bananas, partly because the congested Iranian ports could not handle the flood of imports. The banana shortage was presented by the media as a national calamity and treated as an issue of urgent importance in parliament. The radio and TV broadcast interviews with aggrieved mothers who claimed that shortage of bananas might hamper the normal growth of their children. Satirical sketches filled the newspapers which also devoted editorial comment to the subject. The banana crisis was a substitute for serious political debate, a round-about way of expressing resentment at the fact that almost all major decisions were taken within the narrow circle of the national leadership. The Shah's reaction was, at first, defiant. 'They now want bananas?' he asked his prime minister. 'But since when have they developed a taste for bananas? Did Cyrus the Great eat bananas? Did Prophet Muhammad eat bananas?'[36] Later, however, he decided to 'solve the problem' his own way. He ordered the government to get hold of as many bananas as they could in as short a time as possible. Iranian embassies throughout the world were ordered to treat the matter with urgency and special aircraft were leased to fly in the precious cargo. Even better, the government subsidised the price of the coveted fruit and the crisis ended with a victory for His Majesty. The real message, however, was not received.

The Man from Khomein

In September 1977, on what was to be his last trip to Shiraz, the Shah went to inspect the Shah-e-Cheragh (King of Light) project at the centre of the city. The project was designed to turn the old quarters around the holy shrine of Imamzadeh Ahmad into the world's largest complex of Islamic edifices. The centre of Shiraz was already adorned with a number of mosques, including the oldest in the country, and several theological schools. Under the project a new mosque, to be the largest in the world, was to be built along with luxury hotels, a museum and a public library – also to be the largest in the Muslim world.

Under the Iranian Constitution the Shah was also the temporal head of the world's shi'ite Muslim community. He had quarrelled with a section of the shi'ite clergy over his social and economic reforms for more than fifteen years. Now he was determined to patch things up, to emphasise his credentials as a true believer. The Shah-e-Cheragh project was to be a symbol of reconciliation between the monarch and the conservative clergy who feared his 'foreign' ideas and resented his autocratic style of government.

Walking through the old centre of Shiraz the Shah inspected the demolition work under way. Old and ugly buildings were being demolished to make way for the new Pahlavi monuments. At one point the Shah stopped and pointed at a five-storey block of offices and shops – an eyesore covered with pinkish cement. He recalled that he had ordered the demolition of 'this disgrace' three years earlier. Members of the royal entourage – ministers, governors, national and local dignitaries – stared at their feet or turned their heads away as the monarch fumed about his orders being ignored. 'Why is this building still here?' the Shah kept asking. The answer was finally murmured in a way that only His Majesty and those standing very close to him could hear: the building belonged to Court Minister Amir-Assadollah Alam, a man influential enough to protect his property even against the orders of the King of Kings. The Shah did not pursue the matter: within two years both Alam and the Shah had died in exile and the Shiraz project had been abandoned. The pink office block, however, still stood.

Since the early 1960s the Shah had persuaded himself that he could get what he wanted from his government with a mere nod. This was an illusion. Officials invoked His Majesty's 'special commands' only when and if they themselves wanted something done. Every day the Shah was lavishly praised in official speeches and media reports which portrayed him as the centre of all power in Iran. The machinery of government, however, had its own logic. It was primarily in the service of influential and privileged groups who would go along with the Shah, idolising him, only as long as their interests were furthered.

The 'White Revolution' had created a new urban class of aggressively enterprising businessmen, contractors, speculators and influence-peddlers who treated the state apparatus as an instrument for securing and distributing privileges. The Shah believed that he could stand above social classes and act as a disinterested arbiter of conflicts within society. Iran's economic boom, fuelled by the rising of income from oil, had brought with it an overall improvement in the material living conditions of virtually all sections of society. It also widened the gap between the very rich and the very poor, and created a new urban middle class whose daily lives could never match up to their aspirations for better access to more goods and services. This new class also resented the fact that it was shut out of decision-making.

Over the years the social divisions created or accentuated by the economic boom were reflected in virtually all aspects of life, especially in urban Iran. In Tehran and other major cities, rich and poor began to withdraw into their respective ghettos. In north Tehran and its neigh-bouring villages the nouveaux riches translated their dreams into copies of Versailles or Palm Beach villas, neo-classical mansions with colon-nades and futuristic extravaganza. They also extended their empire into the Caspian coast where they pushed the forest back with bulldozers to build their eyesores. One sumptuous villa near Ramsar, once a natural beauty spot, was made of two huge pink-painted hearts.

Many in the new privileged classes sent their children to foreign-language schools in Tehran and other major cities. In 1978 these schools accounted for some 25,000 children. Women dyed their hair blonde and, led by Empress Farah, became enthusiastic customers of Parisian fashion. Many in the new rich families even spoke English or French at home: Persian was becoming the language of the plebeians.

The 'nouveaux pauvres' watched this strange transformation of Iranian society with a mixture of amazement and terror. The lure of the big cities, especially Tehran, persuaded millions of peasants to leave their villages and march on what they thought was their Eldorado. At first they found the big city fascinating: for the first time in their lives they had access to a new range of consumer goods. Crowded in their shanty towns the new poor often lived in hovels covered by tin sheets or tarpaulins. They lacked piped water but had TV sets, transistor radios and an assortment of furniture they could not have dreamed of in their villages. Through their TV sets and radios they learned about the Shah's peaceful revolution and often found claims made by official propaganda indecent. They saw the new rich driving expensive limousines to official banquets, arts festivals, opera premières and fashion shows. Theirs was a different world: the new rich had created their own Iran within traditional society which fascinated and frightened the new poor at first, but the fear soon began to turn to envy and then to hatred.

Nowhere was this cleavage so dramatically apparent as in Tehran itself. The rising price of housing pushed the poor and the lower middle classes towards the centre and southern districts of the sprawling capital while the north began to look like a prosperous Western suburb. The 2,000,000 people living in north Tehran purchased more than half of all Iran's imported consumer goods. They had 6 times as many private automobiles as the rest of the country and the average north Tehrani family's annual income was 12 times that of its counterpart in the southern parts of the capital.[1] More than 80 per cent of passports issued for travel abroad in 1978 went to people with north Tehran addresses.[2]

The presence of an increasing number of foreign workers in Iran further strengthened the impression that society was divided into two competing realities. By 1978 nearly two million foreigners were working in the country, more than half Afghans who often lived with the Iranian new poor in shanty towns. Tens of thousands of au pairs, nurses, housemaids, governesses and valets from the Philippines, Bangladesh, India and Pakistan catered for the needs of the new rich, further shielding them from contact with the middle and lower sections of their own society.

The expatriate community also included some 200,000 West Europeans and North Americans who lived in the midst of the new rich society and helped further emphasise its isolation. These expatriates – with their own clubs, restaurants, favourite theatres, and even special TV and radio stations – often kept to themselves. They created a colonial atmosphere in Tehran and a few other big cities such as Isfahan. Traditional Iran resented their presence and suspected their motives. New rich Iran tried to imitate them and thus further alienated itself.

The Shah and his government were aware of the deep gap that divided the very rich and the very poor. Throughout the years they tried a number of policies aimed at a better distribution of income, but these had only limited effect. In many parts of the country there were simply no credible channels for income distribution and the flood of peasants coming to urban areas was simply too strong for any government to stem without violence. For a while the Shah was seduced by an idea put to him by the Romanian President Nicolae Ceausescu in the early 1970s. Ceausescu's dream was to reduce the number of villages in Romania to a mere 1200 so that each could be provided with the public facilities of a small town. A similar study was carried out in Iran and it was decided that the nation's estimated 65,000 villages should be 'merged' to create some 8000 'agricultural poles'. Only then could the government provide the necessary public services and stem the depopulation of the countryside.[3] A few dozen model villages were built but most peasants refused to leave their native villages for the new 'poles'. For a while the government toyed with the idea of using force to push peasants out of uneconomic villages but the Shah refused. After all, he was no Ceausescu. He even rejected the idea of forcibly evicting part of Tehran's population so that the capital could become manageable as a megalopolis.

Because the Shah was at the centre of the Iranian state apparatus it was only natural that all those who wished to profit from doing business with the government tried to forge some links with the royal family and the imperial court. Businessmen began to offer a percentage of shares in their enterprises to this or that prince or princess, ostensibly in order to provide funds for charitable purposes. Virtually all members of the royal family had one or more charity outfit named after them which operated under their nominal control. Most of these were fairly small operations but some, like the Red Lion and Sun Society, the Iranian equivalent of the Red Cross, under the presidency of Princess Shams, or the Imperial Society for Social Services headed by Princess Ashraf, were among the largest enterprises in the country. A good part of the money spent by these organisations came from the government's budget but many private companies also offered 'voluntary donations'.

The Shah's own charity, the Pahlavi Foundation, had grown into one of Iran's largest conglomerates with assets exceeding \$1.2 billion in 1978.[4] The Foundation was involved in a wide range of charity work: it offered thousands of scholarships, published subsidised books, financed a number of research projects and a variety of cultural organisations. However, its principal activity was, quite obviously, commercial. It held shares in more than 80 Iranian and some 40 foreign companies and was active in real estate. Under the charter of the Foundation the Shah was entitled to six per cent of the annual income, but he always maintained that he forewent his share after 1965. In the absence of public control over the way the Foundation acquired and spent its money there was no way of knowing whether or not it was used as a means of securing illegal gains. The Shah's opponents, however, had no doubt: the Pahlavi Foundation was the instrument that His Majesty used for the purpose of amassing a personal fortune.

One of the richest members of the royal family was the Shah's half-sister, Princess Fatemeh. On her death in exile in 1988 her fortune was estimated at over \$500 million. Where did the money come from? A good part of it almost certainly came from 'commissions' received by the princess's husband, General Muhammad Khatam, who commanded the Iranian Air Force until his death in 1975 in a sporting accident.[5] Khatam, a close friend of the Shah, was, in a sense, the architect of Iran's modern Air Force which was equipped with the latest in American hardware. It is possible that he received millions in kickbacks from the American manufacturers but this cannot wholly explain the immense fortune the general amassed in just a few years.

Like most of the other nouveaux riches figures in Iran, Khatam made much of his money in land speculation. Acquiring large tracts of land was exceptionally easy, provided one had the right connections. Under Iranian law anyone who 'invested' in unused land could claim ownership, a measure intended to encourage farming and construction. What Khatam did was to spend a small sum planting barbed wire around large areas of the desert east of Tehran. He then claimed the land as his own and obtained the title deeds necessary. The next move was to tell the government that the Air Force needed land east of Tehran. The government had no choice but to accept the judgment of the commander of the Air Force who was, more importantly, the Shah's brother-in-law and personal friend. The worthless land was purchased from Khatam for millions of dollars which he instantly transferred to bank accounts abroad.

Khatam was certainly not alone in using the technique. Nor was he the biggest operator in that domain. Many of the Shah's personal friends and associates were involved in land speculation. Amir-Assadollah Alam inherited much land from his own father, but he would not be content with what he already had. Through his network of relatives he expanded his property, especially in the eastern and southern parts of the country. He was also present as a sleeping partner in dozens of companies – especially those dealing with the Iranian armaments industry.

Khatam and Alam were the only two men who ever came close to being regarded as personal friends of the Shah. They shared with the monarch in some of his indiscretions and were constantly on the watch for an opportunity to arrange a new conquest for His Imperial Majesty. As a Minister of Royal Court Alam had assigned one of his deputies to the task of redamselling the Imperial cot on a regular basis. A small palace, Shahvand, was reserved for his Majesty's private relaxation.

The tremendous success of Khatam and Alam both in terms of personal fortune and the degree of influence they enjoyed with the Shah encouraged other courtiers and courtisans to try and profit from His Majesty's affection for the fairer sex. The Shah's personal physician, General Abdul-Karim Ayadi, became an active scout in Western European circles where companions for His Majesty could be recruited. Ayadi, too, was compensated for his services and by 1978 he was one of the largest landowners in the country.

The Shah's chief pimp was Amir-Hushang Davalloo, a mysterious figure who bore the title 'His Majesty's Special Butler' but who described himself as Prince when travelling abroad. Davalloo was the only person who could go and see the Shah whenever he wanted, including in His Majesty's private quarters. At his home Davalloo exhibited a portrait of the Shah with this inscription by His Majesty: 'Chief Hushang! We are your servant! Muhammad Reza Pahlavi.'[6] There are different accounts of Davalloo's exact role. Empress Farah says: 'He was the court jester. He made the Shah laugh. That's all.'[7] But we know that Davalloo obtained for his wife the monopoly of Iran's caviar exports to Europe. He also received large tracts of land distributed by the government in the 1970s, more than a mere court jester might hope for and deserve.

Davalloo's various duties certainly included the selection of occasional 'adventures' for the Shah. According to some accounts he specialised in very young girls. Others, however, have linked him with the notorious Madame Claude whose *maison* in Paris included such illustrious customers as King Hassan of Morocco.[8]

Davalloo began his career as a go-between in Paris in the 1940s under Nazi occupation where he quickly emerged as one of the most popular procurers of escorts for Nazi officers: Goering himself was at one point one of Davalloo's grateful clients.*

By the mid-1970s it is almost certain that the Shah had neither the time nor the inclination to make full use of the services provided by Alam, Ayadi, Davalloo and many others. These men themselves were also busy in other domains, especially land-grabbing. In this they simply represented the dominant mood among the privileged classes at the time. The absence of a culture of investment in industry meant that many of the new rich turned to land-ownership as their principal form of wealth. In 1977 a survey by the Ministry of Housing and Urban Development showed that some 1300 individuals, belonging to no more than 200 families, owned more than 60 per cent of all land in Tehran and a dozen other major cities.[10]

The apparent Westernisation of the higher echelons of Iranian society in the 1970s did not, as might have been expected, weaken the hold of shi'ite Islam on virtually all classes. Some members of the new privileged classes advertised their irreligiosity by refusing to fast during Ramadan or by going on foreign holidays during the mourning months of Muharram and Safar. A few even converted to Christianity, the religion of the admired West, or reverted to Zoroastrianism, Iran's pre-Islamic faith. One remarkable and angrily remarked conversion to Catholicism was that of the Shah's eldest sister, Princess Shams, and her husband Mehrdad Pahlbod, the Minister for Culture. The Shah did not approve of the

---

*On at least one occasion Davalloo attempted to present a teenage Iranian girl to His Majesty during a stay at the St Moritz ski resort. A timely intervention by Ardeshir Zahedi, then Foreign Minister, saved the situation: the girl never saw the Shah and was sent back home.[9]

conversion but did not intervene as religious faith was a matter of individual choice. Princess Sham's choice, however, gave the Shah's opponents, especially among the mullahs, an excellent excuse for their increasingly bitter attacks on the monarch. 'The Shah wants to destroy Islam,' the exiled Ayatollah Ruhollah Khomeini repeated in his messages to semi-clandestine fundamentalist groups in Qom and Tehran.

Pictures of an expensive church built by Princess Shams as part of a Xanadu-style complex of palaces near Karaj, west of Tehran, were distributed by militant Khomeinists at mosques. Princess Sham's love of dogs – she had a collection of more than 100 – was also seized upon by anti-Shah propagandists as a sign of the regime's hostility towards Islam, as shi'ite doctors regard the dog as a reincarnation of the pig and thus 'untouchable'. Princess Shams provoked further criticism when she organised a wedding ceremony for her daughter on the eve of an important day of shi'ite mourning. To make matters worse the bridegroom was an American.

It is difficult to be certain about the exact origins of social moods and fashions at any given time, but by the mid-1970s the mood of Iranian society as a whole was a religious one and manifestations of religious faith had become fashionable. Was this an unconscious attempt at counterbalancing material wealth with at least a semblance of moral rectitude? Or did all classes of society cling to Islam as the only common ground they still had while material reality divided them as seldom before? Whatever the reasons, between 1970 and 1978 more than 5000 new mosques were built throughout the country; renovation work was carried out in some 1300 holy shrines: the number of pilgrims to the holy city of Mashhad rose from under 500,000 in 1970 to more than 10,000,000 in 1978, 5 times more than the number of pilgrims who went to Mecca, Islam's holiest city. The number of Iranians going to Mecca for the annual Haj rose to 55,000 in 1978, a sixfold increase over a decade.

Religious themes were also popular in literature and art. In the late 1970s religious books often topped the best-seller lists throughout urban Iran and paintings with Islamic motifs attracted viewers and investors. The holding of special religious ceremonies, known as sofreh, became a favourite pastime of rich society ladies. The sofreh ceremony included a sermon by a mullah followed by a feast that could cost tens of thousands of dollars for up to 100 guests. The new rich also went on organised pilgrimages to Mesopotamia, Arabia and Syria. Empress Farah was frequently shown on TV making pilgrimages to Mashhad and other holy shrines in Iran. Her mother, Mrs Farideh Diba, led a delegation of ladies to Mecca. Princess Fatemeh also went to Mecca with a large suite. Princess Shahnaz, the Shah's eldest daughter, went even further and worked as a militant Islamic preacher together with her husband Khosrow Jahanbani. A growing number of famous men – pop singers, poets, artists, business tycoons, ministers, and even army generals –

began to grow stubble or full beards in conformity with shi'ite rules. (According to shi'ite doctors men who shave their beards will end up in hell regardless of all the good they might do in life.) The number of women wearing the *charqad* (designed to cover the hair) also increased dramatically. (According to shi'ite doctors women should cover their hair from the age of nine because it emanates radiation that could render men insane with lust.[11]) The *charqad* made its way into the royal palaces too as several princesses and court ladies began to conform to the Islamic fashion of the day.

The Shah was undecided about what to do with the growing Islamic mood of society. On the one hand he shared the analysis made by SAVAK according to which religion was a useful tool in fighting Communism, especially at universities. Hundreds of mullahs were regularly financed by SAVAK as part of its policy of curbing the radical left. SAVAK also subsidised anti-Communist books written by Islamic fundamentalists.[12] The Shah, on the other hand, had a gut feeling that the mullahs would remain his worst enemies.

Indecisive by nature, His Imperial Majesty tried not to take sides. He continued to go to holy shrines and dutifully attended the 'Ashura mourning ceremonies at Muharram. At the same time he encouraged his twin, Princess Ashraf, who, alone in the royal family not to have caught the Islamic mood, continued to press for more reforms in favour of women. By 1978, however, the Islamic mood of the country was strong enough to block a number of reform projects proposed by Princess Ashraf.[13] The Shah's indecision caused a number of contradictions. While he ordered the government to allocate substantial funds to the construction and repair of mosques and holy places in 1977, he also approved the adoption of a new and totally artificial calendar supposed to encompass the entire pre-Islamic history of Iran. The new calendar had been proposed by Shojaeddin Shafa, Deputy Court Minister for Cultural Affairs, in 1971 and had been rejected by prime minister Hoveyda. In 1977, however, with the Shah's permission premier Jamshid Amuzegar declared it to be the nation's official calendar. Iran suddenly found itself in the year 2537. The starting point of Iranian history was no longer the flight of Prophet Muhammad from Mecca to Medina but the day Cyrus the Great became King of Kings. Not surprisingly the move sent a shock wave throughout Iran and especially outraged the mullahs – including those who had served the Shah and generally supported his reform programme.

The new Amuzegar cabinet went further and ordered an end to government and SAVAK stipends to mullahs. The prime minister took the measure as part of his anti-corruption programme. He had criticised the largesse of the government during the Hoveyda era and was now determined to count every penny that was spent from the public treasury.

Hoveyda's government collapsed in the summer of 1977 while the prime minister rested on the island of Corsica. In his absence Tehran experienced daily power cuts and a water shortage. Prices continued to rise and reports of official corruption multiplied. At the Majlis a number of parliamentarians bitterly attacked the government – disregarding the fact that this was a one-party system. Cabinet ministers present at the parliamentary sessions remained silent, not knowing what to do in the absence of their leader: they were technocrats, not politicians. Some were persuaded that the Shah himself had orchestrated the attacks on Hoveyda in order to prepare the stage for a change of prime minister.

To be sure the Shah had begun thinking about relieving Hoveyda of his post in 1977. There were two reasons for this. First, Hoveyda's cabinet had lost some of its popularity because of rising prices and a number of radical measures taken against powerful sections of society. Early in 1977, for example, the government unveiled a new plan under which social security charges were to be extended to all places of employment, including those that had a single employee. Employers were also required to report their domestic servants and pay social security charges for them. The decision angered tens of thousands of small shopkeepers and all those artisans who employed a few apprentices at wages well below the legal minimum. The government took another unpopular decision: it announced that all rents would be frozen for a period of two years. This was immediately translated into an even more acute shortage of homes for rent and a sharp rise in real estate prices in urban areas. To make matters worse, the government announced a popular campaign against high prices, consisting of raids on thousands of factories and shops by groups of university students employed by the Ministry of Commerce and acting as shock troops for the Iran Resurgence Party. The students arrested thousands of businessmen and merchants, including some of the best known in the country, and dispatched hundreds into internal exile. They ordered thousands of shops and workshops to close for periods of up to six months. Pictures of 'guilty' businessmen were shown on TV and published in newspapers as the 'holy war' against high prices raged throughout the country. The move helped alienate one of the more powerful social groups which would otherwise have supported the Shah in its own interest.

The Shah's other reason for wanting to dismiss Hoveyda had to do with changes in Washington. In the 1976 American presidential election the Shah had put his money on the Republican candidate Gerald Ford. His contribution to Ford's campaign amounted to several million dollars.[14] The Democrat, Jimmy Carter, had made himself unpopular in Tehran by including Iran in a list of countries that violated human rights. Carter's election brought to an abrupt end more than 12 years of close relations that the Shah had maintained with the United States under presidents Johnson, Nixon and Ford. Carter was an unknown quantity and all reports agreed that he could cause problems for Iran.

To forestall pressure from the Carter administration the Shah began to introduce a number of reforms even before the new president had been sworn in: constant harassment of the press was partly abandoned; strict orders were issued that no more political prisoners should be tortured; government departments and Iranian embassies abroad were asked to cut their spending and adopt a more frugal posture; the two wings of the Rastakhiz Party were ordered to become more active to give the impression that a degree of pluralism was acceptable to the Shah. Finally, partly in response to a campaign by the American media which accused the Shah's regime of corruption, the monarch ordered a massive anti-corruption drive. Some dramatic cases were exposed at court but no one was convicted. The Shah also created an Imperial Commission to act as a watchdog on all government departments.

This was an unusual move. The commission began to do what is normally the duty of a parliament. It investigated whatever case it deemed necessary and held ministers, including the prime minister himself, accountable. The full sessions of the commission were televised live. The impression given was that of an entire cabinet being tried by a handful of men appointed by the Shah.[15] The message the Shah intended to send was simple: I know there is corruption and inefficiency, but it is the fault not of my leadership but of the government ministers. I shall expose them and then force them to set things right or be dismissed.

The grim picture of the nation's economy, wildly exaggerated by the commission's selective reports, provided a sharp contrast with the vision of a successful Iran that official propaganda had offered. Again and again the Shah promised Iranians painless economic growth and assured them that there was no need for present generations to tighten their belts so that their offspring would enjoy a higher standard of living. The Shah missed few opportunities for boasting that his government was capable of offering Iran both 'butter and guns'.

The first full indication of the Shah's change of mood came in October 1976 when, in a long interview, he announced the impending end of countless government subsidies that had enabled Iranians to improve their living standards without working harder: 'We have not demanded self sacrifice from the people: rather we have covered them in soft cotton wool. Things will now change. Everyone should work harder and be prepared for sacrifices in the service of the nation's progress.'[16] Two weeks after that interview, which amounted to an indictment of the Shah's own policies over the preceding five years, the Imperial Commission came into being. 'His Majesty wants to apply the brakes,' commented Hoveyda in a private conversation, 'And he is right. The economy is overheated and our income from oil is falling in terms of real purchasing power.'[17]

Applying the brakes was no easy task. Iran had committed vast resources to a number of giant industrial and military projects, many of which were regarded by the Shah as sacrosanct. Thus the inevitable cuts could only affect government projects and subsidies that benefited the lower income groups. Hoveyda, reluctant to introduce the cuts, played for time – a tactic that accelerated the already strong inflationary trends within the economy. It was left to his successor, Amuzegar, to really apply the brakes. Hundreds of projects were either shelved or axed and a wage freeze was imposed in the public sector. The regime began to lose its principal claim to public support: the promise of improved living standards.

The new government, dedicated to tight economic policies, failed to establish effective political communication with the sections of society most affected by its action. Amuzegar saw himself as a serious and hardworking manager – which he undoubtedly was – and genuinely believed that spending time on political communication was a luxury he did not need. Throughout his premiership, a total of nearly 13 months, he made only one trip to the provinces – to Tabriz – where he addressed a mass meeting in March 1978. By that time, however, the Islamic Revolution was already well under way. Unlike Hoveyda, who had constantly toured the country practising a hands-on managerial style, Amuzegar was at his happiest in his office, working alone and letting others look after their own briefs. The result was that the prime minister was seen as remote, detached and ineffective, a serious drawback in a highly centralised regime where no one dared take decisions without the approval of those higher-up. The prime minister himself worked within that tradition and cleared the most trivial of matters with the Shah.

The machinery of state when Amuzegar took over was largely run by Hoveyda appointees who saw his successor almost as a usurper. They dared not sabotage the Amuzegar government but would do nothing to help it either. Amuzegar's dour face, austere style and aggressive manners further alienated the men and women who ran the huge machinery of the Iranian Imperial state.

It was against such a background that the Shah launched his policy of 'opening up the political space'.[18] The move had begun during Hoveyda's premiership but it was under Amuzegar that it was fully spelled out and partly put into effect. The Shah claimed – and perhaps genuinely believed – that he had always wanted to democratise Iran. His argument ran like this: there could be no political democracy without a minimum of economic strength and social progress; poor people sell their votes to the highest bidder; illiterate people vote for anyone supported by demagogic politicians and fanatical mullahs; a multi-party system in Iran would only open the way for foreign intervention; all political parties in Iran were linked with Britain, Russia or the United States. Democratisation must therefore be achieved under the monarch's careful control.

Was 1977 a good time to start liberalisation? The question has been debated for the past fourteen years. Several factors might have persuaded the Shah that this was the right time. Iran had a substantial urban middle class for the first time in its history and the Shah might have hoped to win its support on a democratisation platform. The policy of 'opening up the political space' could also help prevent a clash between Iran and the new Carter administration committed to the defence of human rights. Also, the Shah knew that with oil income on the decline the government could have fewer economic advantages to distribute. Thus, the loss of some economic benefits might be compensated by greater political freedoms. Finally, the defeat of the terrorist challenge from the Left meant that liberalisation measures could not be exploited by groups committed to the destruction of the state through violence.

Equally strong arguments were put forward by opponents of liberalisation within the Shah's entourage. They pointed out that the regime was embarking on what was at best a political adventure from a position of weakness. Rastakhiz, the one-party mechanism, had failed to mobilise support for the Shah's policies. The new prime minister was not yet fully in control and most of his ministers lacked a political profile. Inflation was still on the rise and the housing crisis was running out of control. Relations with the United States, Iran's principal ally and chief arms' supplier, were entering a period of uncertainty. Finally, the defeat of virtually all the regime's political opponents had left the way open for religious extremists.

The Shah was confident that he could keep his liberalisation policy under control. He genuinely believed that he could, at any moment, mobilise popular support on the basis of loyalty to monarchist traditions as well as Iran's undoubted progress during his reign. He was initially encouraged in this belief when one of his principal aides, Hushang Ansary, Minister for Economy and Finance, began a campaign tour of the provinces as leader of Rastakhiz's Constructive Wing. He drew large crowds in places as far apart as Isfahan, Yassuj and Mashhad and his message of liberalisation plus a higher standard of living seemed well received. But all this was no more than a fleeting moment of curiosity and the regime as a whole was unable to liberalise quickly enough to convince the people that something more than a gesture towards the Carter administration was involved.

Some of the Shah's traditional opponents, notably the Mossadeqists, were convinced that the new policy was designed solely as a diversion in anticipation of pressures from Jimmy Carter. Some Mossadeqist leaders believed that the new American administration might want to find a new and more acceptable partner in Iran. Three Mossadeqist leaders even wrote a letter to Carter to ask for his support for the creation of a 'legal and popular government' in Iran.[19] They also began to organise gatherings at their homes and wrote an increasing number of letters to newspaper editors. Their message was: we are still around. However the policy of liberalisation had revealed the weakness of the Mossadeqist groups that had haunted the Shah for nearly three decades. It was clear that history had long passed them by and that new actors would soon appear on the Iranian political scene.

The illegal pro-Soviet Tudeh Party, acting through front organisations, also tried to exploit the new situation with the help of soft-left groups. It was present at a series of mass poetry recitals in the Goethe Institute garden in north Tehran. The party also distributed anti-Shah leaflets, some of them produced at the office of TASS, the Soviet news agency.

The SAVAK chiefs, unhappy about the Shah's new policy, stepped back and watched as opposition groups intensified their activities. SAVAK's hope was that the Shah – once convinced that liberalisation would benefit only his opponents – would restore his former policy of firm control, regardless of pressure from Washington.

Interestingly the policy of liberalisation was never openly discussed or debated within the regime. The Shah consulted a wide variety of individuals about this or that aspect of the policy but no overall consensus was developed. As a result the new policy was supported by some sections of the administration but openly sabotaged by others. Influential groups with something to hide resented the additional freedoms allowed the media and a warning to them came when a leading Tehran daily published a sensational feature on Hozhabr Yazdani, a mystery man who claimed to be the owner of the biggest fortune in Iran.[20] The front page headline said: 'This man can buy all of Iran's wealthy people with a single cheque.' The feature told readers how Yazdani, son of a poor shepherd, had built up his vast fortune in only a few years. What was not said was that Yazdani was, in fact, a front man for a number of other influential people, notably the SAVAK chief General Nasiri. Because various government rules prevented high officials from benefiting from public contracts many used the services of front men like Yazdani.

The publication of the story strengthened SAVAK's opposition to the policy of liberalisation. An attempt was made to arrest the writer of the story on trumped up charges but the Shah firmly ordered SAVAK to keep a low profile. Some SAVAK officials openly criticised the new policy at private meetings with high officials and warned that a sudden lifting of the lid could create a political explosion. 'People are going to learn about all that is wrong in this society – all the corruption, all the injustice – and the government won't be able to do anything about it in a serious way,' said Parviz Sabeti, head of SAVAK's internal operations at a private meeting in January 1977. 'The result could only be a popular revolt. What we have to do now is to tighten our control on opponents of the regime while also hitting hard against corrupt officials and profiteers. Liberalisation could become possible in two years' time.'[21] The Shah might have learned about Sabeti's views through third parties, but he was confident that 'the bond between the people and their monarch' would remain strong. If necessary he could jettison his aides and bring in new faces, including members of the opposition. Everything would remain under control – his control.

The Shah had already established indirect contact with some of the better-known opposition personalities. Mehdi Sami'i, then chairman of the Agricultural Bank, established contact with Mehdi Bazargan, a former Mossadeqist who had moved closer to the exiled Ayatollah Khomeini and his religious supporters. Sami'i formed the impression that the Shah might ask him to lead a coalition government in which Bazargan and his friends could have a place. Sami'i's close relations with business and political circles in the United States and his prestige as an experienced and honest official for more than 25 years made him a suitable candidate for such an operation at the time. At the same time, however, the Shah was in contact with the Mossadeqists – this time through former Commerce Minister Fereidun Mahdavi. Here, the idea was that the Mossadeqists would be allowed to gain a few seats in the next parliament, scheduled to be elected in June 1979. The trouble was that the Mossadeqists had no organisation and very limited support outside Tehran. They were even unable to come up with a list of 25 names to be put forward as candidates.

The organisational weakness of the secular parties opposed to the Shah meant that only religious groups could emerge as the chief beneficiaries of the new policy of liberalisation. The vast majority of the shi'ite clergy had cooperated with the Shah's regime over the years and, despite objections to certain aspects of His Majesty's policies, had no intention of fomenting revolution. Of the six grand ayatollahs that formed the highest echelon of shi'ite theological authority, only one, Khomeini, was an avowed opponent of the regime. During his exile the ayatollah continued his occasional attacks on the government and also maintained contact with a number of fundamentalist groups inside Iran. His two sons, Mostafa and Ahmad, received guerrilla training in Lebanon and were honorary members of the militant shi'ite organisation known as Amal (Hope) led by Imam Mussa Sadr.

After Carter's election a number of anti-Shah Iranian exiles visited Khomeini at Najaf and appealed to him to step up his campaign against the government in Tehran. One was a pharmacist from Houston, Texas, known as Ibrahim Yazdi. Another was the political adventurer Sadeq Ghotbzadeh who had close links with the Syrian security services. Both believed that the new US administration would soon begin to look for new partners in Iran; it was time for the ayatollah to give the many different parties and groups that opposed the Shah the leadership they lacked. The possibility of fomenting a military *coup d'état*, the most frequently used method of changing governments in the Middle East, appeared remote in Imperial Iran. The armed forces seemed totally devoted to the Shah and there was no one among the senior officers who looked likely to betray his Commander-in-Chief. Those who wished to

end the Shah's regime had to find a force strong enough to neutralise the .
armed forces. Such a force could only be unleashed in the streets and
street crowds could be mobilised only in the name of religion. Khomeini
looked like the ideal man for the job.

This analysis of the situation was shared by the Tudeh Party and several
other left-wing organisations. The assumption was that the mullahs in
general and Khomeini, then in his late seventies, in particular would not
want to exercise power directly. Their task would consist of bringing
enough people onto the streets to either frighten the Shah's army or to
persuade it to join the masses. Khomeini, however, had ideas of his own.
He had started his revolt against the Shah's reforms without political
ambitions of his own, but more than fourteen years of exile had changed
all that. Partly because of his own ruminations but mainly as a result of
contact with Ayatollah Muhammad-Baqer Sadr in Najaf, Khomeini had
developed a doctrine of Islamic Government.

Islamic Government, in its simplest form, was derived from basic shi'ite
principles. The government of the community of the faithful must be
assured by the infallible imams. Ali, the fourth Caliph, and his eleven
male descendants had represented divine power on earth. The twelfth
imam, Muhammad ben Hassan, known as Mahdi (The Well-Guided
One), had gone into hiding for an unspecified period of time. On his
return he would restore peace and justice to the entire universe. During
his absence temporal power had to be exercised by a well-known, chaste,
disinterested and knowledgeable theologian. This was the principle of
Walayat-e-Faqih (The Custodianship of the Jurisconsult) or the rule of
the clergy. Thus the Shah's regime was illegitimate and had to be replaced
with a proper 'Islamic' government.

In 1977 Khomeini's views on the subject were well documented in his
own published pamphlets as well as in the discourse of those close to him.
But the non-clerical politicians of the Left as well as the Right simply
chose to ignore them. They persisted in their illusion that Khomeini
would not seek power for himself.

Some of the Shah's opponents described themselves as 'republicans'
but they knew nothing of the republican theories of statehood and the
exercise of power. They were, in fact, only anti-Shah and, because a
presidential system appeared to be the antithesis of monarchy, insisted
that they wanted a republic. Very quickly Khomeini found out that the
Iranian republicans did not precisely know what they were talking about,
so he agreed to endorse the slogan 'Islamic Republic' instead of 'Islamic
Government', the title of his pamphlet. 'Republic' meant no Shah; and
that was all he wanted at the time.

Preparing for his final confrontation with the Shah, the ayatollah first
assured himself of support from his own constituency – that is to say the
section of the clergy that had rejected the royal reforms. Between 1964
and 1977 hundreds of mullahs had been imprisoned for speaking in his

support; dozens had died in prison in suspicious circumstances, some under torture, and thousands had been pressganged into the army. Many hundreds of mullahs were in internal exile while scores were not allowed to mount the pulpit or otherwise address religious gatherings. In 1977 there were some 85,000 mullahs and students of theology in Iran. Many depended on help from government. Large numbers worked as teachers, notaries, public scribes, assessors and clerks. Some 1200 had the title of ayatollah and enjoyed special prestige. They managed endowments, received and distributed vast sums of money paid by the faithful for charity and replied to thousands of religious queries from shi'ites all over the world. A few had secured important functions within the administration. Ayatollah Morteza Motahari, Khomeini's principal contact in Iran at the time, was Vice-Chairman of the Imperial Philosophical Society presided over by Empress Farah. The vast majority of the mullahs, however, consisted of poor, semi-literate preachers in rural areas – men who were too hungry, too frightened and too ignorant of the world to play an active role in politics. A few hundred well-known mullahs in Tehran and other major cities could quickly mobilise the entire clergy against the regime.

The pro-Khomeini mullahs began their assault on the Shah in the middle of 1977. Lacking access to mass media they concentrated on the judicious use of traditional Iranian channels of communication. They used the well-established rumour networks that operated in the bazaars, mosques and tea houses. The idea was to discredit the Shah and desacralise the institution of monarchy. The Shah was accused of having converted to Judaism, Christianity, Zoroastrianism and Mithraism all at once. He was portrayed as an evil man who was pillaging the nation's wealth with the help of 'Cross Worshippers and Zionists'. The rumour mill described him in turn as a sodomite, a womanizer and a poor, impotent husband who had not fathered his own children. The excessive language used was an instant success among the poor illiterate masses who invariably preferred fiction to fact and who were excited by strong images of depravity. Very soon the campaign of calumny was extended to cover a dozen or so of the Shah's closest associates. The impression created was that a small group of men, headed by the Shah, was working to de-Islamicise Iran and give its natural resources to foreigners. When, after weeks of character assassination against the Shah and his aides, the government failed to react, the mullahs began to repeat their attacks from the pulpit and in public. News that the Shah was personally attacked with impunity packed many mosques in Tehran, encouraging mullahs throughout the country to join the rising tide.

Why did the Shah refuse to take action against those who were daily pouring abuse on him? He could have asked the grand ayatollahs who were on good terms with him to intervene. His police could have rounded up the Khomeinist ringleaders and broken up their network of rumours.

Many mullahs had spent years in gaol for lesser offences in previous years, but now it seemed that His Majesty wanted to allow the clergy to vent their hatred of the Pahlavis. The Shah gave a hint of his reasons for remaining uncharacteristically passive in a conversation at Nowshahr, on the Caspian, in the summer of 1978: 'We allowed the reactionary mullahs ample opportunity to reveal their true nature,' he said. 'By now the whole world as well as our own people ought to know who these agents of black reaction really are.'[22] The argument seemed reasonable enough at the time, but subsequent events showed that most people were rather inclined to believe the worst about their rulers and that even educated and well-to-do Iranians were not disturbed by the vile and excessive campaign launched against the monarch. The Shah's passivity was construed as a sign of weakness. 'He dare not unleash his bloodhounds against us because he is afraid of Carter,' said one mullah.

Carter, in fact, never brought up Iran's domestic political issues in his meetings with the Shah. Soon after entering the White House the new president had realised that the Shah was too important an ally to be lectured about human rights. A number of incidents, however, persuaded both the Shah and his opponents that Irano-American relations were heading for a turbulent phase. Carter's reply to a cable from the Shah congratulating the new president's electoral success was inexplicably delayed for more than two weeks. When it finally arrived, the presidential message sounded merely polite. It lacked the adulatory tone of messages from Nixon and Ford. Early in the life of the Carter administration a speech by the new Secretary of State, Cyrus B. Vance, was translated into Persian and published by the US Information Office in Tehran. The speech was mildly critical of Iran's human rights record. The Persian text was initially distributed in the usual limited number of copies fixed by the USIO. Within days, however, the speech was reprinted by mysterious entrepreneurs and distributed in thousands of copies throughout the country with the heading: 'Even US Recognises the Shah's Savagery.' This was followed by the resignation of Richard Helms, a former CIA director and personal friend of the Shah, as ambassador to Tehran. Helms's departure was interpreted by many in the Iranian capital as marking the end of special relations between the Shah and the US administration. Even members of the Shah's entourage were persuaded that 'those American liberals' might be cooking something with regard to Iran. And the Shah himself intimated that, if the worst came to the worst, he was prepared to 'work out new patterns of alliance'.[23]

The first meeting between Carter and the Shah came in November 1977 when the royal couple paid a state visit to Washington. The invitation had been late in coming but the encounter at the White House proved friendly. At the meeting the Shah himself brought up the subject of human rights in Iran and the fact that he had ordered a number of reforms, including the possibility of frequent, unannounced visits by the International Committee of the Red Cross to Iranian prisons. He also reviewed the success of his liberalisation policy and emphasised the fact that there were no more cases of torture in Iran. Carter – and more especially his wife Rosalynne – were charmed by the royal couple. 'Rosalynne fretted about us like a butterfly,' Empress Farah recalled years later. 'She was a simple provincial lady with a certain charm and obviously wanted to please.'[24] The Shah, however, neither liked nor trusted Carter. 'Those frozen blue eyes,' he remarked after his meeting with the president. 'Somehow there are no feelings in them.'[25] The Shah's belief that Carter wanted to play a double game with him was reinforced by an incident near the White House during their meeting. Thousands of pro- and anti-Shah demonstrators were allowed to clash with each other near the White House while the royal couple attended the welcoming ceremony. Police soon used tear gas to disperse the demonstrators as a result of which everyone present, including the Shah, Empress Farah and Carter, had to reach for their handkerchiefs. The whole episode was telecast live to Iran and millions of Iranians saw the humiliation of the King of Kings. The average Iranian knew nothing of the niceties of American law on public demonstrations and the First Amendment and interpreted the incident as a plot by Carter to show that the Shah faced strong opposition from his own people. It is almost certain that the Shah himself, as well as most members of his entourage, were of the same view and secretly believed Carter to be guilty of hypocrisy. 'The Washington Tears', as the incident at the White House was to be called, was seen by the Shah's opponents as a clear signal that their time was about to come.

President Carter and his wife repaid the royal couple's visit to Washington with a 24-hour state visit to Tehran on 31 December 1977. It was from Tehran that Carter sent his televised New Year message to the American people. Some courtiers seized upon this coincidence as a sign that all was now well between the Shah and the president and that Washington fully recognised Iran's importance as an ally. Carter, in fact, went out of his way to persuade Congress to approve massive arms purchases by Iran, including seven AWACS (flying radars). The American media, however, continued its anti-Shah campaign on the issues of corruption and human rights violations. To most Iranians who were unaware of the conflictual relationship between the American media and the administration in Washington, the anti-Shah campaign looked like the continuation of what they thought were Carter's efforts to weaken the Iranian government.

Before Carter's visit to Tehran the exiled Ayatollah Khomeini had issued a *fatwa* formally 'dismissing' the Shah as head of state. The ayatollah had no legal or even theological authority to issue such an edict but this did not worry his supporters inside Iran. All they wanted was a religious endorsement of their anti-Shah activities. Armed with the ayatollah's edict they called on rich merchants and leading businessmen to ask that they stop paying taxes to the Shah's 'illegal and illegitimate' government. Some of those contacted tried to hedge their bets by secretly offering substantial sums of money to Khomeini's representatives in Iran while also informing SAVAK about what was going on. Meanwhile, Khomeini's agents in Paris persuaded the French government to dispatch an emissary to Najaf for a meeting with the ayatollah. This was the first time that Khomeini received the visit of an envoy from a Western power. The encounter immensely enhanced the prestige of the ayatollah in the back-alleys of Najaf and beyond. The French emissary's visit was followed by the arrival of a reporter from the Parisian evening daily *Le Monde*, which had for years conducted a campaign against the Shah. An interview was published in which the ayatollah openly called for revolt against the government. The Persian text of the interview was later printed and widely distributed in mosques in Tehran and other major cities.

At long last the Shah began to take Khomeini's activities seriously, not because he believed the ayatollah could mobilise support in Iran, but on the basis of a suspicion that Western powers were trying to build up the exiled mullah against him. Contact with the grand ayatollahs, broken with Amuzegar's appointment as prime minister, was re-established through various channels. Grand ayatollahs Kazem Shariatmadari and Ahmad Khonsari, in Qom and Tehran respectively, expressed their concern about Khomeini's unorthodox meddlings in politics. The senior mullahs referred to Khomeini as *sharur* (troublemaker), a sobriquet attached to his name in the 1950s. Both Shariatmadari and Khonsari told the Shah's emissaries that they did not approve of Khomeini's agitation but at the same time could not openly condemn the exiled mullah. It was up to the government to arrest the troublemakers and restore order. All they could do was to endorse such government action by remaining silent.

The Shah also created a special 'brains trust' to counter Khomeini's propaganda. The committee included three leading experts on shi'ism, two media specialists, a university teacher and several government officials.[26] The committee quickly decided what the Shah himself had already thought: Khomeini had to be built up as a symbol of opposition to the regime.

This choice seemed logical. The Shah, in a duel with the ayatollah, seemed to enjoy a number of advantages. He would appear as a moderniser, a champion of progress, fighting against a reactionary theocrat who wished to set the clock back. The Shah had given women the right to vote and more or less equal status with men. Khomeini wanted to send women back into purdah and bring back polygamy. The Shah had taken land away from 'feudal barons' and distributed it among peasants. Khomeini was opposed to land reform and wanted to dispossess the peasants in favour of big landowners and mullahs.

The brains trust decided to depict Khomeini as an 'Indian' charlatan whose family had long served British colonialists. The rumour was spread that the ayatollah's mother had been a Hindu temple dancer and mistress of a British captain in Kashmir. Khomeini himself was at once depicted as a crafty British agent and a drunkard who engaged in dervish dances after midnight. Some of Khomeini's old poems were found and quoted to show that the ayatollah had more praise for wine than he had for God. (At that time Khomeini was anxious to hide the fact that he had once been a poet for fear that the public might not take him seriously as a politician.[27]) The language and style adopted by the brains trust in attacking Khomeini fully matched what the ayatollah used in his attacks on the Shah. This was no political debate and the two men never even tackled the serious issues involved.

As long as the exchange of insult and abuse was limited to traditional rumour networks, all sides could keep aloof and pretend that the entire sorry situation was a result of meddling by minor over-enthusiastic members of the opposing camps. Early in January 1978, however, the duel was extended into the pages of one of Tehran's two leading dailies, *Ettelaat*. The newspaper was pressured into publishing a fake letter to the editor by a non-existent Ahmad Rashidi-Motlaq, repeating some of the abuse already directed against the ayatollah through rumours and unsigned leaflets.[28] At first Khomeini's men in Tehran interpreted the letter as a sign that the Shah prepared a crackdown on radical mullahs. Thus they decided to lie low for a while in accordance with their current strategy of avoiding direct confrontation with the police. Khomeini had advised his mullahs to take few risks with their own safety. The idea was that Khomeinist mullahs should hide behind non-clerical opponents of the Shah and thus escape arrest. During the following twelve months of unrest in Iran more than 10,000 people were arrested for various lengths of time because of their role in anti-Shah demonstrations and only two of them were mullahs. Even those two had no role in the Khomeini network. Middle-class politicians were invariably used as front men for the ayatollah's organisation. This flattered their ego but also cost them frequent trips to Tehran prisons where some of them were roughed up by police thugs.

The *Ettelaat* letter served as the detonator for an explosion in the holy city of Qom where tension had been rising for weeks. The ugly, grim and always-moaning city of mullahs and fanatical pilgrims had never been a haven of peace: now it became a veritable inferno of anger and protest. A mob of mullahs and talebehs began to burn copies of *Ettelaat* and ransacked newspaper kiosks. When it encountered no resistance it proceeded to attack government offices and finally arrived at the house of Grand Ayatollah Shariatmadari. Once informed of the contents of the fake letter, Shariatmadari was outraged. He did not approve of Khomeini's behaviour, but he could not tolerate such abuse being levelled against a senior member of the shi'ite hierarchy. Shariatmadari's support encouraged more and much larger demonstrations on 9 January 1978 when the Qom bazaar was closed down in protest against 'insults to our religious leadership'. Very quickly a crowd of several thousand, mostly mullahs and talebehs, formed at the holy shrine of Ma'assumah. After a brief moment of fist-shaking and chanting of anti-Shah slogans, the crowd began to rage through the streets of the city like a burning flood. It made its way to the Faizieh Theological School, Khomeini's former academy, which had remained closed since 1964. The 'liberation' of Faizieh, the symbol of Khomeini's struggle, created a feverish mood in the crowd. Roaming through the city the crowd began to attack and destroy banks, girls' school, public libraries and government offices. The police fled, outnumbered and frightened. Then, when the crowd tried to seize control of the central police station, a few policemen stationed on the roof of the building fired on the demonstrators. Seven people were killed together with two policemen who were trampled under foot by the raging mob. It was not until army units arrived on the scene that order was restored. Khomeini's revolution had its first martyrs.

The events in Qom were reported to the Shah as a minor incident involving a few fanatical talebehs. The following day the Shah addressed a mass rally organised by the Iranian Women's Organisation. He strongly attacked 'the forces of red and black reaction' – his code words for leftist and religious opponents of his regime.

Without naming Khomeini he referred to the ayatollah as 'the dog that barks at the moon'. He told the cheering women that he was determined to pursue reform in favour of women regardless of opposition from Marxists and mullahs. 'My father ended the tyranny of tribal chiefs,' he said, 'and I continued his task by smashing the landed barons, giving land to the peasants. But I know that the supreme test of my reign will be the establishment of full equality for women.'[29]

The Shah's tough speech was not followed by any concrete action against his opponents. The few demonstrators who had been arrested in Qom were quickly released and no government inquiry was ordered to determine the causes of the incident or to identify those responsible.

After a two-day lull, demonstrations were resumed in Qom. On 11 January army paratroops present in the holy city tried to break up a march organised by the mullahs. They chased some of the Khomeinist militants into Shariatmadari's house. According to tradition the residence of a grand ayatollah was an inviolate sanctuary where the forces of law and order would not enter without permission. The commander of the troops on that day, however, knew nothing of the tradition and sent his men chasing the troublemakers right into the ayatollah's home. The soldiers, trained for war not crowd control, fired a number of shots. One talebeh was killed and another was wounded. A number of other seekers of sanctuary were seized. The dead talebeh's corpse was quickly removed from the ayatollah's residence but his bloodstained white turban remained, becoming a symbol of martyrdom in the service of Islam.

Shariatmadari's austere reception room where the bloodstained turban was on exhibit became a place of pilgrimage for the Shah's many opponents during the subsequent twelve months of revolutionary turmoil. The presence of the turban turned Shariatmadari himself into a hostage of the Khomeinists. He now had no choice but to go along with the rising tide of the fundamentalist revolution.

The Qom incident provided the fundamentalists with an ideal base on which to build a whole series of memorial services. The seventh day of the 'martyrdom' of Khomeinist militants was marked with special mourning ceremonies in many cities including Tehran. The police made no attempt to break up the ceremonies despite the fact that some preachers openly attacked and abused the Shah. The government's passivity encouraged the opposition and disheartened the Shah's supporters. Much larger gatherings were organised by the opposition on the fortieth day of the Qom incident. One such gathering in Tabriz, Iran's third most populous city, degenerated into a full-scale riot that affected the bazaar, and some residential districts. Once again the raging mobs targeted banks, girls' schools, women's clubs, public libraries, cinemas, wine shops, restaurants and other 'places of sin'. Thirteen people were killed in clashes between the police and demonstrators armed with knives, iron bars and bricks. The centre of the city presented a scene of destruction that, when seen on TV screens throughout the country, shocked most Iranians.

Iranian society at this time was politically inexperienced, not to say naive. For some fifteen years it had neither seen nor heard of political violence. It had been told again and again that Iran was a haven of security and peace. There had been no strikes, protest marches, no anti-government meetings and, above all, no Third-World style mob politics in the country since 1965. Now all of a sudden everything seemed to be coming apart. What made matters worse was that no one seemed capable of explaining what had happened. The Amuzegar government issued a bland statement to the effect that a number of 'foreign saboteurs' had crossed the border illegally and reached Tabriz in order to cause trouble and destruction. This was a fantastic claim on the part of a regime that guarded its frontiers more jealously than virtually any other country in the world. Not surprisingly not a single shred of evidence was provided in support of the claim.

It seems that every normal society needs a certain dose of strikes, protest movements and other manifestations of conflict at any given time. The Shah, however, believed that he had invented a social system in which there was no need for conflict. He knew what was best for the people and would provide it for them in good time. If there were still some shortcomings to overcome it was because time was required to meet all demands. 'We need just another decade or so,' the Shah said in 1966. In 1978 he repeated the same wish. 'We will look after every Iranian from the womb to the tomb,' he liked to repeat. All that the Iranians had to do was to obey orders and then enjoy the fruits of the 'Great Civilisation', the Persian version of the terrestrial paradise His Imperial Majesty sincerely hoped to create. The Shah's pathological fear of dissent had persuaded him that only traitors, demagogues or madmen might wish to oppose his benevolent policies. His dream was a society free of all conflict in which an intelligent and well-meaning monarch would recognise, indeed anticipate, the needs of everyone and satisfy them within reasonable limits. At a meeting of leading industrialists in 1970 the Shah had advised all those present to anticipate the wishes of their employees. 'Fulfil their desires even before any worker has formulated them,' he suggested. When one of the businessmen present suggested that workers should be allowed to strike so that they could feel they had won something through their own efforts, the Shah lost his temper. At an audience granted to a newspaper editor in 1975, the Shah promised to 'order the government to give you interesting news, all you want' so that there would be no need for 'wasting time and energy on seeking scoops that might cause confusion'.[30] His natural inclination was to try and provide whatever he was asked for – with the exception of the freedom to challenge his policies. He heard that French workers were campaigning for a share in the capital of the companies that employed them. He immediately ordered that a similar scheme be introduced in Iran. 'We must give them 49 per cent of the shares before they ask for it,' he said. 'In this way they would know that no one cares more about their interests than their monarch.' A committee was set up to put the scheme into effect but most workers did not want shares and saw the move as a trick to siphon off part of their savings. As for the industrialists, the Shah's move resembled 'Communism with a crown'. The Shah had been told that some schoolchildren did not have adequate food so he ordered a meal of milk and cakes to be given to every schoolgoer every day. The result was administrative chaos, fresh opportunities for embezzlement of public funds and frequent complaints about the quality of the meals offered. Fundamentalist mullahs made matters worse for the government when they spread the rumour that the milk served at schools was unclean because it came from cows milked by un-Islamic hands and that the cakes given to the children were cooked not with butter but with pig oil. The mention of anything even remotely connected with pig was enough to incite many good Muslims to revolt.

The Shah hated crowds and he was at his best in private conversations. Even formal meetings of more than a dozen or so made him feel uneasy. A shy, lonesome man, he had for years witnessed how street crowds in Tehran had made and unmade Iran's politics and pushed the country to the brink of annihilation. He believed that human beings could be creative and accomplish 'positive deeds' only as individuals or by working in small groups. Large crowds could lead only to frenzy, unleashing man's 'inner urge to destroy'.[31]

In 1978 the Shah was to have all that he intensely disliked: strikes, protest marches, mad crowds; in a word, disorder. Widespread strikes brought important sections of the economy to a halt and attacks by hit-and-run groups on the 'places of of sin' – banks, cinemas, girls' schools – became daily occurrences in many cities and even villages. Undisturbed by the police, convoys of Islamic motorcyclists roamed the countryside, leaving behind a trail of destruction. Local thugs, led by mullahs, terrorised whole districts. They forced men to grow beards and attacked women who refused to wear Islamic headgear. Women who refused to comply were threatened and, on many occasions, disfigured by vitriol thrown at their faces. Local notables known for their support of the Shah were subjected to social ostracism. Pro-Shah merchants and shopkeepers were boycotted and, on some occasions, had their homes and businesses set on fire.

Much of the violence that accompanied the Islamic revolt was the work of urban terrorist groups not necessarily connected with Khomeini and his supporters. These groups, defeated on the ground in the mid-1970s, were now able to regain part of their former strength for two reasons: first, SAVAK and other police forces no longer intervened; second, hundreds of trained terrorists freed from prison as part of the liberal-isation policy immediately began organising terror attacks on symbols of the Shah's authority as well as on his supporters. People who called the police for help against what were, in effect, criminal attacks were told that the Shah had granted his opponents freedom and that there was nothing to do but be patient. This unusual situation persuaded many people into thinking that at least some of the terror attacks were organised by SAVAK and hardline officers in the armed forces in the hope of highlighting the dangers of liberalisation.

Iranian society as a whole seemed prepared to accept the uncertainty caused by the Shah's new policy and, in a sense, even enjoyed the excitement engendered by social and political conflict. It became fashionable to go on strike on just any pretext, or without any pretext at all. And it was certainly a must to take part in at least one of the dozen protest marches that took place every day. The whole thing was a new and exciting game. For years Iranians had seen images of political turmoil in foreign countries on television. Now they could have a taste of it themselves. Poets could write and recite long odes in praise of 'struggling masses' or 'striking heroes'. Young men with designer stubble led protest marches while young women wearing the charqad accompanied them with their admiring looks. Frustrated intellectuals in search of a little glory began to publish open letters to the Shah in which they complained about this or that aspect of his policy and advised him to listen to 'the voice of the nation and the counsel of History'. Local lads had the time of their lives when they seized control of this or that crossroads and diverted traffic from 'the liberated zone'. Like all games that are played collect-ively, the game of fighting the Shah – for it was no more than a game until the autumn of 1978 – created a degree of *esprit de corps* among the middle and lower classes that had not existed for years. For the first time in many years people were doing things together without being ordered to do so.

The protest movement, in its first eight to nine months, remained a largely middle and lower middle class affair. The mass of the peasantry, accounting for nearly half of the population, remained either indifferent or loyal to the Shah. The urban working classes, even when they were dragged into industrial action by their managers, were also reluctant to rise against the monarch. They were suspicious of the students, bazaar shopkeepers and mullahs who formed the backbone of the movement. The attitude of the peasantry and the working class reassured the Shah and convinced him that the so-called 'silent majority' would side with him in the decisive battle. He received news of disturbances from all over the country as indications of the success of his project: 'We have exposed our opponents,' he commented at one private meeting. 'Now the Iranian people and the world as a whole know that our opponents are demagogues and arsonists.'[32] But the 'silent majority' could not remain so for ever. The fundamentalists and their Leftist allies were determined to force that majority to speak out – not in support of the Shah but against him.

By the autumn of 1978 the protest movement had created an efficient nationwide organisation. One important task of this organisation was to take Khomeini's message to all sections of society. Thus came into being a network for the distribution of cassette recordings of the ayatollah's incendiary message. According to a SAVAK estimate some 100,000 Khomeini tapes were sold throughout Iran during 1978. The cassettes were played at private or public gatherings in homes, shops, mosques and even government offices. It was an exciting experience. The ayatollah's colourful and vitriolic language was in sharp contrast to the official discourse people had heard on the government media for more than a decade. The official media referred to the Shah as 'beloved of the nation', 'the Aryan Sun', 'the focus of universe', 'the holiest essence', 'the spreader of justice' and 'The King of Kings'. Khomeini used other adjectives: 'the Jewish agent', 'the American snake', 'the idiot boy', and 'cannibal'.

The ayatollah, unlike the Shah who peppered his speeches with foreign and technical terms unknown to most Iranians, used a simple language accessible to the illiterate masses. His peasant accent, emphasised for the occasion, gave him added authenticity as the leader of 'the poor, the downtrodden'. His was not the complex, flowery and finely-tuned language that the upper classes had developed in order to dissimulate their true feelings. The ayatollah went straight to the point. In a taped speech he commented on the Shah's assertion that the liberalisation policy was a royal gift to the nation. The ayatollah said:

The Shah says that he is granting liberty to the people. Hear me, you pompous toad! Who are you to grant freedom? It is Allah who grants freedom; it is Islam which grants freedom; it is the Constitution which grants freedom. What do you mean by saying; we have granted you freedom? What has it got to do with you anyway to grant (us) anything? Who are you anyway?[33]

As the weeks and months passed the almost daily agitation provoked by the Khomeinists and their leftist allies was established as an almost inevitable background to life in many Iranian cities. The police carefully avoided taking strong measures against the agitators who, in turn, refrained from attacking military targets. Concerned that the movement might gradually die down, Khomeini ordered his men in Tehran to step up their pressure on the regime. In a message he said: 'Our movement is but a fragile plant as yet. It needs the blood of martyrs to help it grow into a towering tree.'[34] The ayatollah's message, broadcast by the Persian service of the BBC, was interpreted by the revolutionaries as an order to attack military installations and provoke clashes with the police.

The first armed attack by the Khomeinists on government installations came in Isfahan, Iran's second city and an important military centre where thousands of American army advisers and their families lived. The attackers, probably helped by leftist guerrillas, went on the rampage and destroyed a number of official buildings by fire. They attacked and wounded two American servicemen. The Shah's most ambitious military project, the creation of the world's largest fleet of combat helicopters with help from the United States, seemed threatened. Many American technicians threatened to leave the city and the local Iranian commanders claimed that they could no longer ensure the security of sensitive bases. The Shah had little choice but to give the green light for a limited period of martial law in the city. It was clear at this point that the policy of liberalisation had failed; nevertheless, the Shah was not prepared to admit defeat. There was to be no crackdown and the few agitators arrested in Isfahan were quickly released together with other militants who had spent years in prison for anti-regime activities. Isfahan spent a few peaceful days under martial law but very soon the usual daily agitation resumed under the helpless gaze of heavily armed soldiers posted throughout the city. Khomeini was trying hard to force the Shah to order his troops to fire on agitators but the Shah would not be provoked. He still hoped that by exposing Khomeini as a cynical politician prepared to wreck the country and provoke bloodshed he would persuade the silent majority to speak out against the ayatollah.

In the absence of real martyrs the Khomeinists staged daily funeral processions and even burial ceremonies using empty coffins to create the impression that innocent people were being killed by the Shah's forces. The mullahs had centuries of experience in staging passion plays on the theme of Imam Hussein's martyrdom in Mesopotamia in the seventh century. The tradition of Muharram mournings put at the disposal of the mullahs a rich treasure of songs, poems, carefully choreographed movements of fanatical crowds and an endless number of dramatic symbols and icons. The funeral processions would bring together thousands of men and women dressed in black and beating their chests or heads. Each procession included one or more *moin al-baka'a* (tears assistant) whose task was to wail and shriek as if in agony in order to incite others to shed tears for the martyrs. These tears assistants, men and women, were specially trained from childhood as part of a *dasteh* (troupe) that staged the passion play for two months each year. The best tears assistants were said to be able to make a mountain cry. Some foreign journalists who had come to Iran to cover the uprising were, understandably, moved by the passion plays they witnessed and reported that scores of people were being killed by the Shah's forces each day. Their reports came back to Iran through the Persian programmes of foreign radios and reinforced the ayatollah's claim that the Shah continued to rule by a daily massacre of the Iranian people.

The leftist guerrilla groups added their own contribution to the mullahs's theatrics. The guerrillas used techniques learned in Cuba, Lebanon, South Yemen and North Korea for the purpose of throwing urban areas into confusion: burning piles of car tyres to cause huge columns of smoke; pouring a red liquid into the gutters and onto the pavements to create the impression that blood had been shed; the sabotage of electricity substations to cause power failures in this or that district; burning cars, shops and homes owned by people who supported the Shah or refused to cooperate with the rebels. Numerically small, the leftist guerrillas used the larger Khomeinist crowds as a shield behind which they could operate without the risk of arrest. Sporting thick beards and wearing black they could, in any case, not be distinguished from the rest of the crowd.

The tragedy that Iran was passing through entered a new stage with what was to be known as 'the Rex Cinema catastrophe'. On 18 August the Rex Cinema in Abadan, Iran's oil capital, was set on fire during a special late-night programme attended by about 1000 people – mostly oil workers and their families. The programme included a special documentary on the Shah's services to Iran, presented to mark the anniversary of the 1 August 1953 uprising that had saved the Shah's throne. Soon after the main feature film had started a fire began to spread as if out of nowhere. Within a few minutes the entire cinema was engulfed in flames. Stampeding towards the exits, the audience found to its horror that all the doors had been blocked from the outside. Fire engines were on the scene within fifteen minutes but could not begin operations, ostensibly for lack of water in the pipes in the street, for a further half hour, by which time the smell of burnt human flesh had spread to much of the city. At least 600 people, including many children, were burned to death and a further 300 were rushed to hospital. This was by all accounts the single most horrific event in Iran's contemporary history. The shock it caused was such that for two days neither the regime nor its opponents were able to offer a coherent account of what had happened. The silence imposed by the tragedy was broken by Khomeini who, in a message from Najaf duly broadcast by the BBC, accused the government of having planned and carried out 'this horrendous crime'. The clue given by the ayatollah was taken up by the Tudeh party's clandestine newssheet *Navid* which even claimed that a General Razmi had been dispatched to Abadan to 'arrange this tragedy'. Neither Khomeini nor Tudeh, however, condemned attacks on cinemas as such. Since January more than 50 cinemas had been attacked, many of them through arson, by Khomeinist and leftist militants throughout the country. The Abadan tragedy did not stop such attacks and cinemas and theatres remained favourite targets for the anti-Shah rebels right to the end of the regime.

After the fall of the Shah a committee of inquiry established by the Interior Ministry concluded that the Abadan cinema tragedy had been the result of a 'mistake by militant youths'. A number of people were charged with having started the fire but most were allowed to go free. It became clear that the cinema had been deliberately set on fire by Khomeini supporters as part of their campaign to disturb the 18 August ceremonies that marked the return of the Shah to his throne. Under the Shah the Amuzegar government should have been capable of conducting an inquiry and establishing the facts. Stricken by panic, however, it did not know what to do. It handed in its resignation to the Shah who promptly appointed Jaafar Sharif-Emami as the new prime minister. Sharif-Emami hushed up the cinema incident: he did not wish to begin work with an open confrontation with Khomeini, the man ultimately responsible for the tragedy.

Sharif-Emami, a former premier and president of the Senate for many years, was the last senior politician the Shah could still turn to at a moment of difficulty. Eqbal, once a trusted counsellor, was dead. Alam was dying from cancer in a hospital in Paris. In any case Alam had already incurred the anger of the Shah and was considered by His Majesty to be 'a two-faced profiteer'. Shortly after leaving Iran for medical treatment abroad Alam ordered that his private papers be transferred to Europe. He also withdrew the bulk of his wealth from Iran. Soon after Alam had left Iran the Shah dispatched one of the younger court officials to the departing minister's home to confiscate the much-talked-about private papers. The official was shown an empty safe. 'The papers are gone,' he was told.[35] A few months later matters became worse when Alam wrote the Shah a long letter in which he complained about 'the effect that bad news from our beloved country' had on his health. Alam told the Shah that the nation's situation was a source of deep concern and the Shah should 'show decisive leadership'. The letter provoked a sharp rebuke from the Shah. In a verbal message the Shah told Alam to 'keep quiet and try and cure the illness that has confused your mind'. The Shah had apparently interpreted Alam's letter as a message from the British to abandon the policy of liberalisation and use force against the opposition. Convinced that the Carter administration still favoured liberalisation in Iran, the Shah, regarding the US as a far more important ally than Britain could ever hope to be, rejected what he thought was a British attempt at meddling in Iranian politics.[36]

The choice of Sharif-Emami as the new prime minister was, at least in part, prompted by the Shah's belief that such a move would please the British. Sharif-Emami was the Grand Master of Iranian freemasonry, an organisation that the Shah regarded as an arm of British influence in Iran. The new prime minister was, in fact, no Anglophile and had spent time in a military prison during the British occupation of Iran in 1941. His arrest had been ordered by the British because of his pro-Nazi activities and his role in the underground resistance movement against the Allies.

Apart from his supposed links with Britain, Sharif-Emami was believed to have yet another asset: he was supposed to have good relations with the mullahs. Himself the son of a mullah, the new prime minister was related to Grand Ayatollah Muhammad-Reza Golpayegani. Within a few days it became clear that Sharif-Emami would be even more helpless in the face of the mounting crisis than his predecessor. He described his government's policy as one of 'national reconciliation' and tried to bribe the opposition movement into cooperation with the authorities. Massive wage and salary increases were granted to all who asked for them. Hundreds of political prisoners were released and instead a number of high officials, including three ministers accused of corruption, were jailed. The 'imperial calendar' that had come into effect under Amuzegar was put aside in favour of the Islamic one. The government also ordered the closure of casinos and many wine shops. The long-serving director of the National Iranian Radio and Television, Reza Qotbi, was forced to leave and the government adopted a pseudo-revolutionary language supposedly designed to steal the show from the opposition.

Sharif-Emami's cabinet was a strange assemblage of politicians with conflicting views and ideas. Many of them had never met before and most intensely disliked one another. All were determined to court the opposition and some practised the worst kind of demagoguery. The cabinet's 'strongman' was Manuchehr Azmun, a turncoat Communist who had joined SAVAK in the 1960s. Remembering the Marxist vocabulary of his earlier years he went around talking about the need for 'popular revolutionary tribunals' to send 'at least 1000 high officials' to the firing squad. He won the support of SAVAK's Parviz Sabeti for a scheme to create a Popular Socialist Party. The operation assumed comical aspects when Azmun solicited the Shah's help in establishing contact with the former west German Chancellor Willy Brandt. The idea was that Brandt, leader of the German Social Democratic party, would help give the Azmun-Sabeti project some legitimacy by supporting the membership of their, as yet non-existent, party into the Socialist International.[37] The episode is worth recalling because it shows that influential individuals within SAVAK and the government continued to believe that the main threat to the regime came from the Left. Khomeini's tactic of hiding behind other forces until he was strong enough to emerge without great risk to himself was working.

Sharif-Emami, who had spent the previous fourteen years looking after his own extensive interests – he was on the board of 33 companies as well as the Pahlavi Foundation's countless operations – had little idea of what was really going on in Iran. He blamed SAVAK for most of the disturbances and toyed with the idea of inviting Khomeini to return from exile and resume teaching at Qom. The picture of a special aircraft waiting to fly to Najaf to bring Khomeini home was shown on television. The ayatollah responded by declaring Sharif-Emami 'an enemy of Islam whose blood must be shed'.

Sharif-Emami's other desperate measure was an attempt to persuade the British government to stop the BBC Persian service from broadcasting Khomeini's messages. The British Ambassador to Iran, Sir Anthony Parsons, tried to bury the issue by referring to the tradition of press freedom in the West. Iran's own Ambassador to London Parviz Raji proved equally unhelpful. A 40-page 'indictment' of the BBC, prepared on orders from the Shah could not be delivered to the British government. One man finally volunteered to take the 'indictment' to London and discuss it with Prime Minister James Callaghan. He was Reza Fallah, a deputy chairman of the National Iranian Oil Company. Once Fallah had received permission to fly to London, however, he just forgot about the whole thing. He had used the mission 'to silence the BBC' as an excuse to get out of Iran as fast as he could.

Fallah was not the only senior official to escape. As Sharif-Emami's government began to crumble Tehran's airport, Mehrabad, began to look like a high society salon where men and women who populated the pages of the Iranian Who's Who? waited to board aircraft flying to any destination out of the country. Former premier Amuzegar was among the first to leave. The Shah's own physician, General Ayadi, fled in such a hurry that he left his suitcase behind at the airport. Senior officials and rich businessmen suddenly discovered that they were in need of immediate medical treatment abroad or that they had to fly to Europe or North America to attend to urgent personal business.

Not all of those who left the country did so for fear of being caught in a revolution. Most were afraid that Sharif-Emami, in his childish attempt at pleasing the mullahs, might send thousands of former officials and leading businessmen to prison. He had already arrested a number of former government ministers and openly threatened to put some on trial on charges of treason. Iran's ruling elite had little difficulty in going abroad for what it was thought would be a brief exile until the storm blew over.

Going into exile was a long-established tradition in Iranian politics. Before Khomeini seized power there were virtually no political killings in the country. Those who won always spared the lives of the defeated by sending them into exile or banishing them to remote provinces. The reason for this magnaminity was that the winners and losers in Iranian politics were often related by blood or marriage: they could not put a member of the family to death. Khomeini, however, brought to power entirely new groups: people who had no relationship to the preceding rulers. Thus the losers could be massacred by the winners.

Those leading Iranians who began going into exile towards the end of 1978 were different from the older generations of political exiles in a number of ways. The older exiles never even dreamed of spending the rest of their lives out of Iran. They avoided buying property abroad as a matter of principle. Going into exile, often for a few months only, was more of a political gimmick to bestow on a politician an aura of importance. Those who went into exile did so in order to sulk, to show their displeasure at the state of affairs back home, and as a prelude to their own return to their homes and to power. The influential and wealthy Iranians who left in 1978 were operating in a different climate. They had already bought property abroad and had part of their fortune safely placed in foreign banks and companies. This had been done perfectly legally, in fact with the encouragement of the Iranian government which saw investment abroad as a sound way of recycling some of the petrodollars Iran earned. Many new exiles also had children at school in Europe and North America. Iran was no longer the exclusive object of their love and personal interest as had been the case with exiles in the old times.

The flight of the elite soon affected the inner circle of the Shah's friends and partners at cards games. Davalloo vanished without saying goodbye soon after Ayadi's hasty departure. Mahmoud Hajebi was ordered by his French doctor to fly to Paris without delay. Senator Jamshid 'Alam, Professor Yahya 'Adl and contractor Majid 'Alam were still in Iran but were not as keen on going to the palace for a gin rummy session with His Majesty as they had been before the troubles. The Shah, deprived of his favourite card game, tried solitary games of patience as the palace became more and more deserted. By September 1978 all members of the Shah's family, including his octogenarian mother and all the royal children, were out of Iran. Only Empress Farah remained by the side of her husband who was beginning to fear that he was reaching the end of the road – both as man and king.

14

From Tehran with Tears

Throughout the revolutionary turmoil of 1978 the Shah desperately searched for the reasons behind what he saw as a sudden – and totally unjustified – revolt against his rule. He believed that he had devoted most of his life to improving the lives of his people and was confident that he had succeeded. For more than a decade everyone had told him that what he had accomplished in Iran resembled a miracle. He had played host and visited the leaders of some 80 states with different ideologies and sociopolitical systems. They had all lavishly praised his leadership and described Iran as the best news in the Third World.

The Shah was convinced of one thing: there could never be any serious political trouble anywhere in the developing world or, more especially, in countries of strategic importance like Iran, without the encouragement of the major powers. In 1978, therefore, he kept asking himself and some of his visitors which of the major powers might be interested in destabilising his regime. In the very early stages of the turmoil his suspicions were directed at the USSR. Moscow had sent as Ambassador to Tehran Vladimir Vinogradov who, according to US intelligence reports, was an expert 'troublemaker'.[1] The Soviets had many reasons to be unhappy about certain aspects of the Shah's policies. Iran had helped crush a Communist revolt in Oman and played a key role in wooing President Anwar Sadat of Egypt away from the USSR and into the Western camp. It had also been under Iranian influence that Somalia had shifted alliances. Iran's high profile policy in Pakistan and Iraq also disturbed Moscow. The Shah's militant anti-Communist posture, at a time when the USSR was expanding its world influence under the cover of detente, seemed out of place. And Iran was buying more and more American weapons, creating a powerful war machine along the USSR's second longest frontier.

Very soon, however, it became clear that Moscow was not only innocent of plotting against the Shah but was, in fact, beginning to get worried about instability in a region so close to the USSR itself. Messages were exchanged between the Shah and the Soviet leader Leonid Brezhnev who assured the Iranian monarch of 'full support and warm friendship.' The Soviet media supported the Shah until the very end. And repeated requests by Tudeh to operate an anti-Shah radio station from Baku, in Soviet Azerbaijan, were approved by the KGB only after the Shah had made it clear he would be leaving Iran. The KGB in Tehran helped print and publish Tudeh's newssheet *Navid* from the middle of 1978, but this was more because the Soviet secret service wanted to keep Tudeh under tight control.[2]

With the Soviets proved not guilty in the Shah's mind it was the turn of the British to fall under suspicion. 'What do the British want from us?' the Shah kept asking trusted visitors. He could find no answer. Britain, then governed by the Labour party with James Callaghan as Prime Minister, was, in fact, a staunch and loyal ally of the Shah. Foreign Secretary David Owen visited Tehran and paid handsome tribute to the Shah. But, His Majesty wondered, how could Britain be a true friend when the BBC 'acted as the voice of Khomeini'? The Shah was convinced that 'the British', meaning the British establishment and not necessarily James Callaghan's cabinet, were interested in putting pressure on Iran ahead of negotiations on the future of Iranian oil. The 25-year old Consortium Agreement was due to end in 1979 and the international oil companies had already asked Iran for talks on a new relationship. The 'oil tycoons' wanted to punish the Shah for his hawkish role within OPEC and to soften up his government ahead of difficult negotiations in 1979. It was on the basis of this analysis that the Shah decided to distance himself from the oil dossier for the first time in 25 years. Hushang Ansary, the Chairman of the National Iranian Oil Company, was ordered to handle the negotiations in consultation with the premier, Sharif-Emami, a novelty for both men. Ansary found himself unable to decide on complex and potentially controversial issues without the Shah's specific approval and Sharif-Emami knew nothing of the dossier. As a result Ansary put his second-in-command in charge of the negotiations pending 'the clarification of the political situation'. This meant that the Iranian side in the negotiations now had virtually no authority to decide on major issues. Frustrated oil company managers who took part in the negotiations ended up by understanding the situation and decided that they, too, had better return home and wait for events to unfold. Their withdrawal was instantly interpreted by the Shah as a confirmation of his worst suspicions. The 'oil cartel' and its 'British masters' did not want a new agreement because they hoped to weaken Iran and force the Shah into offering major concessions.

While suspecting the British the Shah knew enough of the real world to realise that Britain would be in no position to provoke a major crisis in the Middle East without at least tacit approval from the United States. As for Washington's true intentions, it was enough to read Carter's anti-Shah statements during the presidential election campaign of 1976. The fact that Carter, once in office, acted as a strong and enthusiastic supporter of the Shah was, conveniently, overlooked. The Shah could not admit that his beloved Iranians might, for one reason or another, simply not love him any more. 'Our people have been misled by foreign powers who want to destroy our armed forces and push us back into weakness and sub-servience,' His Majesty said at a press conference in August 1978.

The Shah was not totally mistaken about the possibility of 'foreign hands' stirring up trouble in Iran. A number of Democratic senators, Congressmen and former officials from the United States harboured an intense hatred for the Shah on ideological grounds. They encouraged and even partly financed a number of anti-Shah groups and individuals in the United States. Another 'foreign hand' involved was that of the Libyan leader Muammar at Qaddhafi who also financed several Khomeinist groups, including one led by Muhammad Montazeri.[3] Syrian intelligence services had clients of their own among the Shah's opponents, including Sadeq Ghotbzadeh who later became Khomeini's Foreign Minister before being executed on orders from the ayatollah. Finally there was the Palestine Liberation Organisation which regarded the Shah as a friend of Israel. The PLO leader, Yasser Arafat had visited Tehran incognito on a number of occasions and been received by the Shah at least twice, but he had failed to persuade the Shah to allow a PLO office to be set up in Tehran. The Shah regarded the PLO as a terrorist organisation despite the fact that most of its finances came from conservative Arab states such as Saudi Arabia and Kuwait. The PLO repaid the Shah's enmity by training large numbers of Iranian guerrillas, especially urban terrorists.[4]

In the summer of 1978 the modern fleet of Iran Air was busy transporting the Shah's officials and supporters out of Iran and into the safety of Europe and the United States. On the return journey the same aircraft brought to Tehran the hundreds of experts in urban terrorism trained by the PLO or in camps in Cuba, North Korea and South Yemen.

The Shah was confident that his security forces could cope with the terrorist threat. What he was worried about was the growing partici-pation of ordinary people, especially women and children, in anti-regime demonstrations. Every day there were clashes between police and demonstrators and every day one or two demonstrators were killed. The ayatollah's tactic of putting women and children at the head of each protest march was designed to force the police to either retreat or run the risk of causing casualties where it most hurt public opinion. Khomeini's agents in Europe and the United States had already started a massive campaign against the Shah on the theme that his police deliberately fired on women and children and the Shah realised that the battle for Western public opinion could be of crucial importance: 'Western public opinion has been misled by crypto-Communists in the media,' the Shah said. 'The Western media hates us because we are today the only nation standing firm against Communism.'[5] A committee set up to improve Iran's image abroad recommended 'the full exposure of Iran's enemies, revealing their reactionary nature'.[6] In other words it was necessary to tell Western public opinion that the alternative to the Shah's regime would not be a democratic parliamentary system but theocratic rule by a fanatical mullah who wanted to force women to wear the veil and to snatch land back from emancipated peasants. It was necessary to smoke Khomeini out of Iraq, a closed society where Western media had no access. Some of the Shah's advisers doubted the efficacy of the stratagem, warning him that the West would instantly approve 'anything exotic' and reminding him of how a new remake of the film *King Kong* in 1977 had resulted in a great show of sympathy for the captured beast.[7] The West, the Shah was told, would take a look at Khomeini and decide that a man like the ayatollah would be a more representative ruler of 'a remote, oriental land' like Iran than His Majesty who wore European suits and spoke French without an accent.

Sharif-Emami's policy of 'national reconciliation', meanwhile, had encouraged the opposition to step up its activities. Token strikes were now reported from the oil industry and even customs officers were staying away from work at a number of border posts. Some members of the cabinet urged energetic police action to check the spread of the disturbances, but the prime minister continued to preach moderation. 'We can certainly end this agitation,' he said. 'But that would mean the killing of ten thousand people. My government is not in the business of killing people.'[8]

Sharif-Emami's cabinet was regarded with suspicion by the top brass of the armed forces right from the start. General Abbas-Karim Gharabaghi, who joined the cabinet as Interior Minister, was regarded by General Gholam-Ali Oveissi, Commander of the Land Forces, and Chief of Staff General Gholam-Reza Azhari, as 'a question mark'. 'We knew that Gharabaghi was working for foreigners,' Oveissi claimed later. 'His presence in Sharif-Emami's cabinet was a move by foreigners to isolate the truly patriotic officers.'[9] Oveissi did not offer any evidence for his accusations. What mattered in any case was that Oveissi and Gharabaghi hated each other and had for years been involved in personal rivalry within the top brass.

The group of senior officers around Oveissi and Azhari had chosen as their de facto political leader Ardeshir Zahedi, the Shah's Ambassador to Washington. Zahedi now spent most of his time in Tehran where his villa at Hesarak, in the foothills of north Tehran, became the headquarters of those who wanted the Shah to order a crackdown. The group wanted action on two fronts: the arrest and public trial of large numbers of former senior officials, especially Amir-Abbas Hoveyda, and the imposition of martial law to round up tens of thousands of troublemakers throughout the country. Zahedi had held extensive conversations with his Chilean counterpart in Washington on General Agusto Pinochet's successful *coup d'état* against the leftist government of Salvador Allende. Some in Zahedi's entourage had even worked out plans for turning various sports stadia and the Olympics village near Tehran into detention camps for up to 100,000 'troublemakers'. Zahedi was convinced that the people were not angry with the Shah and would calm down once they saw that 'corrupt officials' were being punished. To make sure that a reversal of the Shah's liberalisation policy would be acceptable in Washington, Zahedi enlisted the support of Zbigniew Bzrezhinski who served as Carter's National Security Adviser. This meant that the Carter administration, already unable to develop a coherent foreign policy because of the President's inexperience and indecisive leadership, was further split over Iran. The State Department, which had never been a bastion of support for the Shah, except in the days of Henry Kissinger, was not prepared to endorse a Chilean-style crackdown in Iran. William Sullivan, the US Ambassador in Tehran, was already seeking contacts with the Shah's enemies, and regarded the tough policy proposed by Zahedi and Bzrezhinski as dangerous. To the Shah and his entourage the American Ambassador appeared as 'a militant liberal' who had come to Tehran on a mission to weaken the Persian monarchy. 'We had been warned about Sullivan,' Empress Farah later recalled.[10] The warning had come from a close and trusted friend: Mrs Imelda Marcos, wife of the Filippino president, Ferdinand Marcos. 'He is a snake,' Imelda told Farah in a telephone call. 'When he was Ambassador here we had so much trouble.'[11] In Tehran Sullivan supported Sharif-Emami's efforts to defuse the situation without the use of force.

For nearly two weeks after Sharif-Emami took over it seemed as if his policy might work. Anti-regime demonstrations continued in many cities but the capital was relatively calm. At this point the various leftist guerrilla groups, concerned about the prospect of a retreat by the 'masses', decided to force the government into open confrontation. Several guerrilla groups, mostly working independently of the Khomeinist organisation, launched a series of attacks on police stations in Tehran. They also engaged lightly-armed policemen in gunfire on a number of occasions and killed a few. On 5 September 1978 more than a dozen police stations in and around the capital were attacked and, in two of them, the officers on duty were disarmed. The following day the prime minister chaired a cabinet meeting in the presence of the country's eight most senior military commanders.

This proved a stormy gathering. The military top brass strongly criticised the government's 'policy of weakness in the face of threats to the nation's safety and security'. Sharif-Emami tried to defend his record by pointing to the relative calm that had reigned in the capital for several days. Azmun, however, attacked the commanders as 'men who know nothing but brute force' and threatened to put 'disobedient officers' on trial. The angry military commanders broke the session to telephone the Shah and seek instructions. The monarch said he would abide by any decision taken at the joint meeting of the cabinet and the military chiefs. When the deadlock continued it was Sharif-Emami's turn to telephone the Shah and ask for advice. The monarch sounded evasive: he did not wish to intervene in 'executive matters'. All he would say was that he would support decisions made by the government and the parliament. Sharif-Emami interpreted this to mean that the Shah would not support the government against the military. The prime minister also suspected the monarch of wanting to expose the weaknesses of a civilian government before ordering his generals to take over. He, therefore, decided to appease the military by endorsing their demand for the imposition of martial law in Tehran and 23 other cities for a period of three months. The cabinet was not asked to vote on the issue although a majority might have approved.

The military were reassured. In exchange they agreed not to make the large-scale arrests demanded by SAVAK, but the speed with which army units were brought into the capital showed that the generals had been preparing the ground for the imposition of martial law even before Sharif-Emami was sworn in as prime minister. Had they done so with the Shah's approval? The Shah was Commander-in-Chief of the armed forces and received the Chief of Staff in audience every Thursday. He also gave separate audiences to the SAVAK chief as well as to commanders of the different military forces on a weekly basis. After 18 August, however, these meetings with military leaders had been stopped as part of the Shah's effort to appear a constitutional monarch. Nevertheless, it is almost certain that the generals would not have taken major decisions without obtaining at least indirect encouragement from the Shah. It is possible that Zahedi had led the generals into believing that the Shah would, when the time came, approve of an intervention by the army. Zahedi, however, neither denied nor confirmed that he might have played such a role. 'The generals came to consult with me because of their respect for my late father,' he later said. 'They also knew that I would make their views known to His Majesty.'[12]

The proclamation of martial law put nearly 10 million Iranians under a strict regime which forbade any gatherings of more than three people and envisaged an all night curfew. The following day, a Friday and thus the weekly holiday, Tehran was unusually quiet. Around Jaleh Square, near the parliament building, small groups of people began to gather for a public demonstration announced a week earlier. It was obvious that most of those who were pouring into the square had not heard of the imposition of martial law. Troops guarding the parliament building reported the gathering on their walkie-talkies and, within minutes, orders came from General Oveissi, who had been appointed Martial Law Administrator, to disperse the crowds.

For days there had been a stream of reports from SAVAK suggesting that the rebels might plan an attack on the Majlis and other official buildings. One report claimed that leftist guerrillas planned to seize control of parliament and hold members as hostages. Parliament, however, was not in session on Fridays.

As a show of force at the start of martial law, General Oveissi dispatched a detachment of infantrymen to Jaleh Square. When the troops arrived the crowd was already beginning to disperse without incident. Then, suddenly, a group of motorcyclists who had for weeks wreaked havoc in Tehran through their hit and run attacks on public buildings, drove their machines at top speed in the direction of the soldiers. They shouted 'Allah is the Greatest' and were perhaps intending only to humiliate the soldiers, not to provoke an incident. The soldiers, mostly 18-year-old Kurdish conscripts, were scared and began to fire. A number of riders were killed instantly. The dispersing crowd began to return to the square, partly to see what was going on. Once they saw the corpses on the ground the demonstrators began to charge the troops who fired again, killing more people. Someone with a megaphone shouted that the soldiers firing on the crowds were Israelis. The soldiers shouted instructions to each other in Kurdish, a language that the Tehrani crowd did not understand. The claim that Israelis were killing Muslims was suddenly plausible. 'Massacre the Jews,' the megaphones shrieked from among the raging crowd and some snipers, probably Mujahedeen and Fedayeen guerrillas, began to fire on the soldiers from the roof of the water department building nearby.

By the time calm was restored at least 200 people, including some 30 soldiers, had died, the second-largest number of casualties after the Rex Cinema fire. Religious leaders in Tehran immediately claimed that 'thousands' had been massacred by 'Zionist troops'. The government put the number of dead at 59. Later, the number of Jaleh Square 'martyrs' was inflated to 15,000 and the episode entered history as 'Black Friday'. Odes were composed to mark the occasion and artists tried to immortalise the martyrs in countless paintings and sculptures. A myth was born: the myth of heroic Muslims exposing their bare breasts to the bullets of Israeli troops who had come to save the Shah's throne because another Persian king, Cyrus the Great, had once freed the Jews in Babylon and allowed the rebuilding of the Jerusalem temple 25 centuries earlier. As most Iranian newspapers were already closed down because of a strike provoked by Tudeh Party activists there was no means of offering an objective account of what had happened. The government's version, much closer to facts than the account given by the opposition, was not believed despite the efforts of the state-owned radio and TV networks.

Black Friday all but ended Sharif-Emami's slim chance of obtaining a breathing space for the regime. The Shah began to look for a new prime minister. Through Empress Farah, Zahedi and other trusted figures he sounded out a number of candidates. He swallowed his pride and even agreed to consult with individuals he disliked intensely. Among these was Ali Amini, the former prime minister who had always been regarded by the Shah as an American agent. Amini obtained a royal audience through Hushang Ansary. The Shah also received Karim Sanjabi, an ephemeral education minister under Mossadeq in 1952. Two men especially campaigned for the post: Shapour Bakhtiar, Vice-President of the Tehran French Club and a cousin of General Teymur Bakhtiar the notorious SAVAK chief of the 1950s; and Mohsen Pezeshkpour, leader of the ultranationalist Pan-Iranist party. Amini presented the Shah with the list of 300 top officials, including former premier Hoveyda and 70 other former ministers, who had to be tried by military tribunals and sentenced to death. Sanjabi asked for time to sound out the views of the religious leaders. Bakhtiar's sole demand was that the Shah should leave the country. Pezeshkpour had his own list of people who had to be executed. None of the candidates seemed to know exactly what was happening or to have a coherent programme for dealing with the situation.

The Shah meanwhile pursued his objective of pushing Khomeini out of Iraq and into the glare of worldwide media scrutiny. Ambassador Fereidun Zandfard was asked to leave for Baghdad instantly with a demand that Saddam Hussein should expel Khomeini. Zandfard could not fly to Baghdad because by now the airport personnel, the national airline employees and almost everybody else in the country were on strike. When the Ambassador finally reached Baghdad by road he was told by Saddam Hussein that the reply to His Majesty's demand would be delivered through other channels. A few days later Saddam Hussein dispatched his half-brother, Barzan Ibrahim al-Takriti, to Tehran to meet the Shah. At an audience at the Niavaran Palace, Barzan al-Takriti told the Shah that the Iraqis were willing to arrange 'a suitable accident' that would silence Khomeini for ever. Saddam Hussein wanted His Majesty to stand firm against the mullahs and was prepared to offer whatever assistance was needed. The Iraqi leader's advice echoed the views of President Sadat, King Hussein of Jordan, King Hassan of Morocco, Nicolae Ceausescu of Romania and other friends and well-wishers who could not understand why the Shah was reluctant to crush the insurgents.

That Saddam Hussein was prepared to have Khomeini murdered in order to please the Shah reflected the dramatic change in relations between Tehran and Baghdad. In the 1960s Iran had supported – and partly financed – the Iraqi Ba'ath Party as a rampart against both the Communists and pan-Arab Nasserists. In 1968 the Iranian embassy in Baghdad had helped the Ba'athist plotters in staging their *coup d'état* by providing funds and means of communications. (It is possible that Iran's pro-Ba'ath activities in Iraq had been coordinated with Great Britain through CENTO, a military organisation to which both countries belonged.) Iran's two interlocutors among the Ba'athist plotters were

Colonel Abdul-Razzaq an-Nayef and Air-Marshal Hardan Abdul-Ghaffar al-Takriti. Another faction within the Iraqi Ba'ath, however, regarded Iran with suspicion and wanted to reorganise the party as a vanguard for pan-Arabism in Mesopotamia. This faction was led by Saddam Hussein who was then only 30 years old. By 1969 Saddam Hussein's faction had edged out both an-Nayef and al-Takriti and was establishing its control over the party. Before the end of that year Saddam Hussein had been identified by SAVAK as an enemy of Iran within the Ba'ath leadership and after 1970 Iran began supporting a different faction within the Iraqi Ba'ath. The man who led that faction was Nadhim Kzar, a shi'ite and head of the Iraqi security services. By all accounts Kzar was a sadistic and possibly psychopathic individual who entered Iraqi politics largely to indulge his extraordinary need for inflicting pain on others. He personally supervised the torture and murder of many hundreds of anti-Ba'ath politicians and received high marks from SAVAK because he wiped out nearly a whole generation of Iraqi Communist leaders and intellectuals. In the summer of 1973 Kzar, accompanied by a group of loyal officers, attacked the palace of President Ahmad Hassan al-Bakr with the intention of murdering him together with Saddam Hussein, whose official title at the time was Vice-President. Neither al-Bakr nor Hussein were in the palace and Kzar was soon hunted by troops loyal to the president. Determined to get away Kzar attacked the Interior Ministry and then the Ministry of Defence and seized the two ministers as hostages. He then contacted the SAVAK man in Baghdad to announce that the group, together with their hostages, would make for the Iranian border and would demand permission to enter Iran.[13] The SAVAK man informed Kzar that Tehran could not allow two Iraqi ministers to be brought into Iran as hostages. 'We told Kzar that we could only support a change of government in the usual way – that is to say a *coup d'état*,' the SAVAK man later said. 'We had no special obligations to Kzar besides the fact that we had deposited some money in his account at a Beirut bank. But this was no guarantee that we would back all his adventures.'[14] Convinced that he would not be admitted into Iran with his hostages, Kzar emptied his machine-gun into the two ministers, one of them a four-star general, and set out for the border in great haste.

Iran at the time had no diplomatic presence in Iraq but it is possible that Iranian agents informed the Iraqis of the route taken by Kzar. At any rate Kzar was captured and executed together with 35 other army officers and Ba'ath Party members after a summary trial presided over by Saddam Hussein.[15] Just over two years after the incident Saddam Hussein was preparing himself to become one of Iran's closest friends in the Middle East and in September 1978 the Iraqi strongman had little difficulty in obliging the Shah by issuing an expulsion order against Khomeini.

The ayatollah had expected the move for some time. He had contacted a number of governments in the Muslim world with a view to obtaining a visa but had been turned down. Algeria and Syria had at first agreed to examine his application with sympathy but quickly backed out after it became clear that Tehran would be displeased. Algeria needed Iran's support within OPEC and Syria had just received some $150,000,000 in Iranian aid and hoped for more.

The expulsion order handed to the ayatollah gave him one week to leave Iraq but he decided to set out almost instantly. He was, perhaps, rightly afraid that the Iraqis might organise an 'accident' for him. He and his party drove to the Kuwaiti border and asked for permission to enter on a temporary basis. They were kept waiting for a number of hours until the authorities in Kuwait City could make a decision. The ayatollah's demand was rejected and the group had to travel to Baghdad. Once there the ayatollah was informed that he could go to France. The French Interior Minister, Michel Poniatowsky, had already cleared the matter with the Shah. His Majesty had no objection to 'any Iranian citizen' travelling to France. In any case, holders of Iranian passports required no visas for entering member countries of the European Economic Community in those days and Khomeini could immediately fly to Paris. The Shah was happy: the world would now catch a glimpse of the Islamic 'King Kong' and would decide that Iran was too important to be allowed to fall into the hands of a 'creature out of the Dark Ages'.

The result of the operation was the opposite of what the Shah had hoped for. The ayatollah settled in a modest villa at Neuphle-le-Château, a nondescript Paris suburb. With the help of his advisers he developed a new image for himself – one designed to seduce the West. His stay in France was to last just over four months but within days his face was known to hundreds of millions throughout the world. He gave 132 full interviews and bombarded Iran with his taped messages as his aides kept the telephone and telex lines to Tehran constantly busy. The ayatollah did not speak of the Islamic tribunals he planned to organise, nor did he reveal his plans to impose a one party system in which the slightest sign of dissent could lead to death. He spoke of 'liberty' and 'morality'. His was a 'moral and spiritual revolution'. He was in his late seventies and could not have ambitions of his own. All he wanted was to rid Iran of dictatorship and then allow the Iranian people to choose their form of government and the men they wished to put in charge of the country. The ayatollah's three interpreters added their own contribution to the effort to persuade the world media that Khomeini was, indeed, the 'Gandhi of Islam'.[16]

The ayatollah especially seduced the French leftist intellectuals who are always looking for a cause to support. Convinced that they would not see a genuine revolution in the streets of Paris in their own lifetime, these frustrated intellectuals projected their own hallucinations onto the streets of Tehran where Khomeinist mobs burned, destroyed and disfigured by pouring acid on unveiled women. Professional philosophers of the Left who had only a few months earlier joined the Philosophic Society set up by Empress Farah and received sumptuous gifts in cash and kind now gathered around Khomeini and admired 'the explosion of spiritual energy' he had brought about. Among them were former Communist Party ideologues Roger Garaudy, Henri Lefebvre and Louis Althusser as well as the voguish historian Michel Foucault.[17]

The French were not alone in warming to the ayatollah's cause. He was presented to the American public as 'a frail but determined grandfather' who wished to 'save a nation from moral decrepitude'. The Shah read the international media and could not believe his eyes. When *Time* magazine described Khomeini as 'a kind of philosopher king', the Shah was beside himself with rage. Perhaps for the first time in his life he began to doubt whether he had ever understood the West at all.

As the ayatollah took centre stage the Shah withdrew further into the background. He had become a virtual prisoner in his palace which was surrounded by tanks with their guns pointed towards the interior of the compound. Senior army officers began to murmur that the Shah was thinking of leaving the country and thus bringing about the collapse of the armed forces. Those close to the Shah saw him melt away: between January and December 1978 he lost more than a third of his weight. He looked pale and aged, his athletic vigour all but gone. A sure sign that he was worried was when he took hold of a strand of his own hair and gently twisted it sometimes for more than an hour. This was in contrast with his position when in an upbeat mood: then he would stand erect, put his thumbs into the pockets of his waistcoat and push his chest forward, looking very much like a cock about to crow. In those dark days and nights – Tehran was denied electricity because of the strikes – the Shah's only happy moments came when his children telephoned from the United States. Crown Prince Reza was attending a special course at an American air base in Texas and reported progress in his efforts to become a fighter-bomber pilot. Princess Farahnaz and Prince Ali-Reza treated their exile as something of a holiday and did not much complain. Princess Leyla, the youngest of the royal children, wanted her parents to join her as soon as possible.

At the palace there were no banquets. And even during the day the Shah had fewer and fewer visitors. Many of the people who had once begged to be received by the Shah now did not wish to be seen anywhere near the palace. The Empress still had a few visitors – university teachers who had once operated a research group under her patronage called on her with conflicting ideas about how to save the country from revolution[18]. But she too felt frustrated. All her life as queen she had spent much time touring the remotest parts of the country. Now she could not get out of the Niavaran village where the palace was situated. When one weekend the generals, encouraged by Zahedi, organised a helicopter trip to the Latian hydroelectric centre for the royal couple, the Shah and his wife were all excited. They could have a breath of fresh air and forget the cares of the palace for half a day. At Latian the Shah had created a model farm surrounded by two dozen or so village homes built by a Swiss company. There he might have been reminded of his home in St Moritz in the Swiss Alps where he had spent happy holidays for more than a decade. By the end of September he had begun seriously to think about leaving the country. He raised the matter first with Empress Farah who endorsed the idea but suggested that she stay behind and fight. The Shah dismissed the idea in anger. 'You cannot become our Joan of Arc,' he said.[19]

The crisis brought the Shah and his wife close together as never before. For the first time in years both of them had plenty of time with which they did not know what to do. There were no official trips and no foreign dignitaries to entertain. The two took virtually all their meals together alone. After dinner they retired to a basement projection room where they could watch films thanks to the private palace generator, but most lights in the palace were turned off so as not to provoke the envy of ordinary Tehranis. The Shah was an admirer of the French comedian Louis de Funes and saw each of his films several times. He also spent several evenings watching a French TV serial with the intriguing title of *Les rois maudits* (The Cursed Kings).

By the end of September 1978 the royal palace at Niavaran resembled a haunted castle. Of the regiments of footmen, pages, butlers, adjutants, servants, orderlies, protocol officers, guards and other palace attendants, only a handful of the faithful had remained. Others had either asked for sick leave or simply disappeared. Chief of Protocol, Amir-Aslan Afshar continued to keep up appearances and insisted that at least some of the complicated rules of conduct at the Imperial court be scrupulously observed. Through the years the almost martial atmosphere of life at the Pahlavi court under Reza Shah had been replaced by an elaborate set of rituals partly copied from Great Britain. 'We tried to learn from the Court of Saint James,' Empress Farah later recalled. 'But we knew that we could never penetrate the mysteries of the British royal tradition. Self-styled experts on protocol and court ceremonies appeared from various quarters and imposed their showmanship on us.'[20] The royal couple approved the changes 'without fully realising what was happening'. The net result was that the Shah looked even more remote from the realities of Iranian life. One man who played a crucial role in all this was Hormuz Qarib, a diplomat who served as Chief of Protocol for more than a decade. He argued that because Iran was the oldest monarchy in the world, it had developed the rituals needed to emphasise its unique status. One of Qarib's plans envisaged the revival of titles of nobility that had been abolished by Reza Shah. He succeeded in restoring only one title: Jenab (doorstep) which was given to certain high officials and business-men. One coveted position was that of Adjutant to His Imperial Majesty. Both the title of Jenab and the position of Adjutant were, in later years, offered for sale by 'protocol brokers' without the Shah's knowledge. The honours thus bestowed could cost up to $100,000. On some occasions even seats in the Senate were sold to wealthy businessmen in search of a political profile.[21]

The period of confinement in the palace was especially hard on the Shah because he did not know how to remain idle or pass the time. He did not read books and had no hobbies except his collection of electric trains with which he played every now and then. He did not like to listen to recorded music for any length of time and, after a few weeks, he had seen all the films available at the palace. He thought it unwise to play tennis while his capital was burning. The Empress, who continued to have many more visitors than the Shah, tried her best to give the impression that the business of the court was continuing as usual. She chaired the meetings of the boards of the various cultural and charitable organisations of which she was president and received regular reports from advisers such as Hushang Nahavandi, Sayyed Hussein Nasr and Abdol-Majid Majidi. To keep the Shah busy she also presented him with piles of reports to read. These ranged from a project for a new publishing enterprise financed by the Empress herself to architects' plans for a new royal palace in north Tehran.[22]

Ever since she had married the Shah, Empress Farah had dreamed of building a new palace which would reflect Iran's grandeur while also offering the royal family 'a minimum of decent comfort'. The existing palaces were, in fact, large villas lacking both the charm of original architecture and the space needed for state functions: 'Even in some of the poorest African countries we visited presidential palaces that put Niavaran and Saadabad to shame,' Farah later said.[23] The Shah, however, would not have a new palace. 'At least a third of our people live in substandard homes,' he used to say. 'We have nothing to complain about.'[24] In 1977, however, the Shah, perhaps convinced that Iran was now prosperous enough and encouraged by a government promise to build a million new homes for the people, agreed to invest in a new palace for himself. The first plans were ready in 1978 when the revolution was already on the march. The Empress showed the plans and tried to get the Shah involved in a discussion about the new palace but the monarch was not interested: he had already persuaded himself that it was time for him to leave Iran. Unable to decide why the country was in revolt against him and unwilling to use force to crush his opponents, the monarch concluded that his departure from Iran would open the political safety valve that could save the nation from an explosion.

The Shah was not a fighter by temperament. He had inherited, not won, his crown. In 1953, after he had left the country, it was thanks to efforts made by others that he had been restored to his throne. Unlike his father who only demanded obedience, Muhammad-Reza Shah wanted to be loved and admired by his subjects. And when he was loved and admired, or at least thought that he was, he could become a ferocious fighter. 'If the people are with us we can do virtually anything,' he once said. 'But without the people there will be no point in even trying.'[25] He felt like a betrayed lover. When he received reports that people had demonstrated against him in the remote southern city of Borazjan he was beside himself with sadness. 'Even in Borazjan,' he kept repeating as he paced around his office. 'They have brainwashed my people.'[26]*

The Shah's decision to leave the country was not solely prompted by hurt feelings. He was by now convinced that 'foreign powers', presumably the United States and Britain, were encouraging the Iranian upheaval and would not stop their intrigues until he was out of the country. The objective was to reduce Iran's power and prevent it from creating a solid Persian Gulf bloc under its own leadership. The Persian Gulf contained some two-thirds of the world's oil resources and represented the single most important economic prize outside the industrialised world. Only Iran, because of its geographical size and demographic potential, could offer the coastal states of the Persian Gulf the leadership needed for standing up to the major powers. The Shah was also persuaded that the Western powers wished to get rid of his regime because they feared that the Iranian monarchy would, in the long run, fail to stop the advance of Communism. It was therefore necessary to give Iran a government capable of stopping Communism and defeating it on ideological grounds. Such a government could only be an 'Islamic' one led by the mullahs.

This largely erroneous analysis appealed to the Shah and his entourage for two reasons. First, it turned the Shah into the victim of intrigues by foreign powers: the revolution was not against a regime perceived, rightly or wrongly, as corrupt and brutal but was designed to destroy a patriotic leadership that had begun to frighten 'the enemies of the nation'. Second, the analysis caressed and confirmed deep Iranian beliefs that there could be no political trouble without foreign, especially British, plotting. The Shah, therefore, would leave the country in a gesture of self-sacrifice: a patriot forced into exile by stronger foreign adversaries. In this he would repeat the experience of his father.

Once he had adopted the conspiracy theory the Shah found ample evidence to confirm his own prejudice. He held a long meeting with his long-time friend Nelson Rockefeller on the island of Kish and was partially reassured about continued support from the American establishment. But Rockefeller was, of course, in no position to commit the Carter administration to any course of action in Iran. Later, the Shah dispatched a senior diplomat to Washington to find out about the 'true intentions' of the US government. The diplomat put the question to Vance bluntly: 'His

---

* Borazjan had been proverbial for its poverty and backwardness at the start of the Shah's reign in 1941 but by 1978 it had been developed into a show-case for the promised Great Civilisation. Yet even there people had began to march with cries of 'Death to the Shah'.

Majesty wants to know what the United States wants from him.' Vance's reply was equally direct: 'What does His Majesty want from us?'[27] The Shah saw this as an attempt at evasion by his American allies. Every day he received reports about more and more American businesses withdrawing their capital from Iran despite the exceptional terms offered them by the government in Tehran. Citibank shed its 30 per cent share in the Bank of Tehran, a major private enterprise with investments in a variety of industrial concerns. B.F. Goodrich was already out of Iran and Dow Chemical and Union Carbide suddenly pulled out of negotiations on petrochemical projects in the south of the country. Earlier Rank Xerox of Great Britain had withdrawn from Iran to be followed by IBM which pulled out 'for an unspecified period'. In 1975 the US had been Iran's number one trading partner and accounted for some 20 per cent of the country's non-military imports. By 1978 this share had dropped to just over 10 per cent as the United States fell behind West Germany and Japan. Almost exactly at the time American capital was getting out of Iran, the Japanese came in with a $3 billion project for the world's largest petrochemical complex at Bandar Shahpour. When the Islamic Revolution finally triumphed early in 1979 there was very little American capital left in Iran.

The Shah's suspicions about an Anglo-American plot were reinforced by the fact that many prominent individuals, both from the business community and the political elite, began to leave the country together with all their money. Many of them were, rightly or wrongly, believed to have special relations with either British or American interests. In 1978 more than $4 billion left the country. The State Department in Washington commented that Iranians 'voted with their money long before they voted with their feet'.[28] Much of the money taken out, however, belonged to foreign companies and a few hundred wealthy Iranians. American business had always regarded Iran as a high-risk country. Between 1968 and 1978 Iran bought nearly $30,000 million worth of goods – including military hardware – and services from the United States, but US direct investment in Iran never exceeded $390,000,000, compared to $2 billion in Venezuela, a much smaller oil producer. The $50 billion trade agreement signed between Tehran and Washington in 1975 was partly aimed at changing the imbalance in economic relations between the two countries. In 1978, however, it was clear that, as far as business was concerned, the Americans offered no special advantages to friends.

The Shah had yet another reason to believe that the best course available to him was to leave the country. The events of the previous ten months had all but destroyed the conditions he thought necessary for a Persian king to perform his duties effectively. A Persian king had to be without rival as the first patriot and the father of the nation. Now, however, many Iranians regarded Khomeini and not Muhammad-Reza

Shah as the legitimate head of the national family. To them the Shah had ceased to be 'the father', either because he had identified himself with forces outside the nation or as a result of his weakness and dithering. Further, a Persian king had to be always proved right and seen to be a winner under all circumstances. The Irano-shi'ite cult of the martyr did not include kings. A king had to be a fighter and a winner. The events of 1978 showed that Muhammad-Reza Shah was not prepared to try and win at any cost and that he had made mistakes in his choice of policies and personnel.

The few visitors that still came to the palace gave the Shah a variety of advice. The American and British Ambassadors, in separate audiences, agreed with His Majesty that his departure from Iran might help defuse the situation. The Ambassadors believed that they were doing no more than endorsing the Shah's own judgment. To the Shah, however, their attitude was further confirmation that the United States and Britain wished him harm. General Oveissi insisted that the Shah should stay and allow the armed forces to kill a few thousand demonstrators and arrest a few thousand more. Part of the Oveissi plan envisaged the seizure of 20,000 anti-regime activists and their internment on the island of Kish in the Persian Gulf. Sayyed Hassan Emami, the Friday Prayer Leader of Tehran and one of the few senior mullahs still openly loyal to the Shah, was convinced that an adequate sum of money well spent would buy most of the anti-Shah clerics. 'The mullahs cannot resist two things: money and women,' he told a meeting. He asked the Shah to provide around £9,000,000 to be distributed among the mullahs. The Shah refused. 'We don't have that kind of money,' he said.[29] When Emami approached wealthy businessmen for a contribution they, too, refused. 'The game is up,' said one. 'Otherwise His Majesty himself would have put down at least part of the money.'[30] Another idea put to the Shah was for him to order an invasion of Afghanistan, ostensibly to save it from Communism. The invasion could be presented as a crusade for Islam and divert attention from domestic problems. It could also force the Carter administration into full support for the Shah in an operation that would draw in the Soviets.

Empress Farah still hoped that the moderate mullahs, especially the grand ayatollahs, could be persuaded to come out in support of the Shah in order to save the country from anarchy. She established contact with Grand Ayatollah Shariatmadari in Qom and Grand Ayatollah Khonsari in Tehran. Both men promised support but admitted that they could do little as long as the authorities allowed the rebels a free hand. In contact with the grand ayatollahs, Farah used the code-name 'Ali's Mother'. She also flew to Najaf in Iraq on a brief pilgrimage. From there she drove to Kufa and to the residence of Grand Ayatollah Abol-Qassem Kho'i, number one among the six grand ayatollahs who formed the highest echelon of shi'ite clerical leadership. Kho'i, according to the Empress, practised the mullahs' art of khod'ah: he assured Farah of his full support and expressed the hope that the Shah would make a cash donation to 'our good work here in Najaf'. At the same time he instructed his representatives in Iran to spread the word that the Empress had come to Kufa without invitation and had received no promise of support.[31]

Despite the presence of tens of thousands of heavily-armed troops on the streets in Tehran and other major cities the government was unable to frighten its opponents into obeying the law. Martial law became the subject of many jokes and demonstrators began to engage the troops in conversation and gradually succeeded in inciting some of them against the Shah. Most newspapers remained shut and a journalists' strike soon spread to the state-owned radio and television networks. The national television would go off the air whenever the prime minister or any other senior official wanted to make a statement. Instead, radio and television broadcast news and views favourable only to Ayatollah Khomeini and the other anti-Shah personalities. Power cuts, a shortage of fuel as a result of the strike by oil industry workers, the dwindling stock of food and almost uninterrupted agitation in the streets paralysed the life of the nation. As urban Iranians shivered in sub-zero temperatures they began to prepare themselves for the worst. The Shah's promise of a high standard of living in exchange for an absence of political freedoms, looked no longer relevant. The people lived under martial law and yet had to search hours for food and fuel. The revolutionaries were prepared to starve urban Iran to death, if necessary. Bands of guerrillas, mostly from the People's Fedayeen (Marxist-Leninist) had roamed the countryside in September and burned the harvest in many villages. They also set food stores in several big cities on fire and then blamed SAVAK. Always ready to highlight the farcical even in the most dramatic of situations, the Tehranis greeted each other saying 'Welcome to the Great Civilisation!' They also made fun of the Shah's famous eulogy on the tomb of Cyrus the Great in 1971: 'Cyrus! Rest in peace for we are awake and messing the whole place up.' The Shah heard the jokes and recognised the bitter truth in them. His pride was deeply hurt, both as man and king.

Again and again the Shah rejected suggestions that he allow the army to massacre the demonstrators. This is how he tried to explain his reluctance to use force:

> A king cannot maintain himself on the throne by shedding the blood of his people. A dictator can do this in the name of this or that ideology – a king cannot, should not. A king is not a dictator.[32]

This was very strange reasoning. The people saw the armed soldiers and the tanks in the streets and were firmly convinced that the Shah was maintaining himself in power only by force. They also believed often false reports about the massacre of unarmed demonstrators. In any case every day witnessed incidents that caused casualties. The army, on the other hand, did not understand why it was expected to enter the cities to do the work of the police – work for which it had neither the training nor the equipment. There were no riot control units in Iran at all and the country lacked the tear gas canisters, rubber bullets and water cannons regularly used to disperse crowds. It was only at the end of the year that the first consignments of such goods arrived at Iranian ports, but by then the ports were idle because of strikes. The tools of crowd control were delivered to the Iranian authorities after the Shah had left and Khomeini had seized power. The ayatollah promptly used them against crowds who opposed him.

From the mid-1960s onwards the Iranian army had been trained for major warfare beyond the country's borders. It had units capable of intervening as far as Central Africa and the Indian Ocean, but fighting rioters in the streets of Tehran was something Iranian officers neither knew nor liked. The nation's 55,000-strong police could not cope with the situation either. It had been trained for traffic control, criminal investigation, and other routine tasks. It could not face thousands of well-trained urban guerrillas who, like the proverbial fish in water, operated within the wider context of well-established and highly efficient religious networks. For more than a decade the Western media had lashed out against the Shah's police state. In 1978, however, it was clear that the Shah's regime was anything but a police state; it was a 'soft dictatorship' hiding behind a military mask.[33]

As the political situation deteriorated the Shah's health also declined. The Shah's athletic body, his love of sport and his almost boundless energy for work had hidden the fact that he had suffered from a variety of illnesses in his childhood. Until 1974 his annual check-ups at Professor Karl Fellinger's clinic near Vienna, Austria, had given him a clean bill of health. In the winter of that year the Austrians discovered certain abnormalities in his spleen. The Shah had experienced a nephritic crisis a year earlier and also suffered from allergic reactions to certain foods, caviar for example. A partial account of the check-up somehow found its way into an Austrian newspaper which claimed that the Shah was suffering from cancer. The newspaper 'scoop' was taken seriously enough for the Imperial Court to issue a terse denial. Thought of serious ill health depressed the Shah to the point of disturbing his sleep. He felt nervous and tense. Dr Ayadi, always looking for the easiest way out, prescribed a daily dose of tranquillisers and from then on the Shah was a regular consumer of valium.

Thought of serious illness naturally led the Shah into thinking about death also. The Shah was only 55 years old at the time and planned to stay on the throne for at least ten more years. That would have provided the Crown Prince with ample time to complete his studies and receive some practical training in kingship at his father's side. But the Shah was, somehow, not quite sure that he would live that long. He had, perhaps, received some signs from the metaphysical universe with which he had established contact early in childhood. At any rate he was concerned enough about the possibility of an early death to write and seal his political testament. In March 1974 he convened a meeting of his closest aides – including the prime minister and the senior military commanders – to discuss the problems that might arise if he were to die before the Crown Prince had reached the legal age of 21. The Empress was also present at the meeting. Since no one there could even think of life without the Shah the meeting quickly developed into a formal ceremony in which everyone wished His Majesty a long life. The Shah's testament remained unopened in a palace safe and probably fell into the hands of the Khomeinists in 1979.

By the end of October 1978, the Sharif-Emami government was almost completely paralysed. Cabinet ministers were, at times, unable even to get to their offices because of demonstrations and strikes. The prime minister spent a great deal of time keeping his quarrelling associates together and persuading his ministers not to resign. Meanwhile Khomeinist demonstrators, supported by leftist guerrillas, controlled large sections of the capital under the noses of over 100,000 troops. The hardline generals and what was left of SAVAK after many of its chiefs had either fled or been posted abroad decided to bring everything to a head by forcing the crisis to its logical end. Early on the morning of 5 November bands of thugs, organised by SAVAK and supported by the martial law organisation, began rampaging through Tehran, burning and breaking what they found on their way. Very soon the genuine revolutionaries joined in the exercise: they all thought that orders had come from Khomeini to set Tehran on fire. At the end of the day the Iranian capital was a scene of desolation with flames everywhere. From his palace, situated on the Niavaran hills that dominated Tehran, the Shah could catch a glimpse of what was happening in his capital.

Early in the evening a group of five generals arrived at the palace and met the Grand Master of Ceremonies Amir-Aslan Afshar. 'The Shah must make a move or we shall all be massacred,' they told him. Afshar took the generals to a point where the Shah would board his car to drive from his office within the palace compound to the residential quarters. There a typically Oriental scene occurred: the distinguished diplomat and the five generals, their shoulders covered with stars and their chests with medals, fell at the Shah's feet and began to weep. The Shah tried to console them and asked what was wrong. They reported on the events of the day and asked His Majesty to 'do something'. When they were asked what was to be done they replied that a strong personality should be put in charge of government. The Shah said he would think about it and drove away.[34] Back in his apartments the Shah discussed the incident with his wife. Both agreed that Sharif-Emami had to go. The Empress still hoped for a negotiated settlement of the crisis and opposed the use of force. The Shah expressed concern that his disillusioned generals might take matters into their own hands.

With all the Shah's senior aides and advisers now out of the country or, as was the case with Hoveyda, in virtual disgrace, there was no one that His Majesty could turn to for advice in those crucial moments. Hoveyda had resigned as Minister of the Imperial Court on 7 September 1978, minutes after martial law had been declared in Tehran. Since then he had been confined to his modest apartment in a new block of flats in northwest Tehran. He was allowed occasional visits to his octogenarian mother who lived three miles away. A number of plainclothes policemen provided him with protection round the clock. They were polite and anxious to be of service and he treated them with courtesy, but it was clear that the former prime minister was under something very much like house arrest. At the end of September the new Foreign Minister, Amir-Khosrow Afshar, had tried to force Hoveyda out of the country by suggesting that the former prime minister be named Ambassador to Belgium. When informed of the offer Hoveyda refused. 'This is no time to leave the country,' he told his friends. After this the Shah broke all contact with Hoveyda and the former prime minister soon found himself short of cash — as various government departments said they did not know which one should pay him the pension due to all retired ministers. To the few trusted friends who still visited him, Hoveyda expressed his grave concern about what he saw as 'His Majesty's hesitations'. The former premier believed that a judicious mixture of force and urgent reforms could defuse the situation. He was also aware that he was putting his own life at risk by staying in Iran.[35]

The hardline officers' candidate for premiership was General Oveissi who had won the nickname 'Butcher of Tehran' by crushing the first Khomeinist revolt in the early 1960s. Oveissi was a devout and practising Muslim from the holy city of Qom and believed that, given a chance, he could win over the moderate mullahs and isolate Khomeini. Oveissi's loyalty to the Shah was absolute: the general had been a classmate of the Shah at the Tehran War College and had for years after that served in the Imperial Guard. During the Shah's third wedding Oveissi commanded the guard unit protecting the royal couple. In September 1978 Oveissi demonstrated his negotiating skills by working out an agreement with the mullahs under which Tehran was divided into two sections during the crucial mourning days of Tassu'a and Ashura in the holy month of Muharram.[36] The agreement had left the rebels in control of south Tehran while the army withdrew to the north. The dreaded days passed without incident and the army quickly returned to its positions in the southern districts of Tehran. Oveissi, supported by Zahedi, had also created an advisory board on which a number of intellectuals and academics reviewed the political situation and suggested policy options. High on Oveissi's agenda was the immediate arrest of Hoveyda and dozens of other high officials who were still in Iran. The hardline faction of the army believed that putting Hoveyda on trial as the man responsible for 'all the nation's ills' would be 'like water poured on fire'.[37] Former Justice Minister Muhammad-Ali Hedayati, one of Oveissi's advisers, was the original architect of the idea, which was also supported by Zahedi.

When Sharif-Emami finally offered his resignation – after his government had practically ceased to exist – everyone in Tehran expected General Oveissi to head the new cabinet. Instead, the Shah chose General Gholam-Reza Azhari, the Armed Forces Chief of Staff. Azhari, a mild-mannered grandfather with a poetical bent of mind, had the wit and the courtesy that is associated with the natives of Shiraz, the city of roses and nightingales. The thick dark glasses he wore made him look like the caricature of a Latin American putschist general. Within minutes he was referred to as 'Iran's Pinochet'.

All his life as an officer Azhari had learned to obey His Majesty's orders without question. For the first time that November he was tempted with the idea of refusing the Shah's offer of the premiership, but Azhari was too old and too loyal to become a rebel so late in the day. He was frightened by the idea of being pushed into the furnace of a revolution but he could not defy his sovereign. Leaving the palace after kissing His Majesty's hand, Azhari told those present that this was 'the very last thing I thought would ever happen to me'.[38] He had been brought out of retirement back in the 1970s with the understanding that he would resume his retired life in 1978. Instead, he was now asked to assume a task that his declining health and his temperament did not permit.

Why did the Shah choose Azhari instead of Oveissi? Some of the monarch's aides have claimed that the choice was dictated by the United States and Britain because they knew that Oveissi would cause bloodshed while Azhari would seek reconciliation.[39] This contention, in full harmony with the conspiracy theory so dear to the Shah himself, could not be sustained by the facts. Right to the end the Shah did not want a military government but when he had no other choice he acted in accordance with the logic of the situation. The Iranian armed forces had a strong sense of hierarchy and Azhari was Iran's most senior general and thus easily acceptable to the officer corps while Oveissi had many rivals among his peers; to begin with General Gharabaghi, the Interior Minister and gendarmerie commander, was not even on speaking terms with Oveissi; the War Minister General Reza Azimi, too, would have found serving under Oveissi, his junior in rank, difficult. The appointment of Oveissi might have split the high command.

Oveissi's reputation made him the *bête noire* of the mullahs, especially Khomeini himself. Making Oveissi prime minister would have been a red rag to a raging bull. Among other problems was Oveissi's image as a tough officer, the product, largely, of popular imagination. The general was, in fact, a vain and indecisive man. He dyed his hair and wore high-heeled boots to make himself look younger and taller. His marriage to a lady thirty years younger than himself had helped turn him into a family man – he was the proud father of two small children – and distanced him from the tough life of the gendarmerie garrisons where he had served for years. As Martial Law Administrator Oveissi often threatened to get tough but never did, blaming the Shah for the army's inability to crush the revolt. 'His Majesty would not let us teach these Communist and Khomeinist bastards a lesson,' he liked to say. But was this not a convenient excuse for his own inability to take action? The situation in 1978 was different from 1963. In 1963 Khomeini was the leader of an isolated group opposed to a popular and progressive monarch who had called for rebellion against a reform project that included more rights for women, better treatment of religious minorities, the distribution of land among the poorest peasants and the nationalisation of water and forests. In 1978 Khomeini emerged as the leader of a popular movement against corruption, police brutality and lack of individual and collective political freedoms. This time the regime was on the defensive. It is always easier to fight against unjust privilege than in its defence. In 1963 it was the Shah who was fighting privilege and Khomeini who was defending it. In 1978 the roles were reversed. Oveissi, although not the most intelligent of men, knew this much and was as reluctant to use force as the Shah himself.

General Azhari accepted to serve as prime minister without being told what he was supposed to do. He was simultaneously too excited and too worried to ask any questions and the Shah volunteered no advice. The Shah caused even greater confusion when he made an 'appeal to the nation' through a statement which he personally read on radio and TV. The Shah had been out of public view for nearly ten weeks. His reappearance reassured many of his supporters despite the defeatist content of his message. He told the nation that the appointment of a military government was only a temporary measure and the result of his failure to form a coalition government capable of putting the country back to work. He admitted that much of his rule had been marred by 'corruption and cruelty' and asked the nation for forgiveness. He appeared weak, apologetic and indecisive – the very opposite of the type of leader Iranians admire. For the first time he described the revolt against his own rule as a 'revolution' in which he hoped to participate:

> The Iranian nation has risen against tyranny and corruption. The revolution of the Iranian nation cannot but be endorsed by me both as the Monarch and as an individual Iranian . . . I hereby guarantee [to achieve] what you have offered your martyrs for. . . In this revolution of the Iranian nation against colonialism, tyranny and corruption, I am at your side . . .

Azhari started his premiership by convening parliament to examine his programme and approve his nominees for various ministerial posts. Because he knew very few civilians who could join him in the new cabinet

Azhari brought in the various Army, Air Force and Navy commanders as superministers, each in charge of several departments. He read a sentimental statement spiced with poetic quotations and proverbs and insisted that he was not staging a *coup d'état* but wished to govern in full accordance with the Constitution. His voice choked with emotion, the new prime minister had difficulty holding back his tears. He appeared a pathetic old man asked to do an impossible job.

In the hope of cooling tempers the new prime minister ordered the release of more political prisoners. In their place he had a large number of former officials arrested. His most dramatic move was Hoveyda's detention, a gesture of goodwill towards Oveissi and Zahedi. Oveissi, however, promptly stepped down as Martial Law Administrator and fled the country aboard a military aircraft. His flight accelerated the exodus of senior military and civilian officials. The Shah, increasingly alone in his unheated palace, heard news of each sudden departure from Tehran with a mixture of bitterness and cynical humour. He once commented that he had at least one thing in common with General de Gaulle: 'My supporters, like his in 1968, are marching down the Champs-Elyséees.'[40]

The Azhari government proved a total failure in less than a week. The new prime minister, already in poor health, looked to Washington for a miracle. 'I am sure the Americans would do something,' he told a visitor. 'Iran is too valuable to be jettisoned.'[41] He appeared on television to announce that the cries of 'Allah Akbar' (Allah is the Greatest) that pierced the skies of Tehran every night came from tape recordings of past religious meetings. 'We are facing bombardment by cassettes,' he said. The following day more than half a million people marched through the capital with cries of: 'Is this, too, a cassette? Has anyone ever seen walking cassettes?'

The Shah, who had not believed for one moment that Azhari could succeed where Amuzegar and Sharif-Emami had failed, returned to his earlier idea that only his departure from Iran could end the revolt. He began consultations with a view to the formation of a Regency Council which would take over his constitutional powers and prevent a total collapse of the system. Many Mossadeqists and some of Khomeini's less radical associates, notably Mehdi Bazargan who led the Iran Liberty Movement, shared the Shah's concern and wished to cooperate with him in ensuring a smooth transition. Khomeini, however, would have nothing to do with the monarchist Constitution of 1906 and insisted that the Shah should leave the country and allow the revolutionaries to form their own government.

The Shah spent some time trying to persuade Dr Gholam-Hossein Saddiqi to assume the premiership. Saddiqi, a highly-respected elder statesman, had served as Interior Minister in Mossadeq's last cabinet in 1953. Now in his eighties, Saddiqi had no personal ambitions and was prepared to assume responsibility against the advice of his friends and admirers, but he insisted that the Shah should stay in Iran and act as the constitutional head of state while the prime minister took charge of the executive branch. Saddiqi believed that it was still possible to put the rebellion down by mobilising the forces loyal to Iran's democratic constitution. This required the continued presence of the Shah as figurehead.

Saddiqi's request was rejected by the Shah and the old politician retired to his seclusion. The Shah was now anxious to leave Iran as quickly as possible. Apart from the fact that he believed his departure was desired by the United States and Britain he had other, less complicated reasons for wanting to go. Perhaps unconsciously he wished to avenge himself for what he thought was the injustice being done to him by an ungrateful people. In one of his last statements he warned the Iranians that his departure would usher in a period of 'Great Terror'. He told his people that Iran could not live in peace except under monarchy and that those who had fomented the revolution had nothing to offer but 'death, death again, and more death'. Did he secretly cherish the day when, from the safety of exile, he would see his grim prophecy realised? Many of the Shah's friends and admirers reject such suggestions as unfair. The Shah, they argue, loved his country and his people too much to wish them a tragic fate.

The Shah was not vengeful by nature but was easily hurt. When an official failed to bow to the lowest point possible without falling he would regard the incident as a sign of disloyalty. 'Did you see how so-and-so refused to show respect to us today?' he would ask the Empress once they were alone. 'Don't you think he is turning against us?'[42] He wanted total devotion and was prepared to be totally devoted in return. In 1978 he was angry with his people: they had, in his view, been both ungrateful and stupid in following not someone better than him but a half-literate, reactionary mullah.

Taking his cue from de Gaulle who was said to have loved France without loving the French, the Shah often complained about what he thought was 'the inherent laziness' of Iranians. He looked for an ideal Iranian, a robot who would obey his Shah but at the same time be as intelligent, enterprising and courageous as only a free man can be. He would shed tears of joy when Iranians won gold medals in international athletic competitions and almost lost his self-control when news came that the Iranian soccer team had become Asian champions. At the same time he was not prepared to allow even the best educated and most experienced Iranians the right to take decisions in their fields of expertise without the prior assent of their royal father. It is, therefore, not impossible that the Shah might have believed that by leaving the country he would prove that he had been right all the time and that Iran and the Iranians could not do without him.

The Shah had still another – and perhaps more important – reason for wishing to leave Iran without further delay. He needed medical attention. He had been receiving treatment from a team of French doctors since the summer of 1974. In April of that year he had invited Professor Jean Bernard, the leading French blood specialist, to visit him in Tehran to offer a second opinion on what Karl Fellinger had already detected in Vienna. Bernard brought with him one of his younger protégés, Dr Georges Flandrin. The two French doctors carried out a number of tests on the royal patient and detected abnormalities in the balance of white and red cells in the Shah's blood. A further test on a sample of the Shah's bone marrow indicated cancer-like disorders. The French doctors informed Dr Ayadi, in this case assisted by Dr Abbas Safavian, Chancellor of the National University in Tehran, that the Shah probably suffered from cancer in the very early stages. Both Ayadi and Safavian, however, insisted that the words 'cancer' or 'leukaemia' should not be pronounced in the royal presence. There was no need to tell the Shah the truth before further tests had been carried out. In the meantime the Shah was to be informed that he suffered from a swollen spleen and a blood complaint labelled 'Waldenstrom's disease'.

The decision not to inform the Shah about his true condition was in line with the prevailing rules of conduct at the Imperial Court. An unwritten rule forbade officials from giving His Majesty bad news. Prime Minister Hoveyda tried to justify the rule by claiming that it was essential to keep the Shah's morale high. 'His Majesty is our captain,' he once said. 'We must not undermine his resolve by bombarding him with bad news.'[43] That the Shah did not like bad news was a fact. Those who gave him bad news were labelled *oiseaux de mauvaise augure* (birds of ill omen). Empress Farah herself once received the label from her husband because of a report she offered on the appalling conditions of life in certain villages in the great desert. Nevertheless, the decision to keep the Shah in the dark about his own physical health is difficult to justify. The Shah might have wished to conceal information regarding his health – doubts about his chances of having a long life might have undermined his authority at home as well as his international standing – but news of his ill health would, and almost certainly did, leak in the end. Ayadi must have informed Alam who had been intimately involved in organising the visit of the two French doctors. Alam himself suffered from a similar type of cancer and if Alam knew it was virtually certain that the British would also be informed. The doctors who took the decision together did not even inform the Empress. She was not to know until two years later but even then she was asked by the doctors not to mention the word 'cancer' to her husband.

In hindsight the decision to keep the Shah in the dark about his true condition appears difficult to explain on any grounds. The Shah was not, as yet, seriously ill and had a very good chance of overcoming his cancer. His excellent physical condition and almost spartan way of life provided him with major assets in the fight against serious illness. More important, he had, since early youth, developed a mystical view of life and death. He was not afraid of death, having faced it during at least three major attempts on his life. He took risks with his life that only professional stuntmen might take. On occasions he would fly an aircraft without radio contact over the Alborz mountain range between the Caspian Sea and Tehran. He would guide his plane close to the conic dome of Damavand at a height of over 5600 metres. Disregarding the official speed limits on Iranian roads he would drive his sports cars at speeds of over 200 kilometres per hour through narrow, winding roads in the snowbound mountains. Empress Farah, who at first accompanied her husband on his joy rides was so scared that she closed her eyes and held her head in her hands. In return the Shah would tease her, pinch her cheek and call her 'my frightened lamb'. In later years Farah simply refused to board an automobile with the Shah behind the steering wheel. 'He is a great leader,' she commented. 'But his driving is something else.' The Shah also demonstrated his love of risk while skiing in Iran or in Switzerland. He would disappear on off-piste slopes and court danger at the edge of precipices. On several occasions His Majesty was politely invited by the local authorities at St Moritz not to venture out of designated ski slopes, but he would obey the rules only for a day or two, after which he would seek excitement in the face of death.

Even before the French doctors discovered that he had cancer the Shah had mentally prepared himself for death. He believed that the time and place of his death were predetermined and noted in 'The Book of Time'. This was why he had written and sealed his testament. In 1974, before his cancer was discovered, he spoke of the possibility of an early death in an interview:

> Whatever I do is solely aimed at the progress of my country. I know that I shall take nothing with me into the next world. Doesn't man come into this world naked and alone? Doesn't he enter his tomb in the same condition? Don't I know that I shall not live long enough to see my projects realised?[44]

It is possible to argue that had the Shah known about his illness he might have abdicated in favour of his son, a possibility that he publicly hinted at on a number of occasions.

Farah learned about her husband's illness during a trip to Paris. 'I thought that was the end,' she later recalled. 'I cried all night long. I could not bear the thought of returning to Tehran and facing him. What would I tell him?'[45] She tried to see the bright side of things. The Shah had been on chemotherapy for nearly three years and had apparently responded well. There was no reason why he should not be cured or, at least, continue to live under chemotherapy for several more years. In any case the Empress had to keep her morale high. It was now her duty to nurse her husband and help him overcome his illness. 'The bad news brought me closer to

His Majesty than never before,' she later said.[46] The royal couple often discussed the Shah's illness. Dr Flandrin flew in from Paris every other week and examined his royal patient. The Shah often wondered why he had to take so many drugs so often.

The question whether or not the Shah knew that he had cancer has been debated for more than a decade. Some of the Shah's friends believe that he knew he was terminally ill and it was for this reason that he pushed Iran's modernisation ahead at breakneck speed. This view is not borne out by the facts. The earliest the Shah could have learned about his illness was in 1977 and it was precisely after 1977 that Iran's modernisation slowed down as a result of a fall in the nation's oil revenues. Some historians have tried to explain the Shah's hesitant leadership after 1977 with reference to his illness: once he had learned he had cancer he was no longer motivated enough to fight back; his judgment might have been adversely affected by the drugs he took. This view is also difficult to sustain: the Shah's judgment was more affected by what he saw as a betrayal of his love for the Iranian people. It was not cancer that made him confused, hesitant and ineffective as a leader at a time of crisis. He was convinced that his people had abandoned him and was equally sure that his closest allies wished to stab him in the back.

Officially the Shah was told that he had cancer only in January 1979, after he had left Iran, but it is entirely possible that he had learned about the true nature of his illness even without being told by his doctors. The Shah was told that he suffered from Waldenstrom's disease or lymphoma: he could have looked up the words in one of the many encyclopaedias he had in his palace. He might have questioned one of his closest companions, Dr Yahya Adl, about the meaning of these terms without telling him that he himself was concerned. Empress Farah was convinced that the Shah knew he had cancer as early as 1975. 'He was happy to keep the whole thing quiet both for political reasons and because he did not wish to frighten me,' the Empress recalled.[47] After 1977 the royal couple tried to live with the horrible truth without openly acknowledging it, as Empress Farah later described:

> We talked a great deal about His Majesty's illness. I was sure that he knew that I knew the truth. He might have even known that I knew that he knew. But he played the game as if I didn't know while I pretended not to know what was wrong. It was a strange game: sweet and sour, tender and painful at the same time. I loved him desperately. I wanted to rush into his arms, put my head on his chest and cry. But I kept my cool: *raison d'état oblige.*[48]

The revolutionary crisis of 1978 pushed the issue of the Shah's illness into the background. The royal couple had other bad news to talk about at dinner which they often took alone, not because they did not want any guests but because most of the people they might have wanted to invite had already fled the country. These were candlelit dinners, but the romantic atmosphere was due to the power cuts. The news that most worried the Shah concerned the deteriorating morale of the armed forces. Some conscripts had begun to desert; they did not know why they should repress a revolution which the Shah himself had so lavishly praised and endorsed. The conscripts were also being overcome by physical exhaustion. They were asked to stand on guard in sub-zero temperatures for up to 10 hours a day. In exchange they received a bowl of stew, a loaf of bread and a bottle of water. Some units had been on duty for months and the army's system of rotation was breaking down under pressure. Worse still from the Shah's point of view were reports about secret contacts between a number of generals and Khomeini's agents in Tehran. The Shah's boyhood friend and trusted aide General Fardust himself seemed to have started a double game.

Fardust, accused of being a British agent since his early youth, was believed to have contacted the revolutionary mullahs on orders from his 'masters'.[49] The new SAVAK, chief General Nasser Moqqadam, had also established a channel of communication with the exiled ayatollah. Both Fardust and Moqqadam were experienced security officers and might have contacted the opposition as a matter of course. Their behaviour has been regarded as suspicious because they failed to inform the Shah about contacts with the Khomeinists in Tehran, but they could not have directly informed the Shah because he had decided not to receive them. After September 1978 the Shah insisted that senior civilian and military officials report to the prime minister on all matters regarding internal security. Both Sharif-Emami and Azhari openly sought a dialogue with the opposition. Fardust and Moqqadam were, therefore, acting in line with official policy. More important, the new Armed Forces Chief of Staff, General Gharabaghi, had established his own contacts with the opposition. Many of the Shah's supporters have accused Gharabaghi of treason, but he was doing nothing more than trying to save the army or trying to salvage what he could from the situation. Later he asserted that he had not met any of the opposition leaders until the very last days of the regime and then only in order to prevent armed revolutionaries from pillaging army stores and disarming the conscripts.[50]

The crisis revealed a part of Iranian reality that the Shah had either forgotten or deliberately wished to ignore. In mid-November a rumour started about a pious old lady in the holy city of Qom who had allegedly discovered a hair from the Prophet's beard in the pages of her Qur'an. Mullahs seized upon the incident as a sign from Allah that the honour of the Prophet required the destruction of the Shah. Within days hundreds of the Shah's statues were removed from public places. Later Grand Ayatollah Hassan Tabataba'i Qomi, a rival of Khomeini's, started a rumour of his own. He said that he had seen Imam Reza, the eighth of the 12 shi'ite imams, in a dream. Imam Reza had ordered the ayatollah to ask the faithful to put the Shah's statue back in place. Some faithful obeyed the instruction and restored the fallen effigies of the monarch. On 27 November another rumour spread throughout the country: the faithful would see the face of Ayatollah Khomeini in the full moon: only miscreants and bastards would be denied the privilege. Millions of people gathered on rooftops with cries of 'Allah Akbar' and with tears of joy swore that they had indeed seen the face of Khomeini in the moon. The event was celebrated over the following days in thousands of mosques throughout the country. The mullahs told the faithful that the Mahdi, the Hidden Imam, was about to return. One sure sign of the Return was that the sun would rise from the West. Khomeini, representing the sun of Islam, was now in France and his face was seen shining like a sun in the moon. What was remarkable was that even highly educated and secular politicians, including the Tudeh leadership, swore in public that they had seen the face of the ayatollah in the moon. It was clear that nothing like superstition could mobilise the poor and illiterate masses who were needed for the purpose of providing the revolutionary leadership with vast quantities of muscle in the streets.

A distressed Shah saw these episodes as signs that he had failed to transform Iranian society. When one of his attendants commented that Iran was 'returning to the Dark Ages' the Shah replied: 'I wonder if we ever left them.'[51]

Meanwhile the mullahs, acting through Ayatollah Motahari, began preparing a Regency Council in which a majority of members would be approved by Khomeini. When the plot was discovered by the speaker, Javad Sa'id, he instantly informed the Shah and the list of names already agreed was set aside. The trouble was that almost no one who would qualify wanted to join such a council. It was now clear that the Shah did not wish to stay in Iran under any circumstances and had begun to hate a people he had once loved. 'For me everything is at an end. Even if I return to Iran one day as Shah, nothing will be the same again. It is like a beautiful crystal vase that is broken for good; repair it and it will still show its cracks.'[52]

Zahedi and his friends tried to boost the Shah's morale by organising a small demonstration around the palace. This consisted of a few cars that, claxons pressed to the limit, were driven around the palace while a few hundred spectators shouted 'Long Live the Shah', but the Shah knew that all this was fake and felt even more hurt. In better times tens of thousands of people would have poured into the streets to show their love for him. Now his friends could not even give him a decent rented mob. He was also angry when he was shown a newsreel supposedly showing recent demonstrations in his favour in the city of Rezaieh. This was in December when Rezaieh was snowbound under freezing temperatures and the newsreel showed men and women in summer clothes. It had been dug out of the archives.

By the end of 1978 the Azhari government had disintegrated, several cabinet ministers had fled abroad or gone into hiding in their home towns. The prime minister himself suffered a stroke and had to be taken out of his office on a stretcher. For a few days the country did not have any formal government. The Shah had drawn up a list of elder Statesmen who would form the Regency Council in his absence, but he still found no one who would want to become prime minister – no one, that is, except the ambitious Shapour Bakhtiar.

On 6 January 1979 the Shah, encouraged by the Empress, who had received Bakhtiar in audience a few days earlier, agreed to ask him to form a new government. Bakhtiar, a junior politician with virtually no experience of government – he had once served as undersecretary for Labour for a few weeks in 1953 – had initially promised the Shah to detach the Mossadeqist opposition from the Khomeinists, but no sooner had the Shah asked Bakhtiar to form a government than the Mossadeqist National Front announced Bakhtiar's expulsion from the movement.

Bakhtiar spent ten days putting together a new cabinet. Many of those he approached refused to join a government which lacked popular support and was suspected by the armed forces and the civil service. The Shah was anxious to leave the country as quickly as possible and did not understand why forming a cabinet should take so long. It was finally agreed that Bakhtiar should present his cabinet to parliament on 16 January, despite the fact that some ministerial posts remained vacant for lack of candidates. The royal couple fixed the time of their departure from Iran on the same day. A brief announcement said that His Imperial Majesty the King of Kings had to go abroad for medical treatment and would be accompanied by the Empress. The impression given was that the Shah would return once the situation had been defused.

Few people believed that the Shah would be able to return to his throne. Bakhtiar himself was determined not to let the Shah come back. He compared himself with General de Gaulle and hinted that he himself might take over as head of state once the rebellion had been crushed. Naively, he also tried to contact Khomeini in the hope of persuading the ayatollah to endorse the new government. Bakhtiar had achieved Khomeini's principal objective – the departure of the Shah from Iran. What Bakhtiar did not know was that Khomeini wanted power for himself and detested secular politicians even more than the Shah.

On the afternoon of 16 January the Shah and Empress Farah arrived at Tehran's Mehrabad Airport aboard the blue and white royal helicopter. They had to wait at the royal pavilion until Bakhtiar had obtained a vote of confidence from the Majlis. The Shah was nervous and tense, the Empress already in tears. Bakhtiar finally arrived for a brief farewell ceremony. As the royal couple walked towards the aircraft that was to fly them to Cairo an officer of the guard broke down, broke ranks, seized the Shah's hand and began to kiss it. Other officers present followed suit. The Shah now also broke down and, as he tried to restrain the officers, he let tears pour down his face. Then everyone present, except for a smiling Bakhtiar, also began to cry. The whole episode lasted only a few minutes but it provided a pathetic finale to an eventful reign that had lasted almost 38 years.

The Book of Time

The few officials who had come to see the royal couple off at Mehrabad Airport did not even wait to see the Shah's Boeing 707 take off. They had more urgent tasks to attend to. Special editions of the evening papers had already hit the newstands with headlines screaming: 'The Shah is Gone.' Khomeinist militants stopped cars and forced the drivers to sound their claxons as a sign of joy. Sweets and fruits were distributed and piles of the Shah's pictures were used for making bonfires.

The demonstration of unbridled joy on the streets of Tehran, however, did not reflect the true mood of the nation. Many Iranians cried in sadness and despair in the privacy of their homes. Many more were preparing themselves for what they suspected would be years of instability and violence, but they all belonged to the proverbial 'silent majority' whose inability or unwillingness to speak out keeps the slaughter houses of history busy.

When the royal plane took off the Shah was in the pilot's seat. This was the first time in many months that he had flown and he felt relieved, almost elated: nowhere else did he feel so relaxed as up in the air, piloting his aircraft. The plane took a southwesterly route, leaving behind the snowbound cone of mount Damavand while the ochre desert down below unfurled like a Qashqa'i tribal rug. A squadron of F-4 fighters escorted the royal aircraft over the Iranian space. A few minutes later the Shah handed over command of the aircraft to Captain Behzad Moezzi and returned to the royal suite. For the first time in a month Empress Farah saw her husband smile.

The royal plane had taken the Shah and his wife on numerous state visits to various parts of the world. Every time the couple had been accompanied by a large suite of senior civilian and military officials and protocol personnel. This time they had only a handful of people with them.[1] The party had left in a great hurry, taking a few pieces of luggage. Only the Shah's special cook, Ali Kabiri, had managed to bring what he wanted: two huge metal pans for cooking rice Persian style and an assortment of Iranian herbs and spices. Kabiri did not know that he would get few opportunities to cook in exile and that his two precious pans would be converted to plant pots at a palace in Cairo.

The decision to fly to Egypt had been taken in a hurry, largely because the Shah had not been able to secure an invitation from any other country. Originally he had wanted to go to the United States. The reason for this might have been the naive belief that once in the United States he would be able to use his excellent connections within the American establishment for the purpose of persuading President Carter to 'stop encouraging the forces of disruption' in Iran. Washington had at first expressed doubts about the wisdom of the Shah leaving the country at all, but once it had become clear that the Shah himself was anxious to leave the Americans could not but endorse the royal decision. At the end of December 1978 Ambassador Sullivan had informed the Shah that Washington thought that he should leave the country and that the royal couple would be welcome in the United States. At the same time, however, the Ambassador made it clear that the Shah could not expect to be received like a head of state: in other words he should enter the United States as an exile.

Later the Shah and many of his supporters claimed that he had been forced to leave Iran by the Americans. They also claimed that the Carter administration had refused to let them go to the United States right away. These claims are difficult to sustain. The idea of leaving the country was the Shah's own. He openly talked about it as early as September, nearly three months before the final session with Sullivan. In any case had the idea come from Washington or anywhere else he could, as the leader of an independent country, have told the American Ambassador or anyone else for that matter to go where meddlesome foreigners should go. To blame the United States for what happened in Iran is both disingenuous and misleading. It is the continuation of the conspiracy theory that has prevented Iran – and many other nations in the Middle East – from assuming the consequences of their own choices.

The Shah wanted to manufacture the myth that his forced departure from Iran had not been caused by an uprising against his rule but as a result of a conspiracy by foreign powers who had become jealous of Iran's rising prosperity and prestige. When it suited him he would describe 'the foreigners' as 'donkeys who ought to be kicked'. On other occasions the same 'foreigners' were represented as superhuman creatures who controlled everything under the sun. The Shah was, at the end of his rule, one of the world's most experienced politicians with a remarkable knowledge of how international politics worked, but when it suited his purpose he would pretend that words uttered by a casual foreign visitor represented a mysterious plot hatched by 'the secret government of the world'. In December 1978, for example, the Shah received Lord George-Brown, a former British Foreign Secretary who had, in fact, invited himself. At the audience the Shah told Brown that he was thinking of leaving the country for a while to allow things to cool down. Brown, anxious to say something that would please His Majesty, said this was an excellent idea. The Shah later used the encounter as 'proof' that Britain, too, wanted him to leave Iran.

The decision not to go to the United States directly was taken by the Shah himself with much encouragement from Zahedi. The argument used by Zahedi was strong: the Shah's opponents were accusing him of being a CIA agent. So if he now left Iran and went directly to the United States he would simply lend credence to the preposterous claim. It was necessary for the Shah to begin his travels abroad in a place where he would receive full state honours. At a later stage he could go to the United States for medical treatment. The Carter administration, of course, did not wish the Shah's entry to the United States to be misinterpreted by the Khomeinists who appeared to be the strongest group in Iranian politics. The Shah, therefore, was told that he should not go to Washington. One of the Shah's personal friends, Ambassador Walter Annenberg, even offered his California home as a temporary residence for the royal couple.

The invitation from Egypt had come early in January 1979 in the form of a telephone call from Mrs Jehan Sadat, wife of the Egyptian President Muhammad Anwar Sadat, to Empress Farah. The royal couple had politely declined the invitation.

The Sadats had become personal friends since the early 1970s. The Egyptian President was the only person on earth allowed to call the Shah 'my brother Muhammad'. At the end of 1978 Sadat had telephoned the Shah from Camp David where the Egyptian leader, the Israeli Premier Menachem Begin and President Carter were working on the peace accord between Egypt and the Jewish state. Sadat had urged the Shah to stand firm against the rioters. He had also persuaded Carter to talk to the Shah on the telephone to offer encouraging advice. The Shah had met Sadat for the first time in Rabat in 1978. Both men had been attending the first Islamic Summit Conference. Sadat had come to Rabat as president Nasser's stand-in. At the summit the Shah and Sadat clashed over what policy to adopt to ensure the liberation of Jerusalem. After a harsh exchange at the closed session of the summit the Shah and Vice-President Sadat, as he then was, had been invited by King Faisal of Saudi Arabia to an informal meeting. The Saudi king liked the Shah but believed that the Iranian monarch was still vulnerable to 'youthful errors'.[2] It was essential that Iran and Egypt, the two most important nations in Islam, should come together to face the consequences of the Arab defeat of 1967 and the loss of Jerusalem. At the meeting arranged by Faisal in Rabat, the Shah and Sadat had taken a liking to each other. The Shah found out that Sadat was not the superficial 'gesticulator' that a confidential report had suggested[3] and Sadat realised that the Shah was not the sworn enemy of Arabs as described by Nasserist propaganda.

When the royal plane touched down at the international airport at Aswan, President Sadat, his wife and a host of senior Egyptian officials were awaiting their Iranian guests. The royal couple's arrival was treated as the start of a state visit. Iranian flags and large portraits of the Shah decorated the streets of Aswan and a suitably enthusiastic crowd thronged the road from the airport to the hotel where the royal couple were to stay. Sitting next to Sadat in a state limousine, the Shah could not contain his tears. He said he felt 'guilty and ashamed' for having left the country but had been forced to do so under American pressure and in the hope of saving Iran from destruction. Sadat tried to console him as best he could. Sadat gained the impression that the Shah had not quite written off the possibility of returning to power in Iran. The Egyptian president suggested that the Shah order the Iranian Air Force to fly to Egypt pending a settlement of the political situation at home. The Shah declined the offer: the Air Force was not his personal property. Later, some members of the Shah's entourage claimed that His Majesty had told Sadat that the Americans would not let the Iranian Air Force be transferred to Egypt.[4]

While in Aswan the Shah was visited by Dr Flandrin, the French specialist who had been treating him since 1974. Months of living under stress had weakened the Shah. But his 'condition' – the word cancer was still taboo – had not worsened. His Majesty was told to continue with his drugs and to rest.

The royal couple spent five days at Aswan. They talked to their children on the telephone several times a day. The strike by communications workers in Iran had prevented regular contact between the royal couple and their children in the United States for more than two weeks. At Aswan the Shah received a number of telephone calls from friendly heads of state, King Hussein of Jordan, Morocco's King Hassan, Romania's Nicolae Ceausescu, Yugoslavia's President Tito, Queen Juliana of the Netherlands and her husband Prince Bernhardt, King Baudouin and Queen Fabiola of Belgium and President Leopold Sedar Senghor of Senegal were among those who called. General Gholam-Reza Rabi'i, Commander of the Iranian Air Force, also tried to talk to the Shah on the telephone. Rabi'i, together with a number of senior officers, had decided to prevent Khomeini's return from Iran through whatever means necessary. They were even prepared to shoot down any aircraft that might bring the ayatollah to Tehran. Rabi'i wanted the decision approved by the Shah who was still regarded as Commander-in-Chief by his officers. But the Shah told Rabi'i, through an officer of the guard who was present at Aswan, that all matters regarding military action should be referred to the prime minister in Tehran.

This was also the message that the Carter administration wished to pass on to the Iranian top brass. Carter had dispatched General Robert C. Huyser, Deputy Commander of NATO, to Tehran on a mission to support Bakhtiar and prevent Iranian generals from organising a *coup d'état.* Huyser had slipped into the country without the knowledge either of the Shah or of Bakhtiar. While Huyser was trying to prop up support for Bakhtiar Ambassador Sullivan was already negotiating with Khomeini's agents in the capital. The two men tried to keep their separate activities a secret from one another. Far from pursuing a coherent 'conspiracy' as the Shah pretended, the Carter administration was unable to influence events it did not understand.

At Aswan the Shah tried to disconnect himself from events in Iran and, for the first time in many years, began to examine his own business interests and investments. His personal treasurer, Muhammad-Hassan Behbahanian, a faithful courtier for more than three decades, came from Switzerland and spent several long sessions with His Majesty. Reports about the Shah's fortune have been numerous and contradictory. Khomeinist propaganda claimed that the Shah had 'stolen' more than $56 billion.[5] Less generous estimates gave the Shah and his immediate family no more than $11 billion. King Hassan of Morocco apparently took this latter figure seriously and at one point hoped to get a share of it in the form of investment in Moroccan projects. The Shah himself estimated the wealth of his immediate family at just over $70,000,000, a figure later confirmed by Empress Farah.[6] The Shah owned a sumptuous property in Surrey in southern England as well as his villa at St Moritz. He was also believed to have shares in some 20 international companies. In addition he held cash balances in several bank accounts in Europe and the United States. Empress Farah had managed to bring most of her jewellery out of Iran. It was difficult to estimate the value of the collection which was formed thanks to the presents the Shah gave his wife over nearly twenty years.[7] The figure given by the Shah should, unless there is proof to the contrary, be taken as realistic. His Majesty might have been many times richer had he been able to reclaim the assets of the Pahlavi Foundation abroad but he did not try. Soon after Khomeini seized power, the two men whose signature controlled the assets of the Foundation transferred their authority to two mullahs nominated by Khomeini and the assets of the Pahlavi Foundation were thus transferred to the newly-created Foundation for the Dispossessed in 1979.

The Shah mocked his own business judgment. 'As a businessman I am zero,' he liked to say and there were few indications that he might have tried to amass a personal fortune. To be sure he allowed his sisters and brothers as well as courtiers such as Alam and Davalloo to engage in profitable business transactions and lucrative contracts with the government, but he was careful not to let his own name, or that of his wife, be associated even with legitimate business enterprises. The King of Kings and his Empress could not join the rat race which made some Iranians almost indecently wealthy. While in Aswan the Shah arranged for the transfer of the control of his assets from Behbahanian to himself. Quite clearly he was already convinced that he would not be returning to Tehran anytime soon.

The Shah and his suite were preparing to fly to the United States when the Moroccan Foreign Minister arrived at Aswan with a message from King Hassan II. The Moroccan sovereign wished to invite his 'brother' the Shahanshah of Iran to pay him a visit at Marrakesh before continuing to the United States. The Shah was glad to accept the invitation. It gave him the illusion that he was still in the international game. Members of his entourage encouraged him in this belief and rumours were spread that he was prolonging his stay in the region in order to coordinate some kind of action against the rebels in Iran. The American administration disregarded these rumours and encouraged the Shah to go to Morocco: Carter was in no hurry to have the Shah in the United States.

The royal party left Aswan on 22 January. The send off befitted a head of state but arrival in Marrakesh was a different story. King Hassan was present at the airport to greet his royal guests but there were no ceremonies and the media were kept at a distance. The Moroccan king wished to keep the Shah's visit a private matter without any political significance.

The Shah and King Hassan had first met in 1960 and over the years became close friends. The Shah had sent a 400-man military mission to help the Moroccan army adapt to modern weapons and techniques of warfare in 1971. Later, when Morocco annexed the Spanish Sahara, Iran helped King Hassan's army with the training and arms needed to fight the Polisario guerrillas. Iran also invested in the construction of the Mulai Ismail hydroelectric project on the river Oued Zroud in Morocco. Courtiers in Tehran also claimed that King Hassan had personally benefited from cash gifts from the Shah. It is possible that Hassan hoped that by inviting the Shah he would attract investment from the exiled monarch and other wealthy Iranians. What is certain is that King Hassan had not envisaged a long stay.

At the end of January the US Ambassador to Morocco, Richard Parker, made it known that Washington was still prepared to welcome the Shah to the United States. The Shah, however, wanted to stay in Morocco a bit longer. In later years there were claims that the Shah used his stay in Morocco for the purpose of receiving his advisers and discussing plans for a *coup d'état*, but there is no evidence to support such a claim. The only adviser who visited the Shah in Morocco was Zahedi who flew in from Washington after vacating his post of Ambassador on orders from the new Bakhtiar government. Princess Ashraf also arrived to meet her brother for the first time in nearly six months. The small group spent more of its time gossiping about the past and cursing 'foreign plotters' than planning any political or military move to stem the tide of revolution.

By 11 February Bakhtiar had already gone into hiding and Mehdi Bazargan had taken over the reins of government. Khomeini, who had returned to Iran 10 days earlier, appointed Bazargan. Thus the Iranian Constitution under which the Shah was sovereign and head of state was, in effect, suspended. The new government announced it would hold a referendum to determine whether or not Iranians wished to see their monarchic form of government continued in future. Morocco was among the first countries to recognise the legitimacy of the new Khomeinist government. In this it joined the United States, Britain and all members of the European Economic Community.

With the change of regime in Iran the Carter administration was now reluctant to honour its earlier invitation to the Shah. The United States wished to establish close ties with the new rulers of Iran and did not wish to provoke a backlash in Tehran by letting in the Shah even as an exile. Bazargan's cabinet in Tehran was reassuringly pro-American: in fact it included five American citizens of Iranian origin who had returned to Iran during the revolution after years of self-imposed exile. Anxious not to risk the anger of the new masters of Iran the Carter administration severed its diplomatic contacts with the Shah. At the same time a CIA official was dispatched to Morocco on two occasions to sound out the fallen monarch about his intentions. The CIA man, wearing thick dark glasses and an impressive moustache, never even bothered to present himself under a code name. The Shah's entourage referred to him as 'le moustachu'.[8] During the second meeting with the Shah 'le moustachu' suggested that His Majesty might be able to enter the United States only if he abdicated. A few days later the question of the Shah's abdication was, once again, brought up by Barbara Walters, an American TV reporter who flew in for an exclusive interview. Walters had been close to the Iranian embassy in Washington for years and was included in the list of 'favourite Americans' established by Zahedi in 1974. The Shah, never fully convinced that the American media were independent of the government, regarded Walters and many other journalists as virtual public relations officers for the 'establishment'. Thus when Walters mentioned abdication His Majesty was convinced that he was facing an American plot to destroy all chances of the Pahlavi Dynasty recovering the Iranian throne.

A few days after Bazargan took over as prime minister the Shah received Captain Moezzi and members of the crew of his plane in audience. Moezzi, speaking on behalf of his crew, said they all wished to return to Tehran. The Shah said this was the right thing to do. Moezzi and his crew received around $50,000 in bonuses and were told to fly the royal aircraft back to the capital. 'The plane belongs to the Iranian people,' the Shah said. The airmen wept and kissed the Shah's hand.[9]

On 22 February using the services of a Moroccan courtier, the Shah informed the US Ambassador that it was now time to arrange for the royal couple to travel to California. The following day Carter, surrounded by his national security advisers and Secretary of State Vance, studied the Shah's request and decided to reject it. A compromise formula was found: the Shah would be told that the invitation to visit the United States remained open but should not be taken up immediately. Political tension in Tehran required patience. Carter had never been keen on letting the Shah enter the United States and when the possibility of the Shah's visit to the US had first been discussed in October 1979, long before the monarch had made it clear he wanted to leave Iran, Carter had addressed his advisers in these prophetic words: 'What are you guys going to recommend that we do when they take our embassy and hold our people hostage?'[10] This was an election year and Carter had to take into account not only the fate of the US diplomats but also the safety of thousands of American citizens who still remained in turbulent Iran. Washington's decision to tell the Shah to stay where he was did not reach the Shah until three days later and then only because Zahedi had telephoned Bzrezinski to find out what had happened. The National Security Adviser also informed Zahedi that Washington would help the Shah find another haven pending an eventual settlement in the United States. Zahedi, back at his home in Montreux, Switzerland, sounded out the Swiss officials about the possibility of the Shah settling at St Moritz for a while. The response was a polite but firm no. The British Labour government of James Callaghan did even better than the Swiss and informed the Shah that it would be inopportune for him to apply for a visa to enter the United Kingdom. The arms middleman, Sir Shapour Reporter, who had for years been regarded by the Shah as a reliable contact with the British establishment, was now unavailable whenever someone called on behalf of His Majesty. The Hindujah brothers who had come to Iran in the 1950s from India and became major businessmen after a couple of years as cinema actors in Tehran, sent a message to the effect that they could arrange for the Shah to go to India. The Shah wished to go to the West however. The Empress suggested that France be considered as a temporary home in exile but the French would not have the Pahlavis either. The Count of Marenches, the French secret service chief, had for years rendered services to the Shah. This time, however, he had the painful task of discouraging His Majesty from seeking asylum in his country.

The Shah did not mind staying in Morocco but by mid-March it had become clear that King Hassan was no longer as welcoming as he had been back in January. The Moroccan king was scheduled to preside over an Islamic summit in Rabat in April. He did not wish the summit to be disrupted as a result of controversy with the new Iranian leaders, but how could he ask his 'brother' to pack up and go? Once again it was the Count of Marenches who agreed to break the bad news. The Frenchman was received by the Shah and Empress Farah on 12 March. He told the royal couple a horror story: the mullahs in Tehran had organised a hit squad to send to Morocco where they were to kidnap members of King Hassan's family and exchange them for the Shah and the Empress! The secret service chief asked: What would Your Majesties wish to do now?

The story invented by Marenches had no basis in fact. The mullahs never organised hit squads to kidnap anybody abroad. In any case they had no terrorist capability outside Iran at the time. Furthermore the new government in Tehran had not protested against the Shah's presence in Morocco and was, in fact, happy to let him stay in a fairly remote country where few Iranians were likely to venture. Nevertheless, the Shah had to take Marenches' story seriously. The Count would not have made the move without the approval of King Hassan. Three days later it was the turn of the American Ambassador Parker to call on the Shah for the last time. His Majesty was informed that the Carter administration was no longer in a position to maintain its previous invitation: the Shah had to go somewhere else. Parker also informed the Shah that South Africa and Paraguay were prepared to give him a temporary home. Later, two American lobbyists, working for King Hassan, also asked to see the Shah. Their message was even more brutal: His Majesty would have to get out of Morocco before the end of March. The Shah had not seen King Hassan for weeks and did not wish to ask for a meeting for fear of being refused. His humiliation was total.

The search for a place the Shah could settle in was conducted by more than a dozen people in addition to many more American Ambassadors posted all over the world. Princess Ashraf, Zahedi, Kissinger, David Rockefeller of Chase Manhattan Bank and former Presidents Nixon and Ford, both personal friends of the Shah, were part of the 'search party'. A list of 37 countries was established and, as negative replies arrived, the Empress put a cross in front of the name of the country concerned.

The list of countries that refused to let the Shah in contained a number of surprises. King Hussein of Jordan had been asked to invite the Shah for a brief private visit, earlier in March. The King, who had constantly relied on the Shah's political and economic support, made himself unavailable for anyone who telephoned on behalf of the Pahlavis. Equally unwelcoming was King Khaled of Saudi Arabia who, since the start of his reign in 1975, had developed exceptionally fraternal relations with the Shah.

By 30 March the Shah had decided to fly to South Africa where his father had been an exile in the 1940s. King Hassan's private aircraft was already packed with the royal couple's luggage – nearly 400 pieces – and ready to take off. Only a few hours before the aircraft was scheduled to fly to South Africa came news that Kissinger had found an alternative haven: the Bahamas. The authorities in the island nation had given their consent at the last minute after 'a suitable show of generosity' on the part of Princess Ashraf.

The Bahaman haven had been found for the Shah by Kissinger with help from David Rockefeller. Once on the island the Shah and his suite were in the hands of the Rockefeller machine which provided security and public relations services. A Rockefeller employee, Robert Armao, was attached to the Shah as his 'manager'.

In the Bahamas the Shah and his wife were joined by the royal children who flew in from the United States. The royal couple were housed in a tiny villa which made the Empress feel like 'choking with claustrophobia and heat'. There was nowhere to store the royal luggage which remained piled up in the courtyard. The telephone was often out of order and the air-conditioning worked only every now and then. Worse still the Bahaman authorities imposed strict limits on the number of people who could call on the royal couple. The Shah, the Empress and members of their entourage were also asked not to make political statements to the press. The Bahaman prime minister Sir Lynden Pindoling claimed that 'untoward statements' by the royal visitors might harm his country's 'international standing'. The Empress was outraged: What international standing could the Mafia-infested island state have?

The Bahama sojourn was sweet and sour, the Empress later recalled. The royal couple were united with their children and could indulge in some of their favourite sports. The Shah and Empress Farah played tennis, went water-skiing and relaxed on the beach while the children played around them – all under the watchful eyes of their 'gorillas'. In the evenings they played gin rummy. The few visitors who came to see them in the Bahamas felt that the royal couple wished to distance themselves from Iran's turbulent experience, but this was no more than an impression. Every night the Shah spent hours listening to the radio to find out what was going on in his country. He also jotted down some notes, then immediately tore them up for fear that they might fall into 'improper foreign hands'.

In the first week of the stay in Nassau news came that Amir Abbas Hoveyda had been executed. The Empress cried while the Shah withdrew to his room. Now that they were more relaxed and far from Iran they both remembered how they had been attached to Hoveyda who had served them and their country for nearly 13 years. Did they blame themselves for Hoveyda's tragic death? No one knows. In any case they clung to the claim that they had urged Hoveyda to leave the country and that the former prime minister had adamantly refused. This claim was based on less than the whole truth. True, at one stage Hoveyda had refused to go to Brussels as Ambassador, but at that time he had been a free man still and might have believed himself capable of helping to stop Iran's drift towards catastrophe. Later, when he was out of office, virtually penniless and under house arrest, no one asked him whether or not he wished to leave. Still later, the Shah approved Hoveyda's arrest. The news that Hoveyda would be arrested had, in fact, been broken to the former prime minister by the Shah himself. His Majesty had pretended that the move was needed to ensure Hoveyda's protection. Hoveyda's friends have argued that the Shah could have invited his long-time associate to join him on the flight out of Iran, but by the time the Shah was able to get out he was no longer in a position to take Hoveyda with him. Bakhtiar, who later said he had planned to have Hoveyda tried and executed, would not have allowed that. The Shah almost certainly felt guilty about what had happened to Hoveyda and tried to blame others. One evening at dinner when the subject of Hoveyda's fate came up he turned to Zahedi and said unjustly: 'You must be happy now. You got what you wanted.'[11]

It was at Nassau that the royal couple saw a documentary made by Iranian television, now under the control of the mullahs, about the royal palaces. The Shah and the Empress had taken almost all of their personal effects with them when they flew out of Tehran and the palace keys had been left with Hossein Amir-Sadeghi, the son of the Shah's private chauffeur and himself a highly ambitious young man. On 11 February 1979 Hossein had handed the keys to Mohammad Montazeri, son of the ayatollah, who had come to take over the palace at the head of an armed gang. Montazeri and his companions looted the palace of whatever could be carried away without great difficulty. Thus when the TV documentary team arrived several weeks later it was possible to pretend that the palace had been emptied of its contents by the royal couple before their departure. What shocked the Shah and his wife most, however, was the view of ordinary Iranians who queued to visit the palace and told the TV reporters how amazed they were by the 'incredible luxury' they had seen. Were these the same men and women who had for years thronged the streets to see the royal couple drive by and, whenever they had a chance, rushed to kiss the royal hands and feet? The royal couple were also shocked by the news that many former officials, including ministers and ambassadors, had joined the new regime and strongly attacked the previous one. Tehran's mayor, Javad Shahrestani, who had for years served as a cabinet minister under the Shah, rallied to the Khomeinist side and ordered that 'all vestiges of the hated Pahlavis' be effaced from the capital. The vast majority of the Shah's former associates were in exile, many of them in hiding. Almost none tried to get in touch with the royal exiles and those who were traced refused to take a call from their former master.

The Shah seldom intimated his thoughts, especially on political matters, to anyone. Early in life he had learned the merits of taciturnity in a society where words were quickly emptied of their content, twisted and turned into traps for whoever used them. A deeply emotional man, the Shah had had greater difficulty in bringing his facial expressions under control but nearly 38 years of experience with politics had helped him develop a poker player's mask. During his stay in Nassau he gave no indication that he still hoped to influence political events in Iran. Nevertheless, it is possible, in hindsight, to argue that the Shah did not, as yet, regard himself as a spent force. He was certain that he would not be able to return to his throne. It is possible that he did not even want to. What he did want was to pave the way for his son's accession. He was convinced that the revolutionary regime in Tehran would not last long. In

private conversations he gave 'those people' – as he referred to the
Khomeinists – between six months and a year before their 'incompetence
and criminal stupidity' would be recognised by everyone, especially the
Iranian people. And then? The Shah never explained his views on the
issue, but it is clear that he hoped it would be to the institution of
monarchy that both the Iranian nation and the major powers would
return to stop the tragedy of the revolution. It was in order to keep the
institution of monarchy alive that he refused to abdicate, despite pressure
from the United States. The Crown Prince would be 21 in 1980 and could
claim the Iranian crown under the 1906 Constitution. In the meantime
the Shah had to stay out of the irresponsible schemes discussed by his
generals, many of them now in exile and hiding, who envisaged a *coup
d'état* or civil war as a means of unseating the mullahs. In Nassau the Shah
spent some time with his son and, for the first time, tried to instruct him in
the art of kingship. The Empress took the hint and the father and son were
left alone to walk on the beach and talk.

The Shah had persuaded himself that the United States, once it became
clear that the mullahs could not rule Iran, would throw its weight behind
the monarchist cause in order to prevent a Communist takeover. It was
therefore necessary for the Shah to go to the United States, revive his
contacts and mobilise support for his son.[12] David Rockefeller and Henry
Kissinger, unaware of the Shah's strategy, campaigned on his behalf in
Washington. They argued that the Shah should be allowed to stay in the
United States as a gesture of loyalty to an old friend and ally. In April the
two men held several meetings with Carter, Vance and Vice-president
Walter Mondale to press for an early decision on the issue. Each time they
were told that the United States could not run the risk of upsetting its
relations with the revolutionary authorities in Tehran. The Shah's friends
were also informed that the US embassy in Tehran had already been a
target for attacks by radical elements on three separate occasions and
might be in danger if the Shah were allowed in.[13]

In May 1979 the Shah received news of the Conservative victory in the
British general election with some satisfaction. He had met the new prime
minister Margaret Thatcher in Tehran when, as leader of the opposition,
she had come to acquaint herself with the West's staunchest ally in the
region. The Shah had many personal friends in the Conservative Party and,
once he had left Iran, contacted them about 'the true intentions of Britain'
with regard to the events in Tehran. The possibility of the Shah travelling to
Britain was also brought up. Mrs Thatcher assured the Shah that he would
be welcome in Britain if and when a Conservative government took over.
The Shah had persuaded himself that James Callaghan, the Labour prime
minister, had played a key role in persuading the leaders of the major
industrial nations to abandon the Iranian monarchy, based on erroneous
reports the Shah had received about the 'summit of the rich' on the French
island of Guadeloupe in January 1979.

At the Guadeloupe summit the issue of Iran had been brought up by France's President Valéry Giscard d'Estaing, long considered to be a personal friend of the Shah. Giscard, however, strongly argued that the West should jettison the Shah in order to save Iran from Communism. He painted a disturbing picture of civil war in Iran with eventual involvement by the American military technicians assigned to the Shah's armed forces. This disaster scenario was designed to unnerve Jimmy Carter who had come to Guadeloupe with his own doubts about the Shah's ability to weather the storm. The Shah, wrongly, believed that West German Chancellor Helmut Schmidt, another personal friend, had defended him. Schmidt, in fact, had done the exact opposite, going even further than Giscard in his criticism of the Shah's 'weakness and cruel rule'. The Japanese and the Canadian prime ministers, who had also been present, offered no opinions. The only relatively good words about the Shah as an ally of the West had come from Callaghan.[14] Nevertheless, when Callaghan was defeated at the British general election the Shah believed that one of the enemies of his rule was gone. Mrs Thatcher, the Shah thought, would have a better understanding of Iran's need to have a strong monarchy in order to frustrate Soviet expansionist designs. Very soon, however, the Shah was disappointed. Mrs Thatcher dispatched a former British Ambassador to Tehran, Sir Denis Wright, to Nassau to inform the Shah that he would not be invited to Britain after all.

Nassau, a popular holiday resort, could become excruciatingly boring after a week or two. What is more, the climate did not agree with the Shah whose health began to be affected by the humid weather. Partly to pass the time but also to pursue his political dreams the Shah began writing a book which eventually received the title A Reply To History.[15] He wrote the book with the help of a French ghost writer and an Iranian politician who had once been a Tudeh member. In the book the Shah presented himself as a patriotic leader who had brought his nation out of the Dark Ages and turned it into a regional power. He emphasised his anti-Imperialist credentials, especially with reference to the role Iran had played within OPEC. The Islamic Revolution was described as a conspiracy by 'Imperialists' determined to break Iran and reimpose their hegemony in the Persian Gulf region. The central theme of the book was the claim that the Shah had been 'thrown out of Iran like a mouse by the Americans'.[16] This was, of course, both inexact and self-defeating as proof of the Shah's nationalistic credentials. The readers might wonder why the Shah had to obey Washington's orders to leave the country. The conspiracy theory, however, will always have its adepts if only because if offers a simple and comfortable answer to difficult and disturbing questions.

By June 1979 the question of where he should go next had become an urgent one. His Bahaman visa was no longer valid and the island authorities were not prepared to renew it. All they could do was to give him 10 more days in which to pack and leave. Relations with the Bahaman authorities had soured because of what the Shah believed was 'extortionist prices' charged for his stay. At the end of each week he was presented with a bill of between $120,000 to $130,000 – and payment had to be made immediately. At the same time the Bahaman opposition party used the Shah's presence in Nassau as a good theme with which to attack the government. Ordinary Bahamans began to object to the Shah's presence because they believed the threat of terrorism made against the exiled sovereign might keep tourists away. Each day brought fresh reports or rumours about hit squads being sent to the Bahamas to kill the Shah and his family. An Islamic court in Tehran had, in fact, sentenced the Shah, the Empress, the Crown Prince, Princess Ashraf and the Empress's mother, Mrs Farideh Diba, to death *in absentia* on a charge of 'waging war against Allah'. There were reports that Khomeini had hired 'Carlos', the notorious Venezuelan terrorist, to murder the Shah in Nassau. More seriously, Yasser Arafat, leader of the Palestine Liberation Organisation, was reported to have offered the services of his gunmen to Khomeini for the purpose of eliminating the Shah. Arafat was at that time desperately trying to attach himself to the Islamic Revolution in Iran and attract Iranian support for his campaign against Israel.

Throughout the ordeal the Shah tried to keep up appearances. Anwar Sadat telephoned a number of times to suggest that the royal couple return to Egypt where they would be welcome as long as they wished, but the Shah felt that a return to Egypt would only mean humiliation for him. Worse still, it would diminish the chances of his son acceding to the throne one day; people in Iran would interpret the fact that the Shah could not obtain a visa for the United States as a clear sign that the fallen monarch was totally abandoned by his strongest allies. In those days the American consulates in Tehran, Shiraz and Tabriz were besieged by tens of thousands of Iranians who wished to travel to the United States, most of them to escape revolutionary chaos. Within just a few months more than 100,000 visas were issued to Iranian citizens and twice as many applications were turned down. Now the once mighty Shah, the ruler who had been praised to the skies by eight successive American presidents, was being refused a non-immigrant visa to enter the United States as a tourist. By the end of May the Shah's lobbyists, including Kissinger, knew that President Carter would not change his mind and as a result they speeded up negotiations with the Mexicans.

President Lopez Portillo of Mexico knew the Shah personally and was prepared to grant him a visa for a limited stay. When Zahedi talked to the Shah on the telephone early in June he found the exiled monarch 'in sombre mood'. 'His Majesty showed no sign of weakness in the face of obvious pain, both physical and moral,' Zahedi later recalled. 'But I knew that he was desperate. He told me: "Ardeshir, it's time that we got out of this island." '[17] Just over a week later the Shah, the Empress and the royal suite, including His Majesty's two dogs, left for Cuernavaca, a popular tourist resort that the royal couple had visited during a state visit several years earlier. They had good memories of the place so they arrived in a much better mood: anywhere would have been a relief after Nassau.

For a while the exiles felt almost comfortable. The Shah continued to dictate his book to his French and Iranian ghost writers. The royal children came from the United States to spend the summer holidays with their parents. There was some excitement one day when Crown Prince Reza who, like his father, loved flying, hired a helicopter and flew it over the beach. At one point he directed his chopper right towards the royal villa, hoping to impress his parents. The nervous Mexican guards, thinking this was one of the suicide attacks that Khomeini had promised against the Shah, opened fire at the intruder with their machine-guns. They all missed and the Crown Prince landed his giant toy near the villa, unaware of what had happened. 'I almost wanted to kiss the Mexican guards,' the Empress later recalled. 'I kept telling them how marvellous they were and they couldn't understand because they had been such poor shots.'[18]

The Shah had other visitors. Kissinger called for a two-day stay and helped boost the Shah's morale by discussing high politics with him. Then came President Nixon who, in a sense, wanted to repay the Shah for his kindness back in the 1960s when Nixon himself had been in disgrace. At that time the Shah had invited the former Vice-President, who had suffered a humiliating defeat at the gubernatorial elections in California, to visit Tehran where Nixon had been received like a head of state. After Watergate it was, once again, the Shah who set an example for others by extending to the former president regards and honours normally reserved for the most distinguished leaders of nations.

In Mexico the Shah's health began to deteriorate. He often felt tired and his cancer, never fully acknowledged for reasons of state and still kept a secret, had begun to develop. A team of Mexican doctors were brought in to examine and treat the Shah but they too were kept in the dark about his cancer. The Mexicans said that the Shah might have contracted malaria which the Shah had suffered from in childhood: the Mexicans argued he might now be experiencing a new attack. In any case Cuernavaca, although a resort for the very rich, was not yet quite free of mosquitos. Dr Lucy Pirnia, the paediatrician friend of the Empress, thought His Majesty might have contracted jaundice, a belief encouraged by the Shah's 'face turning saffron yellow'.

When news of the Shah's condition reached New York his lobbyists redoubled their efforts to get him into the United States, this time on purely humanitarian grounds. Princess Ashraf wrote an emotional letter to Carter. 'This was the worst humiliation I had ever suffered in my life,' she later claimed. 'I who had never begged anyone for anything literally begged that heartless man to allow my brother, a dying man, to come to the States for treatment.'[19] Kissinger, Rockefeller and John J. McCloy, the doyen of American politics, also resumed pressure on Carter. The president, however, remained adamant in his decision to keep the exiled monarch out. 'Fuck the Shah,' he told some of his aides. 'I cannot let him come here and play tennis while our people are threatened with death over there.'[20] When David Newsom, Assistant Secretary of State, told a Rockefeller contact that the Shah's application could be reconsidered only if a serious medical case could be made, the lobbyists decided to dispatch a well-known American doctor to Mexico to examine him. The man chosen was Dr Benjamin Kean who was well known and highly respected by many in the American establishment. His views would carry the weight needed to sway opinions within the administration, Rockefeller apparently thought. In Mexico Kean found the Shah in great pain. The doctor decided that his patient was not suffering from either malaria or hepatitis. He began to work on the theory that the Shah might be suffering from pancreatic cancer which causes a form of jaundice. He asked for permission to carry out a blood test which was instantly refused. The Shah had not been comfortable with the Kean mission right from the start. He did not want the Americans to know that he was suffering from cancer and as a result he almost summarily dismissed the distinguished American doctor and, instead, called his French specialist, Georges Flandrin, to fly to Cuernavaca. Flandrin was alarmed by the sudden decline in the Shah's health and suggested that he be hospitalised for further tests.

For Flandrin the Shah put his anti-American disc on. He told the Frenchman to find a hospital 'anywhere except in the United States'. He accused the Americans of having injured his self-esteem and promised 'never to go there even if they begged me'.[21] The next day in early October the Shah was admitted into the university hospital at Mexico City. In mid-October Kean returned and, for the first time, met Flandrin. The American doctor studied a 20-page report prepared by the French specialist on the Shah's condition. The report included a history of the treatment given to the monarch since 1974. Kean concluded that the Shah had not received adequate treatment. (This was, perhaps, because the Shah himself, unwilling to admit that he had cancer, had not allowed the French experts to do more for him.) Kean stuck to his theory that the Shah had pancreatic cancer and urged him to enter a 'proper hospital' where he could receive the treatment needed. Thus began the great wrangle about who should treat the Shah and under what conditions. Flandrin believed that Kean, a specialist in tropical diseases, was not informed enough about the Shah's condition to make a diagnosis. Kean, on the other hand, was manifestly unhappy about what he saw as a situation in which the Shah himself, and not his doctors, had for years managed his own treatment. Kean was now convinced that the Shah could receive proper therapy only in the United States.

The Shah appeared determined not to go to the United States at that time, an interesting change in His Majesty's position. For months he had pressured his friends to do all they could to get him into the country, but now that he seemed to have a chance of obtaining the much-coveted visa he no longer wanted to go. He insisted that Kean, Flandrin and others should get their acts together and arrange for his treatment in Mexico City. Meanwhile the Rockefeller lobby seemed more committed than ever to the cause of getting the Shah into the United States and what happened next was very much like a palace coup. The Rockefeller group, represented at the Shah's bedside by Armao, simply took over. Flandrin was told that he could join a new team to be set up for treating the Shah but should no longer consider himself as the controller of the case. Kean had taken over as the Shah's chief physician. Flandrin was furious and tried to make a scene but he was intelligent enought to realise that he was up against odds that left him little chance. In the meantime Armao continued to work on the Shah by evoking the possibility of terrorist attacks. He told the Shah that the Mexican authorities were not capable of stopping assassins dispatched by Khomeini and that only in the United States would the Shah be safe.

By 17 October the Rockefeller machine had already made the necessary reservations for the Shah at New York Hospital where Amir-Assadollah Alam, the Shah's Minister of Court for years, had died of cancer only a few months earlier. Both the Shah and the Empress regarded the choice of hospital as a sign of poor taste on the part of their American friends. They asked whether it would not be possible to find another institution but their demand was ignored. It seemed that someone had decided that they must go to the United States – and soon – regardless of whether they wanted it or not. The Empress was, by now, even more reluctant than the Shah about what looked like an impending transfer to New York. She was even prepared to return to Egypt where the parliament, urged by President Sadat, had passed a special act that gave the exiled Iranian royal family the right to settle in Egypt for as long as they wished. On 18 October the issue of the Shah's planned trip to New York was raised at the American cabinet and Carter again expressed his opposition. Vance, however, had now changed sides and urged that the Shah be allowed in on humanitarian grounds. The medical report presented to the State Department was used by Hamilton Jordan, White House Chief of Staff, as a strong argument for giving the Shah a visa. 'The man could die in Mexico City,' Jordan told Carter. 'And that would let Kissinger say that you, the president, caused the Shah's downfall and now you have killed him.'[22]

What made Carter change his mind remains a mystery, but two days after the stormy cabinet meeting he agreed that the Shah should be allowed to enter the United States to receive medical treatment on one condition: His Majesty had to leave the United States at the completion of his treatment.

While the Mexican President Lopez Portillo had already assured the Americans that the Shah would be allowed to return to Cuernavaca after his treatment in New York, signals from Tehran remained ambiguous. The pro-American Foreign Minister, Ibrahim Yazdi, informed Washington that the Shah's entry into the United States might create suspicion in Iran that the US was plotting to restore the Shah to his throne, but Yazdi did not formally tell the Americans that giving the Shah a US visa would be regarded as an unfriendly act by the Khomeinist government. The matter was, in fact, never formally discussed between the US administration and the government of the ayatollah. The two sides spoke about it as a side issue but did not seek official clarification about their respective positions.

The Shah, now too ill to walk, left Mexico for the United States aboard a chartered aircraft on the night of 22 October. Farah, tired and shaken, was at his side, trying to remain composed as members of the entourage quietly cried. The aircraft landed at a small airport near Fort Lauderdale in Florida but there was no one to give them permission to enter the United States. Two hours later the immigration officers arrived and formally admitted the party. The aircraft then took off for New York where it landed shortly before dawn. Officials at the airport were told that the aircraft was carrying gold and currency from the Bank of Mexico. The Shah and his party drove to Manhattan where Princess Ashraf had bought a house in the early 1970s, but before they reached the house they were informed on the car telephone that the Shah had to be driven direct to the hospital. The Carter administration had apparently insisted that the Shah should be seen only in the context of medical treatment while in the United States.

At the hospital the Shah was registered under the name of David Newsome – almost the same as that of the assistant secretary of state who had been a strong opponent of the Shah's entry into the United States. No one was quite sure why the Shah had come to the New York Hospital and the doctors there had received no information about the new patient's condition. Flandrin, the only man who had all the information, was back in Paris, sulking. The American doctors carried out tests of their own and gave him a CAT scan. They decided that he had an enlarged spleen and also suffered from gallstones. Dr Morton Coleman joined the team and decided that the Shah's spleen should immediately be removed. The following day, however, Coleman was informed that the Shah had already entered an operating room where his gallbladder was being removed. Confusion was total. What mattered apparently was that the world should be told that the Shah had been admitted into the United States at the very last minute and that he had been taken into an operating theatre almost direct from the airport. Coleman sent a message to the operating theatre to urge that the Shah's spleen be removed at the same time but the surgeons in charge refused: the Shah was too weak to undergo a double operation of that kind. During the operation a sample of the Shah's blood was taken and subsequently tested. It showed that the Shah was suffering from a more serious variety of cancer than the French specialists had diagnosed. The Americans believed that the treatment given by the French to the Shah had been too mild and, as a result, inadequate.

The American doctors had made fun of their French counterparts a bit too early for, a week after the Shah was operated upon, an X-ray showed that the surgeons had left one gallstone well in place to block the bile duct. After extensive wranglings over whether or not a second operation should be performed it was decided that the Shah was too weak to face the ordeal. Iranians, always fond of the conspiracy theory, saw the incident as part of a deliberate plot to kill the Shah. While waiting for the Shah to recover some strength the American medical team decided to use radiation to cure his cancer. But Dr Coleman, the man in charge of treating the Shah's cancer, did not have all the information needed to give the prescribed therapy a real chance of success. The Shah's entourage suggested that he be transferred to the Memorial Sloan-Kettering Cancer Centre just a few hundred yards away. The centre had good relations with the Pahlavis and the dowager Empress had been treated there. The Shah had donated more than a million dollars to the centre as part of a $10,000,000 package of gifts offered to American universities and scientific centres in the mid-1970s. When the issue of the Shah's treatment at the centre was brought up at the centre's board, however, some trustees said they did not want their benefactor as a patient. After bitter disputes the board finally agreed to let the Shah be treated on one condition: the Shah's treatment had to be conducted almost in secrecy. The centre was connected with the New York Hospital through an underground tunnel. It was ordained by the board that the Shah should be taken to the centre through the tunnel in the dead of night and be whisked back to his hospital room immediately after each session of treatment. This was further humiliation for the Shah as he was woken up at 3 or 4 am, placed on a wheelchair and quickly rushed through the tunnel. The exercise soon demoralised and physically exhausted him and he began to fear for his life. He communicated with some of his visitors only in writing for fear that their conversation would be taped. To one visitor he jotted down these words: 'If something happens, know that there was a plot.'[23] Whenever they had a chance to be alone the Shah and his wife shared their apprehensions about what was going on. 'I had a prayer constantly on my lips,' the Empress later recalled. 'It was a simple one: O God, give him strength.'[24] The Empress's prayer was granted. The Shah remained calm and composed despite his obvious great physical pain and tremendous moral pressure.

While the Shah fought for his life and tried to retain his sanity at the New York Hospital his opponents, notably Ayatollah Khomeini, were waging a bitter propaganda war against him. The ayatollah himself was, of course, far away in the holy city of Qom, but his supporters maintained a round-the-clock vigil not far from the New York Hospital. They organised collective prayers and poured abuse against the Shah through loudhailers that could be heard by the patient in his hospital room. He was called 'thief' and 'tyrant' by Iranian students, many of whom had been sent to the United States on scholarships from the Pahlavi Foundation. Ghotbzadeh, Khomeini's chief spokesman, asked for the 'stolen $56 billion' the Shah had supposedly taken from Iran.[25] Khomeini's manager for the Central Bank of Iran, Ali-Reza Nobari, cited the more modest figure of £800,000,000, but he admitted that he had no documentary proof for his claim. After weeks of propaganda the Khomeinist government unearthed a cheque for $16,000 that had been credited to a foreign currency account that bore the name of Princess Shams.[26]

By the end of October the Shah had recovered enough of his strength to sit up in his hospital bed and watch television. American TV at that time was, of course, full of Iranian events. The Shah's presence in the United States had also developed into an election issue within the American Democrat Party with Senator Edward Kennedy, a candidate for the presidential nomination, using the issue against Carter. Kennedy compared the Shah with Hitler and believed that Carter had shamed the United States by letting the fallen 'tyrant' in. Numerous Iranologists appeared on the little screen to echo Kennedy's vitriolic remarks. For the first time in his life the Shah began to realise what American politics was all about. 'These people will do anything to get votes,' he remarked to one visitor.[27] But even then he could not have imagined the storm that was to break out in the next days.

A whole week after the Shah's arrival in the United States the long-anticipated and much-feared attack on the American embassy in Tehran had not yet materialised. There was no sense of tension in or around the embassy and the American Chargé d'Affaires, Bruce Laingen, was the only foreign diplomat who had almost immediate access to the new ministers appointed by Khomeini. At the same time President Carter had chosen a lawyer, Lloyd Cutler, as his nominee for the post of Ambassador to Tehran. Relations between Tehran and Washington were good enough for the two sides to agree on a meeting at a very high level. On 1 November 1979 Khomeini's prime minister, Mehdi Bazargan, who was in Morocco for an Islamic summit conference, held a long and friendly meeting with Bzrezinski who had also arrived in Rabat, ostensibly for talks with King Hassan. Khomeini's foreign minister, Ibrahim Yazdi, a naturalised American of Iranian origin, was also present at the Bazargan-Bzrezinski meeting. The message Bazargan wished to pass on to the American government was simple: All we wanted to do was to get rid of the Shah, otherwise Iran wishes to maintain its privileged relations with the United States. Khomeini later claimed that the Rabat meeting had taken place without his knowledge. Bazargan, however, has written and said that his mission was fully explained to the Ayatollah and explicitly approved by him. Whatever the truth, it soon became clear that the Rabat meeting had alarmed many within the Khomeinist camp.

The Tudeh Communists had supported Khomeini in the hope that Soviet influence would, in time, replace the American presence in Iran. Now they felt cheated out of their share in the victory over the Shah. The various urban guerrilla groups who had also helped Khomeini come to power based their entire ideology on a hatred of the United States. The radical mullahs around Khomeini himself were angered by Bazargan's initiative because they themselves wanted to make a deal with the United States and dominate Iran's politics in the name of anti-Communism. But none of these groups knew exactly what to do to counter what they saw as Bazargan's manoeuvres. Their problem was solved by a group of radical students and unemployed graduates who on 4 November attacked the embassy compound. At first they had meant to create a few dramatic moments in which they could pose as true revolutionaries. Khomeini's revolution had succeeded too quickly and left tens of thousands of excited young men and women almost frustrated. By the time most of them had joined the revolution the whole thing had been over. Now they thirsted for some action and a little bit of glory.

For years many radicals had been chanting the slogan: 'Iran is the Next Vietnam.' But Iran had not become the next Vietnam. There was not to be a long civil war. The Iranians had proved too clever, some might say too opportunistic, to divide into two large camps and fight each other to the bitter end. Once it had become apparent that the Shah, for whatever reason, did not have the stomach for a fight, most of his supporters either joined the revolution, becoming more radical than the radicals, or simply stayed at home. As the first day of the attack on the embassy wore on someone announced that the attackers would not leave until the Shah and all his wealth were handed back to Iran by the United States. Once that had been said there was nowhere else that the seekers of revolutionary glory could go. Khomeini, after a day's hesitation, decided to side with the raiders of the embassy who took over 120 people, including 53 diplomats, hostage. Khomeini, then still in Qom, could have told the attackers to leave the embassy and liberate their hostages, but had he done that he might have run the risk of appearing too soft at a time when tough and uncompromising leaders were in demand by the crowds. The Shah had lost because he had been perceived as *sholl* (indecisive), incapable of ordering one of those massacres that have saved many a Middle-Eastern tyrant from destruction. Khomeini knew that and was determined to let no one upstage him in revolutionary fervour. Thus the irresponsible action of a bunch of bored adolescents became the official policy of Iran and provoked one of the longest and toughest international crises in contemporary history. It caused 444 days of captivity for 53 men and women and in the end cost Iran billions of dollars in losses incurred as a result of the freeze Carter imposed on Iranian assets.

The whole world, of course, blamed the crisis on the Shah, but the dying man in New York Hospital was no more than an excuse for a drama that had to be acted out on the stage of Iran's revolution. At the end of 1979 history still hesitated as to which course to take in Iran. One course was to maintain the traditional Iranian society in place with a number of long-overdue reforms. The Shah was gone but there was no need to destroy the entire constitutional and legal structures of society. A limited amendment of the 1906 Constitution could have turned Iran into a republic without pulling the whole country apart. Better still, Khomeini, determined to exercise personal power, could have declared himself king and founded a new dynasty. But he had grown to hate anything even remotely connected with the word Shah and the institution of monarchy and he had instilled enough of that hatred into the souls of enough people to make a smooth transition virtually impossible. The revolution needed a hate symbol and that hate symbol was the Shah. And now that he was dying it was necessary to merge his image into a new symbol of hate: the American Great Satan.

While President Carter wondered what to do about a crisis that threatened not only his chances of a second term at the White House but also the unity of his administration, the Shah's doctors quarrelled about how best to treat their patient. Dr Coleman was dropped from the team after Dr Kean found his methods 'too aggressive'. Dr Coleman, of course, believed that he had been right all along: the Shah's spleen should have been removed immediately and chemotherapy should have been stopped at least for a while. The Shah no longer seemed to care. All he wanted was to get out of the United States as fast as he could. A special aircraft was chartered to take him and his entourage back to Mexico on 3 December. On 30 November, however, the Mexican Consul General in New York informed the Shah that the Mexican government was no longer prepared to readmit the royal party. The best the Mexicans could do was to let the Shah go back to Cuernavaca for a few days to 'collect his personal effects and settle his bills', but a longer stay in Mexico would be impossible. President Lopez Portillo had decided that readmittance would be contrary to Mexico's national interests.

Once again, the exile was without a home while every day Carter stamped his feet and insisted that the Shah be removed from US soil as fast as possible. The hospital staff also insisted that the Shah ought to vacate his room on 3 December as already decided. On 2 December the royal suitcases were packed and the Shah was getting ready to leave the hospital for his sister's home less than a mile away, but then came news that a special emissary from President Carter would call on His Majesty for an urgent meeting. The emissary was Lloyd Cutler, the ambassador-designate to Iran who was, of course, convinced that he could not go to Tehran before the crisis unleashed by the seizure of the hostages had been sorted out.

Cutler told the Shah that he had to leave New York immediately. He was polite but firm: the royal couple should fly to Lackland Air Base in Texas where the Shah could use the facilities of 'the excellent hospital there'. Everything had to be done in secret: even the royal children were not to be told where their parents were going. The Shah and the Empress were not to take anyone with them: only the Shah's favourite dogs, two Great Danes, could accompany their master. The Shah was, of course, made to understand that he had no choice. Cutler was, in fact, delivering an arrest warrant. And when a bunch of rough 'gorillas' poured into the Shah's room in the middle of the night and asked him to get moving the whole operation began to look more like kidnapping. The Shah, put in a wheelchair, was taken out of the hospital through the basement and quickly pushed into a car already full of security agents. The Empress was whisked to another car by another group of agents. At La Guardia Airport the royal couple boarded an Air Force plane headed for Texas. There were no smiles and no service on board apart from cold coffee served in plastic cups. At Lackland Air Base the Shah and his wife were quickly bundled into an ambulance which drove at top speed towards an unknown destination. Minutes later the ambulance stopped and the royal couple were asked to get out. They were led into a building where they were greeted by a number of male nurses all dressed in white. This was the base's psychiatric ward. The commander of the base muttered some explanation to the effect that this was the safest place on the base and that no terrorist would be able to penetrate it. The Shah was directed into a narrow room at the centre of which stood a high metal bed. The room had no window. The Empress was given the room next door with a small window which could be opened a couple of inches to let some fresh air in.

The Shah and the Empress exchanged questions through their glances. They believed that they had been arrested: but was Carter cynical enough to hand them over to Ayatollah Khomeini in exchange for the American hostages? The Shah apparently did not think so: he still believed that his American friends would rescue him and during his last days in hospital he had had visits from a number of them including Rockefeller, Kissinger, Senator Goldwater and even Frank Sinatra. No, Carter could not send them back to Iran which would mean certain death. The Empress was not so sure. 'At that time we thought Carter was capable of anything to ensure his re-election,' she later recalled.[28]

An hour after they had been pushed into their rooms the Shah and the Empress managed to obtain an interview with the commander of the base. 'Are we under arrest?' the Empress asked point blank. 'No Your Majesty,' came the answer. She was allowed to make a telephone call to New York to inform her mother, Mrs Farideh Diba, of what had happened. Mrs Diba reported that Princess Leila, the youngest of the royal children, had been crying all day long because she did not know where her mother had suddenly disappeared to and why. The Empress talked to Leila, then aged only eight, and reassured her. Then she talked to Princess Ashraf, who could not control her emotions.

A few hours later the Shah and his wife were transferred to another wing of the hospital. This one looked less sinister: the Shah's room had a window and there were no iron bars. The royal couple knew they were under some kind of arrest but they no longer felt as if they were in prison. The following day the situation improved still further as the royal couple were moved into a tiny apartment used for visiting officers and their families. Initially the couple were told they should not venture out of their apartment for fear of assassination. Later, however, the commander of the base, General Acker, agreed that the danger had been much exaggerated and the Empress could take the Shah, still in a wheelchair, our for short walks. The royal couple were also invited to dinner by the base commander and met some of the officers who had either served in Iran or had helped train thousands of Iranian pilots and Air Force engineers at Lackland over the years.

While they were at Lackland the royal couple received news that Prince Shahryar, the second son of Princess Ashraf, had been murdered by an unknown hit squad in Paris. Shahryar, one of Iran's youngest naval commanders, had arrived in the French capital a few weeks earlier to establish contact with political groups opposed to the ayatollah. He was determined to organise a revolt the spearhead of which would be the Persian Gulf fleet which he had commanded until Khomeini seized power. Shahryar was probably murdered by Communist urban terrorists. His sister, Princess Azadeh, suspected 'certain foreign powers' who did not wish to 'see Iran make a comeback on the regional scene'.[29] In Tehran, however, Ayatollah Sadeq Khalkhali, a close friend and associate of Khomeini, announced that Shahryar had been murdered on his orders. Khalkhali, nicknamed 'the Hanging Judge' by his opponents, also said that he had dispatched other hit squads to kill the Shah, his wife and their children.

Once again efforts to find the Shah a safe haven found a new momentum. There was more bad news from Tehran as the execution of former officials and military commanders continued: Khomeini's Imam Committees also arrested the Shah's youngest brother, Hamid Reza, who had stayed behind in Tehran. Hamid Reza had been divested of his titles and expelled from court many years earlier for misbehaviour that included the abuse of drugs and chronic indebtedness. His arrest showed that the ruling mullahs were determined to pursue their vendetta against the Pahlavis at all costs.

Meanwhile Senator Edward Kennedy and his friends continued their attacks on the Shah, some newspaper columnists even suggesting that the

Shah should voluntarily give himself up to the Khomeinist authorities in order to facilitate the liberation of the American embassy hostages. Princess Ashraf was convinced that someone might develop the idea of murdering the Shah in the United States in order to impose a solution to the hostage crisis. It was early in December when Panama's strongman, General Omar Torrijos, informed the Carter administration that he would be prepared to offer the Shah a temporary refuge. The offer was passed on to the Shah at Lackland by Cutler and Jordan. Once again he was made to understand that he had no other choice. It was left to Armao to negotiate terms. The agreement reached was that the Shah would go to Panama on the understanding that he could return to the United States for medical treatment when and if that became necessary. Why did Torrijos, a macho dictator who had amassed considerable personal fortunes from dubious sources, invite the Shah? The reason he himself gave was that he wanted to help get Carter out of a tight corner. Carter had negotiated a new treaty with Panama that transferred control of the canal to the Panamanian authorities before the end of the century. The treaty had been strongly opposed by the American Republicans who promised they would abrogate it at the first opportunity. Torrijos therefore wished to see Carter remain in the White House. The Shah's entourage had other theories. They believed that Torrijos was after the Shah's money. Torrijos was involved in countless shady deals, often in partnership with his close friend and associate Manuel Noriega, and there was no reason to believe that he would be interested in a purely political move.

On 15 December the Shah, his wife, a few servants and attendants and the inevitable Great Danes, were flown to Panama City aboard a chartered jet. The royal party were housed at the former residence of a wealthy Panamanian diplomat on the island of Contadora. A detachment of the Panamanian National Guard commanded by Noriega – then only a colonel – was given the mission of protecting the Shah against would-be assassins. A day after the royal party had arrived at Contadora, Torrijos flew in aboard his helicopter to welcome the Shah. The Shah found the Panamanian dictator 'vulgar and uncouth' and he could not understand how Carter, who made so much of his Christian values and love of human rights, could have struck such a close friendship with an adventurer who seemed oblivious of ethics. Before leaving for Panama the Shah received a telephone call from Carter who wished to say goodbye. Carter had not talked to the Shah since September 1978 and now, more than three months later, he called to say that he was sure the Shah would have a good time in Panama.

In his meeting with the Shah, Torrijos kept talking about 'my friend Jimmy Carter' and pretended that he and the American president were 'almost like family'. What the Shah especially disliked about Torrijos was the Panamanian's expansive and chummy attitude. Torrijos admitted that he had never seen a king before and did not know how to address the royalty correctly and kept referring to his guest as 'Señor Shah', an appellation that infuriated the monarch. There was another problem: Torrijos seemed to take an unusual interest in Empress Farah and on a number of occasions he invited her to visit him alone. The excuse given was that the Shah might not be well enough to attend a party. The Empress politely refused the invitations but the sticky general would not give up, sending messengers and flowers. It was both comical and irritating. On a few occasions when the royal couple attended lunches and dinners given by Torrijos, the Latin dictator tried to play the role of a world statesman and offered opinions about issues he knew little or nothing about.

Despite the irritation caused by Torrijos's behaviour the royal exile in Panama was an undoubted improvement over Lackland. At Lackland the Shah had, for the first time perhaps, stopped playing 'the King of Kings' and made it clear how deeply dependent he had become on his wife's love and affection. 'It is here and now more than anywhere else and any other time that I feel you are my wife,' he once told the Empress. 'And I want you to know that you are also my best friend.'[30] The Shah had always used the royal we even in private conversations with his wife, but now, gravely ill and deeply humiliated, he was content to say 'I'. He had returned to earth, a demigod reincarnated as a frail, suffering and fragile man. On Contadora he was the attentive husband and, when the royal children flew in for holidays from the United States, the loving father. He continued to coach the Crown Prince in the art of Persian politics. He laughed at Prince Ali-Reza's imitation of the ayatollahs. He played tennis with Princess Farahanaz and, for the first time, found time to enjoy the presence of his youngest daughter Princess Leila. He also pursued his political plans – or, rather, illusions.

Initially the Shah had forecast that the mullahs would be out of power within a year. Now he pinned his hopes on the belief that Khomeini's death would mean the end of the ayatollah's regime. And with Khomeini gone the Iranian people would have no one to turn to but their Shah. At that point he would simply suggest that his son be put on the throne. By that time too Carter would be out of the White House and Ronald Reagan, an old friend, would be President of the United States.* Everything would then go back to normal and the revolutionary episode would be wiped from memory.

The Empress did not get directly involved in the Shah's political projects, but she helped by writing countless letters and making numerous telephone calls. Princess Ashraf was also busy organising supporters of the monarchy in exile. The first pro-monarchy bulletins in

*The Shah had received Reagan in audience in Tehran in May 1978 when the former governor and his wife had come on a private tour of Iran as guests of Zahedi. Reagan and his wife had also been Zahedi's guests at the Iranian Embassy in Washington. Reagan had been impressed by the Shah.

exile had already started publishing and the Egyptian authorities had
provided a radio transmitter for programmes beamed into Iran. General
Oveissi had gathered a group of exiled officers and ministers around
himself in the name of the Shah and was in contact with the monarch
through Ahmad Ansari, a cousin of Empress Farah. The Empress also
maintained contact with former Premier Bakhtiar who had created his
own organisation in exile in Paris. Much of the finance for these diverse
activities came from Princess Ashraf who had gathered around her an
impressive group of former officials that included Abdul-Reza Ansari
and Akbar Etemad.

The Khomeinist authorities in Tehran were aware of the political
activities directly or indirectly inspired by the Shah and were determined
to destroy the man they considered to be the only real threat to their rule.
Ghotbzadeh, Khomeini's Foreign Minister, established contact with
Torrijos and tried to whet the general's appetite for money by evoking the
prospect of generous financial aid from Iran to Panama. Ghotbzadeh who
had for years worked for the Syrian secret services, also offered money to
PLO freelance terrorists in the hope of one day using them for the purpose
of eliminating the Shah. In the meantime he also spent money among
Panamanian opposition parties who staged protest marches against the
Shah's presence in the country. One argument they used was that the
Shah's visit had led to a sharp drop in the number of tourists coming to
Panama. The North American clientele of Panama's best hotels were
terrified of getting caught in terrorist crossfire or mob riots staged against
the Shah. In the meantime Jordan, strongly supported by Carter,
established direct contact with Ghotbzadeh in the hope of securing the
release of the hostages. At a later stage Jordan was to meet Hassan
Ibrahim Habibi, a special envoy of Ayatollah Muhammad Beheshti, then
the strongman of the Khomeinist regime and leader of the pro-American
faction among the mullahs. News of Jordan's unorthodox diplomacy
soon leaked out in the European press. Torrijos began to think that Carter
and his close aides would do virtually anything to get the hostages out
before the American presidential election. Couldn't he, Torrijos, kill two
birds with one stone by handing the Shah over to Ghotbzadeh? Such a
move would ensure Carter's re-election and also restore Torrijos'
declining fortunes to robust health. The general had made lots of money
but also had lots of expenses. And Ghotbzadeh had hinted at serious
money – one of the figures mentioned was £800,000,000. Ghotbzadeh,
who was at that time himself running for president in an election
organised by Khomeini, knew that getting the Shah into his hands would
make him the first ever president in Iran's multimillennial history. Every
night he was on the telephone to Torrijos offering the general money,
women, a share in Iran's oil exports and whatever else he could think of.[31]
At one point he suggested that Torrijos put the Shah behind bars,
photograph him there and send the pictures to Tehran. 'We could then tell

the ayatollah that we have the man he wants,' Ghotbzadeh said. 'This would cut ten years off the old man's age.'[32] Torrijos however was noncommital: he wanted the money but he was not sure about the possible reaction of his friend Jimmy Carter. Noriega, a CIA agent as well as a Torrijos associate, must have learned about all this and reported it back to his controllers in Panama City and Washington DC. That the Carter administration did not choose to probe into these reports, compounded by other rumours, was an indication that Carter didn't care what happened to the Shah.

The idea of murdering the Shah had been put to Jordan by Ghotbzadeh at a secret meeting the two men had in Paris. Jordan had vehemently rejected the idea but he continued to negotiate with Ghotbzadeh and later remained in touch with him for several more months, showing that the idea of putting the Shah to death – maybe through an injection arranged by the CIA, as Ghotbzadeh had suggested – was still a proposal being put to him.

One who was certain that the Shah could be in danger in Panama was Princess Ashraf. She visited her brother in his new exile home a number of times and had meetings with both Torrijos and Noriega. She found the Panamanian strongman and his associates 'a bunch of gangsters in uniform, very much like characters out of old Humphrey Bogart movies'.[33] Soon still shadier characters arrived on the scene and the business of getting Carter off the hook developed into an international industry in which a variety of adventurers sought personal fame and fortune. Among them was an international fixer who had once worked as chauffeur to the Argentine dictator Juan Peron. The fixer negotiated a deal under which Tehran would present Panama with a demand for the Shah's extradition and Panama would promise to examine that demand through legal channels. In exchange, Torrijos would become the beneficiary of 'a gesture of appreciation' from Ghotbzadeh and the former chauffeur would end up several times richer. Carter, who met the fixer and his associates in his Oval Office at the White House, encouraged the deal. On 23 January 1980 Ghotbzadeh announced in Tehran that the Shah had been arrested by the Panamanian authorities. Torrijos was furious: he had hoped to make himself richer without actually provoking a larger international crisis by handing the Shah over to the mullahs. But would Torrijos be as furious if the Shah simply died as if of natural causes? Ghotbzadeh's agents had already started working on that possibility also. There were enough people who would do anything for money.

Soon after taking up residence on Contadora the Shah was subjected to constant pressure – at first subtle but later more aggressive – to invest in Panama. Torrijos's friends and mistresses appeared at the royal residence with all manner of projects, mostly related to real estate, in which they wanted the Shah to invest. The fact that the Shah told all of them that he did not have the kind of money they believed he had made them angry and rude. On a number of occasions Noriega offered to arrange for the Shah to meet prostitutes. Later Noriega even claimed that the Shah, then too ill to engage in gallant escapades, had in fact taken up the offer and spent a night of indiscretion with a young companion at a hotel at Panama City. On that occasion the Shah had, indeed, been absent from Contadora for a few hours, but the monarch's own version of the disappearance was different: he had gone to Panama City for a meeting with the American Ambassador who wished to convey to him a message from Carter.

The political and moral pressure the Shah had to endure on Contadora did not help his condition. His spleen continued to enlarge and his cancer developed further. The debate between his French and American doctors was now joined by the Panamanian doctors who had been virtually imposed on him by his new hosts. In March the possibility of removing the Shah's spleen was raised once more. Everyone agreed that it had to be done. The Panamanians wanted to do it themselves in consultation with Flandrin who had flown in from Paris on one of his frequent visits. Dr Kean and his American group, however, had other ideas: it was Dr Michael DeBakey and his team who were to carry out the operation. The Panamanian doctors saw this as an insult: their macho pride was hurt by what looked like a deliberate provocation by the gringos. Matters became worse when a number of American friends of the Shah began to tell the media that they believed the Shah should come to the United States for the operation since Panama might not have the necessary equipment and personnel. DeBakey's arrival at Panama City brought the dispute to a head. The Panamanians insisted that the American doctor and his team had been invited to join the operation, not to monopolise it. DeBakey for his part was adamant: either he was in charge or he would withdraw. The possibility of taking the Shah back to Lackland for the operation was raised. The Shah himself was not keen on the idea and Carter, making his views known through Cutler, said the Shah would not be readmitted into the United States in spite of the earlier promise. There was no way for DeBakey and Kean to force their way into the operating theatre of the main hospital in Panama City and even if they did there could be no guarantee that the vengeful Panamanians would not pull some stunt to make sure that the operation failed.

With the Shah in urgent need of an operation and the United States closed to the royal exiles, once again there was nowhere to turn to except Egypt. Empress Farah telephoned Mrs Jehan Sadat and informed her of what was happening in Panama. 'Come and have the operation here,' Mrs Sadat told the Empress, who was delighted. Later Sadat himself called his sick friend: 'Come to your second home Mohammad,' he said. 'You can have the best care and facilities needed.' The Shah was grateful: he could no longer wait for his various doctors to settle their quarrels.

The Shah hoped that he would be able to set out for Egypt on 20

March, on the eve of the Iranian New Year. It turned out, however, that Carter was strongly opposed to the Shah's return to Egypt and meant to try and stop the enterprise. Carter believed that the Shah's presence in Egypt would add to Sadat's political problems including opposition from radical elements who regarded his bilateral peace with Israel as a betrayal of the Arab cause. That Sadat himself did not share these apprehensions was apparently not enough to reassure Carter. Accordingly, the American president dispatched Jordan to Panama with instructions to stop the Shah's flight to Egypt. A day before Jordan's arrival another visitor had come to Panama City with the same mission. He was Christian Bourguet, a Frenchman working for Ghotbzadeh. With him he had brought a formal demand for the Shah's extradition to Iran, duly signed by Ghotbzadeh and the Khomeinist Justice Minister in Tehran. The presence of the two men in the same city was supposed to be the product of pure coincidence, but Jordan and Bourguet quickly met to discuss a full agenda. Bourguet said that if the Shah returned to the United States or flew back to Egypt the American hostages in Tehran would be put to death. Jordan believed the threat which, at least in hindsight, appears to have had absolutely no foundation in reality. The Khomeinist hostage-takers were not mad enough to kill anybody: they needed the hostages alive and meant to use them as bargaining chips in an eventual settlement with the United States.

Torrijos met Jordan and told his gringo friend that there were ways of preventing the Shah from leaving Panama. Jordan remained silent, a fact that encouraged the strongman that his friend would not object to unorthodox methods being used. Later Jordan met the Shah himself and urged him to accept surgery in Panama. The Shah said he would rather return to Lackland, in accordance with the wishes of his American doctors. Jordan said he would ask the president. When Jordan called Carter he was told that all the president's senior advisers were with him at the Oval Office: Carter renewed his opposition to the Shah's return to the United States; Bzrezinski was, once again, in favour of welcoming the Shah; Vance said he, too, would agree if the Shah would abdicate and renounce all claims by himself and his family to the Iranian crown. The president agreed that this 'compromise' be put to the Shah. The assignment was given to Lloyd Cutler and Arnie Raphael.

Once in Panama Cutler and Raphael tried to see the Shah alone; even Empress Farah was to be kept out. The idea was to isolate the Shah, then more indecisive than ever, and force him into accepting the final humiliation of his life. The Americans, however, had underestimated the Shah's capacity to fight back when something essential was at stake. He regarded himself as heir to Cyrus the Great and would not relinquish his birthright simply because two indelicate cigar-smoking Americans asked him to do so.

The meeting took place on the first day of the Iranian New Year. The

U.S. Government gave the impression of being anxious to offer a special present to Khomeini. The meeting started with the usual banalities as the Americans waited for Empress Farah to leave the room but she remained at his side. Cutler opened discussions by suggesting that the Shah remain in Panama. The Shah said he knew that he was a dying man and was prepared for 'the final stage in my life', but he wanted to die with honour and not as a result of a medical error or a conspiracy financed by his enemies. Cutler then brought up the Vance 'compromise': the Shah's abdication would calm down the Khomeinist radicals and allow Washington to welcome His Majesty back into Lackland where DeBakey could operate. At this the Empress turned to her husband and, speaking in Persian so that the Americans would not understand, said that the demand made by Washington was 'out of the question'. 'Tell them to pack up and go,' she suggested.[34] The Shah only smiled. The Empress then turned to Cutler and, speaking in English this time, said that the Shah's abdication would not solve anything. Iran's monarchy would stay alive. 'My eldest son will claim the crown,' she said. 'And if he gives up my second son will come forward. Monarchy is a gift from God to the Iranian nation and the Shah is its personification.'[35] This argument, based on Persian mythology, history and constitutional tradition, was too complex for the visitors to fully appreciate but the message was clear: there would be no abdication. The Shah concluded the meeting by saying: 'Thank you gentlemen. I'll inform you of my final thoughts tomorrow.'

In Washington Carter continued his efforts to stop the Shah from going to Egypt. He telephoned Sadat to suggest that the Shah be told to stay in Panama until the end of the hostage crisis but Sadat would not change his mind: the Shah was 'like a brother' and Egypt was 'his second home'. He even informed Carter that a special presidential aircraft had already set out for Panama to pick up the Shah and his party.

The Shah could not wait for the Egyptian plane to arrive. He asked Armao to charter an aircraft and the contract went to an American firm which took £150,000 and sent an almost derelict machine. On 23 March 1980 the aircraft with the Shah and his party of nine people and two dogs, flew out of Panama en route for Cairo via the Azores where a refuelling stop had been negotiated at the last minute. Throughout the day Ghotbzadeh had continued to ring Jordan, Torrijos and Bourguet in Panama City with a variety of scenarios about freeing the hostages in exchange for keeping the Shah in Panama until Iran's extradition demand was examined by a Panamanian court of law. What was remarkable was that the Carter administration had not yet realised that Ghotbzadeh had no real power in Iran and was no more than an adventurer pursuing his own ambitions. Ghotbzadeh continued his desperate campaign even after news of the Shah's departure from Panama had been announced. Jordan was still in Panama City, relaxing at the poolside of his friend Torrijos, when Ghotbzadeh called again to suggest that the Shah's plane be stopped at Azores for forty-eight hours so that the release of the hostages could be arranged. Did Jordan agree to play the game as suggested by Ghotbzadeh? In his memoirs the American says that he refused; he even claims that he got angry with his Khomeinist interlocutor.

The Shah's plane was stopped in the Azores even after it had refuelled. The excuse given was that permission for the route had not arrived yet. The delay at Azores lasted more than two hours during which Torrijos called Ghotbzadeh and said that a way could be found to prevent the Shah from reaching Egypt provided Ghotbzadeh could take control of the hostages himself. Ghotbzadeh, who was the kidnappers' *bête noire* and was himself in danger of being taken hostage, continued to bluff: he would deliver the goods in 24 hours. Torrijos lost his temper. 'Go put your face in . . .' he shouted and put the receiver down.[36] He informed Jordan that Ghotbzadeh could no longer be taken seriously. Jordan agreed and twenty minutes later the Shah's aircraft was given permission to leave the Azores.

Death by the Nile

'The worst flight of my life' is how the Shah described the journey from Panama to Cairo aboard the aging DC8 he had chartered with help from the Carter administration. During the long Atlantic crossing the Shah felt unwell most of the time. This was unusual for a trained pilot who had many thousands of hours of flying in a wide variety of aircraft on his record. Although he did not yet know it, the Shah was, by now, a dying man.

At Cairo Airport President Sadat and his wife Jehan were on hand to offer a state welcome to the exiles. From there the Sadats and their guests flew to the Qubbah Palace aboard a helicopter. The Shah remembered the Qubbah well. It had been at Qubbah where, some 40 years earlier, he had courted Princess Fawzia who later became his first wife. Now Qubbah was to become his exile home. After a brief rest at the palace the Shah and his wife, still accompanied by the Sadats, flew to the Maadai military hospital. Sadat wanted the Shah to have a complete and immediate medical check-up. The Egyptian leader did not know what exactly might have happened to his sick friend in Mexico, the Bahamas, the United States and Panama. Had Sadat suspected the Americans of having been less then trustworthy in their relations with the Shah? The president himself said nothing on the subject but his wife Jehan later revealed that Sadat had come to believe that the Americans had, at one point, toyed with the idea of sending the Shah back to Tehran.

The Shah's entourage at any rate suspected the Carter administration of harbouring the vilest of intentions against the fallen monarch. They even believed that the derelict chartered aircraft had been chosen as a death trap: an air crash could have killed the Shah, solved the problem of the hostages and ensured Carter's re-election.

The Egyptian doctors who examined the Shah at Maadai described his condition as serious. His spleen had swollen to ten times the normal size and an operation was urgently needed. On 25 March Dr DeBakey arrived at the Shah's bedside where he was met by Dr Flandrin who had already flown in from Paris. DeBakey's team included four Egyptian doctors, one of them Sadat's son-in-law, and carried out a 45-minute operation on the Shah. Empress Farah and the royal children watched the operation on closed circuit television at the hospital. The operation was declared a complete success and everyone congratulated everyone. Sadat distributed Egyptian decorations among the doctors and the nurses involved.

The euphoria produced by the successful removal of the Shah's spleen was shortlived. A test of the Shah's liver tissue showed that it was in an advanced state of malignancy and when Dr Kean saw the results he concluded that the Shah did not have long to live. Kean's view, however, was rejected by the Shah's entourage and disputed by other doctors. Within a few days American, French, Egyptian and Iranian doctors were at each others' throats once again.

In April DeBakey returned to Cairo where Dr Coleman, who had earlier been eased out of the team by Dr Kean, was now at the Shah's bedside with support from Princess Ashraf. For his part Flandrin had strengthened his alliance with the Empress and was preparing a counter *coup* to oust the Americans, his revenge for a previous *coup* by the Americans in New York Hospital. The doctors quarrelled but could not even agree on a diagnosis. None was prepared to take the hard decisions needed and at one point even President Sadat was dragged into the dispute and tried to negotiate a settlement. He had less success than in negotiating peace with Israel.

The American doctors found it impossible to carry on and gave Flandrin an opportunity to complete his takeover of the case. By the end of June he had achieved complete victory by expelling the last of the Americans although Kean, in New York, was still theoretically in charge. On 30 June a French surgeon carried out a second operation on the Shah, this time to drain the infection that had filled his abdomen. The Egyptian press, meanwhile, conducted a campaign against 'foreign doctors' who were supposed to have made major mistakes in the first operation. Flandrin's takeover was angrily received all around. Kean announced that he had severed his links with the case. Furious, the Egyptian doctors went to see Sadat who told them to stay out of the *mêlée*. Meanwhile the Shah continued to bleed and had to undergo several more operations supposed to stop his haemorrhage.

At Maadai the Shah was often so sick that he could not work for more than an hour or so each day. He spent what little time he had on the American version of his book. An American ghost writer helped him with it and Empress Farah checked the prepared text. The Empress also assigned Hushang Montasseri, a former Communist turned ardent monarchist, to the task of preparing 'the political testament' of the Shah. Montasseri wrote a text which, after numerous corrections by the Empress, was ready for submission to the Shah by mid-July. He never saw the text; by then he was already too ill to take important decisions.

Both the American version of the Shah's book and the so-called 'testament' prepared by Montasseri tried to offer a coherent account of what had happened to the Shah. The thesis put forward was simple: the Shah, a great patriot and moderniser, had transformed Iran from a backward peasant country into a modern medium-size power: the United States saw this development with concern; how could she allow a regional power dominate the Persian Gulf which contained two-thirds of the world's oil resources? Thus Iran had to become weak, divided and subject to internal discord; and the best way to achieve that was to overthrow the Shah. The revolution had been fomented by American and British agents with the help of the Soviets who had their own reasons for wanting to destroy Iran.

Did the Shah himself believe the analysis that was subsequently put forward in his name? We shall never know for sure. He had on occasions harped on similar themes but he was too experienced a politician to be satisfied with so crude an explanation of so complex a phenomenon as the Iranian revolution.

On his deathbed at Maadai the Shah had brief moments of joy. He mobilised his very last ounces of energy to talk to his son in the hope of instructing him in the art of statesmanship. But did the son see his father, now a broken man and a half-living symbol of political defeat, as a worthy model? The answer must be no. In subsequent years the son missed no opportunity to point out his father's 'many errors' and insisted that when and if he himself won the Persian crown he would not reign as his father had. The dying Shah also spent some time with his other children and tried to cheer them up. He kept his dry sense of humour until the very end and when Zahedi tried to console him by saying that he would soon recover, the Shah replied: 'I always knew you were a good doctor, Ardeshir.'[1] Zahedi was now the only former senior official to be at the Shah's side. 'I loved the man,' Zahedi later recalled. 'But it was not until I saw him on his deathbed that I realised his inner nobility. He suffered immensely; everyone knew that. But you would see no sign of it in his eyes. They were as sad, as dignified as ever.'[2] The dying Shah was remembered by his former wives. Fawzia, now living in Alexandria, sent him flowers and from Soraya came a message of 'eternal affection and undying friendship'. Princess Ashraf was constantly present: she had been with her twin brother even before their birth, now she wanted to be with him as he died. Until the very last moment she desperately tried to find doctors who could promise to cure the Shah. Every night she prayed and cried as she had done many many years earlier when Mohammad-Reza had been sick with typhoid.

President Sadat and his wife were frequent visitors. The love and respect Sadat manifested for the Shah went far beyond the debt of gratitude he might have had to his dying friend because of past political support. In the struggle for power that had followed Nasser's death in Cairo the Shah had persuaded the Americans to back Sadat. Later, the

Shah had played a crucial role in persuading Sadat to abandon Egypt's alliance with the USSR and instead firmly join the Western camp. Iran had also helped with initial contacts between Sadat and the Israelis, contacts that eventually led to Sadat's historic visit to Jerusalem and the Camp David accords in 1978. In 1973 Iran had thrown its support behind Egypt in the Ramadan war against Israel. In doing so the Shah had alienated many of his Jewish American friends. Iran had given Egypt non-military assistance – food, medicine, field hospitals, petroleum products and £40,000,000 in cash. But the Shah had also allowed Soviet planes to fly emergency military cargo to Syria while Iranian military transport aircraft had carried Saudi troops to Syria overflying Iraq. All these gestures had changed Iran's image in the Arab world from that of an ally of Israel to one of a potential source of support for the Arabs. In July 1979, however, Sadat's treatment of the Shah was not motivated by any narrow political calculation.

The Shah's presence in Egypt was seized upon by fundamentalist Muslims and Communists as an excuse for attacking Sadat. Anti-Shah slogans were daubed on Cairo walls and preachers in downtown mosques compared the dying Shah with Hajjaj Ibn Yussuf, a ruler of Mesopotamia whose name is synonymous with tyranny. In the city of Assiout, in Upper Egypt, the fundamentalists went even further and murdered seven Coptic Christians as a sign of protest against the Shah's presence in Cairo. In Tehran almost daily demonstrations were organised against Sadat, the Shah and the United States. Ayatollah Khalkhali even went as far as declaring that Sadat deserved to be put to death for his 'crime' in welcoming the Shah.

The attitude of the Khomeinists on the issue of the Shah's presence in Egypt underlined their departure from traditional Islamic values. The God of the Qur'an is constantly referred to as 'the merciful' or 'the One who forgives'. Only once is he described as 'the avenger'. Traditional Muslims were horrified by the news that a dying exile was being persecuted right down to his deathbed in the name of political revenge. But modern Islam had already entered a civil war of ideas that was to shake it to its very foundations. The Shah simply happened to be the best known victim of that war at the time.

The Shah heard the news, mostly from Zahedi, and, whenever his condition permitted, listened to radio news programmes. Was he hurt by the Niagara of abuse that constantly fell on his name, his work, indeed his very existence as a man? We shall never know. He never complained. His suffering seemed to have made him oblivious of worldly concerns.

In the third week of July the Shah's condition deteriorated suddenly. The royal children were in Alexandria for a brief holiday and Empress Farah had planned to join them for the day, but on 26 July she telephoned the children to ask them to return to Cairo immediately. Throughout the night the Shah underwent long sessions of blood transfusion but it was no use. In any case no one knew what to do. The Empress bit her lips to stop herself from breaking into tears. She wanted to remain reassuring and dignified. She was already thinking of all the things she had to do to ensure their son's acceptance by Iranian monarchists as the legitimate heir to the throne. Princess Ashraf had no such preoccupations. She let herself go. She cried as she kissed her brother all over. She kissed his head, his hands but also his feet. She wailed: 'I must come with you. We came together and we must go together.'[3] The Shah tried to restrain her. 'Lady,' he said, 'please behave. The will of God will be done.'[4] At the same time, however, he caressed her hair. The princess, almost hysterical with crying, eventually fell unconscious and the Shah's doctors had to carry her out and put her under observation in another room in the hospital.

The end came at 10 am on 27 July 1979. The Shah opened his eyes and examined each face in the room one by one: there was Empress Farah, Zahedi, Dr Pirnia, the butler Pour-Shoja'a, Eli Anotniades, a friend of the Empress, the bodyguard Jahanbini and a few others. Then the Shah closed his eyes and was gone. Zahedi performed the initial religious rites, an unusual role for the fast-living diplomat who had turned the Iranian embassy in Washington into a favourite rendezvous of the international jet set.

President Sadat arrived at the hospital shortly afterwards. He was truly moved, his hands trembling and tears running down each cheek. A state funeral was organised with a 5km cortege to carry the Shah's mortal remains to a 'temporary' grave at the Rifa'i Mosque in the centre of Cairo where, almost thirty-five years earlier, the embalmed corpse of Reza Shah, Muhammad-Reza's father, had also been deposited pending reburial in Iranian soil. Richard Nixon and former King Constantine of Greece – who had forged many business links in Iran under the Shah – flew in for the funeral. Also present were the Ambassadors of France and West Germany plus the British Chargé d'Affairs in Cairo. The American government sent no one. Of the Muslim countries only Morocco was present through its Ambassador to Egypt. One surprising absence was that of Jordan whose ruler, King Hussein, had been like a younger brother to the Shah for nearly three decades. Some of the Shah's generals and a few of his former ministers were also present but the most senior of his generals, Azhari, Jam and Oveissi, stayed away. The first said he was too ill to travel. The second invoked family problems in London. The third said that he had been told by American contacts not to go to Cairo.

Immediately after the burial members of the Shah's entourage dispersed but not before a big row over the 'political testament' that Montasseri had prepared. Some members of the entourage wanted to publish the text regardless of the fact that the Shah had not seen it. Others, led by Zahedi, were strongly opposed: it would be an insult to the Shah's memory to forge a testament for him. A compromise was found and it was agreed that the Empress publish a statement in which the Shah's last wishes were cited in his own words. The Empress immediately set to work to prepare the ground for Crown Prince Reza's succession. The Crown Prince would turn 21, the legal age under the Iranian Constitution, in October and could take the oath as the new King of Kings. A committee of former officials was appointed by the Empress to advise the Crown Prince on how best to prepare for the succession. It was an informal committee, chaired by Alinaqi Alikhani, a former Economy Minister and one of the brightest technocrats who worked for the Shah.[5] The committee was quickly split by constitutional disputes. Some members insisted that the Crown Prince could not declare himself Shah unless he took an oath at the Majlis in Tehran. Others said that an oath of allegiance to the nation and the Constitution could be taken anywhere. The Crown Prince had his own agenda: in October he declared himself Shah.

After President Sadat's assassination in 1980, his successor Muhammad Honsi Mubarak continued to manifest the same warmth and friendship towards the Shah's family, but he was also concerned about the fact that the presence of the Shah's temporary tomb in the heart of Cairo could cause trouble with the fundamentalists. The possibility of giving the Shah a permanent burial place near Cairo was brought up. One idea was to bury the Shah in the same mausoleum as Sadat. Another idea was to construct a mausoleum for the Shah in the outskirts of the Egyptian capital and a number of Iranian and Egyptian architects even submitted plans for what would become a tribute to the fallen ruler. The Shah's family could not get their acts together and decide what was to be done. Nor did they think of creating a foundation to honour the memory of the Shah and to try and understand, if not politically explain, his work. A few hagiographic pamphlets were published in exile and some exceptionally poor examples of sycophantic goo were handed out. The number of family members and friends who gathered at the Shah's tomb on 27 July each year was smaller than the year before.

Many of the men who had played a role in bringing about or speeding up the fall of the Shah were themselves pushed out of the limelight in the years that followed. The leaders who had decided at Guadeloupe that the Shah should no longer be supported were all defeated at elections and forced out of office. Carter, Callaghan, Schmidt and Giscard d'Estaing never fully admitted that they had misjudged the situation in Iran, but in their respective memoirs they showed that they were no longer as sure as they had been at Guadeloupe that Iran would do better without the Shah. Giscard d'Estaing, not always the most warm-hearted of politicians, went even further and expressed his sorrow at the fact that he had not invited the Shah to go to France after he had been refused entry into the United States.

None of the Shah's long-time Iranian associates came out in his defence. Most remained silent on an important era of Iranian history and those who broke their silence took every care to distance themselves from the Shah as much as possible. Their standard position was something like this: Whatever good that the Shah did was done by his ministers and other aides, notably ourselves. We told the Shah that he was making mistakes but he wouldn't listen to us. There was corruption and brutality in the Shah's regime but it had nothing to do with us. We either didn't know about it or tried to limit it as best we could.

Most of the Shah's bitterest enemies were assassinated, executed, forced into exile or imprisoned by the ruling mullahs in subsequent years. Some others forgot about lifelong campaigns against the Shah and became ardent monarchists; one even became the leader of the principal monarchist movement in exile. Inside Iran Ayatollah Khomeini continued to attack and vilify the Shah every time he spoke for as long as he lived. He even tried to eliminate the very word Shah from the Persian vocabulary.

Many ordinary Iranians, who had neither supported nor opposed the Shah during his rule, began to feel nostalgic about their monarchist past. As the mullahs massacred more and more of their opponents and made life increasingly intolerable for ordinary Iranians, the Shah's reign began to be imagined as something of a Camelot. Poets who, in many cases, had made cryptic attacks on the Shah a central theme of their work, now changed their symbolism to express a rather pathetic nostalgia about the good old days of the monarchy. At times this was done in the name of Persian – or Aryan – nationalism as opposed to the supposed Arabisation of Iran under the mullahs. Many Iranian intellectuals had thrown all discretion to the wind by joining Khomeini in the name of social justice in the 1970s. A decade after the establishment of Islamic government in Iran they went full circle and emerged as bitter opponents of theocracy in the name of nationalist and secular values that the Shah had tried to uphold against his many opponents.

The decade that followed the Shah's departure from Iran was one of untold sufferings for the Iranian people. During that period more than a million people were killed in urban guerrilla operations, by firing squads, in prison under torture and, above all, during the eight-year Iran-Iraq war. This means that every hour of rule by the mullahs cost the lives of at least ten Iranians. In nearly 38 years of the Shah's reign, a total of 312 people were executed – many of them for murder. In the decade that followed the Shah's fall the number of Iranians executed by the new regime rose to more than 12,000 according to Amnesty International.[6] In the same period the number of political prisoners, which had never exceeded 4000 under the Shah, rose to more than 55,000 according to the lowest estimates. The Iran-Iraq war left more than 4,000,000 Iranians homeless and caused massive destruction in 6 out of the nation's 23 provinces. Iranian industrial output in the first decade of the ayatollahs fell to less than 20 per cent of what it had been under the Shah. Oil production was cut by nearly 40 per cent. Agriculture suffered even more:

the value of farm produce in Iran in 1990 was less than half what it had been in 1977. One of the important aspects of the Shah's policy, criticised as a plot against Islam by Khomeini, had been family planning. The mullahs abolished the national network created during the 1960s and 1970s and launched a campaign 'to multiply the number of mouths that shall cry: There is no God but Allah.' The result was the fastest rate of population growth in the world. Iran's population, 38,000,000 in 1979, had reached 58,000,000 in 1991. Less than a third of school-age children were receiving a formal education in 1991 and only 7 per cent of those who wanted higher education could enter university. More than 12,000,000 people, a good half of the work force, were either unemployed or engaged in 'ephemeral occupations'. The value of the rial, the Iranian currency, had fallen to less than 5 per cent of its worst levels before the revolution. Inflation, around 30 per cent in 1978, was over 100 per cent in 1991.

After the Shah's fall more than 2,000,000 Iranians, including many highly educated men and women, went into exile. In 1991 there were more Iranian doctors and medical technicians in Canada than in Iran itself.[7] Of the teaching staff of Iranian universities, more than half left the country after 1979.

The Iran-Iraq war and the various tribal and ethnic revolts inside Iran cost the country more than £250 billion in war damages, but the social cost was even higher. In 1991 there were more than 200,000 war widows and some 300,000 war orphans in Iran. Tens of thousands of war prisoners also returned to Iran from Iraq, many of them suffering from mental imbalance caused by years of torture. Some prisoners were teenagers when they were captured; they returned home as embittered men who had spent the best years of their lives in enemy camps. Some were immediately sucked into the criminal networks that combined political violence with the pursuit of personal profit and terrorised the bigger cities.

When the Shah flew out of the country, Iran had some £15 billion in foreign exchange reserves. In 1991 these were down to around £4 billion, despite the fact that the country had earned more than £75 billion in oil revenues, more than the oil income earned in the preceding half a century. And yet not a single major development project was started in Iran between 1978 and the middle of 1991.

Iran's international status also changed. The new regime became an ally of radical and revolutionary movements and was involved in extensive terrorist activities in the 1980s, including the seizure of Western hostages and suicide attacks on Western positions. Under the Shah Iran had acted as the 'gendarme' of the Persian Gulf, keeping the peace in the region. After 1979 Iran's role in the region became more and more limited. In 1988 the US Navy virtually took over control of traffic in the Persian Gulf and during the 1990–1 Kuwait crisis Iran was reduced to the role of spectator. It made a virtue of necessity by declaring its neutrality. After Iraq's defeat the victorious alliance saw no reason why Iran should be given a role in reshaping the future of the region. Many of the Shah's critics in the West and in the Arab world suddenly realised what a good job he had done of keeping Saddam Hussein's Iraq firmly at bay for nearly a decade. The simple truth that not all change is necessarily for the better came home to many who suffered as a result of a decade of instability provoked by the Shah's fall from power.

The new regime changed the appearance of Iran and of Iranians. Men were forced to grow full beards and women were required to cover their hair with the Islamic headgear and refrain from wearing bright colours. The rich, the better educated, those with aristocratic connections or Western tastes were chased out. Their places were taken by some of the poorest, the least educated and the most culturally backward elements in Iranian society.

The 'downtrodden' enjoyed their newly-won place in the process of decision-making. For the first time in Iran's history they felt they were in charge of the nation's destiny. Over the years, however, they too became disillusioned. The sufferings inflicted by the war, of which they bore the brunt, combined with the social and economic dislocations caused by revolution and political instability, destroyed their hopes of achieving an Islamic paradise and made them nostalgic for the peace and the relative prosperity that they might have aspired to during the reign of the Shah. Nostalgia, the religion of the vanquished in history, now became the opium of the victors who began to realise how empty their triumph had been.

Because the very mention of the Shah's name entailed the risk of falling foul of the new authorities most people developed a code name for the monarch who died in exile. They called him *Khoda Biamorz* which, translated literally, means 'forgiven by God'. But this was also a term of endearment for a man whose sufferings in the last year of his existence seemed to have put him beyond the judgment of a world he had so vainly tried to reshape.

Notes

Introduction

1 This was how Henry Kissinger described the Shah in July 1979 after President Carter had refused to let the exiled monarch travel to the United States.

2 Johnson visited Iran when he was still Vice-President.

3 The following personalities were members of the informal group: Hushang Ansary, Raymond Aron, Henry Kissinger, Edward Heath, Helmut Schmidt, David Morse and Lee Kwan-yu

Chapter One: The Giant

1 The officer later became known as General Fazlallah Zahedi and played a major role in Iranian politics in the 1950s.

2 Reza Khan's first daughter, Hamdam al-Saltaneh, was born in 1904. His second daughter, Shams (later Princess), was born on 18 October 1917.

3 The slave market of Khivah continued to function until the late 1920s.

4 The Shah also had a gendarmerie, commanded by Swedish officers, and charged with the task of protecting order in the capital.

5 Dar al-Fonun (The House of Techniques) had been founded in the nineteenth century with the hope that one day it would develop into a full university. It never did.

6 'Asr-e-Enhetat, in Persian, covered the period 1800–1921.

7 Variation's of Mohammad's name were also popular, eg Ahmad, Mahmud, Hamid.

8 In later years this became, for obvious reasons, a very popular name.

9 Princess Ashraf in conversation with the author, Paris 1987. (This was part of a series of interviews between April 1987 and March 1989.)

10 Duodecimal (Ethna-'Ashari) is the Iranian version of shi'ite Islam, also known as Twelver Shi'ism.

11 The names cited are those of mythological heroes and not of actual historical rulers of Iran. (*The Mind of a Monarch*, p 30)

12 This is how Dr Mossadeq and, later, Ayatollah Khomeini referred to Reza Khan and Mohammad-Reza.

13 *The Mind of a Monarch*, p 31.

14 A more senior person was Ata-beyg (father chief) who raised the orphaned children of aristocratic families.

15 Iranian New Year coincides with the spring equinox, 20 or 21 March.

16 The Twelfth Imam of Shi'ism, Mohammad Ibn Hassan, who went into hiding in the tenth century.

17 *Sharh-e-Hall-e-Rejal-e-Iran* (Biography of Iranian Statesmen), vol II, p 2, Tehran, 1971.

18 Cf G. de Villiers in *L'irrésistible ascension de Mohammad Reza*, p 31, Paris, 1977.

19 *The Mind of a Monarch*, p 31. Cf *Mission for my Country*, p 27.

20 Some accounts suggest that Maryam Khanom died in childbirth.

21 A unit of the Cossack Brigade was known as an Atriyad, a Russian word signifying a company of soldiers.

22 Among those who committed suicide was Lieutenant-Colonel Fazlallah Khan who had been appointed liaison officer with the British military mission.

23 Between 1906 and 1911 a number of political parties came into being. But they all disappeared before the First World War.

24 He had attended theological seminaries in the holy cities of Mesopotamia.

25 Ali-Reza was the only one of Taj al-Moluk's four children not to have been born in October. By a strange coincidence he was to die in October 1954.

26 The rule regarding concubines is for shi'ite Muslims only. Sunni Muslims, the vast majority, do not recognise temporary marriages as valid.

27 The four sons were Abdul-Reza (7 June 1924), Ahmad-Reza (21 August 1925), Mahmud-Reza (4 October 1926) and Hamid-Reza (4 July 1932). The daughter was Fatemeh (30 October 1928).

28 Princess Ashraf, see note 9 above.

29 Ahmad Shah never returned to Iran and died in the south of France in 1928.

30 *Khaterat va Khatarat* (Memoirs and Dangers), p 324.

31 Under the 1906 Constitution, the institution of monarchy belonged to the nation as a whole. It was, therefore, up to the elected Majlis to bestow the custody of that institution on an individual and his family. In 1911 the Majlis had already exercised that right by removing Mohammad-Ali Shah and appointing Ahmad Shah instead. Reza Khan was named 'provisional monarch' because his position had to be confirmed by a Constituent Assembly.

32 The five were: Muddaress, a mullah; Taqizadeh who later became minister; Ala, another future prime minister; Mossadeq, yet another future prime minister; and Dowlat-Abadi who continued as a parliamentarian. The wily Mossadeq, in his opposition speech, used the convoluted arguments that Reza Khan must not become Shah because the nation needed his services as prime minister.

Chapter Two: Child Exile

 1 The new army came into being largely on paper at the time. It was not until 1926 that Iran had a truly unified army controlled by the central government.

 2 *Mission for My Country*, p 52.

 3 Abol-Fath Atabay in interview with the author in New York, December 1989.

 4 Princess Ashraf in interview with the author in Paris, November 1989.

 5 *Ibid.*

 6 *Mission for My Country*, pp 54–5.

 7 *Ibid.*

 8 Ali Izadi, Mohammad-Reza's special assistant at the time, in interview with the author in June 1979.

 9 *Mission for My Country*, p 55.

10 *Ibid.*

11 *Ibid.*

12 *The White Revolution of Iran*, p 16.

13 Among the poets and writers who used the theme were Iraj Mirza, Bahar, Dehkhoda, Aref, Parvin Etessami and Jamal-Zadeh.

14 Princess Ashraf, see note 4 above.

15 *Answer to History*, p 46.

16 *Ibid.*

17 *Ibid*, p 47.

18 *Ibid.*

19 Tabriz retained this position until the mid-1970s when it was overtaken by both Isfahan and Mashhad.

20 The American boy was Charlie Child. The most complete account of the incident was given by another American contemporary of Mohammad-Reza at Le Rosey, Frederick Jacobi Jr, in an interview published by *Newsweek* on 20 February 1949.

21 He skied almost every weekend between mid-October and mid-March at one of the resorts near Tehran. In later years he also spent part of the winter in Switzerland where he had purchased a house at St Moritz and skied in the most dangerous spots possible.

22 *Mission for My Country*, p 62.

23 Princess Ashraf in interview in Paris, November 1988.

24 *Ibid.*

25 *Mission for My Country*, p 62.
26 *Ibid*.
27 *Ibid*, p 63.
28 When he became king he tried to make up for his father's harsh treatment of the Teymurtash clan and offered Mehrpur a number of governmental posts.
29 Princess Ashraf, see note 23 above. Cf *L'irrésistible ascension de Mohammad Reza'*, p 72. Also, article on Perron in the weekly *Asiay-e-Javan*, vol IX, 1954.
30 At least two members of the royal family have told the author that they and the Shah knew that some of the foreign governesses and butlers employed at the palaces had been approached and recruited by British and American intelligence services in the 1950s and 1960s.
31 Empress Farah in interview with the author, Paris, March-April 1988.
32 Cf *Mission for My Country*, p 64.
33 The anthem was called 'Hymn to the Shahanshah' and replaced the national anthem after 1930.
34 Reza Shah's speech at the ceremony, quoted by Mrs Ziba Karami in *The Day the Veil Was Shed*, Tehran, nd.
35 The association was led by Mrs. Safiyeh Firuz, a Qajar princess, who died in Paris in 1990.
36 This was not quite the case; Persians had always sported long beards at a time the Arabs actually shaved theirs.
37 This is best illustrated in the popular hymn 'O, Iran!', composed in 1933.
38 The building was completed in 1941 when Reza Shah had to go into exile. It remained unused for several years and, in 1961, was turned into the headquarters of the Mortgage Bank!
39 For more on this see the author's *The Spirit of Allah*.
40 This happened on 12 May 1930, an important date in Iranian economic history.
41 The new Iranian Navy was officially launched on 1 May 1931.
42 A three-day holiday was, nevertheless, allowed. This coincided with the anniversary of Imam Ali's assassination in Kufa back in the seventh century.
43 Princess Ashraf, see note 23 above. Also Ali Izadi, Mohammad-Reza's personal assistant at the time, quoted in *L'irrésistible ascension de Mohammad Reza*, p 79. Cf M. R. Majd in *Khatarat Rejal az Reza Shah* (Memoirs of Statesmen about Reza Shah), Tehran, 1975.
44 Ali Dashti in *Panjah va Panj* (Fifty-Five), p 119, Tehran, 1977.

Chapter Three: Playing King
1 Author's interview with Lady F. who had a brief friendship with Mohammad-Reza in 1938. She spoke on condition that her full name not be given. The interview was conducted in the United States in 1988.
2 *Ibid*.
3 Cecil Beaton in *Near East*, London, 1949. The author first met Fawziah in her house in Alexandria in 1971 and found her still as beautiful as Beaton had described. Here is how Beaton saw Fawziah: 'If ever Botticelli were reincarnated and wished to paint an Asiatic [sic] Venus or Primavera here is his subject. He would delight in the Queen's features contained in a perfect heart-shaped face: strangely pale but piercing blue eyes; crimson coloured lips curling like wrought-iron volutes; and the way in which the dark chestnut hair grows beautifully from the forehead.'
4 This was achieved more than seven years later as a result of complicated negotiations between the shi'ite theological hierarchy in Iran and its sunni counterpart in Egypt.
5 Iraj Eskandari, *Khaterat Siyassi* (Political Memoirs) in two volumes, Paris, 1986. Eskandari was one of the founders of the Soviet-sponsored Tudeh Party.
6 *Reza Shah Kabir dar Ayneh Khaterat* (Reza Shah the Great in the Mirror of Memoirs) by Ibrahim Safa'i, Tehran, 1975. Mohsen Ra'is in his article names Professor Wolfe, the famous Jewish-German Iranologist, as one of the scholars invited to live and teach in Iran.
7 Princess Ashraf in interview with the author, Paris, April 1988.

8 *Towt'eh hay Almaniha dar Iran* (German Conspiracies in Iran) by Karim Nava'i, Tehran 1972, p 34.
9 Quoted in *Mission for My Country*, pp 71–2.
10 *Ibid.*
11 *BBC va Iran dar Tayye Chehel Saal* (BBC and Iran during Forty Years) by Mahmoud Jaafarian, special paper prepared in 1978 by the National Iranian Radio and Television's research team, pp 11–13.
12 Cf. *Russia and the West in Iran* by George Lenczowski, Ithaca, NY 1949.
13 Cf. *Aryamehr, the Shah of Iran* by Ramesh Sanghvi, London, 1969.
14 *Mohammad Reza Pahlavi, Shah d'Iran* by Fereidoun Sahebjam, Paris, 1971, p 18.
15 *Iran dar 'Asr Pahlavi* (Iran in the Pahlavi Era), vol IV, p 23. Cf *Memoirs of General Fardust, Kayhan* airmail edition, vol 706, December 1987.
16 This account of the Shah's encounter with Foroughi is based on several sources including an interview with Massud Foroughi, the prime minister's son, in Tehran in 1975. Cf *Iran: Anatomie d'une révolution* by Houchang Nahavandi, Paris, 1983, pp 25–6.
17 Sanghvi, see note 13 above.
18 *Mottaefqin dar Iran* (The Allies in Iran), by Abbas Hakimi-Rad, Tehran 1974, pp 44–5.
19 *Ettelaat*, 18 September 1941.
20 Princess Ashraf in interview with the author, Paris, April 1988.
21 Princess Sham's husband, Lieutenant Fereidun Jam, also joined the exile party.
22 M.K. Dast-Ghayb's account of the transfers is given in *Reza Shah Kabir dar Aynehe Khaterat* (Reza Shah the Great in the Mirror of Memoirs), pp 135–6.
23 *Persia, the Immortal Kingdom*, p 192.
24 *Under Five Shahs*, p 306 for the army officers' view of the young Shah.
25 Author's interview with the Shah, Tehran, 20 October 1976.
26 The group included Dr Mohammad Mossadeq, Ahmad Qavam, Vosuq ad-Dawleh, Mohammad-Taqi Bahar, Ibrahim Hakimi and Zaynalabedin Rahnema.
27 Princess Ashraf's initial investment in the *Kayhan* remained a well-guarded secret for more than 40 years. It was revealed by Dr Mostafa Mesbahzadeh, the paper's founder and director, in 1984 in conversation with the author.
28 Princess Ashraf in interview with the author, Paris, November 1987. She added that she loved her son Shahram who was the only fruit of her marriage to Qavam Shirazi.
29 *Ibid.*
30 Ali Izadi in interview in Tehran in 1974. Izadi was in charge of Reza Shah's personal office in exile.

Chapter Four: The Return of the Demons
1 *Mission for My Country*, p 77.
2 Black turbans are worn by those who claim to be descendants of the Prophet. Other clerics wear white or cream turbans.
3 *Reza Shah dar Aiyneh Khaterat* (Reza Shah the Great in the Mirror of Memoirs), p 452.
4 *Iran dar 'Asr Pahlavi* (Iran in the Pahlavi Era), p 244.
5 Mahmud Hajebi, one of the Shah's confidants, in conversation with the author in Tehran in 1978. Also confirmed by others including General Parviz Khosravani.
6 They are, in fact, Zoroastrians. See *To Us Spoke Zarathustra* by Emir Muawyyah, the Leader of the Yazidis, Paris, 1983.
7 Including the Naqshbandi, the Ali-Allahi and Haqju tariqats (paths).
8 He had fought for the independence of Iraq which had been a British protectorate since 1918 and had also supported Rashid Ali Gilani's anti-British *coup d'état* in Baghdad in 1941.
9 Colonels Hamid Samadi and Abdallah Yadegari in interviews with the author in Hamburg and Paris in 1988 and 1989.
10 For more on Tchapkin see Iraj Eskandari's *Khaterat Siassi* (Political Memoirs) vol II, pp 6, 7 and 8.
11 *Ibid.* p 5.
12 *Ibid*, p 25. Also speech by Khomeini in Qom on 25 March 1979.

13 Eskandari, pp 10–12.
14 Cf Sir Claremont Skrine's *World War in Iran*, London, 1962, pp 302–3.
15 Princess Ashraf in interview with the author, Paris, November 1988.
16 *Mission for My Country*, p 67.
17 *Ibid*, p 79.
18 *Ibid*.
19 The Soviets, however, had had a full embassy since 1921.
20 Eskandari, vol II, p 38.
21 Senator Reza Divan-Beygui in conversation with the author in Tehran in 1977.
22 Zaynalabedin Rahnema, the propaganda chief at the time, in conversation with the author in Tehran in 1979.
23 Mahmud Hajebi in conversation with the author in Paris in 1988.
24 Study carried out by Isfahan University Faculty of Medicine, Department of Psychotherapy in May 1977.
25 This theory is developed in memoirs attributed to General Hossein Fardust and published in Tehran in 1988. Fardust knew Perron well since the days of Le Rosey. The authenticity of the published memoirs, however, is still being debated by Iranian scholars.
26 Fardust memoirs, Tehran 1988, p 137. Cf *Iran dar Asr Pahlavi* (Iran in the Pahlavi Era), vol IV, pp 67–8.
27 Princess Ashraf in interview with the author, Paris, November 1988.
28 *The Mind of a Monarch*, p. 67

Chapter Five: Six Bullets

1 In interview granted to the author in 1971 in Tehran.
2 After the US, the USSR and Venezuela.
3 Cf *Mardom* editorial on 9 November 1944 written by Ehsan Tabari, the Tudeh Party's principal theoretician.
4 Eskandari, vol II, p 112.
5 *Ibid*. p 113.
6 *Ibid*.
7 The text of Mossadeq's letter was published in several newspapers at the time.
8 Eskandari, vol II, p 114.
9 *Mission for My Country*, p 87.
10 Eskandari, vol II, p 146 (quoting the historian Mahmud Mahmud).
11 *Ibid*. p 124.
12 Qavam's own account reported by Amidi Nuri who was present during the visit. Cf *Iran in the Pahlavi Era*, vol IV, p 364.
13 The Shah in Olivier Warin's *Le Lion et le soleil*, Paris 1976, pp 120, 173 and 212.
14 Eskandari, vol II, p 132.
15 General Hassan Arfa in conversation with the author in Tehran in 1977. Cf Arfa's *Under Five Shahs*, London 1964. Also cf *Iran in the Pahlavi Era*, vol I, pp 400–402. Firuz substantially confirmed these reports in a series of conversations with the author in Paris in 1983.
16 The two were Ahmad Qassemi and Nureddin Kianuri. She finally married Kianuri.
17 Cf James Bill in *The Eagle and the Lion*, New Haven and London, 1989, pp 37–8.
18 George Allen in his memoirs, quoted in *Iran in the Pahlavi Era*, vol IV, p 453. In conversations with the author Princess Ashraf confirmed that she had a number of 'altercations' with her brother but could not remember the exact words used.
19 Partly because of the first-past-the-post system in effect at the time, in Tehran Tudeh could win thousands of votes without getting a single seat.
20 The account of the trip was given to the author by Princess Ashraf in a series of conversations. Cf Ashraf Pahlavi in *Faces in a Mirror*, New York, 1981.
21 For more details see *The Spirit of Allah*, London, 1985, pp 105-6.
22 Shah in interview with G. de Villiers, Zurich, February 1974. The Shah's 'special way with horses' was confirmed by Abol-Fath Atabay in conversations with the author in New York, 1989.
23 *Mission for My Country*, p 56.
24 *Ibid*, p 57.
25 *Ibid*.
26 *Ibid*.
27 Princess Ashraf in interview with the author, Paris, November 1988.
28 *Ibid*.
29 Hazhir, who was Court Minister at the time of his murder, and Ahmad Zangeneh the Minister for Education and Culture.

30 For more on the Fedayeen see: Amir Taheri's *Holy Terror: The Inside Story of Islamic Terrorism*, London, 1987.

Chapter Six: The Man from Ashtian

1 For Army Mission. A Military Assistance Advisory Group (MAAG) was added in 1950. The two structures were later merged as ARMISH-MAAG.

2 *Mission for My Country*, p 66.

3 *Ibid*, p 89.

4 Moscow, however, refused to return to Iran 11 tonnes of gold that the Red Army had taken from Tehran during the occupation.

5 E.A. Bayne in *Persian Kingship in Transition*, New York 1968, p 132.

6 Princess Ashraf in interview with the author, Paris, November 1988.

7 The other three kings were Cyrus the Great, Darius the Great and Shah Abbas the Great.

8 He changed his Arabo-Turkish name into the purely Iranian one of Mehrdad Pahlbod. His father had rendered great service to music in Iran and was the founder of the first conservatory of western music in the country.

9 Soraya in *Ma vie*, Paris 1963, p 27.

10 *Ibid*, p 41.

11 *Mussadiq's Memoirs*, London, 1988, p 265.

12 This story is regularly repeated by Mossadeq supporters. In fact, Mossadeq's youngest daughter Khadijeh was committed to a Swiss psychiatric hospital in 1942, more than a year after Reza Shah had abdicated and gone into exile.

13 *Musaddiq's Memoirs*, p 424.

14 *Ibid*, p 265.

15 Mossadeq as-Saltaneh was an honorific title given by Mozaffareddin Shah. It means Endorser of Monarchy.

16 The charge was even raised during Mossadeq's trial in Tehran in 1954.

17 At the Constituent Assembly session that chose Reza Khan as the new Shah, Mossadeq spoke against the move but did not vote against it. The only person who voted against was Soleiman Mirza Eskandari, an old friend of Reza Khan who then broke with him.

18 Related by an old associate of Qavam in conversation with the author in Paris in 1982. The source demanded anonymity. Qavam's low opinion of Mossadeq has also been reported by numerous other sources.

19 This was unfair because Qavam was a Persian scholar and a poet.

20 Among the delegation received at the palace were Dr Mozaffar Baqa'i, Hossein Makki, Allahyar Saleh and Karim Sanjabi.

Chapter Seven: A Prisoner of the Marble Palace

1 The proverb originally came from Arabic: al-'awam ka-al 'in'aam!

2 In those days everyone called everyone a British agent. The allegations against Eskandari were based on documents seized during a mob raid on the home of a British official in Tehran. Mozaffar Baqa'i, then a close friend of Mossadeq, gained possession of the 'documents' and used them for political blackmail against opponents – and some friends, too! – but he did not allow any independent examination of them.

3 Iran had traditionally used the Bank of England for depositing its foreign currency reserves.

4 Sir Anthony Eden in *Full Circle*, London, 1960, pp 200–1.

5 Mossadeq had spoken against the building of the railway at a session of the Majlis during Reza Shah's reign. He defended his idea that Iran, being sparsely-populated, would do better with roads rather than railways to the very end.

6 Princess Ashraf in interview with the author, Paris, November 1988.

7 *Mussaddiq's Memoirs*, p 35.

8 Fatemi in a speech on 17 August 1953 in Tehran revealed his 'years of reflection' on the desirability of a republican system for Iran.

9 Soraya in *Ma vie*, p 173.

10 The phrase comes in many of Mossadeq's speeches and is also quoted by politicians who met him during his premiership.

11 *Mission for My Country*, p 97.

12 Mossadeq, in his memoirs, denies this

and insists that the suggestion came from the Shah himself.

13 The figure was cited by Senator Mohammad-Ali Massudi, then an associate of the Rashidians, in interview with the author in Paris, 1980.

14 He had spent several years in exile in Palestine in the 1940s for his anti-British activities in Iran during the early phase of Allied occupation.

Chapter Eight: Back from the Brink

1 Princess Ashraf in interview with the author in Paris in November 1988.

2 Woodehouse, in his *Something Ventured*, claims that his deputy met Ashraf. He also does not mention the name of the American officer. He further gives the place of the meeting as Switzerland. So many modifications to keep operational patterns a secret?

3 Shafiq had also been sacked as head of the Civil Aviation Organisation but was not put under arrest.

4 The list of Tudeh officers fell into the hands of the authorities when a key member of the clandestine network, Captain Abbasi, defected to the police. The list of Pro-Tudeh NCOs, however, was never discovered.

5 *Eterafaat Kianuri* (Kianuri's Confessions), Tehran, 1984.

6 Roy Melbourne in 'America and Iran in Perspective: 1950 and 1980', *Foreign Service Journal*, April 1980, p 16.

7 E.g. Margaret Laing in *The Shah*, London, 1977, p 135. Soraya, who could not have known, gave a figure of $6,000,000 in her ghost-written autobiography, p 99.

8 Amir Taheri in *Nest of Spies*, London, 1987, p 36.

9 Ardeshir Zahedi in interview with the author in Switzerland, June 1988.

10 On Lavrentiev's role see *Nest of Spies*, p 38.

11 In interview with the author, Paris, November 1988.

12 Soraya in *Ma vie*, p 78.

13 The council members were the Prime Minister, the Speaker of the Majlis, the President of the Senate, the Friday Prayer Leader of Tehran, the Court Minister, two senior army generals and a constitutional jurist.

14 Hajebi, a confidant of the Shah, in interview with the author, Paris, April 1987. He was a member of the mission.

15 Princess Ashraf, see note 11 above.

16 Contrary to reports at the time, no monthly 'salary' was fixed for the ex-Queen.

Chapter Nine: Playing Revolutionary

1 Assadollah Alam in interview with the author in Tehran, 1972.

2 Ardeshir Zahedi in interview with the author, Switzerland, June 1988.

3 *The Mind of a Monarch*, p 149.

4 *Nest of Spies*, p 52.

5 *France Soir*, 14 February 1959.

6 Maria-Gabriella and her family remained good friends of the Shah. Maria-Gabriella's brother, Victor Emanuel, the pretender to the Italian crown, moved to Tehran and became active in several major projects.

7 The female form of Sayyed (Master), a title assumed by those claiming descent from the Prophet.

8 Empress Farah in interview with the author, Paris, March 1988.

9 *Ibid*.

10 *Ibid*. The students played on the sound of the word Shah which was the same as *chat* (cat) in French.

11 *Ibid*.

12 *Ibid*.

13 These details were provided by an associate of Bakhtiar in interviews with the author. As the source lives in Iran, he required anonymity. This account is supported by other sources: Cf *Newsweek*, 12 May 1961 and *Time*, 16 June 1961. On other aspects of Bakhtiar's moves at that time cf *Peygham Emruz*, 27 December 1961.

14 Based on information supplied by several high-ranking Iranian diplomats in interviews with the author. Cf *The Eagle and the Lion*, pp 138–40.

15 Related by General Pakravan in conversation with the author in Tehran, 1978. Also corroborated by Shahpur Zand-Nia who was then special assistant to General Bakhtiar.

16 *Ibid*.

17 The six-point programme was later extended to cover 13 more points. It

was also renamed 'The Sixth of Bahman Revolution' because it had been approved on the sixth day of the Persian month of Bahman in a referendum. Cf *Answer to History*, pp 91–6.

18 For Khomeini's role see *The Spirit of Allah*, pp 138–40.

19 This account was given by Alam in conversations with the author in Tehran in 1973 and confirmed by accounts given by General Pakravan and Alinaqi Kani who was deputy prime minister at the time.

20 Deputy prime minister Alinaqi Kani in conversation with the author in Cannes, France, June 1988. Kani put the number of people killed during the June 1963 riots at 'over 2000'. Pro-Khomeini sources have spoken of '15,000 martyrs', but both figures appear to be wildly exaggerated.

Chapter Ten: On the Peacock Throne

1 Morghab is a mythological figure.

2 The term Mossadeqism began to be used from 1960 onwards. It denoted the essentially personal affection that many middle-class Iranians felt towards the former prime minister.

3 Address to the nation by the Shah. Cited in *Answer to History*, p 96.

4 In *Kavusnameh*, a classical Persian text on statecraft.

5 The immediate occasion was provided by the June 1963 riots. Also present were NIOC Chairman Abdallah Entezam, Chief Justice Mohammad Soruri and Senator A.R. Daryabegui.

6 *Iran in the Pahlavi Era*, vol III, p 413.

7 In interview with the author, Tehran, October 1975.

8 *Ibid*.

9 Alam in interview with the author, Tehran, January 1972.

10 *The Spirit of Allah*, p 152.

11 *Ibid*.

12 Figure cited by Ayatollah Mahdavi-Kani at a press conference in Tehran, February 1980.

13 Hoveyda in conversation with the author, Tehran, March 1971.

14 Empress Farah in interview with the author, Paris, April 1988.

15 *Ibid*.

16 *Ibid*.

17 *Ibid*.

18 *Ibid*. Cf *L'irrésistible ascension de Mohammad Reza*, p 316.

19 Alam, see note 9 above.

20 Later research established that there was no plot. Qarani had only tried to establish a personal relationship with American military officers in Tehran.

21 Empress Farah, see note 14 above.

22 This part of the narrative is based on interviews with various Bakhtiar aides, notably Shahpur Zand-Nia, and information supplied by the Iranian Foreign Ministry in 1970.

23 *Ibid*. SAVAK never officially admitted the murder. Unofficially, however, many SAVAK chiefs boasted about it.

24 Shojaeddin Shafa in interview with the author, Paris, January 1989.

25 *Ibid*.

26 Empress Farah, see note 14 above.

Chapter Eleven: The New Achaemenians

1 *Mission for My Country*, p 77.

2 Shafa in conversation with the author, Paris, January 1989.

3 In Olivier Warin's *Le Lion et le soleil*, Paris 1976, p 113.

4 Quoted in Shafa's *Jenayat va Mokafat* (Crime and Punishment), Paris 1988, vol IV, p 2097.

5 *Selection of Speeches by His Imperial Majesty the Shahanshah Aryamehr*, Tehran, 1975, p 97 (henceforth *Selection*).

6 The term Pahlavism was coined by journalist and politician Dr Mostafa Alamuti in a book he published in 1969.

7 Members of the commission included Dr Ahmad Fardid, Dr Hossein Nasr, Dr Anvar Khameh'i and Dr Ehsan Naraghi.

8 Hoveyda in conversation with the author, Tehran, June 1977.

9 Iran's population topped 57 million in 1989, making the country the world's 17th most populous nation.

10 The Persian term was qodrat manta-qeh'i. It became part of the regime's vocabulary.

11 Hoveyda in conversation with the author in Tehran, March 1971.

12 Saudi Arabia, Kuwait and Iraq also joined OPEC after a series of consultations in Baghdad in 1960. The organisation's membership later expanded to include Indonesia, Qatar, the United Arab Emirates, Nigeria, Libya, Algeria, Gabon and Ecuador.

13 Fuad Ruhani in conversation with the author in Paris, 1986.

14 New estimates changed that in 1986 by showing the presence of substantial additional oil reserves in Iran.

15 In an address to the Plan and Budget Organisation staff in Tehran, 29 December 1971.

16 Press conference in Tehran, 5 February 1971.

17 In conversation with the author in Tehran, 8 September 1977.

18 General Reza Azimi in conversation with the author in Paris, April 1989. General Azimi served as War Minister between 1969 and 1978.

19 Ibid.

20 In an exclusive interview with the author in Tehran in July 1968. Additional information on Ba'ath party links with Iranian intelligence services were supplied to the author by Sayyed Mehdi Pirasteh and Ezaatallah Ameli who served as Ambassadors to Baghdad during the 1960s and early 1970s.

21 This account of the events was supplied to the author by General Azimi. See note 18 above.

22 Ibid.

23 Ibid.

24 Mulla Mostafa Barzani in interview with the author in Tehran, March 1975.

25 In 1971 the Shah sacked his Chief of Staff, General Bahram Aryana, because of the latter's suggestion that Iran launch a pre-emptive attack against Iraq.

26 Khalatbari in conversation with the author in Tehran in December 1974.

27 Jaafar Ra'ed in conversation with the author in London, 1989. Ra'ed served as the Shah's Ambassador to Saudi Arabia and was a member of Khalatbari's team that negotiated with the Iraqis.

28 Barzani, as in note 24 above. A résumé of the interview, the last by the Kurdish leader, was published in Kayhan in 1975.

29 Shah in his book Tamadon Bozorg (The Great Civilization), Tehran 1977, p 18.

30 Ibid. p 33.

Chapter Twelve: Empire of Gold and Fear

1 Iran had no Ministry of Defence, except for a few months under Mossadeq in 1952.

2 General Esmail Riahi served as Agriculture Minister and General Zargham held the Commerce portfolio during the 1960s.

3 Alinaq Alikhani served as Minister of the Economy in successive cabinets. Valian was Minister of Land Reform for many years. Azumn became Minister of State in 1978.

4 Hushang Ansary, a businessman originally based in Tokyo, served in various ministerial posts throughout the 1970s. Fereidun Mahdavi served as Minister of Commerce.

5 Parviz Raji became Ambassador to the Court of St James, and Iraj Amini was posted as envoy to Tunis.

6 Including Ardeshir Zahedi who served as Foreign Minister and Abdul-Reza Ansari who held the Interior portfolio in the 1960s.

7 In private conversation with the author in Tehran, 1976.

8 General Azimi in interview with the author, Paris 1989.

9 This account is based on numerous interviews by the author with SAVAK victims in the 1970s.

10 Interview with Karen Shapiro, Sa'edi's girlfriend at the time, in London 1989.

11 Parviz Sabeti, head of SAVAK's Third Directorate, in conversation with the author in 1988.

12 Based on accounts given to the author by a number of top officials and leading industrialists at the time.

13 Alam in interview with the author in Tehran, 1973.

14 Shah's speech at the inauguration of the Darius the Great hydroelectric complex.

15 The Shah in conversation with the author, Tehran 1977.

16 Empress Farah in interview with the author, Paris, 1988.

17 See note 15 above.

18 Related by Hushang Ansary – who accompanied the Shah as Minister of the Economy – in conversation with the author, New York, 1989.

19 For more on Sadr see *Holy Terror*, Hutchinson, London, 1987.

20 Related to the author by aides to premier Hoveyda who spoke on condition of anonymity.

21 For more details see *Nest of Spies*, Hutchinson, London 1988.

22 This account based on author's conversations with a number of former SAVAK agents and informers in the 1970s.

23 V. Kuzishkin in his autobiography quoted by *Kayhan*, 11 October 1990.

24 *US Embassy Documents*, vol VII, p 78, quoted in *Nest of Spies*, p 102.

25 The Shah himself admitted this in a private interview with the author in Tehran in 1977. He said that he had ordered SAVAK to change that policy forthwith and to stop all torture in accordance with recommendations made in a report submitted to him by Hoveyda.

26 *Mission for my Country*, p 173.

27 Related to the author by court officials in Tehran.

28 Empress Farah in conversations with the author in Paris, 1988.

29 Sir Anthony Parsons, who served as British Ambassador to Tehran, in his *The Pride and the Fall*, London 1984, p 72.

30 *Mission for My Country*, p 323.

31 Related by several members of the cabinet during the 1970s.

32 Related to the author by General Abbas Gharabaghi who served as Ground Forces Commander, in conversation in Paris, 1989.

33 *Ibid*.

34 In interview granted to the author in Tehran, October 1976.

35 Related by Jaafar Ra'ed who served as the Shah's ambassador to Saudi Arabia and corroborated by accounts given by several naval officers in conversations with the author in 1979.

36 Related to the author by Hoveyda in conversations in Tehran in April 1975.

Chapter Thirteen: The Man from Khomein

1 Estimate by the Plan and Budget Organisation in 1977.

2 Annual report, the National Police, Passport Office, Tehran, 1977.

3 Agriculture Minister Mansur Ruhani was the architect of the scheme. He exposed his ideas to the author on a number of occasions in 1975 and 1976.

4 This is an estimate. The foundation never made its accounts public. Some sources claim that the foundation's assets in Iran and abroad exceeded $12 billion.

5 At the time there were rumours that Khatam had been killed on orders from the Shah. He died when his hangglider hit a mountain near Dezful.

6 Related to the author by Hushang Ansary who saw the autographed portrait at Davalloo's home in Tehran. In interview with the author in St Martin, 1990.

7 In interview with the author, Paris, 1990.

8 Cf Gilles Perrault in *Notre ami le roi*, Paris 1990.

9 Ardeshir Zahedi in interview with the author, Montreux, Switzerland, May 1989.

10 The list was shown to the author by Minister for Housing and Urban Development Homyaun Jaberi Ansari in Tehran in 1976.

11 Some of Khomeini's supporters initially even suggested that this had been 'scientifically proven' through laboratory research. Abol-Hassan Bani-Sadr made such a claim in a speech at Tehran University in March 1979.

12 Ali Shariati's pamphlet, *Marxism Against Islam*, was published and freely distributed by SAVAK despite the fact that the author was a known opponent of the regime.

13 These included the lifting of restrictions on foreign travel by married women. Under the law these women could not obtain a passport without the written permission of their husbands. The issue was important enough to provoke the resignation of Mrs

Mehrangiz Manuchehrian, a leading feminist, from the Senate.

14 Figures of between $3,000,000 and $6,000,000 have been cited by various high officials of the time in separate interviews with the author.

15 The commission had only four permanent members: General Hossein Fardust, head of the Imperial Inspectorate; Nosratollah Moinian, the Shah's chief of cabinet; and two journalists representing the media. Ministers and other ranking officials attended the commission's meetings on invitation.

16 *Kayhan International*, 26 October 1976. The interview was conducted by the author at Saadabad Palace.

17 Hoveyda in conversation with the author, October 1976 in Tehran.

18 The phrase was originally coined at a meeting of a committee chaired by Hushang Ansary in 1976. Also present were Mehdi Sami'i and Manuchehr Taslimi.

19 The three were Shapour Bakhtiar, Dariush Foruhar and Karim Sanjabi.

20 The feature, including an interview with Yazdani, was by the *Kayhan* reporter Nushabeh Amiri.

21 Sabeti made the remarks at a meeting with Hushang Ansary in Tehran in August 1978. His remarks were reported to the author by Ansary. Later Sabeti confirmed this position in a conversation with the author in the United States in 1978.

22 The meeting in August 1978 was attended by Empress Farah, premier Amuzegar, Court Minister Hoveyda, radio and TV director Reza Qotbi and the author.

23 In interview with the author, 20 October 1976, Tehran.

24 In interview with the author, Paris, April 1989.

25 *The Spirit of Allah*, p 213.

26 Names could not be given because some of the members of the committee are still in Iran. One active member even became special adviser to President Rafsanjani in 1989.

27 The fact that the ayatollah was a poet was made public after his death when his son, Ahmad, published several collections of his verse.

28 A smiliar letter was sent to *Kayhan* whose editor refused to publish it.

29 Speech broadcast by Tehran Radio on 11 January 1978.

30 The Shah said this in the audience granted to editors of the *Rastakhiz* daily, the organ of the ruling party, in April 1975.

31 The Shah's hatred of crowds has been mentioned by many of his relatives, friends and associates. At a meeting in September 1978 in Tehran he told the author that the crowds on the streets of Tehran reminded him of 'earthquake energy gushing out to destroy everything'.

32 At the Nowshahr meeting, cited in 22 above.

33 *The Spirit of Allah*, p 206.

34 *Ibid*, p 219.

35 The court official was Kambiz Atabay. He related the episode in an interview with the author in Nice, France, in April 1989.

36 Alam's letter to the Shah was delivered by Alinaqi Kani who had once served as Alam's *chef de cabinet* in the 1960s. The Shah's reply was given to Hassan Behbahanian, deputy Court Minister. Behbahanian did not relay the message and Alam died shortly afterwards. The incident was related to the author by Kani in an interview in Paris in May 1989.

37 The author learned about this through interviews with Azmun, Sabeti and Farrokh Dadashpur, who was at the time tipped to become the new party's secretary-general. Dadashpur, however, told the author in 1978 that the whole scheme was 'stupid and dangerous'.

Chapter Fourteen: From Tehran with Tears

1 There was no evidence to support this and Vinogradov continued to recommend support for the Shah right to the end.

2 *Eterafaat-e-Kianuri* (Kianuri's Confessions), Tehran 1986, p 45.

3 Mohammad Montazeri was the eldest son of Ayatollah Hossein-Ali Montazeri, Khomeini's heir-designate until

his dismissal in 1987. Mohammad earned the nickname 'Ayatollah Ringo' because of his gun-toting tactics.

4 Hani al-Hassan, the PLO's envoy in Tehran, claimed in 1980 that his organisation had trained 'more than 10,000' Iranian anti-Shah guerrillas. This, however, was almost certainly an exaggeration designed to enhance the PLO's status in post-revolutionary Iran.

5 In interview with the author, Tehran, July 1978.

6 The committee was formed by Hoveyda in 1977 and included among its members the Foreign Minister, the SAVAK chief and the director of the National Iranian Radio and Television.

7 *The Spirit of Allah*, p 229.

8 In interview with the author in Tehran, August 1978.

9 In interview with the author in New York, December 1980.

10 Empress Farah in interview with the author, April 1990, Paris.

11 *Ibid.*

12 Zahedi in interview with the author, July 1990, Montreux, Switzerland.

13 Account given to the author by a former SAVAK officer who requested anonymity in interview in Palm Beach, Florida, February 1990.

14 *Ibid.*

15 Cf Samir al-Khalil in *Republic of Fear*, London 1989.

16 The sobriquet was invented by Dariush Shayegan, an Iranian philosopher, who later joined the opposition to the ayatollah.

17 Foucault, a homosexual, changed his mind about Khomeini after the ayatollah ordered the public hanging of a number of gays in Tehran.

18 The group had come into being in the mid-1970s under the title The Thinkers. They presented critical papers to Empress Farah. The Empress later recalled how she, in turn, sent the papers to Hoveyda who 'immediately threw them into his waste-paper basket'.

19 *The Spirit of Allah*, p 236.

20 Empress Farah in interview with the author, Paris, April 1989.

21 The Shah appointed half of the sixty members of the Senate. The other half were elected at the same time as members of the Majlis.

22 Empress Farah as in 20 above.

23 *Ibid.*

24 *Ibid.*

25 During audience granted to the author together with Reza Qotbi and Manuchehr Ganji, Niavaran Palace, 23 September 1978.

26 *Ibid.*

27 *Nest of Spies*, p 95.

28 Quoted by Mark Hulbert in *Interlock*, New York 1982, p 100.

29 *The Spirit of Allah*, p 236.

30 Emami's account given to the author in Tehran, September 1978.

31 Empress Farah as in 20 above.

32 Shah in interview with the magazine *Now*, 7 December 1979.

33 'Soft dictatorship' is a translation of 'dictablanda', a term used in Latin America to describe milder forms of dictatorship.

34 Related to the author by General Mohammad Yamin-Afshar, one of those present, in conversation in Tehran in December 1979. Cf William Shawcross's account in *The Shah's Last Ride*, p 25.

35 The author discussed the matter with Hoveyda in Tehran on a number of occasions between September and November 1978.

36 Tassua (the ninth) and Ashura (the tenth) days of Muharram mark the martyrdom of Hussein, the third Imam of shi'ism, in Mesopotamia in the seventh century.

37 General Manuchehr Khosrowdad in conversation with the author, October 1978 in Tehran.

38 Azhari quoted by Reza Qotbi who saw the new prime minister minutes after the audience with the Shah. Qotbi related the episode to the author in conversation in Paris in 1980.

39 Cf Amir-Aslan Afshar's account in *The Shah's Last Ride*, p 25.

40 *The Spirit of Allah*, p 237.

41 Azhari in conversation with the author in Tehran, 15 November 1978.

42 Empress Farah in interview with the author, as in 20 above.

43 Hoveyda in conversation with the author in Tehran, 1976.

44 The Shah in interview with the German weekly *Die Zeit*, 5 April 1974.

45 Empress Farah as in 20 above.

46 *Ibid.*

47 *Ibid.*

48 *Ibid.*

49 There was no independent evidence to support this and the Shah himself did not accuse his old friend of treason. Fardust was captured by the Khomeinists and died in prison in mysterious circumstances in 1989.

50 Gharabaghi in conversation with the author in Paris, May 1989.

51 Related by Aliqoli Ardalan, then Court Minister, in conversation with the author in Tehran, November 1978.

52 *The Spirit of Allah*, p 243.

Chapter Fifteen: The Book of Time

1 The following were with the Shah and the Empress on the flight out of Tehran: Amir-Aslan Afshar, Grand Master of Ceremonies, Colonel Kiumarth Jahanbini and Colonel Yazdan Navissi, bodyguards, Ali Kabiri, special cook, Amir-Pur-Shoj'a and Mahmud Eliassi, royal valets, Lieutenant Ali Shahbazi, royal orderly, and Dr Lucy Pirnia. Dr Pirnia, who had for years served as paediatrician to the royal children, joined the royal party at the last moment. She was a friend of the Empress.

2 King Faisal made the comment in 1972 when the Shah cancelled a scheduled trip to Saudi Arabia. Related to the author by Jaafar Ra'ed who served as the Shah's Ambassador to Riyadh at the time.

3 A copy of the report was shown to the author by foreign ministry officials in Tehran prior to the Rabat summit in 1968.

4 This was the opinion of Amir-Aslan Afshar.

5 The claim was made by Sadegh Ghotbzadeh, one of Khomeini's close associates, at a press conference in Tehran on 10 November 1978.

6 In interview with the author, July 1989, Paris.

7 The Empress later sold most of the jewels and made 'heavy losses'. A childhood friend apparently sold some of the royal jewels without transferring the proceeds to the Empress.

8 Farhad Sepahbodi, then Iran's Ambassador to Rabat, in conversation with the author, April 1989, New York.

9 On their return to Tehran they all claimed that they had been forced to leave Iran by the Shah. Captain Moezzi later joined the Mujahedeen urban guerrilla group and piloted a hijacked airforce plane out of Iran. Aboard was Abol-Hassn Bani-Sadr who had acted as President of the Islamic Republic between April 1980 and June 1981, and Massoud Rajavi, the Mujahedeen leader who later went to Baghdad to work for the Iraqi government against Iran.

10 Quoted in *Interlock*, p 131.

11 Farhad Sepahbodi who was present at the dinner related the incident in conversation with the author in New York, April 1989.

12 This is based on several accounts by the Shah's entourage at the time. But the monarch himself did not openly discuss his hopes and plans.

13 Various accounts of the meetings are given by Carter, Vance, Bzrezinski and Jordan in their respective memoirs. But they all agree that Carter was against granting the Shah a visa.

14 This view of Callaghan's position is based on accounts given by Helmut Schmidt, Valery Giscard d'Estaing, Jimmy Carter and Callaghan himself in their respective memoirs.

15 The American edition of the Shah's book appeared under the title of *The Shah's Story* in 1980.

16 This phrase came from General Rab'i'i, Commander of the Air Force under the Shah, during his trial in Tehran in February 1979.

17 Zahedi in conversation with the author, July 1989. Montreux, Switzerland.

18 Empress Farah, in interview, with the author, July 1989, Paris.

19 Princess Ashraf in interview with the author, April 1989 Paris.

20 Interlink, p. 109.

21 Farah as in 18 above.

22 Cf Hamilton Jordan in *Crisis*, p. 113

23 Ahmad Ansari in conversation with the author, September 1980. Atlanta, Georgia.

24 Empress Farah as in 18 above.

25 At a press conference in Tehran, 22 November 1979.

26 Princess Shams subsequently claimed that the cheque was a fake.

27 Ansari as in 23 above.

28 Empress Farah as in 18 above.

29 Princess Azadeh in conversation with the author, November 1989, Paris.

30 Empress Farah as in 18 above.

31 Related by Mrs Fereshteh Mussavi, Ghotbzadeh's interpreter at the time in conversation with the author, June 1989, Stockholm, Sweden.

32 Ibid

33 Princess Ashraf as in 19 above.

34 Empress Farah as in 18 above.

35 Ibid.

36 Mrs Mussavi as in 31 above.

Chapter Sixteen: Death by the Nile

1 Zahedi in interview with the author, Montreux, Switzerland, July 1989.

2 *Ibid.*

3 Princess Ashraf in interview with the author, Paris, November 1989.

4 Zahedi, as in note 1 above.

5 Former deputy prime minister Halaku Rambod, former Director of the Atomic Energy Commission Akbar Etemad and former Director of the National Iranian Radio and Television were among the other members of the informal committee.

6 Other estimates cite figures of more than 50,000. Opponents of the regime claim that more than 100,000 people were executed between 1979 and 1991.

7 Estimate contained in an open letter by Iranian doctors to Health Minister Iraj Fazel in Tehran in December 1990.

Titles of the Shah

The Aryan Sun
Superior Presence
Shadow of God on Earth
The Focus of Universe
Holiest Essence
Spreader of Justice
Power of Fate
Strong Glory
King of Kings
Inspirer of Joy

Select Bibliography

Abrahimian, Ervand, *Iran Between Two Revolutions*, Princeton, NJ, 1980.

Acheson, Dean, *Present at the Creation, My Years at the State Department*, New York, 1969.

Akhavi, Sharough, *Religion and Politics in Contemporary Iran*, New York, 1980.

Alexander, Yonah and Nanes, Allan (eds), *The United States and Iran*, Maryland, 1980.

Amirie, Abbas (ed), *The Persian Gulf and the Indian Ocean in International Politics*, Tehran, 1975.

Amirie, Abbas and Twitchell, Hamilton (eds), *Iran in the 1980s*, Tehran, 1978.

Amirsadeghi, Hossein and Farrier, Ronald (eds), *Twentieth Century Iran*, London, 1977.

Arasteh, Josephine and Reza, *Man and Society in Iran*, Leiden, Holland, 1970.

Arberry, A.J., *The Legacy of Persia*, London, 1964.

Arfa, Hassan, *Under Five Shahs*, London, 1964.

Avery, Peter, *Modern Iran*, Tonbridge, Kent, 1965.

Banani, Amin, *The Modernization of Iran 1921–1941*, Stanford, California, 1965.

Bashirieh, Hossein, *The State and the Revolution in Iran*, New York, 1984.

Bausani, Alessandro, *The Persians*, London, 1971.

Bayne, E.A., *Persian Kingship in Transition*, New York, 1964.

Behnam, Muhammad Reza, *Cultural Formations of Iranian Politics*, Salt Lake City, Utah, 1986.

Bharrier, John, *Economic Development in Iran 1900–1970*, London, 1971.

Bill, James Alban, *The Eagle and the Lion*, New Haven and London, 1988; *The Politics of Iran: Groups, Classes and Modernization*, Colombus, Ohio, 1972.

Binder, Leonard, *Iran: Political Development in a Changing Society*, Berkeley, California, 1962.

Bonine, Michael E. and Keddie, Nikki R. (eds), *Modern Iran: The Dialectics of Continuity and Change*, New York, 1981.

Brzezinski, Zbigniew, *Power and Principle*, New York, 1983.

Burrel, R.M., *The Persian Gulf: The Washington Papers*, volume 1, Beverly Hills, California, 1971.

Carter, Jimmy, *Keeping Faith*, New York, 1982.

Carter, Rosalynn, *First Lady from Plains*, Boston, 1984.

Chubin, Shahram and Zabih, Sepehr, *The Foreign Relations of Iran*, Berkeley, California, 1974.

Cottam, Richard W., *Nationalism in Iran*, Pittsburgh, 1979.

Denman, D.R., *The King's Vista: A land reform which has changed the face of Persia*, Berkhampstead, 1973.

Diba, Farhad, *Mohammad Mossadegh: A Political Biography*, London, 1986.

Douglas, William D., *Strange Lands and Friendly People*, New York, 1951.

Dulles, Allen W., *The Craft of Intelligence*, New York, 1963.

Eden, Anthony, *The Reckoning*, London, 1964.

Eisenhower, Dwight D., *Mandate for Change, 1953–1956: The White House Years*, New York, 1963.

Elwell-Sutton, Lawrence P., *Persian Oil: A Study in Power Politics*, Westport, 1976.

Fischer, Michael, M.J., *Iran: From Religious Dispute to Revolution*, Cambridge, Massachusetts, 1980.

Ford, Alan W., *The Anglo-Iranian Oil Dispute of 1951–2*, Berkeley, California, 1954.

Frye, Richard, *Iran*, London, 1960.

Goodell, Grace E., *The Elementary Structures of Political Life: Rural Development in Pahlavi Iran*, New York, 1986.

Graham, Robert, *Iran: The Illusion of Power*, New York, 1978.

Grayson, Benson L., *United States–Iranian Relations*, Washington DC, 1981.

Green, Jerrold D., *Revolution Iran: The Politics of Countermodernization*, New York, 1982.

Grummon, Stephen, *The Iran–Iraq War*, Washington DC, 1982.

Harriman, W. Averil and Ellie, Abel, *Special Envoy to Churchill and Stalin 1941–1946*, New York, 1975.

Helms, Cynthia, *An Ambassador's Wife in Iran*, New York, 1981.

Heravi, Mehdi, *Iranian–American Diplomacy*, New York, 1981.

Hooglund, Eric, *Reform and Revolution in Rural Iran*, Austin, Texas, 1982.

Hoveyda, Fereydoun, *The Fall of the Shah*, New York, 1979.

Hulbert, Mark, *Interlock*, New York, 1982.

Hurewitz, J.C., *Middle East Politics: The Military Dimension*, New York 1969.

Huyser, Robert E., *Mission to Tehran*, New York, 1986.

Ioannides, Christos P., *America's Iran: Injury and Catharsis*, Lanham, 1984.

Issawi, Charles, *The Economic History of Iran (1800–1914)*.

Jabbari, Ahmad and Olson, Robert (eds), *Iran: Essays on a Revolution in the Making*, Lexington, 1981.

Jacobs, Norman, *The Sociology of Development: Iran as an Asian Case Study*, New York, 1966.

Jacqz, Jane W. (ed), *Iran: Past, Present and Future*, New York, 1976.

Jordan, Hamilton, *Crisis*, New York, 1983.

Kazemi, Farhad, *Poverty and Revolution in Iran*, New York, 1980.

Keddie, Nikki R. (ed), *Religion and Politics in Iran*, London, 1983.

Kennedy, Moorehead, *The Ayatollah in the Cathedral*, New York, 1986.

Khomeini, Ruhollah, *The Islamic Government*, Rome, 1983.

Kissinger, Henry, *White House Years*, Boston, 1979.

Kuniholm, Bruce R., *The Origins of the Cold War in the Near East*, Princeton, NJ, 1980.

Laing, Margaret, *The Shah*, London, 1977.

Lambton, A.K.S., *Landlord and Peasant in Persia*, London 1953.

Lenczowski, George, *Russia and the West in Iran*, New York, 1949; *Iran under the Pahlavis*, Stanford, 1978.

Limbert, John W., *Iran at War with History*, Boulder, Colorado, 1987.

Looney, Richard, *The Economic Development of Iran*, New York, 1973.

Louis, William R., and Bill, James Alban (eds), *Mussadiq, Iranian Nationalism and Oil*, London, 1988.

Lytle, Mark H., *The Origins of the Iranian–American Alliance 1941–1953*, New York, 1987.

McDaniel, Robert, *The Shuster Mission to Iran and the Persian Constitutional Revolution*, Minneapolis, 1974.

McGhee, George, *Envoy to the Middle East*, New York, 1983.

Milani, Mohsen M., *The Making of Iran's Islamic Revolution*, Boulder, Colorado, 1988.

Millspaugh, Arthur, *The American Task in Persia*, New York, 1925; *Americans in Persia*, Washington DC, 1946.

Nakhleh, Emil, *The Persian Gulf and American Policy*, New York, 1982.

Paalberg, Robert, 'The Advantageous Alliance: US Relations with Iran 1920–75' in *Diplomatic Disputes*, Mass., 1978.

Pahlavi, Ashraf, *Faces in a Mirror: Memoirs from Exile*, Englewood Cliffs, NJ, 1980.

Pahlavi, Mohammad-Reza, *The White Revolution*, Tehran, 1967; *Mission for my Country*, London, 1960; *Answer to History*, New York, 1980.

Parsons, Anthony, *The Pride and the Fall*, London, 1984.

Powell, Jody, *The Other Side of the Story*, New York, 1984.

Powers, Thomas, *The Man who Kept the Secrets: Richard Helms and the CIA*, New York, 1979.

Ramazani, Ruhollah, *The Foreign Policy of Iran 1500–1941*, Charlottesville, 1973.

Roosevelt, Archie, *The Lust of Knowing: Memoirs of an Intelligence Officer*, Boston, 1988.

Roosevelt, Kermit, *Countercoup: The Struggle for Control of Iran*, New York, 1979.

Rubin, Barry, *Paved with Good Intentions: The American Experience and Iran*, New York, 1980.

Saikal, Amin, *The Rise and Fall of the Shah*, Princeton, NJ, 1980.

Sampson, Anthony, *The Seven Sisters: The Great Oil Companies and the World they Shaped*, New York, 1975.

Sanasarian, Elin, *The Women's Rights Movement in Iran*, New York, 1982.

Scott, Charles W., *Pieces of the Game*, Atlanta, 1984.

Shawcross, William, *The Shah's Last Ride*, London, 1989.

Sheehan, Michael K., *Iran: The Impact of United States Interests and Policies 1941–1951*, Brooklyn, 1968.

Shuster, W. Morgan, *The Strangling of Persia*, New York, 1912.

Stemple, John D., *Inside the Iranian Revolution*, Bloomingdale, Ind, 1981.

Sullivan, William, *Mission to Iran*, New York, 1981.

Taheri, Amir, *The Spirit of Allah: Khomeini and the Islamic Revolution*, London, 1985; *Nest of Spies: America's Journey to Disaster in Iran*, London, 1988.

Turner, Stansfield, *Secrecy and Diplomacy*, Boston, 1985.

Upton, Joseph M., *The History of Modern Iran: An Interpretation*, Cambridge, Massachusetts, 1961.

Vance, Cyrus, *Hard Choices: Critical Years in America's Foreign Policy*, New York, 1983.

Walters, Vernon A., *Silent Missions*, New York, 1978.
Wilbur, Donald, *Adventures in the Middle East*, Princeton, NJ, 1986.
Woodehouse, C.M., *Something Ventured*, London, 1982.

Yar-Shater, Ehsan (ed), *Iran Faces the Seventies*, New York, 1971.

Zabih, Sepehr, *The Mossadegh Era*, Chicago, 1982.
Zonis, Marvin, *The Political Elite of Iran*, Princeton, NJ, 1971.

Index